SWASTIKA
NATION

SWASTIKA NATION

Fritz Kuhn and the Rise and Fall
of the German-American Bund

Arnie Bernstein

St. Martin's Press
New York

A note on dialogue: Any words or sentences said by the characters in this story were quoted directly from firsthand sources, including books, newspaper and magazine accounts, and legal documents. Fritz Kuhn spoke with a thick Bavarian accent, which was often lampooned by writers through mocking transliteration. Other journalists quoted his bad English grammar verbatim throughout their stories. His own writings were neatly massaged into proper American English. I've relied on these varied sources to bring Kuhn's voice to life, which accounts for discrepancies and anomalies within his syntax throughout the story.

www.stmartins.com

Design by Phil Mazzone

Library of Congress Cataloging-in-Publication Data

Bernstein, Arnie.
    Swastika Nation : Fritz Kuhn and the Rise and Fall of the German-American Bund / Arnie Bernstein.—1st U.S. edition.
        pages cm
    ISBN 978-1-250-00671-4 (hardcover)
    ISBN 978-1-250-03644-5 (e-book)
    1 Kuhn, Fritz (Fritz Julius), 1896–1952.   2. German American
Bund—History.   3. Germans—United States—History—20th
century.   I. Title.
    E184.G3B353 2013
    973'.0431—dc23

                                                    2013013486

St. Martin's Press books may be purchased for educational, business, or promotional use. For information on bulk purchases, please contact Macmillan Corporate and Premium Sales Department at 1-800-221-7945, extension 5442, or write specialmarkets@macmillan.com.

First Edition: September 2013

10 9 8 7 6 5 4 3 2 1

For Jan Pagoria
My guardian angel and true believer

CONTENTS

Our battlefield is right here, and here is where we must fight it out.

—FRITZ KUHN, *BUNDESFÜHRER*, GERMAN-AMERICAN BUND

In acts he was like a lion, and like a lion's whelp roaring for his prey. And he pursued the wicked and sought them out, and them that troubled his people he burnt with fire.

—1 MACCABEES: CHAPTER 3, VERSES 4–5

When Der Führer says we is de master race
We heil *pffft!* heil *pffft!* right in Der Führer's face
Not to love Der Führer is a great disgrace
So we heil *pffft!* heil *pffft!* right in Der Führer's face

—"DER FÜHRER'S FACE," OLIVER WALLACE,
POPULARIZED BY SPIKE JONES & HIS CITY SLICKERS

SWASTIKA NATION

PROLOGUE

February 20, 1939

PANDEMONIUM SURROUNDED MADISON SQUARE Garden. Seventeen thousand-plus policemen strained to keep the crowd at bay. It was tough going; by one estimate some 100,000 strong swarmed the streets. Fights broke out. Cops on foot and cops on horses fought back the melee. And yet, though his officers were overwhelmingly outnumbered, Police Commissioner Lewis J. Valentine claimed there were enough of his men on the streets to "stop a revolution."

There was a preponderance of Jews backed up with a healthy number of Christians. Veterans of Foreign Wars (VFW) members were out in force. So were businessmen, housewives, students. Trade unionists. Democrats, Republicans, Socialists, Trotskyites. Old and young. White and black. A crazy quilt New York crowd, united as one, trying to get inside the Garden, which was open only to ticket holders of an exclusive event.

Though police sympathies largely matched the crowd's, the cops had to protect the Garden, the speaker, and his audience. It wasn't something they wanted to do, but the law was the law. The people backing tonight's event had signed contracts and paid rental fees and thus, according to both business arrangements and the First Amendment of the United States Constitution, had every right to speak at the Garden tonight.

Inside the crowded arena was a stark contrast to the street chaos. The place was also packed, the audience joyous and orderly, row upon row of men and women dressed in uniform similarity. They clutched pamphlets, books, and other souvenirs bought from the many vendors lining the hallways of the Garden. Banners, festooned with a glorious emblem, fluttered from the balconies.

Tonight was a rally for their people, their cause, and a celebration of President George Washington's birthday. The speaker they were anticipating was—like Washington—marshaling a great movement toward the thunderous legacy of a world to come. Above the speaker's platform, dominating the hall with stoic presence, was a thirty-foot-tall banner, a portrait of Washington himself, bathed by ethereal light, face solemn, resplendent in regalia, and with a ceremonial sword firmly clasped in his left hand. On either side of this banner, hanging just as tall, were the forty-eight-star American flags; Betsy Ross banners of thirteen circled stars, representing the United States presided over by the great Washington, hung on the far end.

Between these towering versions of Old Glory was another magnificent set of banners. They were adorned with the group's party symbol, configured into a rising geometrical shape, almost phallic in its upward thrust—strong, mighty, ever powerful as Washington and ready to take on all enemies:

The swastika.

In perfect precision, men wearing crisp uniforms of black pants and brown shirts, military-style Sam Browne belts, and garrison caps marched down the aisles. They were the *Ordnungsdienst*—"OD" for short—a highly trained division of well-dressed bodyguards who undertook their duties with brutal seriousness. Next came the drum line, wielding enormous bass drums and beating a strong tattoo resounding throughout the arena. Finally were flag bearers, a snaking line of American red, white, and blue, tempered with men bearing swastika banners. It was as dramatic as it was impressive.

They took their place behind the speaker's podium, the drummers continuing their thundering rhythm, the OD falling in behind them, and the American flag bearers anchoring the rear. On either side of the dais, uniformed men, each one bearing an elaborate banner centered with a swastika, took solemn stances. The drums silenced, and the crowd roared.

A series of speakers addressed the gathering. And then, at last, to tumultuous applause, their leader Fritz Kuhn forcefully strode to the podium. Decked out in his dress uniform, ample belly held in tightly by his Sam Browne belt, Kuhn surveyed the loyal assembly, studying them through his thick glasses, a smile broadening his fleshy face. Followers packed every seat on the floor, overflowed into the rafters, tiny little dots of people from Kuhn's point of view, a mosaic of pure Aryan humanity. Right arms shot aloft en masse, straight out, palm down, in a uniformly powerful salute. A rallying cry thundered throughout the Garden in fierce unison. "Free America! Free America! Free America!"

Kuhn stepped to the microphone to address his people. Guaranteed by the First Amendment, written by his beloved Washington's peers into the American Constitution, it was time to exercise his right to speak his mind, freely and fully.

Kuhn had come a long way to this moment of glory. Once a criminal on the run in his own German Fatherland, a refugee in Mexico, then an American immigrant and naturalized citizen, he found his voice while working as a chemist for the visionary industrialist Henry Ford, author of *The International Jew*, a searing volume exposing the sinister Judaic forces seeping into every corner of society. Like Ford, Kuhn spoke out against the Jew. In 1936 Kuhn founded the German-American Bund with dreams of a fascist America run by and for German Aryans and German Aryans alone. Predecessors of the Bund stretched back to 1918, when Americans of Teutonic heritage banded together against the hatred fired at them during the Great War. Immigrants from the Fatherland and their native-born offspring, pegged as enemies in their adopted country, joined in a constantly evolving amalgamation of groups. People came and left. Many were repelled by an increasing devotion by some groups to the rise of Hitler and the Nazi party back home. But others stayed, finally uniting in the mid 1920s in an organization dubbed The Free Society of Teutonia, which morphed into The Friends of New Germany in the early 1930s, and finally coalesced in 1936 as Kuhn's German-American Bund. Tempered by fierce anti-Semitism, their determination to stand up against Jewish domination in America (and beyond) was echoed and enhanced by others: radio priest Father Charles Coughlin, for one, and like-minded groups such as William Pelley's Silver Legion of America (also known as the Silver Shirts) and the Friends of Progress led by Robert Noble and Ellis Jones. They looked up to unofficial fellow travelers: Kuhn's onetime boss Henry Ford, America's International Olympics standard bearer Avery Brundage, and the family-friendly movie impresario Walt Disney.

With his natural leadership skills and fiery passion for the great cause, Kuhn—known by his followers as the *Bundesführer*—earned what he assumed were the blessings of no less then the great Adolf Hitler. The German-American Bund swelled into a national movement under Kuhn's masterful command, with divisions from New York into the Midwest and stretching out throughout the United States to the West Coast. Members brought their

families to Bundist vacation retreats, and organized boys and girls in a robust
youth program. They sold newspapers and pamphlets, held social meetings,
screened films, staged public and private rallies. They pledged allegiance to
the American flag, venerating George Washington while scorning President
Franklin Delano Roosevelt—a man they were convinced hid his Jewish past
and true family name of "Rosenfelt." As protection against enemies real and
perceived they relied on the OD, the Bund's equivalent to Nazi Germany's
Schutzstaffel—the SS.

In February 1939, the German-American Bund was a force on the
march. Tonight, with the Washington's Birthday Rally, years of hard work
were culminating. Though Kuhn's accent was thick—a still-dominant ves-
tige of his German origins—his voice was clear and strong. "Ladies and
gentlemen," the *Bundesführer* began, "fellow Americans, American patriots:
I am sure I do not come before you tonight as a complete stranger. You will
have heard of me through the Jewish-controlled press as a creature with
horns, a cloven hoof, and a long tail."

The audience roared with laughing approval.

On the floor directly in front of the dais, a man snapped out of the
crowd. He was determined, angry, hurling himself at the stage like a Rang-
ers hockey linesman on the attack. The podium shook, a microphone tum-
bled to the floor. For a moment, Kuhn was flustered.

Several OD bodyguards, a mass of muscle, swarmed the man and pummeled him into submission through the power of fists and the thrilling
crack of boot heels. The show of force was met with loud cheers some twenty
thousand strong. The attacker's pants were ripped from his legs during the
struggle. Later identified as an unemployed Jewish plumber's assistant from
Brooklyn, the man was shoved into the waiting arms of New York's Finest,
handcuffed, and hustled out of the Garden.

It was an unexpected surprise in a night of order.

With the interloper now removed, Kuhn again looked over his people.
He knew that beyond the followers packed in Madison Square Garden tonight were thousands more throughout the United States, eager to follow his
every command in their shared dream of a great fascist Jew-free America.

But outside Madison Square Garden, beyond the 100,000 protestors
swarming New York streets were other adversaries, disparate, unconnected
and as improbable a confederation that ever existed. They came from the
halls of justice, from the annals of show business, and from the dark

underbelly of America. Though far from united, they were singular in their goal to bring down Kuhn and smash his movement.

Ensconced at New York City Hall was Mayor Fiorello LaGuardia. "The Little Flower" as he was known, a loose translation of his Italian name, would have been impure under Kuhn's American Reich, not for his Mediterranean blood—albeit that certainly wasn't Aryan. Rather, the beloved Italian who ran New York City was a half-Jew. LaGuardia embodied New York's ethnic melting pot, the son of a Jewish mother and lapsed-Catholic father: Irene Luzzato Coen, of Hungarian-Jewish heritage by birth and Italian via her home in the Triestine section of northern Italy, near the Slovenian border; and Achille LaGuardia, who hailed from the Cerignola region of eastern Italy along the Adriatic Sea. By Judaism's Halakhah laws, LaGuardia was considered Jewish by virtue of his Hebrew mother. Moreover, the name "Coen" linked him back to the Kohanes, the ancient priestly lineage descended from Aaron, brother of the prophet Moses. And this half-Jewish leader of noble birth would not stand for Nazis running amok in his beloved city.

LaGuardia's partner in the fight was a rising legal star, a man in his mid-thirties but already a feared prosecutor. Thomas Dewey was a few years shy from New York governorship and near-presidency and—unlike the Manhattan born and bred mayor—came from humble Midwestern roots. Dewey didn't like Kuhn's lot either. Yes, they had freedom of speech and every right to speak at Madison Square Garden—or anywhere else, for that matter. Yet a man like Dewey didn't get where he was without knowing every legal nuance and loophole. There was more than one law on the books to get Kuhn and his ilk. And both LaGuardia and Dewey knew how to work the law.

In Washington D.C., another New Yorker had his eyes on the Bund. Congressman Samuel Dickstein, a larger-than-life personality with a flair for drama, was a longtime foe to the American Nazi movement. In 1934, along with fellow Democratic firebrand, Massachusetts representative John W. McCormack, Dickstein formed a unique alliance. Their goal: root out and eradicate fascists and communists within the United States. Three years later, in an unlikely partnership, Dickstein teamed up with Texas congressman Martin Dies, a man gifted with a similar self-aggrandizing personality. They named the Congressional Nazi and Commie hunting organ the House Committee on Un-American Activities, better known as the Dies Committee. Dickstein, a Lithuanian-born Jew, understood that if he wanted to bring down American Nazis, it was best to let a Gentile lead the attack—at least for appearance's sake. The official veneer meant nothing; Dickstein was a determined man who knew how to play the game from behind the scenes. He merged a ruthless blend of personalities and politicians in an unyielding pursuit of the country's internal enemies—and Kuhn was the ideal blackguard.

Back in New York, pounding pavement and typewriter keys was Walter Winchell, bon vivant columnist and radio commentator, a man alternately feared and loved by show business personalities, politicians, and business figures of all stripes and ethics. Winchell had worked his way up from two-bit vaudeville performer to feared journalist. One biting sentence from Winchell could make or break a career. With an ever-present fedora fixed smartly on his head, he ruled New York City perched from behind his typewriter or microphone, as well as his home away from home, table 50 at New York's famed Stork Club.

Great-grandson of a venerated Russian rabbi and grandson of a cantor—the singer of Jewish prayers at synagogues—Winchell was thoroughly assimilated into Gentile America but was fiercely loyal to his people. Other reporters treaded carefully toward the subject of Hitler, Nazis, Kuhn, the Bundists, and their kind; Winchell blasted through niceties, insulting the lot of them with the glib nickname "Ratzis." He fired verbal salvos and bombs via the power of his media might. And when Bundists came searching for revenge on their public tormentor, Winchell eagerly returned fisticuffs.

There were other Bundist foes with a keen understanding of the brute level. They lurked in the underworld of New York and metropolises across the country. Sons of Israel, like LaGuardia, Dickstein, and Winchell, these were Jews whose means and methods operated outside the law. Dark-skinned Yiddish-speaking men in fancy suits, they considered themselves to be businessmen, strictly businessmen, though their trade was rough. They included the likes of mob pioneers Meyer "Little Man" Lansky, a tough fighter with a head for numbers and the vision of running organized crime like a corporation—one that, in his words, would become "bigger than U.S. Steel"; Lanksy's childhood friend Benjamin Siegel, an enforcer who had the guts and violent temper needed to pull necessary triggers (that reputation earned him the nickname "Bugsy," since Siegel was considered "as crazy as a bedbug," albeit no one called him that to his face unless they wanted to suffer the consequences); Abner "Longy" Zwillman, king of the rackets in New

Jersey, mentor and lover of a Hollywood legend, and commanding general to an army of Jewish prizefighters; and Mickey Cohen, a former street thug and Al Capone flunky turned Benjamin Siegel protégé, who then became a colorful character within southern California's seamy landscape of movie stars, studio moguls, pimps, prostitutes, dope dealers, and other assorted miscreants. Lansky, Siegel, Zwillman, Cohen, and their peers were a violent lot who knew the code of the streets, the crunching of bones necessary to vanquish enemies. Like modern-day versions of the Golem, that legendary man of clay brought to life by the great Rabbi Loew of sixteenth-century Prague, they were summoned by judges, politicians, Hollywood power brokers, and even the highest figures of official Jewish leadership to protect fellow Jews from a common enemy. These *shtarkers*—strong, if less than noble big shots—were bad guys, but they were bad guys with Jewish hearts.

Kuhn and his Bundists didn't give a damn what a Jew's job was; they only cared about his blood. Blood, of course, was stock in trade for Lansky, Siegel, Zwillman, and Cohen. Though not always respected by their fellow Jews, these men had no qualms about doing what was necessary when it came to defending their people.

None of this mattered inside the Garden right now. Tonight the German-American Bund was on the verge of great victory, a march into history. Kuhn thundered ahead, words pouring out of him. Let the mob outside revel in their hate! Soon they would all be under his command. A Swastika Nation with Kuhn at the helm.

Fritz Kuhn had the loyalty of thousands. The passionate love of a golden-haired Aryan woman. His adoring children. And his wife.

The stage was set.

PART I

The *Bundesführer*

"I, personally, shall do everything possible to lead the Bund to the top."
—*Bundesführer* Fritz Kuhn,[1] Bund Command No. 1
Detroit, Michigan, October 20, 1936

1

Fritz Julius Kuhn

ON THE EVENING OF November 8, 1923, three thousand men packed the *Bürgerbräukeller*, a beer hall in Munich, Germany, waiting to hear a speech by Gustav Ritter von Kahr, the controversial leader of Bavaria's chaotic postwar government. Outside, where a uniformed and adversarial mix of stormtroopers and police uneasily mixed, it was wet and cold. Inside the hall was a choking miasma of stale smoke, beer, and sweat.

A foppish man outfitted with a Charlie Chaplin toothbrush mustache sat nervously at the bar and ordered three beers. In the wake of Germany's crippling postwar recession the price was hard: one billion marks per glass.[1]

Austrian by birth, German by choice, Adolf Hitler was a failed art student and veteran of the Great War; a brooder overflowing with ideas and prepared for action. It was time to live up to his name "Adolf," an old Teutonic word meaning "fortunate wolf."[2] Tonight, within the packed confines of a Munich beer hall, this fortunate wolf felt poised to change the world. The dismal late autumn weather had compounded a daylong headache. What's more, his jaw throbbed from an ugly toothache. "See a dentist," his friends had implored, but Hitler had paid them no mind. There was work to be done, work of national importance—nay, world importance. His physical maladies were nothing compared to the rot pervading his adopted country.[3]

As Kahr outlined the aims of his government, a colleague approached Hitler at the bar. The time was now.

Hitler whipsawed one of the billion-mark beers to the floor, smashing the mug with a loud crash. Pulling his Browning pistol from its holster Hitler, surrounded by a thug entourage pushing and elbowing bewildered inebriates out of the way, defiantly took the stage. Hitler held his pistol high, squeezed the trigger, and sent a bullet into the ceiling.

The Browning's loud *bang!* did the trick. The confused and rambunctious crowd fell into uneasy silence, a moment that lasted all of an eye blink. From outside storm troopers poured into the packed hall, crying "*Heil* Hitler! *Heil* Hitler!" It was a dictum more than a salute, barked out by loyalists to a cause greater than themselves.[4]

"The national revolution has broken out!" Hitler declared. "The hall is surrounded!"[5]

History would remember this night as the "Beer Hall Putsch," Hitler's attempt to seize the government for Nazi control. Though the night ended in failure with Hitler's arrest, it marked the beginning for a nascent movement that grew into a New World Order the fortunate wolf dreamed of: Germany's conquering Third Reich.

As the cult of Hitler expanded over the years, many of his acolytes would proudly say, "I was at *Bürgerbräukeller*. I stood with our *führer* from the start." Among those who declared he boldly followed the future dictator into the melee was a plump, nearsighted chemist named Fritz Julius Kuhn.[6] In the end, it didn't really matter whether or not Kuhn was part of the putsch mob. Throughout his life, he would claim many things.

Fritz Julius Kuhn was born on May 15, 1896, in Munich to Karl and Anna Kuhn.[7] The Kuhns raised a large brood; Fritz was one of Karl and Anna's twelve children.[8] His childhood was nondescript at best. Certainly nothing emerged in later investigations of Kuhn's past that would show any glimmer of what he was to become.

In 1913, during Kuhn's high school years, Hitler moved to Munich from Vienna. He was twenty-four, a failed art student with a dismal future and completely taken with his new surroundings. "A *German* city!" he later rhapsodized in his autobiography/manifesto *Mein Kampf*. "[T]here was . . . heartfelt love which seized me for this city more than any other place that I knew, almost from the first hour of my sojourn there."[9] Munich provided fertile ground for Hitler's growing Jewcentric ideologies. This "German city" was teeming with anti-Semitic salons and Hitler soaked it in.[10] He plunged himself into studies, while eking out a meager living selling architectural drawings to afford the tiny room where he lived. After long days of creating art and voraciously devouring book upon book, Hitler would head to beer halls for the always lively, sometimes drunken political discussions hurled back and forth on any given night.[11] In some quarters, a greeting was traded between friends to indicate their anti-Semitic political bonds. It was a simple but effective word: *Heil!*[12]

On June 28, 1914, the Austro-Hungarian archduke Franz Ferdinand and his wife Sophie paraded in an open car through the streets of Sarajevo. The pleasingly plump couple seemed not to have a care in the world as they soaked in the cheers of a mostly adoring crowd lining the streets. Yet among the happy faces were some stern looks, silently holding in their contempt for the royal pomposity.

Lurking within the crowd, slipping in and out of the throng, five teenagers all wracked by tuberculosis tightly held their coats, guarding secrets. The minutes dragged until one of the young men saw his chance. He hurled a pocket-sized explosive at the archduke's car. Evasive moves by Ferdinand's sharp-eyed driver couldn't stop the bomb from landing in the automobile. Quickly realizing what was happening, the archduke threw up his arm to shield Sophie from the incoming firepower. His actions had limited effect; shrapnel from the explosion cut her slightly along the neck. The chauffeur floored the gas pedal, smashed cars, and injured pedestrians in the confusion.

Not ones to let an assassination attempt ruin the day, Ferdinand and Sophie next attended a mayoral welcoming ceremony at Sarajevo's city hall. After the ritual pomp and circumstance, the archduke insisted on going to the hospital to meet people hit by his car during the royal getaway.

Apparently the change in plans confused the chauffer. He drove down the scheduled motorcade route but was corrected on his mistake and told to change direction.

The car stopped. Five feet away, Gavrilo Princip saw his chance.

Princip, the brains of the tubercular quintet, pulled a handgun from his coat and squeezed off two shots. Ferdinand, the intended target, was neatly hit. The second bullet penetrated the car door, then struck Sophie. Seconds after pulling the trigger the assassin tried to turn the gun on himself. A mob grabbed him, deflecting any chance for Princip to commit suicide. His second option, chomping down on a vial of cyanide, was an equal failure. The poison within was old, its lethal potency long evaporated.[13]

Princip's bullets cut down two people. The war sparked by this assassination ultimately would kill millions, military and civilian alike.

One month to the day after Ferdinand's assassination, Austria-Hungry declared war on Serbia. Four days later, on August first, Hitler joined the exuberant crowd in *Odeonsplatz*, Munich's central square, celebrating Germany's declaration of war on France and Russia.[14]

Like Hitler, and so many young men of his generation, eighteen-year-old Fritz Kuhn volunteered in the fight for his country. Joining a Bavarian combat unit, Kuhn developed adept skills as a machine gunner, providing firepower support to brethren in the war-torn trenches of France.[15] He served four years, rising to the rank of lieutenant. For bravery on the field of battle Kuhn was awarded the Iron Cross First Class, the German military's highest honor. It surely was a proud moment, as this esteemed laurel was rarely bestowed on enlisted men.[16] And in this award, Kuhn's life invisibly crossed Hitler's, another enlisted man who earned the coveted medal.[17]

Luster ultimately dimmed in the wake of German defeat in the Great War. The devastating loss was followed by the Treaty of Versailles, a forced contract on Germany from the American, French, and English victors demanding reparations be paid from a people shattered by postwar economic recession.

With no job and no future in sight, Kuhn joined many disillusioned veterans in the *Freikorps*, a paramilitary force determined to restore honor to the Fatherland. These freelance troops were funded surreptitiously with money funneled into an anti-Bolshevik movement by leaders of German heavy industry, including Alfred Krupp, Emil Kirdorf, Hugo Stinnes, Albert Vögler, and Hermann Röchling. The country may have been in turmoil and deep in an overwhelming recession, but the barons of business were taking no chances that upstart rebels might cut into their profits via revolution.[18] *Freikorps* volunteers, still bitter from Germany's loss, were lured by patriotic broadsides and newspaper advertisements, crying out for men to defend honor of country and "prevent Germany from becoming the laughingstock of the earth."[19]

They operated under the eye of Gustav Noske, Germany's postwar Minister of Defense. In the terrible wake of Germany's humiliation in the Great War, the *Freikorps* served as a sort of internal protection force. Their law enforcement techniques were highly unorthodox, driven by a mob psychology specializing in intimidation and brutality.[20]

The bankrollers behind *Freikorps* had reason to worry. The Spartacus League, a leftist force that took its name from the leader of the ancient Greek slave revolt, was making inroads. Under the leadership of Rosa Luxemburg— a Jewish Russian–born Marxist—and her colleague, fiery German attorney Karl Liebknecht, a Bolshevik takeover similar to the recent Russian revolution loomed. The Spartacist movement was gaining momentum in Berlin, taking control of public utilities, transportation, and munitions factories. Friedrich Ebert, the postwar German Republic's first president, panicked. He fired Berlin's chief of police, declaring the man a Spartacist sympathizer.[21]

On Sunday, January 5, 1919, Spartacists held rallies and demonstrations throughout the streets of Berlin. Luxemburg issued a broadsheet imploring people throughout Germany to join the fight. "Act! Act! Courageously, consistently—that is the 'accursed' duty and obligation . . ." she wrote. "Disarm the counter-revolution. Arm the masses. Occupy all positions of power. Act quickly!"

Overthrow of the government was quelled through efficient and merciless means.

During what became known as "Bloody Week," *Freikorps* volunteers from throughout the country flocked to Berlin. Forces amplified to thousands of men salivating for street battles against the paltry opposition.

Using an abandoned school as his headquarters, Noske took command as *Freikorps* men brought down wave upon wave of the enemy throughout the week. On January 11, *Freikorps* shock troops, armed with flamethrowers and machine guns, unleashed their furies on the headquarters of the leftist newspaper *Vorwärts*. Spartacist snipers scattered throughout the building held out as best they could. Finally seven of the rebels came out waving white handkerchiefs. One member of the group was sent back into the building, with the message that *Freikorps* would only accept unconditional surrender. The remaining six were beaten and shot. As they fell into gruesome heaps, three hundred remaining Spartacists inside the building were rounded up. Seven people in this final group were turned into helpless targets, blasted with a fusillade of ammunition as their comrades were taken into custody en masse.

Next were Luxemburg and Liebknecht. The duo, holed up in the flat of

one of Liebknecht's relatives, was found on January 15th. They were hauled
to the ironically named Hotel Eden in the center of Berlin. Liebknecht was
clubbed insensible with rifle butts.[22] Battered and helpless, he was dragged
off to nearby Tiergarten, a public greenery described by author Erik Larson
as ". . . Berlin's equivalent to Central Park. The name, in literal translation,
meant 'animal garden' or 'garden of the beasts . . .' "[23] Liebknecht was ordered to walk. As he stumbled forward *Freikorps* guns riddled his back with
bullets. The bloodied corpse was dumped off at the Berlin Zoo like a slab of
freshly butchered meat meant for animal feed.[24]

Once Liebknecht was dispatched attentions turned to Luxemburg. Like
her now-dead comrade, she was slammed in the skull with merciless rifle
butts. Bleeding from her nose and mouth, unconscious yet still alive, she was
thrown into a car and spirited away. Hotel workers heard pistol shots as the
automobile peeled off.[25] Upon reaching Berlin's Landwehr Canal, Luxemburg's killers secured heavy stones around her body with tightly bound
wire, and then threw the weighted corpse into the water. "The old slut is
swimming now," sneered one of the assassins.[26] Five months later Luxemburg's remains, a bloated caricature of a woman, were found in one of the
canal locks.[27]

Emboldened by the unchecked Berlin slaughter, men throughout the
country clamored to join *Freikorps*. Kuhn signed on with a unit organized
by Colonel Franz Ritter von Epp, a highly decorated hero of Germany's
doomed war efforts.[28] The division—known as *Freikorps Epp*—was formed
in the violent wake of Bloody Week. Its members were mostly former enlisted men such as Kuhn and became the largest *Freikorps* regiment in Bavaria.[29] Determined not to let any rebels create new threats, Kuhn and his
fellow soldiers in the *Freikorps Epp* kept tight and brutal rings surrounding
cities throughout the region. "No pardon is given," one member of the
group wrote. "We shoot even the wounded. . . . Anyone who falls into our
hands first gets the rifle butt and then is finished off with a bullet. We even
shot ten Red Cross nurses on sight because they were carrying pistols. We
shot those little ladies with pleasure—how they cried and pleaded with us to
save their lives. Nothing doing! Anyone with a gun is our enemy . . ."[30]

Like many of his *Freikorps* volunteers, Kuhn joined Hitler's growing
Nazi Party, officially becoming a member in 1921. Intellectual ambition
separated him from the majority of his peers, most of whom were working
class men of limited schooling. Kuhn enrolled in the University of Munich

and in 1922 earned the American equivalent of a master's degree in chemical engineering.[31]

Higher education afforded Kuhn opportunities outside the classroom. He developed a penchant for pilfering the overcoats of fellow students, a crime that earned Kuhn four months at Munich's Stadelheim Prison in 1921.[32] Again, Kuhn and Hitler crossed inadvertent paths. On April 16, 1922, Hitler was arrested and taken to Stadelheim for inciting an Easter Sunday riot, shouting, "Two thousand years ago, the mob of Jerusalem dragged a man to execution in just this way!"[33]

Fearful for his son's future, Karl Kuhn sought out Reinhold Spitz, a Jewish manufacturer whose clothing factory was down the street from Kuhn's business. Spitz empathized with the situation, having known Fritz since he was four years old, and in 1924 hired the wayward young man as a shipping clerk.[34]

Within a few months Spitz noticed that bolts of cloth used in factory machinery were coming up short. On further investigation, he realized the actual lengths of cloth were not as stated on inventory tags. Spitz's first thought was that his suppliers were cheating him, but this proved wrong. Next he traced how the cloth bolts were transported within his factory. Somewhere between the first-floor stock room and the third-floor manufacturing plant on the top of the building, an employee was altering inventory. Watching carefully through a workroom door, Spitz found his culprit. Fritz Kuhn was using tailor's shears to remove several yards of cloth from each bolt, and then slip the purloined material to an accomplice outside the factory.

Spitz called Fritz Kuhn to his office, promptly fired him, then summoned Karl Kuhn to come fetch his son.[35] All told, Kuhn had stolen some three thousand marks' worth of material. Karl implored his son's boss not to press charges. Spitz was a forgiving man, for he agreed to help give Fritz a fresh start and helped raise money so his now ex-employee could move to Mexico.[36] Perhaps this radical change in scenery was what Fritz needed to get on the straight and narrow. Besides, the man now had a wife to support, having gotten married May 28, 1923.[37]

Kuhn's move to Mexico with his new bride, Elsa, was not an unusual strategy for the times. Strapped by their Fatherland's battered economy, many Germans of his generation sought better opportunities in the United States.[38] The American consulate told Kuhn a quota system regulated immigration so it might be easier if he first went to Mexico. In theory Kuhn would only have to wait a few months to establish Mexican residency, and then relocate to the United States.[39]

In Mexico Kuhn was hired as a laboratory chemist with the La Corona Oil Company. He later found work with a cosmetics firm, and briefly taught at the College of Mexico City.[40] The Kuhns' two children, daughter Waltraut and son Walter, were born in 1924 and 1928 respectively. On May 8, 1928, three days after his thirty-first birthday, Fritz Kuhn at last arrived in America, officially checking in at the immigration office of Laredo, Texas.[41] Elsa, Waltraut, and Walter joined him seven months later on December 8.[42]

The America Kuhn found was not the paradise he might have imagined. Rather, it was an oppressive, almost totalitarian world when it came to Germans, both newcomers and generations-old Americans with Teutonic lineage alike. Americans with a German background numbered one-fourth of the United States population at the dawn of the twentieth century.[43] Holding close ties to the Old World, they banded together through national German-American organizations and newspapers, extolling the beauty of their heritage within this adopted homeland. This was hardly unique; the United States was the "nation of immigrants" and just about every ethnic or émigré group had similar outlets. But as war raged throughout Europe the American frame of mind radically changed on Germany, Germans, and German-identified citizens within the United States. Although the United States was officially neutral in the conflict, it was clear the government sided with the Allied cause. That position ratcheted up in May 1917 after a German U-boat torpedoed the British ocean liner RMS *Lusitania*, killing 1,198 passengers and crew, including 128 American citizens. And once United States forces hit the battlefields of Europe the following year, rhetoric exploded into a homeland security that cared little for rights guaranteed by the United States Constitution.

In the fall of 1917, six months after the United States officially entered the war, all German-born U.S. citizens or foreign nationals over age fourteen had to register with the government; any property they owned was subject to governmental control.[44] Music by German composers was removed from symphony repertoires, schoolbooks eliminated any favorable mentions of German history, and even food fell under suspicion.[45] The ethnic sounding "sauerkraut" was rechristened to the more patriotic name "liberty cabbage."

Frankfurters became "hot dogs," a lasting moniker that over the decades evolved into a symbol of American culinary culture.[46] German language books were removed from public libraries, then torched in patriotic celebrations. In some towns, German-Americans were ordered to confess their love of country by kneeling in public squares to kiss the Stars and Stripes.[47]

Throughout the postwar United States, German-Americans were still looked upon in some circles as pariahs. President Woodrow Wilson led the way declaring, ". . . any man who carries a hyphen about with him carries a dagger that he is ready to plunge into the vitals of this Republic whenever he gets ready. If I can catch any man with a hyphen . . . I will know that I have got an enemy of the Republic."[48] Wilson had spoken out strongly against these "hyphenates" in the past, a not-too-subtle phrase many German-Americans took as a code word aimed directly at them. Some members of the German-American press were publicly outraged over this scurrilous insult; others, such as the *Express und Westbote*, a Columbus, Ohio newspaper, urged its readers to "quietly and coolly refute all attacks against us."[49]

Respect and tolerance, a path back to the American mainstream, was forged through the work of conscientious groups like the German-American Citizens League and the Steuben Society of America, the latter symbolically named after the Hessian hero of the Revolutionary War. In August 1920, leaders of these and other groups convened a national meeting in Chicago for the purpose of developing avenues to mainstream German-Americans back into acceptable circles.[50]

But in other pockets of German-America, resentments of these persecutions did not go away. Out of dogmatic and jingoistic discrimination, friends grew and new alliances were forged. And for inspiration they looked back to the Fatherland and Hitler's expanding Nazi movement.

This was the America where Fritz Kuhn hoped to reestablish himself. After crossing the border into Laredo, Kuhn headed north to Michigan at the suggestion of a Mexican acquaintance. Jobs in Detroit were plentiful in the many branches of Henry Ford's sprawling automobile empire. There was a strong community of new German immigrants living in the area, so culture shock would be minimal.

In short, Detroit and the Ford Motor Company was a place where Kuhn could begin to forge his new life.

Kuhn was hired as an X-ray technician at the Henry Ford Hospital, a health institution funded by its namesake.[51] Given Kuhn's Nazi party membership, Ford Hospital must have been his version of the ideal employer. The facility, operating under the direction of Henry Ford's right-hand hatchet man Ernest Liebold, had a strict policy against hiring Jewish doctors.[52]

Ford's well-known anti-Semitism permeated his vast operations, from the close-knit leadership at the top to workers on factory floors. The Ford-backed newspaper, *The Dearborn Independent*, was probably best known for its ongoing feature "The International Jew," a personal screed by the automobile magnate (cowritten with Ford's ghost collaborator, William J. Cameron) warning of Jewish influence throughout every stratum of modern American society and around the globe. Public outrage over "The International Jew" boiled over into a consumer boycott with significant impact on national automobile sales. Ford felt the bottom line pressure. He publicly claimed to renounce "The International Jew" and all it stood for via a widely disseminated letter to prominent Jewish officials. However, Ford neither read nor signed the letter. It was drafted and affixed with Ford's name by Harry Bennett, head of the company security and a master at replicating his employer's signature.[53] Regardless of Ford's pretense of contrition he continued propagating the screed via a sly loophole. The newspaper series was published as a four-volume book set in the early 1920s but never copyrighted, an unusual choice for a man of Ford's business acumen. With no legal means to prevent anyone from reprinting, distributing, or translating his work, in essence Ford vaulted *The International Jew* into worldwide perpetuity.[54] His supposedly renounced views spread freely from country to country through many editions and translations, eventually winding up in the hands of Adolf Hitler. A voracious reader of all things anti-Semitic, Hitler dived into *The International Jew* with gusto, finding revelation and inspiration on every page. In his own book, the 1925 volume *Mein Kampf*, Hitler paid homage to Ford's visionary understanding of social forces. "It is Jews who govern the stock exchanges of the American Union," Hitler wrote in a typical phrase for the tome. "Every year makes them more and more the controlling masters of the producers in a nation of one hundred and twenty millions; only a single great man, [Henry] Ford, to their fury, still maintains full independence."[55]

Employment at Ford provided a good life for Kuhn. The security of a steady paycheck and anti-Semitic work environment aside, this new career offered other benefits: women.

Remarkably, in spite of his pudgy frame, fleshy face, weak eyes, and marital status, Kuhn possessed an arousing spark that ignited feminine passions. He brazenly flirted with female coworkers. Perhaps realizing that his status as a lowly X-ray technician with thick glasses, thick middle, and thick German accent did not exactly make him movie-star attractive, Kuhn inflated his credentials with faux allure, proffering himself to potential conquests as "Doctor" Fritz Kuhn. Some would-be paramours repelled the sexual overtures. Others reciprocated his affections, swept off their feet by Kuhn into broom-closet liaisons.

Despite his flirtations and affairs with female staffers at Ford Hospital, not all of Kuhn's peers were impressed with his Romeo handiwork. One former coworker with clear disdain for Kuhn's hyperactive sex drive viewed the technician-*cum*-physician not as a conquering ladies' man, but rather "a queer."[56]

Kuhn had a mixed employment record in the Ford Corporation. Hired on August 20, 1928, he was subsequently out of a job the following year on December 12. Official reports indicated Kuhn was "laid off because of slow hospital and laboratory work." He was rehired in July 1930 for a position at the Ford Heat Treatment department, a job that lasted all of four weeks. Six months later, in February 1931 he came back to Ford, landing a position in his trained field as a chemist. This proved to be Kuhn's longest tenure with the company, a position that lasted through July 1936. At that time new circumstances demanded a leave of absence. Kuhn never returned and in January 1937 his employment with Ford Motor Corporation was officially terminated.[57]

Though his employment within the company came to an eventual end, leaving Ford Motors would not be Fritz Kuhn's concluding moment with its founder Henry Ford.

2

Friends

IN GERMANY KUHN HAD been a soldier in a mighty—albeit failed—army; a strong-willed member of the *Freikorps;* and a proudly loyal acolyte of a rising political movement. Petty theft forced an end to these glories and into uneasy refuge in Mexico, a country far removed from his native culture and language. New life in Detroit offered financial security, a home for his family, and a string of dalliances. But something was missing. Kuhn needed to be part of something larger than himself.

Kuhn found his cause seething along the fringes of Ford's mighty empire. Throughout the company and into Detroit's German enclaves of immigrants and second- and third-generation German-Americans was a collective association known as The Friends of New Germany. Like Kuhn, The Friends, a group of similar-minded individuals steeped in German politics and culture, openly admired the growing power of the *Nationalsozialistische Deutsche Arbeiterpartei,* commonly known as the NSDAP, the Nazi Party. Unknowingly Kuhn stumbled onto his future.

The Friends seemed like a solidified organization. In reality it was born from turmoil and always on the verge of self-destruction. The group had its roots in the National Socialist Teutonia Association, a ragtag German-American collective devoted to the NSDAP. Incorporated on October 12, 1924, nearly one year to the day after Hitler's failed putsch, Teutonia was founded by two German immigrant brothers, Fritz and Peter Gissibl. The Gissibls, both in their early twenties, were too young to have participated in the Great War but old enough to suffer through the aftereffects of Versailles and Germany's struggle against crushing recession. Through Teutonia, their hope was to support the burgeoning Nazi party while building a similar movement in the United States.

Teutonia was driven by bluster and sheer will. Membership was largely made up of disaffected factory workers toiling hand to mouth to support their families. Yet these men eagerly scraped together a portion of their meager earnings to provide for a greater cause, the eternal battle against worldwide Jewish control. Through Teutonia they were no longer soulless cogs twisting wrenches in eternal drudgery on an assembly line floor. They were transformed into stalwart German men decked out in uniforms and badges, driven by the illusion that Teutonia was a force to be reckoned with.

In a bold move to link Teutonia to the Fatherland, in April 1925 Fritz Gissibl sent Hitler a birthday present consisting of a few extra dollars out of the organization's thin pockets. It was enough to impress the fledgling Nazi leader, who expressed his thanks in a postcard. "If the affluent ones among the Germans and Germans in foreign countries would sacrifice in equal proportion for the movement," Hitler wrote his American patron, "[then] Germany's situation would soon be different."[1]

For all their efforts, the Gissibl brothers had pitiful return on the investment. Though Teutonia's reach extended from its base in Detroit and Chicago into New York City, Los Angeles, and points in between the coasts, overall the organization never amounted into anything resembling a solid and unified body. At its height, the group maintained a core national membership of around five hundred people, although record keeping was notoriously inaccurate. By 1932 Teutonia's influence on expatriates loyal to the NSDAP movement had evaporated.[2]

Still, the ideas continued to flourish. Disparate groups met in private homes and clubs throughout German quarters, praising Hitler, grousing about Jews, and wondering when the United States would throw off its democratic yoke in favor of a fascist state. There was enormous frustration that the movement was not taking hold on a wider scale. Seeking to unite as a stronger force separate from the Gissibl brothers' spiraling movement and realizing the time for action was now, one such backroom cell contacted Hans Nieland, the NSDAP bureaucrat charged with overseeing foreign affairs. What America needed, this anonymous group believed, was not a disgruntled and fading band of pretend Nazis, but an official branch of the Party complete with an endorsement from Berlin.

Looking at Teutonia and the overall disorganization of other American factions, Nieland did not like what he saw. Unhappy drinkers gathered in the saloons throughout New York's largely German Yorkville neighborhood and other German-American enclaves in Detroit, Chicago, and Los Angeles, hoisting glass after glass of beer and achieving nothing was not in keeping with the Nazi ideals of strength and order. Nieland dictated that all American pro-Nazis should unite under the general title of *Gauleitung-USA*, commonly known as "Gau-USA." It was hoped a streamlined organization would be effective, but Nieland's choice as leader, Paul Manger, was a significant blunder.

Manger was a German native with impressive credentials as an authentic member of the NSDAP. His professional position was considerably less stellar. A janitor by trade, Manger was unemployed, as were the majority of his followers. At its best Gau-USA could pull in ninety members at the weekly Saturday night Yorkville meetings. Nieland provided some assistance, sending propaganda for the organization's intermittently published newspaper *Amerika's Deutsche Post*.

Given the rough financial circumstances of Gau-USA's membership and Manger's overall ineptness as a leader, continued turmoil was inevitable in the struggle for a strong American Nazi Party. Manger was often challenged by unhappy members trying to bring him down in a series of failed putsches. Other factions within Gau-USA broke loose from the parent group to form new associations. The chaotic state of affairs left officials in Berlin with no choice. On April 16 the official word hit Manger's desk: Gau-USA was *kaput*.[3]

Enter Colonel Edwin Emerson Jr., a cog in the Nazi machine with a most unusual pedigree. He was born in Dresden, Germany in 1869 to American parents, academian Edwin Emerson Sr. and Mary Louise Ingham.[4] Emerson earned a Harvard degree, then rode with Theodore Roosevelt up San Juan Hill during the Spanish-American War as part of the fabled Rough Riders. After the war he worked as an itinerant journalist, filing stories from various conflicts throughout Mexico and Central and South America, and fighting in the occasional skirmish himself as a soldier-for-hire. He returned to Germany during the Great War, where his American background made him an ideal agent to spread propaganda among English-speaking Allied forces. During the postwar era he was kicked out of Guatemala, Austria, and Switzerland as a German spy. In 1928 Emerson authored a biography, *The Adventures of Theodore Roosevelt*, for E. P. Dutton and Company. Then, in March 1933, as Gau-USA was spewing out its last desperate gasps, Emerson was appointed NSDAP emissary to the United States. His mission: reconcile and unite the disparate Nazi supporters in New York and the rest of the country.[5]

Emerson's office was in the Whitehall Building at 17 Battery Place, the same location as the German consulate at that time. Once ensconced in the new job, Emerson sent his feelers out to the thriving German-American community in Yorkville. It was hoped this outreach would finally develop a definitive Nazi foothold in America through Emerson's benignly named collective "The Friends of Germany."

But back in the Fatherland, a former colleague of Fritz Gissibl's hungered to remake himself in America. Heinz Spanknöbel previously worked with Gissibl at Ford in the factories as well as in Teutonia, where he earned high status. After the group's dissolution Spanknöbel went back to Germany, still fostering a dream to make his fascist mark on the United States. Through various social maneuvers, he managed to ingratiate himself to Hitler's top lieutenant Rudolf Hess. Spanknöbel seized the chance, concocting for Hess a grandiose fantasy of thousands of German expatriates longing for a robust Nazi movement in their adopted homeland. All they needed was the blessing of the NSDAP top leadership. That, coupled with Spanknöbel's brilliant vision and this grand movement, could begin its triumphant march.

The tale won over Hess, who authorized Spanknöbel to create the definitive American organization supportive of Nazi Party objectives. Armed with a renewed sense of purpose, plus official papers signed by Hess, Spanknöbel once more decamped to the United States and in May 1933 promptly began coopting The Friends of Germany.

Setting up headquarters in Yorkville, Spanknöbel spent the summer connecting with the unhappy remnants of Teutonia and Gau-USA. Through his old friend Gissibl, Spanknöbel found inroads into the community of pro-Hitler Germans living in New York and beyond, making numerous personal visits to massage egos so badly bruised by previous years' infighting. Presenting himself as a man aligned with the changes unfolding back home, Spanknöbel quickly won over hearts and minds. His credentials as Hess's handpicked choice opened numerous doors, earning instant approval from former members of Teutonia, Gau-USA, splinter groups, unaffiliated people in search of a like-minded community, and of course those sympathetic to everything National Socialism represented.

Spanknöbel christened his movement *Bund der Freunde des Neuen Deutschland*, best known in English as The Friends of New Germany. In theory, these Friends were not in competition with Emerson's Friends of Germany, as the latter group was supposedly aimed at German-Americans rather than German immigrants. It mattered little; eventually Emerson's organization fell way to Spanknöbel's more strident efforts.

In July the burgeoning Friends of New Germany met in Chicago for a two-day convention. Spanknöbel felt it would be best to split the United States into an efficient organizational model with three separate districts in the East Coast, Midwest, and West Coast.

Spanknöbel declared himself the group leader, *Der Bundesleiter*. The title was deliberately chosen over *Führer*, which translated in English as "leader" or "guide." When delivered in its original German this word commanded a bold and forceful tone. Yet *Führer* was a supreme designation, and as such could be held only by one man: Adolf Hitler. Hungry for power though he was, Spanknöbel did have a sense of decorum and thus deferred to the world's only *Führer*.

Spanknöbel adopted a key aspect of Hitler's rule. He demanded The Friends adhere to the NSDAP *Führerprinzip*, the so-called "Leadership Principle." This precept, a common law among dictatorships, declared that a leader's word was law. All actions, major and minor, would be fulfilled according to *Der Bundesleiter*'s decree, and obeyed to the letter. His wisdom was not to be questioned. Charged with this ultimate power Spanknöbel decided that the Leadership Principle was personal license to commandeer all things German in the United States.[6] His ego and sense of purpose inflated to zeppelin-sized proportions after Emerson agreed to fold The Friends of Germany into Spanknöbel's organization. In September, in what felt like a coronation of sorts, *Der Bundesleiter* went to the docks of New York, joined crewmembers and passengers aboard the German ship S.S. *Resolute* and was feted in a night of song, beer, and revelry. Surely he was poised for greatness.[7]

But the majority of German-Americans was not NSDAP-inclined and held other views on the matter. Spanknöbel made his first great blunder by storming the offices of *New Yorker Staats-Zeitung und Herold*, a long-established newspaper for new German immigrants and their predecessors. The journal was by far the most important of its type in the United States, neutral in position on the unfolding changes in German government, and—in Spanknöbel's fevered lust for power—ripe for the taking. Waving his letter from Hess, he barked an order that the paper henceforth devote increased space to pro-Hitler material. Rather than acquiesce to this bold and seemingly official demand, the newspaper's editor called the police and unceremoniously threw *Der Bundesleiter* out on the street.[8]

Sullied but undeterred, Spanknöbel next attempted to wrest control of the United German Societies (UGS), an organization that brought together German-American groups of common cultural and historic interests. On September 18, 1933, a UGS meeting was held to plan New York's annual October German Day festivities. Spanknöbel and his security detail ignored decorum as they shouted anti-Semitic slurs to the collective gathering. Representatives from four Jewish affiliated German groups, outraged by this unprecedented display, stormed from the hall. But Spanknöbel sat on the UGS board of directors and managed to get a majority vote on a key German Day issue. Thanks to his intense lobbying, Spanknöbel's beloved national German flag, the bloodred banner centered by a circle of white emblazoned with a black swastika, would fly proudly throughout the festival alongside the American Stars and Stripes.

Spanknöbel believed this strategic move would solidify his position as *bundesleiter*, pulling all UGS into his fold. Instead, the hijacking sent UGS into complete disorder. The entire board of directors, save Spanknöbel, handed in a collective resignation as did the organization's treasurer. German-American groups long associated with UGS quit the federation outright.

He remained defiant, though nowhere to be found. In the days that followed his aborted takeover of UGS, synagogues throughout Manhattan were defaced with swastikas. Rumors swirled as to who were the culprits. By all accounts, it was believed Friends-associated thugs slathered on the graffiti at the orders of *Der Bundesleiter*.

Throughout these debacles, given the outrage over the Nazi government having passed laws earlier in the year banning Jews from working as doctors, lawyers, civil servants, and in universities, coupled with the closing of many Jewish shops, by pushing German Day as an NSDAP-friendly celebration, Spanknöbel unwittingly attracted attention from beyond Yorkville.

New York mayor John O'Brien teamed with Samuel Untermeyer, a Jewish attorney with impressive connections in business and politics, and pressured the remnants of UGS to cancel German Day. In the halls of Congress, Samuel Dickstein—Chair of the House Committee on Immigration and Naturalization and a formidable New York powerhouse concerned about anti-Semitism percolating in the German immigrant community—took special interest in Spanknöbel and his activities. At Dickstein's command, a federal grand jury ordered Spanknöbel's deportation for not registering with the U.S. State Department as a representative of a foreign government.

Three days before the scheduled October 26 festivities German Day was called off. Now a wanted man, Spanknöbel fled New York for clandestine refuge in Washington D.C. On October 29, the day he had been scheduled to speak beneath the new German banner at the Manhattan Amory building, Spanknöbel escaped Dickstein's grasp, secretly boarding the Bremen-bound ocean liner S.S. *Europa* to safety back in Germany. His personal quest for an American Swastika Nation was shattered.[9]

Given their position as American representatives of the Fatherland, The Friends' clumsy propaganda skills and bitter infighting created a potential political nightmare for Nazi Germany's already shaky relations with the United States government. Spreading NSDAP ideology around the globe required finesse. Hess wanted someone he knew and trusted running The Friends. To counter any potential problems, Ernst Bohle, one of Hess's key lieutenants, met with top German foreign ministry bureaucrats and hammered out a solution: The Friends of New Germany should be led by a United States citizen who was not a member of the NSDAP.

Emerging as the leading candidate was Dr. Ignatz Griebel, whose professional credentials as a surgeon at New York's Harlem Hospital certainly provided the veneer of public respectability. Furthermore, Griebel was a German-born naturalized American citizen. Clearly he fit the bill as a worthy successor to Spanknöbel.

However, the good doctor lacked one important quality: Hess didn't like him. Hess wanted his own man as *bundesleiter*, Fritz Gissibl. As founder of Teutonia and proven Nazi-friendly Gissibl was ideal, though he came with two potential drawbacks: he was still a German citizen and a member in good standing of the NSDAP—qualities declared *verboten* by Bohle. Both of these obstacles were easy to fix with a little bureaucratic choreography. On his end Gissibl began the paperwork for American citizenship, while in Germany his Nazi Party affiliation was officially "suspended," a purely symbolic wink-and-nod move by Hess.

What Hess and Gissibl didn't count on was Griebel, who refused to go away. Bolstered by loyal Spanknöbel factions, the spurned leader insisted he was still at The Friends' helm. Gissibl, taking no chances on Griebel's presumptions and his own perceived destiny, fled to Chicago where he hunkered down with a cabal of loyalists. They brainstormed a disinformation campaign of the highest order, concocting a glut of falsehoods smearing Griebel's credentials as a defender of Germany's New Order. Griebel was a Freemason. And a Communist. His wife Martha was a Jew. Of course none of this was true. It mattered not. The strategy unfolded exactly as planned, turning fiction into perceived reality and for the time being forced out Spanknöbel's heir apparent.[10]

And yet, The Friends of New Germany survived. Though top leadership operated in a state of perpetual topsy-turvy, local units remained calm and productive. Spanknöbel's big-picture plan to unite the national organization via three regional umbrella groups proved to be a model of good German order. Divisions throughout the United States remained relatively intact as Friends groups spread westward throughout German enclaves in Philadelphia, Cincinnati, Chicago, and other cities.[11]

In Detroit, The Friends of New Germany had a natural base, given the numbers of Germans working at Ford Motors coupled with the company's top-down, deeply entrenched anti-Semitism. Certainly their employer's words provided moral support to Hitler. Though officially denied, it was long rumored that the NSDAP movement received financial assistance from Ford himself.[12] When cornered by an American reporter, Hitler vehemently denied taking any money from "Heinrich Ford," albeit in his personal office a portrait of the American auto magnate was displayed with pride.[13] In addition to Ford and his conglomerate, another important anti-Semitic voice emerged from Michigan, in the Detroit suburb of Royal Oak. At the National Shrine of the Little Flower Catholic church, Father Charles Edward Coughlin delivered weekly radio sermons, holding audiences spellbound with his unfettered broadcasts blaming the world's woes on Jewish influence.

Within the Friends of New Germany's Detroit chapter Kuhn saw rich potential to fulfill his yearnings to serve a higher cause. With a national power vacuum in the wake of Spanknöbel's departure, opportunity within the organization was ripe. Anyone with determination, talent, and ambition could rise to the top.

It was Kuhn's American dream, as refined through a swastika filter.

3

The Rise of Fritz Kuhn

On June 28, 1934, Kuhn filed petition for citizenship. The request was approved by the United States Department of Immigration and Naturalization in five short months, and on December 3 he was reborn as a full-fledged American.

Though he adopted the rights and responsibilities of his new homeland, Kuhn was still loyal to Germany and found kindred spirits within The Friends. FBI reports indicate Kuhn officially joined the Detroit branch in November 1934—just weeks before becoming an American citizen—though it is probable he was involved in the organization much earlier.[1] As with his membership in the *Freikorps*, and its later incarnation *Stalhelm*—The Steel Helmets, a loose confederation of *Freikorps* veterans—Kuhn devoted himself body and soul to a cause bigger than himself.

Like all members in good standing, Kuhn joined The Friends with their prescribed oath:

I herewith declare my entry into the League of the Friends of the New Germany. The purpose and aims of the League are clearly known to me and I obligate myself to support them without restriction. I acknowledge the "Leadership Principle"; I do not belong to any secret organization of any kind . . . I am of Aryan descent, free of Jewish or colored racial traces.[2]

Loyalty was also sworn to Adolf Hitler "and everybody designated by him . . . the respect and absolute obedience, and to fulfill all orders without reservation and with my entire will, because I know that my leader does not demand anything from me illegally."[3]

Kuhn's world expanded beyond the mundane world of family and workplace. Again, time was stolen from the job for broom closet actions. But these spaces were no longer secret hideouts for extramarital liaisons. Kuhn used them as rehearsal rooms to practice oratory skills.[4] Though these moments earned Kuhn periodic employment suspensions, the practice sessions paid off in other dividends. He took these carefully honed speeches to Friends meetings. The results earned Kuhn considerable respect from his peers—and soon overall control. In September 1935 he was appointed leader of the Detroit Chapter of The Friends of New Germany.[5]

Gissibl's woes seemed to have no end. In spring of 1934, Hess changed his mind about who should head up The Friends. "Suspending" Gissibl's NSDAP membership was too transparent; it would be best to have a *bundesleiter* who—unlike Gissibl—was never a member of the NSDAP in the first place. However, the move would merely be for show; behind the scenes Gissibl was still Hess's man in America.

Reinhold Walter, a longtime associate of The Friends, was selected as the titular front man. When it quickly became obvious Walter wanted all the glory that came with his position, Gissibl removed him from power and chose Hubert Schnuch, an old friend from Teutonia, as the new figurehead. Like Walter, the German-born Schnuch was never a member of the Nazi Party. With degrees from the University of Chicago and Yale, Schnuch seemed like an impressive individual. Hess agreed. To give the group a more "American" appearance, Schnuch's title was changed from *"bundesleiter"* to "president." Regardless, his position as leader of The Friends was ceremonial. It was understood that Gissibl, who ostensibly was shifted to head the Midwest gau, was still top man.[6]

But another German-born American, Anton Haegele, was tired of the shenanigans. Leading a faction of anti-Gissibl Friends, including spurned *Bundesleiter* Walter, he attempted to wrest control of the organization from Gissibl in 1934. Gissibl fought back in a political tug of war, with accusations, slanders, and egos boiling over into an ugly mess.[7]

With top leaders in constant flux and fighting, individual chapters looked elsewhere for disciplined inspiration. It wasn't difficult. The strict regimented order instituted by Hitler's government served the ideal model for developing a political party, with systematic elements that could grow into a powerful national organization. Local chapters worked harmoniously to bring together a network uniting East, Midwest, and West Coast gaus.

As the head man in Detroit, Kuhn demanded change—and with that change there would be complete obedience to his command. The Friends, he firmly believed, behaved like a weak-willed organization afraid to raise a collective voice against the Jew-dominated United States government and their comrades in the Jew-controlled press. What, he asked his new subordinates, were they so afraid of?

It was not fear, members tried to explain. Rather it was a matter of political tact. Still scarred by the anti-German bile and biases of the Great War and its aftermath, a German in America had to be careful. One member of the Detroit chapter had direct experience in this arena. His father-in-law was victimized by the Alien Property Custodian Act of 1917. These statutes enacted by the Wilson administration allowed for complete seizure of property and possessions of any foreigner suspected as an enemy agent lurking in the United States. It was by these dictates, Kuhn was told, that this man had been scapegoated, with a "sizeable sum" of his money confiscated by the authorities. Now the man was working his way through the court system in hopes of regaining what was rightfully his. This was a delicate process, one that required a certain amount of discretion. Though the Detroit Friends longed for a New Order, they were straightjacketed by the Federal system.

Nonsense, Kuhn said. Such men were a weak-willed disgrace and undeserving of the title as a "Friend" of the New Germany. These cowards must be dealt with accordingly and with no sympathy.

He watched closely, looking through his underlings for any sign of wavering from the strength of German discipline. Kuhn took down names of members he believed did not display proper respect to Adolf Hitler and NSDAP ideals. Their names and addresses were collated into a sizeable list, which Kuhn then brought to the German Consulate. This action, Kuhn believed, would serve as stern warning to any man who doubted his resolve.[8]

Exactly what the German Consul might do with this information, Kuhn did not know. The point, he insisted, was to make sure those disloyal to the *Führer* were ferreted out and made examples of to others. These men were citizens of the Fatherland, not naturalized Americans, yet were not loyal to their exalted bloodline. "I did not want them in the organization," Kuhn declared, "and I wanted [the German Consul] to know who they were. . . . I don't know what authority he had, or what action he could take." What was important was throwing down the symbolic gauntlet. A new man with clear vision for The Friends of New Germany was emerging from the Motor City.[9]

Kuhn was promoted to head of the Midwest gau in 1935. In less than a single year he'd risen from member to Detroit head and now was commander of an entire region. Fritz Kuhn was a man filled with potential.

The Friends, for all their problems with leadership, developed a framework that would have long-term benefits for Fritz Kuhn. For inspiration they looked to the Fatherland and its unique brand of marshaling all aspects of the country's folk. The centuries-old Teutonic reputation for order and discipline infused Hitler's bureaucracy in fine detail to create the infrastructure vital to Nazi Germany's success. A paramilitary order to guard and enforce the law. A propaganda machine for effective communication. A well-oiled youth program for developing and nurturing new generations of Third Reich leaders for decades to come. All these elements of the NSDAP provided ideal models for the vision of an American Swastika Nation.

The Friends developed their own brand of protective marching enforcers, the *Ordnungsdienst*, German for "uniformed services," or some sort of police force. Commonly referred to as the OD, the men in this disciplined unit served as security at Friends events and as bodyguards for higher ups. A potential OD man filled out an application which read, in part: "I put myself at the disposal of the Friends of New Germany for the Protection of its members, friends, and guests, as well as its property, using all my strength and ability, and that I do not make any demands upon its Leader and upon the League." OD men also promised to maintain the highest of military discipline standards and "to follow the orders of the Leader at any time."[10] The OD started loosely as a protective unit during the Teutonia days, and further developed under Spanknöbel through his lackey Josef "Sepp" Schuster, who was well qualified for the position.[11] In postwar Germany, before his immigration to the United States, Schuster belonged to the *Sturmabteilung* (commonly known as the SA), the brown-shirted thug force of guardsman and enforcers that evolved into the Nazi paramilitary brute force *Schutzstaffel*, the infamous SS squads.

Beyond guaranteeing security, OD men were a disturbing presence on

Manhattan streets, hooligans foisting Friends leaflets and Nazi-provided pamphlets into the hands of unsettled pedestrians.[12] The newsstands in York-ville and other New York German neighborhoods were neutral territory from this propaganda, with proprietors content to peddle community news-papers, *The New York Times, Time* magazine, and other stock fair. This changed in August 1933, when a new publication crept into the stacks: *Deutsche Zei-tung*, "A Fighting Paper for Truth and Right—A Bridge between the United States and Germany." The Friends of New Germany was now in the news-paper business.[13]

The *Deutsche Zeitung* editor was Walter Kappe, who, while no Joseph Goebbels, had stellar credentials for the job. A longtime associate of Gissi-bl's, Kappe got his start in the 1920s editing Teutonia's tabloid *Vorposten*, "News of the German Freedom Movement in the United States." His work was earmarked by comically grammar-free prose, stringing together clichés and stereotypes straight out of Ford's *The International Jew*, coupled with a heavy dollop of material imported from Germany.[14]

This tradition was carried on in *Deutsche Zeitung*. Most of its content was made up of verbatim reprints of propaganda brought in from Germany. Kappe also tried to reach out to a broader audience, combining Nazi anti-Semitism with American racial fears and prejudices. The day was coming, Kappe liked to warn readers, when Jews of all stripes would unite with the darker-skinned races to overthrow the natural order of Aryan dominance. German-Americans must be prepared for the onslaught.[15]

Such groundwork required long-range thinking. Like the NSDAP Hit-ler Youth initiative, The Friends developed activities for German-American children. There was no subtlety to this branch of the organization. Swim-ming, athletic competitions, and other standards for any American summer camp were coupled with marches and drills where the American flag flew side by side with swastika banners. In the battle for supremacy of Aryan order a well-trained child was the foundation for adult warriors. Typical of these Friends havens was Camp *Wille und Macht* (Will and Might), located just north of Princeton, New Jersey. In the summer of 1934, some two hundred children from throughout the New York/New Jersey region, ex-tending up into Buffalo and from German communities in Philadelphia, participated in camp activities.[16]

Shortly after Hitler's rise to power Samuel Untermeyer rallied for a boy-cott of imported German goods, insisting his initiative be aimed at goods brought to America by German vessels. Yet the follow-through itself was not always neat. In many cases German merchants sympathetic to the plight of Jews in their homeland—particularly grocers and delicatessen owners— were unfairly hit hard in the cash register. This boycott, The Friends declared, was part of a Jewish plot to destroy German commerce for their own nefarious ends. Fears of new persecution stirred up and rekindled German-American anxiety of the postwar era. But this time, The Friends insisted, there was safe haven among united kinsmen. Seizing the opportunity to bolster their ranks and promote their ideology, The Friends rallied members of the German-American Business League to their cause, forming the German-American Protective Alliance, an organization commonly known as DAWA after its German name, *Deutsch-Amerikanischer Wirtschafts-Ausschuss.*

A guide to German-friendly businesses was released, stores put signs in the window declaring kinship with DAWA, and stickers exhorting customers "Don't Buy from Jews" were distributed. The campaign spread from Yorkville into German enclaves throughout Brooklyn and the Bronx. Storeowners, businessmen, and their respective customers saw the strength in numbers and eagerly joined The Friends, an unintended result of Untermeyer's initiative.[17]

Strong bonds were developed through this counter boycott. A yearbook provided to members at a formal dance, held by a Brooklyn chapter on June 3, 1934, looked like any other fraternal order annual, with standard pictures of smiling members, the women's auxiliary, and youth group activities. One photo depicted unit leader Josef Schuster delivering a fiery speech on a podium decorated with an American flag while stoic OD men stood guard. The photo caption boldly (and perhaps hyperbolically) declared an unseen crowd of six thousand was soaking in the *gauleiter*'s oration.

The yearbook was filled with advertisements typical for such a publication. Neighborhood photographers, tailors, travel agencies, hardware stores, merchants of women's undergarments, and shoe salesmen—some probable members of The Friends—all bought space. Several merchants emphasized Germany loyalty in their advertisements with a hearty *"Sieg Heil!"* in the copy.

The main event of the evening was a music program and dancing, with a selection of compositions by mostly German composers. Another high point was a flag presentation of the American Stars and Stripes and the NSDAP government's swastika, coupled with the singing of the two national anthems, "The Star-Spangled Banner" and the *Deutschlandlied* (*"Deutschland über alles"*).[18]

Wherever The Friends met, enemies followed. Meetings were broken up by demonstrators. Police were called, arrests were made, and newspapers in major cities reveled in stories about brawling Nazi thugs. None of it looked good.

The Friends didn't endear themselves to the public any further by their association with one of America's most hated men: Bruno Hauptmann. On February 13, 1935, Hauptmann was sentenced to death for the kidnapping and murder of eighteen-month-old Charles Lindbergh Jr., son of America's beloved aviator. Factions within The Friends were convinced their fellow German immigrant Hauptmann was nothing more than a patsy. Before his notoriety, Hauptman spent time with fellow immigrants, many of whom belonged to The Friends. At one point his landlady attempted to evict Hauptmann, complaining he held too many late-night drinking parties, often with Friends members.[19]

Granted, Lindbergh—a man of Swedish heritage—physically defined the Aryan Nazi ideal and his murdered baby was a model of "Gentile perfection." Hence, an alibi proving Hauptmann's innocence was concocted, with a tortured explanation typical of age-old anti-Semitic canards. The arrest, trial, and conviction were all part of a conspiracy, official Friends propaganda declared, "to shift public sentiment against Hauptmann and his home country . . ." This cabal was funded by "Jewish money" and in collusion with "the Jew press."[20]

Congressman Dickstein felt the time had come to look into The Friends, telling one reporter he wanted to remove any trace of Nazism from the United States. As he pushed for a congressional investigation, Dickstein inherently understood that as a Jew he would be accused of using his political power to punish German-Americans for filial devotion to their homeland. This point was emphasized in the pages of *Deutsche Zeitung*, where Kappe decried Dickstein's committee as nothing more than a "Jewish Inquisition."[21] Even Martha Griebel, once slandered by the Gissibl factions of The Friends, weighed in on the matter, writing to President Roosevelt that "Congressman Dickstein, as a Jew, cannot under existing conditions, be tolerant and just in his conclusions," asking that he be replaced in any official actions with "a neutral congressman, preferably an American Gentile."[22]

To avoid any possible suggestion of ulterior motives Representative John

McCormack of Massachusetts, son of Irish immigrants, was selected to head the newly formed Special Committee on Un-American Activities, with Dickstein serving as vice chairman. Their so-called "Dickstein-McCormack Investigatory Committee" was formed with the express idea of looking into Nazi activities in the United States.[23]

From the start, the committee was charged with controversy. The appropriately-named Texas representative Maury Maverick declared the whole investigation a farce, stating, "Un-American is simply something that somebody else does not agree to."[24] Dickstein, while officially the second in command, quickly asserted himself as lead investigator. His abrasive personality was countered by McCormack's more reticent demeanor, but the two worked well together as a sort of bad cop/good cop congressional team. The committee held hearings throughout the country, with twenty-four closed executive sessions and seven public hearings. Gissibl and his rival Griebel were called to testify, as were several hundred of The Friends and other suspected Nazi sympathizers.[25]

Dickstein made no pretenses about his true feelings, often badgering witnesses and pushing them to emotional limits. Without any proof, Dickstein declared all German seamen were secret Nazi agents and the Hitler government was running guns into the United States.[26] Ignoring condemnations from some congressional peers, Dickstein took his crusade to radio and newspapers. His pronouncements and accusations were natural fodder for sensational reporting, exactly the kind of whipped up publicity the congressman had hoped for to get the public behind him.[27]

The Friends pushed back. At a New York public hearing on October 17, 1934, some two hundred members packed the hearing room, continually interrupting the proceedings with jeers and catcalls. The tense atmosphere ratcheted up as Dickstein and onlookers heard the testimony of Ludwig Werner, an ousted Friends member. He was kicked out of the organization, Werner declared, because "I was too smart to obey orders blindly."

His assessment set off a mass psychological trigger. The hecklers barked out cries of "*Heil* Hitler!" Desperate to bring back some sense of decorum, Congressman McCormack cried out, "I desire to ask the people not to construe this action as representing Americans of German blood. Actions of this kind reflect discredit on the Friends of New Germany." His response got swallowed in mob action bordering on near-riot. For safety's sake, the hearing was shut down.

The melee spilled out into the hallway. Police officers managed to hold off a crowd of Jewish spectators, determined to counter the hearing room pandemonium by The Friends with some healthy fisticuffs of their own.[28]

After ten months of contentious hearings, the Dickstein-McCormack Committee released its findings in February 1935. According to the report, the Nazi government was providing propaganda for dissemination in the United States, money was being funneled through clandestine channels to aid The Friends of New Germany, and the youth camps were devoted to indoctrination of Nazi principles and un-American ideals. Mandatory registration for foreigners circulating propaganda in the United States was recommended; furthermore, congressional committees were to be allowed an extension of subpoena powers for hearings held outside of Washington. Congress agreed and both items were passed into law.[29]

Theodore Hoffmann, top man at the Steuben Society, understood that loyal German-Americans must take action against The Friends. In the wake of postwar anti-Teutonic sentiments, German-Americans founded the Society and named it after Friedrich von Steuben, the German-born chief of staff to General George Washington. Steuben Society members had worked hard to rehabilitate the image of their homeland and countrymen in America. The good will and fragile coalitions built by Society members was rapidly being undermined by The Friends of New Germany, a group that viewed Hoffmann and his kind with deep mistrust and contempt. As one member of The Friends later recalled, "[Our] origin was that young, truth-loving Germans in this country were enraged over the Jewish hate propaganda [against Germans] and unable to get the old established German American societies . . . to act and to fight this hate campaign . . ."[30]

In what must have been a move of sheer desperation to quell troubles whipped up by The Friends, Hoffmann took the ultimate in ironic action: he finagled an audience with the *Führer* himself, hoping this could rectify all difficulties. The Friends of New Germany, Hoffmann implored Hitler, were no friends of the Fatherland. Rather, they were denigrating the Nazi government's already unsavory image within the United States. Something had to be done and soon. To Hoffmann's dismay, Hitler appeared to show little interest in the American dilemma.[31]

The *Führer*'s apathy was apparent veneer. He sent a note to Hess, asking if there was any substance to Hoffmann's concerns. On this matter, the German Foreign Ministry already was on point. It was understood that The

Friends were an increasing liability in America.[32] Between the constant internal squabbling and unpopular public actions, coupled with burgeoning Congressional heat, the group was a monumental embarrassment. With representatives like The Friends of New Germany, the NSDAP couldn't have chosen a worse public face in the United States for propagating Hitler's ideals.

Yet between the OD, the publication division, youth and family programs, and DAWA The Friends had a foundation in place. For this infrastructure to build into its mightiest potential, a visionary leader must be found to cultivate the future.

In July 1935 during a national gathering of The Friends in Pennsylvania, Kuhn asserted himself as a bold thinker proffering a unique challenge to the organization as a whole. Extending Berlin's edict that The Friends of New Germany leader be an American, Kuhn argued that The Friends could be a mighty political force in their adopted country if membership was the exclusive domain of United States citizens—albeit those with Teutonic roots. No German nationals should belong, he argued, otherwise the organization would be nothing more than Germans for Germany hunkering down in a foreign land, attracting unwanted attention from a country already suspicious of the Fatherland's affairs. If they became a strictly American organization with a focus on developing influence as United States citizens, The Friends of New Germany could better ingratiate Nazi ideology into mainstream American society.[33]

His outlook gathered no traction with higher-ups, but Kuhn continued to impress. A remarkable gift for administration, public speaking, and what was considered a "methodical mind" earned him considerable attention beyond convention halls. Kuhn's star power was starting to take hold among the rank and file in Friends chapters across the country.[34]

The death knell for The Friends came in October 1935. Under direct instructions from Hitler, Rudolf Hess decreed that German nationals living in the United States must cease all political activity, including membership in the Friends of New Germany.[35]

It was a stunning blow. How could the beloved *Führer* turn against his loyal American supporters? Walter Kappe declared this order was just another "Jewish lie by a Jewish paper." In disbelief, Gissibl went to Berlin to get the facts for himself.[36]

To his shock and dismay, the edict was indeed true. Two months later Hess again ordered all German nationals to leave The Friends. Embarrassed and defeated, The Friends of New Germany leadership sent a statement presenting the "clarification of our attitude" to the membership, as well as members of the press.

The edict released on Christmas Day was unequivocal: "The leaders of the Friends of New Germany will require from its members who are German nationals an unconditional compliance with this order. The severance of such members from the organization must be complete by December 31, 1935. This includes also those who have only their first American citizenship papers."[37] The Friends of New Germany appeared to be at their end.

In Detroit, Fritz Kuhn had other ideas.

PART II

The Rise of the German-American Bund

"We Germans must become a power in the United States."

—*BUNDESFÜHRER* FRITZ KUHN[1]

4

Bundesführer

IN THE WAKE OF Berlin's official Christmas edict, Gissibl's days clearly were numbered. His cause was on the brink of collapse, pulled into an ideological abyss by petty infighting and foolish power struggles. If there was any hope for survival of the Friends of New Germany, Gissibl quickly needed to install a fresh and bold leader, someone with the power of imagination to forge the remnants of the organization into a cohesive whole. In essence, this man must be strong, intelligent, resolute, unyielding, and inspirational. An American parallel to Adolf Hitler.

Gissibl found that man in the outspoken and charismatic leader from Detroit—a contradictory, maddening, wholly unlikely figure, part Caesar and part popinjay, bursting with potential.

Gissibl took the plunge. In December he ceded his power, conferring Fritz Kuhn as provisional leader of The Friends of New Germany.

In his position as Detroit and then Midwestern leader, Kuhn demanded his members take a more aggressive attitude, and regularly suit up in garb patterned after the NSDAP uniform. Now, as The Friends' pro tem authority, Kuhn's daily attire was commensurate to that of *Der Führer* himself. A military-style jacket. Crisp pants with sharp crease. A black leather Sam Browne belt, wide at the waist with a diagonal supporting strap looping over the right shoulder. Decorations on the left breast pocket. And despite his soft body and weak eyes, a hardened stance and fierce look that commanded respect from loyalists.[1]

In January 1936, not even a month after Kuhn's appointment, word circulated among The Friends that Gissibl was returning to Germany for good. With the founder in exile and other would-be commanders rendered obsolete by their own doing, Kuhn could not afford to make the same mistakes as his predecessors. His power must be complete, unchallenged, and quickly solidified. A missive was sent out to Friends chapters throughout the country. A convention was to be held in Buffalo, New York come March. Change was imminent.

From Yorkville, Brooklyn, the Bronx, Newark, Cincinnati, Detroit, Chicago, Milwaukee, Los Angeles, and other chapters across the country they came. On March 29, 1936, The Friends of New Germany began its transformation to the New Order of Fritz Kuhn's coveted Swastika Nation.

Buffalo, New York lies on the eastern shores of Lake Erie, about twenty miles south of Niagara Falls. In 1936 it was a decidedly blue-collar city with a population including various extractions of Irish, Polish, Italian, and German immigrants. Buffalo's German community was also comprised of a thriving Jewish neighborhood. Despite this latter demographic, Buffalo was apparently hospitable enough to the German cause, and as such a place for The Friends to regroup when their new leader convened his first national meeting.

Delegates flocked into Buffalo's Hotel Statler for the two-day event held the weekend of March 28 and 29. Hotel staff fielded angry phone calls from a score of angry protestors furious that such a historic city landmark would host a Nazi convention.[2] With delegates openly displaying Sam Browne belts and military-style, swastika-festooned shirts, Buffalo's citizens might have thought it was a demi-invasion of Hitler acolytes straight off the boat from Germany. No, Kuhn insisted, this gathering was nothing of the sort. "We are one hundred percent Americans," he proclaimed, "and therefore not Nazis."

Some opponents felt differently. Waiting to greet Kuhn and The Friends of New Germany was a feisty band of American Communists. They staked their political ground on the sidewalk, hurling anti-Nazi chants at any Friends delegate trying to enter the Hotel Statler. The last thing police needed was a potential street brawl between brown shirts and Reds. The Bolshie protestors were hustled from the scene.

Kuhn applauded the move, publicly aligning his group with the spirit of the police action. The Friends, he declared, "is solemnly pledged to expose and help the government to eradicate Communistic groups like this one here in Buffalo . . . camouflaging their real purpose of spreading Soviet Russia's doctrine . . ."[3]

Police actions weren't enough to stop the Reds from making one last symbolic public statement. Sometime during the night of March 28, an unknown number of local Communists snuck into the hotel. The next morning delegates were stunned to see a proud Communist flag poking out of a seventeenth-story window, flapping in all its glory as a final Red thumb in the eyes of Friends conventioneers.[4]

With the Communists in check, Kuhn next turned his attention to another potential source for agitation: the prying eyes of any interlopers. It was given that The Friends had plenty of enemies beyond the realms of Jews and Bolsheviks. Such forces must not be allowed into the convention. A strict order was enacted forbidding entrance into the meeting room for anyone other than delegates. The Friends of New Germany was a private organization holding an exclusive meeting. Outsiders—including Kuhn's perceived menace of Jewish-controlled newspapers or any public-at-large gadflies—were *verboten*.[5]

Anti-Red fervor continued inside the hall once formal business got under way. A resolution was passed declaring communism, "the greatest conceivable danger for all peoples of the world and particularly our own country." Presumably "our own country" meant the United States.

And yet, while strongly maintaining they were Americans first, The Friends remained loyal to Germany. Three weeks earlier Hitler terminated the *Reichstag*, remilitarized the Rhineland, and called for a national plebiscite to be held in late March—by sheer coincidence the same time that The Friends were gathered in Buffalo. The election results provided exactly what the fiery chancellor demanded. By a margin of nearly 100 percent, German citizens agreed that only Nazi Party candidates would be allowed on the ballot for upcoming general elections. The electorate also gave vehement approval for Hitler's military actions. William L. Shirer, the American journalist who witnessed the rise and fall of the Third Reich firsthand, reported that this was a referendum with no secrets. Given the ominous scrutiny of Gestapo poll watchers, few Germans would be so foolish as to publically cast their vote against the NSDAP.[6] Regardless of how the Reich accomplished its electoral goals, The Friends of New Germany were inspired with the results, passing a second resolution applauding Hitler for his absolute victory at the ballot box.[7]

The convention culminated with the election of Kuhn as the new leader, thus solidifying the position handed to him by Gissibl. Standing on a podium swathed with American Stars and Stripes and Nazi swastikas, Kuhn heartily accepted his now official position.[8]

While inside the hall the Fatherland was exalted, outside Kuhn knew any American group supporting the Hitler government would be treated as a pariah in the United States. An image change was paramount for survival and expansion. Kuhn returned to his vision, first proposed at The Friends of New Germany's 1935 gathering in Pennsylvania. Building the organization on traditional American principles would be more effective in winning hearts and minds. It was time to march into a new era. Henceforth, under Kuhn's leadership the Friends of New Germany would be known as *Der Amerikadeutscher Volksbund*, the German-American Bund, an all-American organization with supposedly nothing more than tangential loyalties to the Fatherland.

An official booklet, *Awake and Act!* penned by the new *bundesleiter*, laid out the reasoning for this name change. "The Friends of the New Germany did great and glorious work during the past years," Kuhn wrote. "It was always at all times an aggressive organization, and the German American Volksbund will continue to be as active and aggressive, yes, it will even intensify its attacks upon lies and political incendiarism, against Marxism and Bolshevism, and will not shirk its duty to wage war with every available power. But a change of name seemed dictated by good judgment if we are now to accomplish our ends."

This was not, Kuhn insisted, a matter of simply jettisoning the honorable former name, one that should always be looked on with pride. As The Friends of New Germany, they had engaged in a noble cause. That illustrious name, however, no longer reflected the organization's larger mission.

[T]he exercise of our objects demands a wider field and our movement a broader foundation," he wrote. "During the first years of our movement no better title could have been selected for our activities, but today every German by birth or descent should be a friend—an assumption we take for granted—a friend of present-day Germany.

As an organization of American citizens, it [the Bund] proposes to take an active part in the affairs of the country while complying unqualifiedly with its duties to the United States. We shall educate the American people to become friends of the new Germany. As American citizens [we shall] advance our political interests, defend our native land against lies and slander. We shall always observe loyalty as citizens of this country, linked as it is with the destiny of our ancestral race. Hence we call ourselves American Germans and our movement the German American Volksbund. The Bund is American in its inception and in its field of endeavor.[9]

Two weeks later, on April 17, three days before Hitler's forty-seventh birthday, *Awake and Act!* was handed out to some fifteen thousand zealous partisans at a meeting hall in New York's Yorkville neighborhood. Kuhn was officially sworn in as the German-American Bund *bundesleiter*. His inaugural address pulled no punches.

"Our task over here is to fight Jewish Marxism and Communism!" he thundered. "So long as there's a swastika, there'll be no hammer and sickle in this country."[10]

Only three years ago Fritz Kuhn had been nothing more than a minor cog in the Henry Ford complex. Now, through hard work, conniving moves, and seeming sheer will, he was the *Bundesleiter* of *Der Amerikadeutscher Bund*, a man poised to emulate the great Adolf Hitler and bring a glorious fascist government, a Swastika Nation of his own making, to the United States of America.

5

Order

OFFICIAL STATEMENTS FROM THE German-American Bund emphasized it was a patriotic organization of naturalized citizens brimming with allegiance for their adopted country. This red, white, and blue veneer was an obvious cover. Kuhn was determined to infuse the ideals of the New German Order within the American political and social landscape. Bundists were German to the core, loyal to their Teutonic bloodline, the Fatherland, the NSDAP, and Hitler. "We cannot and must not deny our racial characteristics," Kuhn proclaimed, "because if we did we would be useless to America."[1]

Kuhn amplified his intentions by purging the last title used by The Friends for their supreme leader, "president." It stank of assimilation, a seeming renunciation of every Bundist's exalted heritage. Kuhn demanded a return to the robust *Führer*, the title dropped by The Friends since Hitler was the only man worthy of this exalted rank. Kuhn felt differently. If *"Führer"* was good enough for the German Nazi leader, then the United States commandant must have the title as well. Still, Kuhn held deep reverence for Adolf Hitler. The title was slightly altered in deference to the one and only *Führer*. Henceforth Fritz Kuhn, the duly elected commander-in-chief of the German-American Bund, would be officially known as the *Bundesführer*.[2]

As *Bundesführer*, Kuhn inherited *Der Führerprinzip*, the Leadership Principle. Spanknöbel and Gissibl had struggled to enforce the concept, but Kuhn, using his gifts for seduction, easily sold it to his Bundists.

Having watched and studied Hitler, Kuhn understood how the Leadership Principle worked on a political level. And as an employee of Henry

Ford—who used a tycoon's variation of the Leadership Principle to oversee a vast oligarchic business empire—Kuhn witnessed how one man with vision and determination could control his people on a monumental scale.

This business aspect of the Leadership Principle was vital to the continued growth of the German-American Bund given the economic landscape of the mid-1930s, still a time of financial struggle throughout the United States. President Roosevelt's New Deal reforms had cracked some millstones of the Great Depression, but in December 1935 as Gissibl officially bestowed leadership of The Friends to Kuhn, many American businesses remained in dire straits. Kuhn's quick solidification of The Friends' fragmented infrastructure was a business model that other failing enterprises might have been smart to adopt. If the *Bundesführer* had been handed over the reins of a conventional but wheezing corporation rather than the struggling factions of a quasi-Nazi party, he might have been considered a commercial genius.

One of Kuhn's first actions upon his appointment by Gissibl, even before his official election, was to take complete charge of the OD. They became his personal bodyguards, responding to Kuhn's every demand with unquestioning allegiance. Everything about Kuhn's revamped OD was sacrosanct. Uniforms commanded respect, with black shoes, long black pants sans cuffs, gunmetal grey shirts with black necktie, black Sam Browne belts, light gray tunics similar to that of the U.S. Army, and black caps. Chevron badges were designed for easy removal so members could walk freely after meetings without identifying themselves to the public at large as OD men. They were forbidden from carrying firearms, though a protective truncheon was de rigueur. Weekly training meetings emphasized physical strength and psychological loyalty. Together an OD unit gave a steely impression that for all intents and purposes was a menacing and highly ordered human machine. The OD men provided Bundists with "the assurance that our movement will, at the sacrifice of life if necessary, *remain* the inexorable opponent of Jewish Marxism and the uncompromising champion of the demands of American Germans."[3]

With protection in place, a lengthy constitution, originally developed by The Friends at their 1935 convention, was massaged in early 1936 to Kuhn's liking. The revised document amounted to a corporate mission statement for the German-American Bund, bland but thorough to the core in its bureaucratic structure. The bund conglomerate broke down into a series of subdivisions, with each level administered by a carefully prescribed management structure. At the top, of course, was Kuhn, the all-powerful *Bundesführer*/chief executive officer. The Friends national three gau structure of East Coast, Midwest, and West Coast remained; this troika was then broken down into territorial sectors. The constitution spelled out in exact minutia what was expected at each level of the corporate hierarchy, drilling down into a complex network of departments, regions, districts, sections, units, branches, cells, blocks, and assemblies in private homes. A system of community activities was also laid out, including recreational and educational divisions for women, children and teenagers, various cultural events, and "others deemed as necessary over time."

In keeping with their mission to be looked on as patriotic Americans, the Bund constitution lifted the opening passage of the Declaration of Independence, altering with Nazi flourish what John Adams dubbed Thomas Jefferson's "felicity of expression." The reworked phraseology, calling for German-American loyalty to "Common Blood," was punctuated by the Bundist promise to "endow every American of German Origin with that absolute Equality with any and all other Americans, that is essential to the preservation of the inalienable Right to Life, Liberty, and the Pursuit of Happiness in a truly sovereign United States of America, ruled in accordance with Aryan Christian Precepts!"

At the heart of the document was the ironclad dictate of the Leadership Principle. Members were told categorically that the ". . . Office of National Leader renders the final decision in all matters pertaining to the Movement and has the absolute power of ownership over the Bund, its monetary or other property and its policies; to remain ever aware that the Bund is not limited to the Unit or any other Subdivision or Part, but that the primary Loyalty of the Member is due the Bund as such, personified in its National Leader."[4]

Like his figurative mentors Hitler and Ford, Kuhn maintained a loyal inner circle, a Bundist board of directors that oversaw various wings and business interests to make sure his word was followed to the letter. They were also loyal to NSDAP ideals and equipped with proper Aryan heritage. Gerhard Wilhelm Kunze, a New Jersey–born grease monkey turned limo driver turned fanatical National Socialist, was appointed national publicity director and Kuhn's second-in-command.[5] James Wheeler-Hill, a man of Latvian parentage, was Kuhn's national secretary. Various other men, loyal to Kuhn and fully understanding of how the Leadership Principle was to be carried out, filled additional subordinate positions. A headquarters was established at 178 E. 85th Street in New York's German Yorkville neighborhood where Kuhn ran his empire.

Membership, as per the constitution, was open "to all Americans and prospective citizens of Aryan blood of German extraction and good reputation." This was in blatant violation of Hess's 1935 order forbidding anyone other than American citizens from joining The Friends. Under Kuhn's directive, an easy loophole was found giving German nationals a demi-membership via the heading "Prospective Citizens League," which allowed participation in the Bund to any German in the process of becoming a naturalized American citizen. While such associates could not have high-rank inclusion privileges such as becoming a divisional leader, they were readily accepted into the rest of the fold, including membership in OD squadrons. Another subcategory was a simple moneymaking operation that allowed anonymous participation by "those persons who sympathize with our struggle and work and who express this sympathy by paying regular donations of money."[6]

More income was generated via annual dues coupled with creative ancillary fees. Individuals paid nine dollars per year at a rate of seventy-five cents per month. On top of this was a required twenty cents more for a membership card. A propaganda campaign demanded each member contribute an additional dollar and fifty cents. The mandatory purchase of *Mein Kampf* and other prescribed reading brought in further dollars. Compulsory uniforms for rank-and-file and OD squads must be purchased from Kuhn-approved tailors. Bundists had to purchase various armbands, signet pins, and badges for auxiliary functions, which naturally required an entry fee. Items for home use, ranging from bookends to dishware to records of Bund choral groups were also mandatory purchases.

The AV Publishing Company was the propaganda wing, taking its name from the initials of the Bund's German name, *Amerikadeutscher Volksbund*. Walter Kappe, editor of many publications for The Friends, continued to serve in this capacity for the Bund. The weekly flagship newspaper, *Deutscher Weckruf und Beobachter*, which translated as "The German Wakeup Call and Observer," was published in New York, with regional editions focusing on stories of local interest distributed in Philadelphia, Chicago, and Los Angeles. Readers enjoyed a bevy of articles, features, editorials, and regular columns. Some content was in German and some in English; and in both cases the tabloid pulled no punches. *Deutscher Weckruf und Beobachter*—nicknamed "our battle press"—specialized in anti-Semitic sensationalism and zealous pro-Nazi rhetoric. Editorial directors made no secret that some of their stories, copious illustrations, and transcriptions of Hitler's speeches were reprints of material supplied by the German propaganda office, ballyhoo that was gladly accepted. Advertising placed by German businesses and tourist agencies was a lucrative source of revenue for newspaper operations.

An annual subscription, an obligation for all Bundists, was three dollars per year. But subscribing to the *Deutscher Weckruf und Beobachter* by rank-and-file members was not good enough. Bundists received a harsh order from Kuhn: they were expected to help "spread the fight through our newspaper." It was absolute duty to increase revenues through recruitment of additional readership and drumming up advertising dollars.[7]

Bund-friendly printers churned out the newspaper across the country. Beyond the tabloid Kuhn provided them plenty of other work. AV Publishing was in the propaganda business. Myriads of pamphlets, leaflets, booklets, and other staples developed for dissemination to the faithful and would-be recruits. Many of these items required that the checks be made out to *Bundesführer* Kuhn. Under the Leadership Principle he had sole discretion of Bund expenditures. There would be no questioning of this wisdom.

At least for the time being.

Still, this was the midst of the Depression, and financially strapped German-American Bundists were just as affected by the country's economic woes as their non-Aryan counterparts. Kuhn dismissed any grousing and ended all arguments with an anti-Semitic spin. "It is only through a spirit of joyous self-sacrifice that we shall prevail," he told followers. "The Jewish spirit of materialism must not be permitted to enter the Bund or we shall be destroyed individually and collectively."[8]

Deutscher Konsum Verband (DKV), the German Business League, was a key element in Kuhn's moneymaking operations. In essence the DKV was a rejuvenated manifestation of DAWA, the merchants association organized by The Friends. Resentments left over from the postwar boycotts of the early 1920s coupled with the rise of Hitler and his sweeping anti-Semitic reforms rippled throughout the United States, particularly in urban centers with large Jewish populations such as New York City and Chicago. These sentiments translated into a new homegrown economic embargo. Given the resulting financial pressures, the need for this businessmen's alliance remained vital. DKV-associated businesses found friendly and sympathetic Bund customers through advertisements in *Deutscher Weckruf und Beobachter*, which gave ample editorial space to the organization. Advertisements whipped up slogans appealing to the sacred Teutonic bloodlines of consumers: "Patronize Gentile Stores Only." "Aryan Buying Pays Aryan Men."[9]

AV Publishing produced guidebooks directing customers to DKV merchants. "[T]he present time makes economy in all matters a necessity," read one directory. "We, therefore, ask you to make it a habitual [sic] to consult the D.K.V. Trade Guide." "Always ask for D.K.V. stamps," commanded another booklet. "Buy only in D.K.V. stores."[10] A listing cost three dollars annually, and the benefits were well worth the fee in terms of business generated. The guidebooks contained saving stamps, which provided discounts to customers. These stamps also racked in monetary returns to the DKV bureaucracy in general, and Bund coffers overall. Stamps could be earned for each purchase of ten cents, with books holding space for five hundred stamps or fifty dollars worth. Once a book was filled, it could be redeemed for one dollar and twenty-five cents.[11]

The DKV held Christmas shopping extravaganzas in meeting halls and marketplaces in New York, Chicago, and other cities. Customers browsed from booth to booth at the "Buy German for Christmas" marketplaces, procuring various goods, services, and propaganda books and pamphlets. Door prizes were part of the fun, and lucky winners might end up with a round-trip ticket to the Fatherland.[12] Yet this nationwide Yuletide effort was more than just shopping for holiday baubles and NSDAP-friendly reading material. It was billed as "the living expression of the iron determination to form commercial relations between America and Germany, as well as to put up on the other hand a resistance . . . against the Jewish boycott of German goods, a resistance in an unspeakably difficult struggle which on the side of their enemies is being waged with equal bitter determination a fight for the continued existence of the German racial Christian businessman in our new home country."[13]

At one Christmas sale a Ford sedan was offered as a door prize, an expensive and unusual item for any mid-Depression-era giveaway. Just how the German-American Bund could afford to hand out a free car from Henry Ford's assembly line is a mystery.[14]

At long last, after so many misfires from too many incompetent leaders and too much interparty strife, *Bundesführer* Kuhn had created the solid structure within which a legitimate brand of American Nazism could thrive. What was needed now, as symbolic benediction for the German-American Bund and their bond to *Deutschland* was official recognition from the NSDAP government. With all eyes on Berlin and the 1936 Olympics, the time was ripe for Kuhn to make a return visit to his homeland for an audience with Adolf Hitler, a man Kuhn insisted he followed from the very beginning of National Socialism at the Beer Hall Putsch. Petty squabbling of past days was over; through the Bund, Kuhn declared, Germans in the United States worked together as a cohesive nationalist group that found inspiration from the stoic New Order of Berlin.

PART III

Swastika Nation

"Our enemies call us Nazis and we proudly confess that we are. YES, WE ARE THE AMERICAN NAZIS!"

—*Deutscher Weckruf und Beobachter,*
    September 8, 1938[1]

6

Olympia

THE INTERNATIONAL OLYMPIC COMMITTEE (IOC) named Berlin as host city for the 1936 Olympiad in 1931, while Germany was still ruled by the Weimar Republic. Five years later, a radically new German government was in place. Through this prism, the games were to be a sparkling showcase for the New Germany, reinvigorated from its shattered state during the postwar era to domineering status as a world leader under the all-powerful rule of Adolf Hitler.

No expense was too great for this serendipitous opportunity. A majestic stadium was built for ceremonial events and athletic contests. An array of pageants, parades, and artistic displays was organized. Hitler's henchmen Joseph Goebbels, Hermann Göring, and Joachim von Ribbentrop planned extravagant parties for world visitors.[1] Leni Riefenstahl, the gifted filmmaker who changed the face of documentary cinema with *Triumph of the Will*, her visualization of the 1934 Nazi rally at Nuremberg, was hired to orchestrate what became *Olympia*, an impressionistic nonfiction film lauding athletic virtues of the modern Aryan.[2]

In Jewish circles throughout the United States there was a growing demand to boycott what was now dubbed "Hitler's Olympics." Leaders of the Jewish community made personal and public appeals to officials of the American Olympic Association (AOA; today's American Olympic Committee), declaring the anti-Semitic pronouncements in Germany as unacceptable to the very spirit of what the Games symbolized. Avery Brundage—head of the AOA and a proud alumnus of the 1912 Stockholm games as a participant in both the decathlon and pentathlon—seemingly neutralized these concerns in a written statement declaring ". . . the Games will not be held in any country where there will be interference with the fundamental Olympic theory of equality of all races." What was left out of this statement was Brundage's deep-seated feeling that any call for a boycott was a damning criticism of the entire Olympic movement.[3]

The statement did nothing to quell lobbying efforts against the games, which Brundage found deeply offensive. Ultimately the AOA board agreed to look further into this pressing issue. In September 1934 Brundage was sent to Germany to personally assess social conditions under the Hitler regime. Karl Ritter von Halt, a German member of the IOC and one of Brundage's longtime friends, served as personal escort and translator throughout the trip. Brundage met with several Jewish athletic representatives, though these conferences were always held in the company of Nazi officials, including Arno Breitmeyer, a deputy of the Reich's official Sports Office. Breitmeyer wore his SS uniform during these sessions as a symbolic insurance policy to guarantee the silence of any Jew who might dare speak out.

Von Halt and Breitmeyer had no need to worry about hiding anti-Semitic laws from their guest. Privately Brundage confided to his hosts that he belonged to a Chicago men's club with steadfast restrictions against Jews.

In his report to the AOA Brundage pronounced conditions for Jewish citizens and athletes of the host country as perfectly acceptable, with no unsavory attitudes or issues whatsoever. His findings were satisfactory to other board members. There would be no American boycott of the 1936 Olympiad.[4]

Manipulating Brundage's ready-made observations was relatively simple for the German government. But in light of the 1935 Nuremburg Laws, which stripped Jews of nearly every basic civil right, maintaining a veneer of national contentment and freedom for all German citizens required more finesse. To save face, all signs of public anti-Semitism were scrubbed from the scenery. Placards forbidding Jews from stores, hotels, restaurants, pubs, public parks, and theaters were quietly removed. This facade changed little of the realities behind the scenes. Jews were still forbidden from civil service employment, journalism, radio, farming, public office, teaching, theater, and film. Half of the country's Jewish population had no jobs.[5]

"I'm afraid the Nazis have succeeded with their propaganda," journalist William L. Shirer, the American foreign correspondent wrote in his diary on August 16, 1936. "First, [they] have run the games on a lavish scale never before experienced, and this has appealed to the athletes. Second, the Nazis have put up a very good front for the general visitors, especially the big businessmen. . . ." Shirer was horrified after one well-heeled American attending the games told him, ". . . [Göring] assured us there was no truth in what you fellows write about persecution of religion here.'"[6]

Throughout early summer, Kuhn trumpeted his upcoming Olympic trip as a jubilant return to the Fatherland. Bund members were invited to join, although each person had to pay his own way for travel, lodging, food, tickets to Olympic events, and other expenses. Numerous fund-raisers were held across the country to help defray costs. In New York the single-night tally of a June 13 extravaganza held at the Yorkville Casino, a German gathering hall at 210 East Eighty-Sixth Street, came to three thousand dollars.[7] That night Kuhn announced to a cheering rank and file that all financial goals were achieved. Now on to Berlin and what surely would be a veneration of Kuhn's hard work.[8]

Still, more money was needed. Bund units across the county raised another three thousand dollars for the Fatherland's *Winterhilfswerk*, the annual Winter Relief Fund overseen by Goebbels flunky Erich Hilgenfeldt. This endowment was ostensibly a national charity with generous German citizens providing alms to help the poor with food, coal, and other necessities for surviving cold winter months. As with so many programs under Nazi rule the Winter Relief Fund was orchestrated propaganda, giving pretense that Germans were united to help the destitute amongst them. Members of both Hitler Youth and the SS enforced collection, in essence making the Winter Relief a charity via shakedown.[9] Those who did not contribute, or whose contribution was deemed to small risked losing their jobs for "conduct hostile to the community of the people . . ."[10] Said Hitler of the fund, "We want to show the whole world and our *Volk* that we Germans regard the word 'community' not as a hollow phrase, but as something that for us really does entail an inner obligation."[11]

Of course a good number of Germany's poor were members of undesirable castes, including the infirm, handicapped, and mentally ill. Under Nazi persecution such charity cases were removed from polite society and dealt with accordingly.

Kuhn allocated a portion of the Bundist Winter Relief donations to pay for a custom-made gift he hoped to present to the führer personally. The so-called *Goldene Buch der Amerika-deutschen*, or "The Golden Book," was beautifully bound with leather covering. Its pages were inscribed with the names of some six thousand Bundists, and picture-packed with an overview of pro-Nazi American activities from the infancy of Teutonia to the culmination of the German-American Bund. Its opening paragraph read:

> In America the hearts of the German people also beat for the great leader of all Germans. Thousands upon thousands have found new hope and faith through him and his work. The German-American Bund is the expression of his National Socialist worldview. May the bonds between German-Americans and the German people be everlasting.[12]

Kuhn boarded the ship S.S. *New York* on July 23. Joining him was a retinue of close associates, a squadron of OD guards, a troupe of fifty flag bearers, and representatives from Bund units throughout the United States totaling two hundred people. They arrived in Hamburg on August 1, the same day that the Olympics officially commenced, and were greeted by Bundists who'd arrived earlier, an estimated two to three hundred individuals, though it's possible these numbers are exaggerated.[13] In an adjective-laden memoir of the journey, published in the 1937 Bund yearbook George Froboese, head of the Midwest gau, wrote, "After an incomparable beautiful crossing, and after arriving on German ground, events precipitated in such a manner that my brain hardly found time to register all the vigorous happenings which dashed in upon me." The group was treated to a reception by the mayor of Hamburg and a hearty welcome in Berlin by the *Volksbund für das Deutschtum im Ausland*, or the VDA, a cultural organization for outreach to Germans living abroad. Froboese rhapsodized on the "signs of love existing between the Motherland and us German-Americans . . . it was to me as if I were experiencing a German 'Midsummer Night's Dream'—a German wonder of gracefulness."[14]

The next day was, in retrospect, perhaps the finest of Fritz Kuhn's life. At dawn the *Bundesführer* led a group of associates to Berlin's memorial grave for the Unknown Soldier of the Great War. As a veteran of the conflict, Kuhn certainly shared a kinship with his nameless comrade. With great solemnity, he placed a symbolic oak wreath on the grave. The cortege then moved on to the next item on their agenda, marching in a grand parade through the tree-lined boulevard of Berlin's historic Mitte district. Josef Schuster, the former OD administrator for The Friends, had arranged this honor.[15] Now a repatriated German, Schuster held a position of some importance in *Deutsche Arbeitsfront*, the Nazi Labor Front. With the government having dispensed of trade unions through a combination of laws and arrests the Labor Front was essentially a tightly controlled facade masquerading as a worker's collective. Rank-and-file workers were compelled to join the organization, allowing employers to operate as they pleased without any fear of union interference.[16]

The Mitte parade was a magnificent display of NSDAP talents for public choreography. "Everywhere our gaze wandered there were happy, celebrating people, festoons, pictures and banners," Froboese wrote. The Bundists were in their element, proud representatives of their adopted country, and as loyal as any native German to the New Order. Kuhn's entourage was in prime position when the parade came to a halt beneath Hitler's headquarters at the Imperial Chancery. The overflowing crowd spilling through the streets bellowed in unison for their leader with a rhythmic chorus of *"Heil Hitler!"* A stiff right-armed Nazi salute was repeatedly thrust into the air en masse. Blessed with a gift for the power of political theater, Hitler remained inside the Chancery, keeping his people on edge. At last, with dramatic flourish, he emerged on the balcony, Field Marshall Göring at his side. The multitudes cheered.[17]

Certainly Kuhn must have swelled with pride to be part of such a monumental event. And still, he had not reached the pinnacle of the Olympic journey. That came when Schuster pulled the necessary strings for Fritz Kuhn and his lieutenants to have their much-hoped audience with the *Führer* himself.

That afternoon Kuhn, and his lieutenants George Froboese, Karl Arndt, Rudolph Markmann, and Karl Weiler were ushered into the reception room of the Imperial Chancery.[18] Hitler exchanged handshakes with the *Bundesführer*, who presented the precious Golden Book and the Bund's Winter Relief contribution. The *Führer* thanked Kuhn for the gift, asked trifling questions about Germans living in America, and praised the Bundists for their vigorous opposition to "the infamous false provocations of a custom-corrupted press . . ." At the end of this brief audience the entourage was presented with a memento of the occasion, an autographed picture of their host.[19]

And then Hitler gave Kuhn stunning words: "Go over there and continue the fight."[20]

To Kuhn's ears, this was his longed-for official endorsement. It was Hitler's command that under Fritz Kuhn's great leadership, the German-American Bund must promulgate NSDAP philosophy and action in the United States.

The reality of Hitler's remark was poles beyond poles apart from Kuhn's interpretation. Throughout the Olympic festival, Hitler greeted many foreign dignitaries, large and small, high and low, powerful and mundane. Kuhn's short visit was little more than a trifling meet-and-greet session arranged by their mutual connection, and certainly with no sanctified command intended by Hitler's generic well wishes.[21]

That afternoon the Bundists made pilgrimage to another grave, that of Horst Wessel, exalted NSDAP martyr and composer of Nazi Germany's official national anthem *"Horst Wessel Lied"* ("the Horst Wessel song").[22]

In the late 1920s Wessel was a denizen of Berlin's low life district, friend with pimps and prostitutes alike. Tough and cocksure, Wessel impressed Joseph Goebbels as a rabid anti-Communist and efficient street brawler. Ultimately, hatred of Reds proved to be Wessel's undoing. He refused to pay back rent owed to his Communist-associated landlady. Knowing Wessel's reputation among her fellow travelers, she appealed for help from a violently versatile Communist cell, who were happy to oblige the spurned proprietress. While lookouts held the streets outside the building, an armed confederate surprised Wessel at his flat with point-blank precision. The mortally wounded Wessel lingered for about three weeks, finally succumbing on February 23, 1930. Goebbels, though wracked with sorrow, did not let emotion overcome his keen instinct for powerful agitprop. Wessel was upgraded from murdered NSDAP thug to fallen Nazi demigod. Fortunately for Goebbels, Wessel left behind a tailor-made artifact to enhance the fiction. In 1929 Wessel penned a song, *"Die Fahne hoch"* ("Raise the Flag on High"), a rousing melody with simplistic lyrics venerating fighting men bearing Swastika banners. Goebbels crafted a dramatic mythology for its composer, renamed the song *"Horst Wessel Lied,"* and made it the official song of Nazi Germany.[23]

"Horst Wessel Lied" was a staple at meetings of The Friends and then the Bundists. Now Kuhn and his men paid their respect at Wessel's revered resting place. "An honor guard was especially impressed by these few moments,"

Froboese dutifully recorded. "In reverence our storm flags bowed before the great hero who gave the new German the new National Anthem as well as his life."[24]

As the days passed, Kuhn was in his glory. He reunited with his mentor Fritz Gissibl, now an official with the German Foreign Institute, who held a dinner party in *Der Bundesführer*'s honor. Another gala afforded Kuhn the opportunity to hobnob with National Socialists from several European countries and even South America. Other Bundists on the trip reunited with family and old friends, hoisting mug upon mug of beer in pubs throughout Berlin, Munich, and other cities.

As a natural social animal, drinking and parties were Kuhn's forte. But outside of the amusements, beyond the pomp and circumstance, once the photo ops were done, Kuhn was shut out. NSDAP officials wanted nothing to do with Kuhn or the German-American Bund. Even Gissibl had nothing to offer his former protégé other than dinner and kind words. The only substantive thing Kuhn could wheedle out of his German hosts was more propaganda for dissemination in America.[25]

On August 14, Kuhn and his entourage paid a call on American ambassador William E. Dodd. The ambassador recorded the visit in his diary, a sparse entry tinged by subtle hints of contempt for his visitors. "Fritz Kuhn, Nazi Fuehrer in America, brought a group of German-Americans to my office," Dodd wrote. Noting that he was aware of Kuhn's background with Henry Ford's empire, he referred to the *Bundesführer* as "a Nazi propagandist.... He is guiding his party of visitors about Germany to convince them that Nazism is the salvation of modern peoples. He kept his purpose from me but I have since learned that he represents [Ernst Wilhelm] Bohle of the Foreign Office of the Nazi Party."[26] Given that Bohle was a subordinate of Rudolf Hess's, whose disdain and hands-off approach to The Friends and their successors were well known, it's unlikely Dodd's last assessment was true. Three years earlier during his speech at the Nuremberg Rally of 1933 Bohle had declared, "We recognize only one idea: a German always and everywhere remains a German and nothing but a German—and thereby a National Socialist."[27] This was long before Kuhn's rise to power and Dodd's observations quite possibly are from information he received based on conjuncture rather than solid facts.

———

On October 20, three months after his return, Kuhn issued a "Bund Command" to all unit leaders for dissemination to members. "The Olympia Journey of the German American Bund was a great success," he proclaimed. This was not only because Bundists experienced "the real Third Reich," but also gained a better understanding of what must now be done in the United States. "From the hearty reception we received in the cities of Germany . . . it was proved that the work and will of our Bund has been correctly valued . . . I realize today as never before what track our Bund has to follow and in which direction it has to go. I know that there is more than one point to the continuation of our work—that the German American Bund is called upon to take over the political leadership of the German element in the U.S.A."[28]

"Go over there and continue the fight," Hitler had said. Now it was time to flex political muscle. The German-American Bund must be vocal in the upcoming presidential election in November and make an endorsement of either current president Democrat Franklin Delano Roosevelt or Republican Alf Landon, the governor of Kansas.

Paramount to Kuhn's decision-making process was electing a man who would ". . . pursue a policy for the Fatherland which is also favorable to this country. . . . [T]he German and the American viewpoints have to be combined in all our considerations . . ." He emphasized that the Bund was not now nor ever would be aligned with a political party. "Naturally, it is forbidden for anyone to support Jewish or Marxist candidates for any office whatsoever," he added.

It was a given that President Roosevelt was unfit for the office. "His preference for the Jewish element and the filling of many government positions with Jews is generally known."[29] Kuhn's edict was redundant at best. The Bundists despised Roosevelt and routinely twisted his surname into the Jewish variant, "Rosenfelt."[30]

A second man, North Dakota congressman William Lemke, who was the presidential candidate for the obscure Union Party, was also dismissed. Kuhn claimed that Father Coughlin once favored Lemke, but had since withdrawn his support. Lemke was simultaneously running under his regular Republican banner for reelection to his congressional seat, an office Kuhn misidentified as the United States Senator from Kansas. Perhaps the worst element to Lemke's character was what Kuhn saw as the congressman's rejection of his Teutonic heritage. "The only thing German about this man is his name," the *Bundesführer* wrote.

The Bund's choice for president, in Kuhn's opinion, was obvious: Republican candidate Governor Alf Landon of Kansas. From a German point of view, Kuhn believed Landon would be more favorable to doing business with the Hitler government. "[T]hat must be the deciding thing for us," he wrote.[31]

There was, however, one nagging factor about Landon that Kuhn needed to address. Upon garnering the nomination of his party, Landon received countless telegrams of congratulations, including many from Jewish leaders. "Just for your information," Kuhn wrote, "I would like to inform you that the 50 congratulatory telegrams of rabbis to Landon are not based on the truth; it is only a trick."[32] Just exactly how he knew this was a trick was not explained. And Kuhn apparently did not investigate his candidate to the core. Just three years earlier Landon publically condemned Hitler's sweeping changes in Germany and "the inhuman treatment now accord the Jews . . ."[33]

Kuhn's lengthy endorsement closed with an odd coda. "I would like to take a position on the lies recently spread concerning the influence of Ford on me," he wrote. ". . . [I]t is pure invention that I have been influenced in any way at all by Ford or a Ford official. I have not even mentioned the political question with anybody."[34]

Why did Kuhn include this statement? Ford's anti-Semitism and the influence of *The International Jew* on Hitler's *Mein Kampf* was well known. Many of The Friends, including Heinz Spanknöbel and Kuhn, were employed at Ford Motors in some capacity from the late 1920s through the 1930s. Rumors persisted of a link between Kuhn and Ford. Certainly a free giveaway of a Ford sedan at the Bund's Christmas sale was an unusual and expensive door prize for any organization in the Depression era.

The German government immediately sought to distance itself from Kuhn's endorsement. Dr. Hans Thomsen, counselor of the German Embassy in Washington D.C., released a statement, emphasizing that the NSDAP had no interest in how people voted in the United States. Furthermore, Thomsen said, he was one of the German diplomats present when Kuhn and his men met Hitler in August. The reception, he insisted, was a routine affair with no discussion of Roosevelt, Landon, or any other issues involving American politics.[35]

Kuhn ignored the snubs from Berlin and Thomsen. As far as he was concerned Hitler's words still rang true: "Go over there and continue the fight." His bureaucratic machine was in place. The Bund's business divisions were blossoming. Plans to unite Bundists across the country through youth programs, summer family camps, and other recreational activities were becoming reality.

Just how many people belonged to the German-American Bund at any one time is impossible to pin down. At one point Kuhn claimed they were more than 200,000 strong, a genuine Swastika Nation coast to coast. Membership numbers went unreported by some locals. In later investigations of the Bund by the FBI and other government entities, it was believed membership was somewhere in the range of six to eight thousand total, give or take a few hundred.[36] A study by the American Legion estimated Bundist membership numbering at twenty-five thousand people. Most lived in large cities of the East Coast, Midwestern, and West Coast gaus, though it's conceivable there were members outside of urban areas. And given there were twenty thousand in attendance at the 1939 Washington's Birthday rally in Madison Square Garden, clearly there were numerous uncounted members and sympathizers. The vast majority of the Bundists were blue-collar workers, employed as mechanics, at restaurants, lowly office clerks, itinerant job hoppers. There was a smattering of professional people within the ranks, some working as technicians or chemists, like Kuhn. Then there were others such as members of the women's auxiliary units, children, and the unseen sympathizers channeling money into Bund coffers. A hodgepodge cross-section of immigrant and native born Americans.[37]

Kuhn's outreach to other American fascist groups, notably William Dudley Pelley and his Silver Shirts, the Friends of Progress founded by Robert Noble and Ellis Jones, and members of the Christian Front, was well received. These American fascist movements, in conjunction with the Bund, complemented one another in vision and support of fascist ideologies.

All the while, there were other Americans unsympathetic to the German-American Bund keeping watchful eyes on Fritz Kuhn. The *Bundesführer* was not a trivial man to be brushed off or ignored.

7

Nazi Fighter with a Typewriter

A JOURNALISTIC COMBINATION OF Greek chorus, Puck, and gadfly, in his prime Walter Winchell was unofficially perhaps the most powerful man in New York City. Broadway producers and Hollywood stars loved, feared, and hated him—sometimes all at once. Politicians courted his good graces. Gangsters enjoyed his company, even though Louis "Lepke" Buchalter, the only mobster ever to earn the death penalty for his sins, ended his criminal career turning himself over not to the FBI, but to Winchell, who served as FBI director J. Edgar Hoover's emissary.

He was born Walter Winschel, son of Jacob and Jennie, on April 7, 1897 in New York's Harlem neighborhood, then one of the city's biggest Jewish enclaves. His grandfather Chaim Weinschel, himself the son of a Russian rabbi, was a respected cantor. Chaim brought his family to America after a job offer from a New York temple. The family's surname seemed a continual ethnic work in progress, with spellings switching between Wienschel and Weinschiell, until one of Chaim's sons nailed it down as an Americanized "Winchel."[1]

Winchell (who managed to work in a second "L" later on) was, like many New York Jewish boys of his generation, done with school by age thirteen, lured away from P.S. 184 by the sirens of show business. He joined two fellow refugees of the classroom, singing ditties at the neighborhood movie theater to entertain audiences while the projectionist changed reels. Winchell, his friend Jack Wiener, and the son of the theater's ticket seller, a kid named George Jessel, called themselves "The Imperial Trio." The boys were signed up by Gus Edwards, a vaudeville song plugger and producer, and ended up touring in Edwards's *Song Review of 1910*.[2] Edwards clearly had an eye for emerging talent; he later cast shows with up-and-comers like Eddie Cantor and a bunch of brothers named Marx.

Winchell knocked around vaudeville for a few years as a cut-rate song-and-dance man, then did a short stint in the Naval Reserve at the end of the Great War. Discharged after a little under five months' service, he returned to vaudeville in a music and comedy act with Rita Greene, a partnership that extended into offstage romance and eventual marriage.

In February 1919, Winchell's life was forever altered during an engagement in Chicago. Being Chicago and it being winter, the city was hit hard by a snowstorm. Jo Swerling, a friend of Winchell's who wrote for the *Chicago Herald-Examiner*, was unable to cover the entire city by himself. Winchell volunteered to help, so Swerling sent him to a downtown railway station for that angle of the story. The would-be journalist phoned in a tidbit about snowbound commuters, which Swirling worked into the article, much to Winchell's delight. As an apparent joke, another reporter gave Winchell a press card naming him a "traveling correspondent." The authorization was flimsy at best, but it didn't matter. Walter Winchell was bit hard by the newspaper bug.[3] (Swerling later took his talents to Hollywood, where he wrote the screenplays for a string of motion picture classics including *Pride of the Yankees, It's a Wonderful Life, Lifeboat*, and uncredited assistance on *Gone with the Wind*.)

Winchell kept on writing. During down time on the vaudeville circuit he banged away on a typewriter, filling reams of paper with jokes, gossip, and behind-the-scenes show business news. The aspiring reporter sent his material to the showbiz trade journal *Billboard*, would-be columns with the inklings of what would become the trademark Winchell style: short rat-a-tat-tats of newsy items, opinions, speculations, and corny one-line jokes. Every once in a while *Billboard* published his submissions.[4]

He built on the *Billboard* success by developing a paper all his own, *The Daily Newsense*, a one-sheet tabloid for fellow vaudevillians.[5] On the strength of his little rag, Winchell was hired as a jack-of-all-trades office assistant, with tasks ranging from janitor to errand runner to writer by editor Glenn Condon of *The Vaudeville News*.[6]

In September 1924, Winchell joined a start-up newspaper, *The New York Evening Graphic*. "Graphic" was the daily's operative word. The tabloid specialized in lurid stories saturated in purple prose and illustrated with salacious photo montage recreations—called "composographs"—of sensational news items like the oddball wedding of middle-aged millionaire playboy Edward "Daddy" Browning to teenaged flapper Frances Belle "Peaches" Heenan. Journalists at more respectable papers like *The New York Times* pooh-poohed *The Graphic* and its torrid headlines like "I Hated My Mother So I Killed Her."[7] The paper was despised by polite society; the New York Public Library ended its subscription after just six weeks.[8]

Winchell thrived within the hyped-up tabloid atmosphere. He clawed his way through New York's kaleidoscopic world of Broadway and the social scene, with a headlong fixation on gossip that could neatly be surmised in just a sentence or two. Winchell played with language, creating his own lexicon that he dubbed "Slanguage."[9] Gangsters were "Chicagorillas." Shapely female legs became "shafts." Booze, illegal but plentiful, was "giggle water." "Intelligentlemen" and "debutramp" spoke for themselves. His beloved Broadway got a cynical treatment: "Hardened Artery," "Bulb Belt," "Baloney Blvd." Sentences were often punctuated at the end by Winchell's derisive prose laughter: "heheheh."[10] "Winchell wrote like a man honking in a traffic jam," said Ben Hecht. "His energy was amazing, and his style was as arresting as a café brawl."[11]

He became the toast of Broadway, a man both courted and shunned. When the Shubert Organization banned him from their theaters, Winchell fired back: "A certain columnist has been barred from all Shubert openings. Now he can wait three days and go to their closings."[12]

In 1929 Winchell jumped from the *Graphic* to the Hearst-owned New York *Daily Mirror*. His column "Walter Winchell On Broadway" became a "must read" for his legions of fans as well as his many detractors and enemies. Love him, hate him, they read him. For the next thirty-four years Winchell's column was a staple for the *Mirror*, as well as for hundreds of newspapers across the country that picked him up in syndication.[13]

Now a Broadway bon vivant and celebrity journalist, Winchell needed the proper atmosphere for a man of his flair and discernment. He found what he needed in the Stork Club, the swanky establishment founded by Sherman Billingsley, an ex-bootlegger from Nowheresville, Oklahoma. Billingsley built the club into the epitome of style and sophistication, *the* Manhattan nightclub to see and be seen. Winchell, who held court nightly from his permanent seat at table 50 dubbed the Stork Club "New York's New Yorkiest place . . ."[14]

In 1932 Donald Flamm, who operated New York's CBS radio affiliation WMCA, got the bright idea of transposing Winchell's newspaper personality to the airwaves.[15] Within a matter of weeks Winchell's distinctive nasal-voiced delivery was a hit from coast to coast. His signature sign-on burned its way into the American cultural consciousness, a staccato greeting accompanied by the clickity-click of a manic telegraph key. For millions of radio listeners Sunday night began when Winchell barked out, "Good evening, Mr. and Mrs. America and all the ships at sea—let's go to press!"

At the *Daily Mirror* he became more than just a peddler of gossip. Walter Winchell turned into a real reporter with his dogged pursuit of the 1932 Lindbergh baby kidnapping. He shocked, surprised, and scooped every other journalist when he told radio listeners that wood used in the kidnapper's ladder found at the Lindbergh home matched that of flooring in the attic of prime suspect Bruno Hauptmann.[16]

In his metamorphosis from gossip columnist to gossip columnist *cum* serious journalist Winchell developed something no one expected of him: an unabashed liberal political conscience. He praised President Roosevelt with words that sounded like something written by a schoolgirl in the throes of her first crush. "They should give the Nobel Peace Prize to FDR's smile," he gushed in one column. Another plaudit read, "They're making the postage stamps bigger so that when the time comes to put President Roosevelt on it there'll be enough room for his heart."[17]

He'd long given up religious observance, but Winchell remained keenly aware that he was the great-grandson of a respected rabbi. He didn't wear Judaism on his sleeve, but Winchell had his own idea of Jewish sensibility at his core. In the 1920s he took on a very public feud with an anti-Semitic detractor. Rather than earn praise, Winchell was shocked by the negative reaction from fellow members of his tribe. One letter writer told him, "It is not good for Jews like you to disgrace us with a defense. It would do more honor of the Jews if you didn't make others look ridiculous: you are not what is known as a Jew." Winchell was mortified. It was one of the few times in his life that someone was able to get under Winchell's thoroughly calloused skin.[18]

Arnold Forster, a top official with the Anti-Defamation League, would have none of it. As far as he was concerned, the Jews had no better defender than Walter Winchell. "Winchell never forgot his beginnings . . . ," Forster wrote. ". . . [He] became a prominent voice in exposing anti-Semitism [and] pro-Nazism . . ."[19]

That he did. Winchell was one of the first American journalists who understood the darkest implications of Adolf Hitler and the dreams of the NSDAP. He sensed something in the German dictator that few of his peers seemed to understand: the man was a dangerous threat to the world. A chilling firsthand account came to the United States from George S. Messersmith, the American consul general to Germany. "I wish it were really possible to make our people at home understand," he wrote to his superiors at the State Department in June of 1933. ". . . With few exceptions, the men who are running this Government are of a mentality that you and I cannot understand. Some of them are psychopathic cases and would ordinarily be receiving treatment somewhere."[20]

Three months before Messersmith's communication, Winchell took on Hitler with an item in his *Daily Mirror* column. Winchell hated Hitler with a passion, but understood that any high-minded criticism from a gossip columnist would come off as pretentious, uninformed, and easily dismissible. He needed to apply the Winchell brand of verbal attack. But how? He found his hook from an off-color assessment of the German dictator by fellow journalist Quentin Reynolds. Reynolds, an internationally respected foreign correspondent put it succinctly when he told Winchell, "Hitler is a fag."[21]

In an era where homosexuals were easy subjects for scorn, derision, and cheap gags, what better way to attack the self-important *Führer*—strutting around in his uniform, parading through the streets, a man whose thunderous speeches were punctuated with wild physical and facial gestures—than by insinuating all this added up to Hitler as an effeminate and lowbrow comic caricature? "The best way to fight a person like Hitler is to ridicule him, of course," Winchell concluded.[22]

The first salvo came in his column on March 28, 1933. "Cable. March 26, Berlin—to Walter Winchell, care of Paramount Theatre, Brooklyn—What are you doing over the weekend? Would you like to spend it with me? I think you are cute—Adolf Hitler." By the time Messersmith was expressing his concerns in June, Winchell had perfected his gay baiting of the *Führer* to lowbrow comic virtuosity. "Hitler turned down the chance of entering a beauty contest because he found out the first prize was a free trip to the Bronx," Winchell wrote. "Henceforth this column will call him Adele Hitler."[23] Winchell had no compunctions taking this blatantly slanderous route. "I cannot refrain from flaunting the fact that [Hitler] is a homo-sexualist, or as we Broadway vulgarians say—an out and out fairy . . ." he declared.

Though inartful by twenty-first-century standards, Winchell's continued attacks were far and away stronger than just about anything anyone else in the press or public office was saying. The snipes on Hitler's sexuality—and hence, his masculinity, the very source of *Der Führer*'s perceived psychological power—were unrelenting. Winchell himself acknowledged in "On Broadway" that his gay bashing Hitler often roared out of respectable bounds. Not that it mattered. "I believe that a man's private life and preferences are his own," Winchell wrote, "but Hitler is so dangerous and such a faker, that any weapon can be used with justification."

In some quarters Winchell was referred to as "the most rabid anti-Hitlerlite in America," criticism he proudly wore as a badge of honor.[24] In the fall of 1933 he raved with unmitigated glee after the German National Socialist newspaper *Völkischer Beobachter* published a photo of the columnist accompanied by the caption "A New Enemy of the New Germany." "I wondered for a long spell if my barbs were being seen by the Nazis—and if they were irked by them, even a little," he wrote on September 27. "It is so nice to know that my efforts haven't altogether been snubbed."[25]

Winchell understood the Nazi menace wasn't limited to Germany. In the early 1930s the United States was rife with Nazi sympathizers and Winchell's journalistic instinct detected something afoot in Detroit. There, in the backyard of Henry Ford, the only American mentioned in Hitler's autobiographical manifesto *Mein Kampf*, Winchell found his nemesis in Fritz Kuhn. Early on Winchell sensed that this Ford employee was a rising force in The Friends movement, and thus a perfect target for the bully pulpit of "On Broadway." What would transform into one of the most legendary battles of Winchell's career began with a simple one liner: "Fritz Kuhn, who poses as a chemist for a motor magnate, is Hitler's secret agent in the United States."[26]

In many ways, this was a typical Winchell item, facts wrapped with half-truths that played better than the reality. Kuhn was indeed a chemist at Ford, he was a rising star in the American pro-Nazi movement, but he never was "Hitler's secret agent." If anything, Kuhn became a public embarrassment for Hitler and the NSDAP command in Berlin. So what? Winchell was not someone who let veracity get in the way of a great hyperbole. "On Broadway" was not bound to conventional notions of journalism. The column was Winchell's and Winchell's alone, with free rein to attack whomever he wanted and however he pleased. In Fritz Kuhn, Winchell found his quintessential punching bag and over the next few years took great delight in smacking away at the *Bundesführer*.

New slanguage and Winchellisms were developed for Nazis both home and abroad. "Ratzis," "swastinkas," and "swasti-cooties" were regular euphemisms. As Kuhn's influence and power grew, Winchell took delight developing new riffs on the name of a man he regarded as a third-rate circus clown decked out in a Sam Browne belt. Some of the creative cognomens were razor sharp, others happy buffoonery, and a few were downright puzzling, enigmatic insults that were perhaps a gag in Winchell's mind alone. Among the choice sobriquets hurled at Fritz Kuhn were:

- Phffftz Kuhn
- Kuhnazi
- The Shamerican
- Fat Fritz Kuhn
- Fritz Kuhn, the local anesthetic
- Communist Fritz Kuhn (an odd choice, given Kuhn's hatred of all things communist)
- Life's Little Ironist
- Fritz Kuhnfucius
- Son-of-a-Fritz
- Beef Bundit
- Chief of the Ratzis

Kuhn's retort to Winchell's attacks was swift and not in the least bit surprising. He took to referring to his media antagonist as "dot Choo Vinchell."[27] On another occasion, Kuhn proclaimed Winchell was using a pseudonym to hide his Jewishness. Walter's real last name, he insisted, was "Lipschitz." "*Ja*," was Winchell's reply, "me *und* President Rosenfeldt!"[28]

The Bund newspaper declared Winchell "Kuhn's worst enemy." Kuhn was quoted by news wire services with a threat to "blacken Walter Winchell's eyes because of all the lies he has written about Germany and the Nazi Party."[29]

Winchell enjoyed the public battle and dismissed the threats as trivial. This cavalier attitude changed one cold December night. As he stepped out onto Seventh Avenue, fresh from a quick trim at the Dawn Patrol Barbershop by his barber Sam Schmer, the columnist was jumped by two men.

One assailant held Winchell down, while the other applied some chin music to his face. Winchell's nose was smashed and a punch to the mouth loosened a crown. Schmer roared out of the barbershop, razor in hand. The mugs took off, disappearing into the Broadway night.[30] As if the bloody nose wasn't bad enough, the repair for Winchell's crown rang up to a hefty $4,500.[31]

The men were never caught, but Winchell was convinced this pummeling was a blunt response to his unrelenting strikes on Fritz Kuhn and Hitler. A bubble of fame was not enough protection from determined assailants. Winchell started packing heat. "If they know I carry a gun," he told his assistant Herman Klurfeld, "the Nazi creeps will be scared shitless."

"To my knowledge, he never fired a shot in anger," Klurfeld later wrote.[32] Winchell's real bullets were the words firing out his mouth on the radio and blasting from his typewriter.

8

Family and Youth

ON JULY 18, 1936, a twenty-five-car caravan brought the Medford, Long
Island Republican Club for a combination family picnic/Alf Landon rally to
nearby Heckscher State Park, a recreation area on the edge of Long Island.
Children played games and held races while adults ate, drank, and talked
politics. All in all, a splendid way to spend a midsummer Saturday.

The Republicans were wildly outnumbered the next day by another
Long Island family gathering, held at a private retreat located on the outskirts of nearby Yaphank. At ten o'clock in the morning a fourteen-coach
caravan from New York City pulled into the town train station. A welcoming party hundreds strong greeted the travelers; many were fellow New
Yorkers and had been in Yaphank since Friday. A fife and drum corps led a
parade down Main Street—where else but Main Street?—through town.
Apple-cheeked youngsters, boys smartly dressed in khaki uniforms and girls
in matching white blouses and blue skirts, accompanied by proud parents
and other adults—many also in uniform—marched toward their secluded
haven.

Their get-together bore some similarity to that of the Medford Republicans. Children laughing and playing; adults eating, drinking, and talking
politics. By one estimate, some five thousand people were in attendance.
Beyond size, there were other significant differences.

People entered via gate doors beneath a sign emblazoned with a swastika
and a sign reading *"Herzlich Willkommen,"* "Hearty Welcome." Most of the
partiers spoke exclusively in German.[1] The 187-acre compound was hidden
from the general public by thick landscaping.[2] Street signs inside the camp

marked pathways such as "Goering Street," "Goebbels Street," and, of course, "Adolf Hitler Street."[3] A sporting greens was designated "von Hindenberg Athletic Field."[4] Other signs scattered throughout emphasized traditions old and new: *Deutschtum Erwache* ("Germans awake"); *Wir Amerikaner Deutschen Blutes Ehren die Heimat* ("We Americans of German Blood Honor the Fatherland"); *Ein Volk, Ein Reich, Ein Führer* ("One People, One Realm, One Leader.") Swastikas festooned clothing as jaunty buttons or blazed with pride on armbands of uniformed guardsmen.[5]

All in all, a typical Sunday.

Later in the afternoon, an honored guest spoke to the adults. He praised the virtue of this exclusive retreat, its importance to home, heritage, and honor. It was, he told these disciplined parents, a place where families could "combat Communism by instilling the principles of Germany in the youth!" His political rhetoric heated up, taking on New York's governor, Herbert H. Lehman. The governor—a family member of the Lehman Brothers investment-banking firm—was a pariah who should not get any support from German New Yorkers in the November election. Emphasizing the point, he stressed that Lehman was a Jew and that "Jews are the fathers of Communism!"

A roar of approval thundered throughout the multitudes. This man, revered in their community, knew his audience well, for Walter H. Kappe edited the newspaper of choice for this crowd, the German-American Bund's *Deutscher Weckruf und Beobachter.*

Thus it would be every weekend for the next six weeks, with thousands of people coming and going to the private Bundist-owned Camp Siegfried, named after the legendary Teutonic hero immortalized in music by Hitler's favorite composer, Richard Wagner. It was a sanctuary where Bundists could relax with families and like-minded friends, far away from the foul summer stench of Jew-filled New York City.

The train that faithfully shuttled people back and forth throughout the summer was dubbed "The Camp Siegfried Special."[6]

Camp Siegfried, established in July 1935 as The Friends were falling into twilight, offered picnic grounds, hiking trails, a swimming pond, cabins, a private pro-Nazi mini-resort for family getaways, and children's summer camps.[7] On paper the camp was owned by Ernest Mueller of the German-American Settlement League, a seemingly innocuous business based in

Brooklyn. In reality Mueller's business was a shadow front for the Bund, another element within Fritz Kuhn's extensive revenue generating monopoly.[8]

Kuhn declared that "all camps of the German-American Bund are for the recreation of the children of German-American parents," as well as weekend and holiday retreats for the entire family. Camp Siegfried and other such facilities were, he insisted, "absolutely without ulterior political significance."[9]

Information about Camp Siegfried in one piece of Bund literature spoke of something radically different. "Our Camp is designed principally to be a place which breathes the spirit of the new Germany," it stated. "We want to be helpers and advisers who are ready at all times to do any work; to provide for order and to make propaganda for the ideals of our great German racial community. Hereby we consecrate you as a little piece of Germany soil in America, as a symbol of our motto, 'obligated to America, tied to Germany.' " Siegfried provided homes for OD men, with swastikas either part of the building brickwork or incorporated into painted additions.[10]

To residents of Yaphank, hordes of New York brown shirts parading from the train station to Camp Siegfried every weekend grew unsettling. The local police force cracked down on the weekend processions, keeping the swastikaed marchers in single file and shutting down their music whenever a church was passed.[11]

People parading in Nazi-styled uniforms through town was bad enough, but others Bundists in more casual attire crossed different bounds of decorum. "I saw a 250-pound woman walking around . . . in only shorts and a halter top . . . ," reported Judge Gustave Neuss, Yaphank's justice of the peace. "She was bubbling out all over." He saw another man strolling through town ". . . wearing only a pair of shorts rolled down as far as they would go and up as far as they would go."[12] One Bundist, when told to get off of private property, turned belligerent and demanded to see the owner's deed.[13] Others ransacked area strawberry patches and apple orchards. Flowers were ripped from family gardens.[14]

Campers bearing swastika banners outside of campgrounds sans Stars and Stripes prompted more outrage.[15] A retired Army major stopped a group of boys when he noticed one of them brandishing a knife emblazoned with a distinctive crest.

"What is this emblem on here?" the major demanded of the young man.

"That's a swastika," was the answer.

The major was outraged. "That should be an American flag there," he snapped and confiscated the offensive item. A camp official saw the situation and managed to get the knife back. The issue went to court, with the judge agreeing that the knife, swastika and all, was the property of Camp Siegfried. "The knife doesn't mean anything to us," Ernest Mueller declared after the trial. "It's the principle we are concerned with."[16]

Judge Neuss was outraged. "The situation is so acute that Yaphank is on the verge of insurrection," he declared.[17]

By the end of summer in 1937, the town board agreed. Building permits were temporarily denied until camp officials provided a survey of the property citing where the proposed buildings would be constructed. Mueller fired back with pallid threats. If Yaphank didn't want the Bund, then fine. "If they want a fight, they can have it," he told a reporter.

Perhaps Siegfried would be put on the market and sold to the lowest bidder, "a Negro group," Mueller said. "How would you like Father Divine here?" Replacing the swastika with a reviled black Christian cult leader certainly wouldn't help property values, would it now? "All we want is to be left alone," Mueller said.[18]

Far and away, the most important aspect of the camps and retreats was the youth program run by Theodore Dinkelacker, the Bund's National Youth Leader.[19] "We must make every conceivable effort to obtain a tight grip on all German-American youngsters," he thundered to a meeting of Bund parents. American schools were polluters of impressionable young Teutonic minds. Furthermore, Dinkelacker reminded fathers and mothers, raising children loyal to the Third Reich was ". . . the duty of every person of German blood in this country . . ." Through the Bund summer camps, a new generation would blossom, young men and women ". . . destined to carry forward our Nazi ideals, and who will ultimately bring victory to the glorious German ideals here."[20]

The Bund Youth Movement was split into divisions by age and gender. *Jungvolk* was the children's division for boys and girls six to thirteen. At age fourteen girls enrolled in the *Mädchenschaft* and boys in the *Jugendschaft*. From there young women were inducted into the Women's Command, the supportive women's auxiliary group of the Bund. Older boys could move forward in the Bund as full members and into leadership positions. Young men blessed with "a personality of strength and will" were steered toward the ranks of OD protective goon squads.[21] Youth Movement members wore uniforms, much like any other scouting group, but with distinctive Bund features. Boys' uniforms included the Sam Browne military belts worn by their Bundist fathers, swastika buttons, and emblems of a short flash of jagged lightning set against a blue background.[22] Daggers sported on belt loops, similar to Hitler Youth counterparts, bore the inscription "*Blut und Ehre*," or Blood and Honor, to signify "eternal allegiance to the Fatherland."[23] Both genders were affixed with caps consciously modeled after their counterparts overseas enrolled in Germany's male-only Hitler Youth and the female counterpart League of German Girls. Activities, while emphasizing outdoor fun and athletics, were skewed toward a specific goal: *Der Tag*, or "The Day." This was a solemn commitment. No one knew when *Der Tag* might come, but every Bundist knew what it was about. On this critical day the fight would break out on American soil between Aryans and violent Jews determined to install a Bolshevik system within the United States government. Young men must be ready for that battle, with support from good German women. "These young boys must carry on our fight in the days to come," Dinkelacker told the parents of potential Youth Movement campers. "Urge your children and the children of your friends and relatives to join us. . . . The children will benefit by this training indoors and outdoors and will learn to understand the true meaning of our cause . . ." This education, he promised, would be a powerful investment in the future. ". . . [W]hen they have reached mature life, they will rise to fight with us and send their children to us."

The Bund 1937 Yearbook tried describing the combination of Bund Youth and *Der Tag* in more poetic terms. "To this youth we bind ourselves in duty to the end that some day it may feel bound in duty to our nationality and complete what we have begun. To have trained and straightened and schooled them for national and racial responsibility, to be clean, healthy and strong men and women, that some day shall be the fairest reward of our pains, activity and sacrifices."[24]

Junges Volk, an irregularly published magazine for Bundist children, emphasized the might and order Adolf Hitler brought to the Fatherland. German impact on the American Revolution was another theme found within *Junges Volk* pages, enhanced with a Nazi-tinged slant on the contributions

made by Friedrich von Steuben and others. The purity of Aryan blood was
stressed in short stories and poems. One perverse moment of supposed nonfiction intertwined the biographies of two fallen martyrs brought down by cowardly assassins: Abraham Lincoln and Horst Wessel. The tortured logic within
praised Lincoln and Wessel as fighters for national harmony in the face of civil
war and men who died in the name their great causes. In Lincoln's case, this
may have been confusing to some readers given *Junge Volk*'s editorial propen-
sity for decrying the infestation of racial rot within the United States at the
hands of America's black population. Jews, of course, lurked everywhere within
the pages of the magazine, a constant enemy bent on the destruction of
America through infiltration into schools and the political process. A United
Soviet States was what the Jews wanted and nothing would stand in their
way. Only a combined fighting force of Aryan youth could hold off this terrible scourge of a racially impure people.[25]

The energy and enthusiasm of youthful Bund members was channeled
into activities not found at other American summer camps. Laborers necessary for building cottages and other camp structures were expensive. What's
more, trade unions were rife with Jews and Communists. Why not employ
the many recruits at the disposal of camp leaders? Child labor was used in
construction, heavy and dirty work, and dangerous when undertaken by
untrained hands. If a parent dared complain, Dinkelacker fired back with
unnerving intimidation. What would life be for any family who crossed fellow German-Americans? Would they like to fend for themselves in this Jew-
controlled nation without Bund protection? Blackballing threats did the
trick. Besides, Dinkelacker maintained, "if the children were forced to do
work at the expense of their recreational time for games and sports, that's
nobody's business but our own."

Camp leaders emphasized strict German discipline. Teenagers bearing
knapsacks stuffed with as much as thirty pounds of gear were sent on grueling twenty-mile hikes under hot summer suns and compelled to bear this
weight for the duration.[26] Throughout their rigorous marches the campers
bore aloft a blue and white "Victory Sign" flag decorated with a majestic
white swastika. Other hikes were staged in the darkest of night. Campers,
working hard to hold the strict formation demanded of them, struggled
through pitch-black trails while ignoring the bites and scratches scraped into
their skin by underbrush. Complaining showed forbidden weakness. Cuts
on arms and legs were badges of honor. Enduring pain was sacramental.

At the end of these hikes, exhausted and bleeding campers built fires, then held arms aloft in Nazi salute with triplicate cries of *Sieg Heil!* Firelight danced off young faces as their rendition of *"Horst Wessel Lied"* resounded through the night air.[27]

The Youth Movement inadvertently provided the Bund with a juicy plum: a martyr for their cause. Tillie Koch was a teenaged leader of the South Brooklyn girls unit and was responsible for helping other young women obtain uniforms.[28] But Koch, while loyal to the Bund cause, was concerned about a growing issue within the camps.

There were other problems adult leaders were ignoring, Koch told Helen Vooros, a close friend and confidant. Something had to be done about it. In August 1937, Koch volunteered to stand guard outside the sleeping quarters of her sister campers. This devotion became her undoing. Koch developed a cold after standing overnight as a guard on behalf of other young female campers.[29] Her infection turned into pleurisy and by August 12 Koch was in desperate need of a doctor. Dinkelacker refused her any medical attention. No German child would turn into a soft Americanized sissy under his watch.

Koch's condition spiraled downward. Her chest rattled from unending coughs, her body shook with fever. Tillie Koch died on August 17.

A dead camper was the last thing Kuhn and Dinkelacker needed on their hands. They went into heavy damage control. Both wrote lavish obituaries in *Deutscher Weckruf und Beobachter*, praising Koch for her devotion and courage. Three days later a grand funeral was held. Under the shadow of the swastika banner and the watchful eyes of an OD honor guard several dozen strong, Tillie Koch's grieving family, her peers in the Youth Movement, and Bund officials laid their fallen young warrior to rest.[30]

Koch's father, a janitor of modest means, paid for everything.[31]

While the Nazi government officially would have nothing to do with the Bund, Hitler Youth leaders were always glad to fill young minds with NS-DAP philosophies. In spring 1938 leaders of both groups coordinated a trip of thirty select Youth Movement teens, fifteen boys and fifteen girls. They traveled aboard the German ship *Hamburg*, although the group was cautioned about wearing their uniforms during the voyage lest they upset the sensibilities of another passenger, Joe Jacobs. Though Jacobs was a Jew he had a certain cachet among some Nazis as the manager of Germany's revered

heavyweight boxing champion Max Schmeling. Given Schmeling's status
and his loyalty to Jacobs, Dinkelacker and other Youth Movement leaders
weren't about to risk angering one of the few exceptions to the Fatherland's
Jewish policies.

Once on Teutonic shores, the visitors were housed either in the homes of
host families or relatives living in Germany. Politics was downplayed during
the visit. Hitler Youth instructed their counterparts in German culture and
Aryan ideals.[32] The American teens were given material to take back home,
notably books by Julius Streicher, the NSDAP's leading propagandist whose
work was infused with white hot anti-Semitism. One volume they received
was a popular children's picture book, rife with caricatures of Jews as subhu-
man monsters bent on destruction, only to suffer the inevitable defeat at the
hands of superior Aryan adversaries.[33]

On April 29 the Youth Movement visitors were brought to a Berlin rally
for an event Bundists back home could only dream about: the chance to hear
the *Führer*, Adolf Hitler himself address a rally at the Olympic Stadium.
Joseph Goebbels, Minister of Public Enlightenment and Propaganda, personally doled out the invitation.

The oration itself was a by-the-numbers speech, with Hitler emphasizing the importance of loyalty to Germany no matter where the Fatherland's
children might be. Be it the South Pole or the North Pole, he asserted, the
Führer was *führer* for anyone with Teutonic blood coursing through their
veins.

The Americans were treated to a post-speech banquet, an anticlimactic
event given the excitement of the past few hours. It was their only meal of
the day, and amounted to nothing more than heaping plates of sauerkraut
and pigs knuckles.

The rest of the trip was basic indoctrination sessions extolling Germany
and the Aryan race, denouncing democracy, and vilifying the inherent evils
amidst Jews, blacks, and Masons. Christianity also took a drubbing, with the
visitors informed that the only true religion was National Socialism. They
also received a lecture by a German physician on the importance of mandatory sterilization for children of Jewish/gentile couples. More pamphlets and
propaganda, emphasizing NSDAP principles and the Jewish menace throughout the world, were provided for distribution back home.[34]

Helen Vooros, who had succeeded her friend Tillie Koch as leader of the

South Brooklyn *Mädchenschaft*, was one of the honored young women who participated in the German excursion. Beyond the official events and presentations, Vooros witnessed other activities during the trip, things that reminded her of the goings-on Tillie Koch had divulged; and that Vooros experienced herself as a Youth Movement camper.

For the time being, she remained silent. The time to speak out would come.

9

It Can't Happen Here

ON JULY 18, 1937, the Bund opened Camp Nordland, a ninety-seven-acre facility in Andover Township, New Jersey, about forty miles from Newark. Presiding over the festivities was August Klapprott, one of Kuhn's most trusted loyalists and head of the New Jersey gau. Eight thousand people were in attendance, some brought in via a special train chartered from Hoboken. Swastikas were everywhere throughout the grounds—on flags, uniforms, badges, armbands, pins, and other adornments.

Klapprott presided over the festivities like a happy mini-*Führer*. Both he and Kuhn made speeches, diverting any discussion of Jews to code words readily understood by the crowd: "a certain minority." The event seemed to have official government sanction in the presence of New Jersey state senator William A. Dolan, who was warmly introduced by his host. Dolan expressed no animus against Swastika New Jersey, instead welcoming the addition of Camp Nordland to his district.

An elected official embracing Bundists was bound to cause reaction. In Washington D.C., Congressman Dickstein was outraged. He called for the state senator's impeachment and suggested Dolan might have financial interests in Camp Nordland. The congressman's insinuations were spot on. Dolan's law office took care of the title work when the Bund acquired the land where Nordland was built.

Veterans groups of all stripes, including the American Legion, Jewish War Veterans, the VFW, and Order of the Purple Heart demanded investigations. One member of the Irish War Veterans called for anti-Nazi education programs throughout area school districts. It was important, he emphasized that students learn the evils of the fascist "goose-step, Hitler salute, and disregard for our flag."

Camp Nordland did not shut down but the protests and political sabre rattling had a mighty impact. The second weekend of the camp's operation, attendance dropped off by six thousand people, far less than what was anticipated. Klapprott was furious. The Bund, he said, was a private organization just like any other. They had rights. After all, Kuhn, Klapprott, and their minions "never investigate[s] Jewish synagogues."[1]

Such backlash against Bund camps was felt throughout the country. At Camp Hindenburg, about twenty miles north of Milwaukee, Wisconsin in the small town of Grafton, Bundists were smacked with a counterpunch wielded by a group they perhaps did not see coming: angry German-Americans outraged by the growing danger of Hitler in their Fatherland, the antics of Fritz Kuhn in their own country, and the blind loyalty of the *Führer*'s and *Bundesführer*'s followers. The Wisconsin Federation of German-American Societies were incensed by the Bundists from Milwaukee and Chicago marching through Grafton and into a secluded camp located on the outskirts of town, hidden within thick groves of trees. Their response was municipal rather than private and in full cooperation with Grafton officials: the creation of a public space saluting all of the patriotic good brought to the United States by the contributions and actions of German-Americans.

About a mile from Camp Hindenburg, the Federation leadership developed Carl Schurz Park, which was named in honor of a Wisconsin German immigrant who fought in the Civil War. The Bundists could have their vision of Swastika Wisconsin; through Schurz Park, Federation members demonstrated to their neighbors that not all German-Americans were marching in Kuhn's goose steps.

This goodwill action was not enough to stop Kuhn's loyal followers. To the consternation of residents and public officials, Bundists pockmarked the town with arrogant regularity. Uniformed Youth Movement participants attended church services. Bund leaders passed the time in local bars, downing steins of hearty German ale. These brazen actions were doubled down when the Bundists rented a train bound for downtown Milwaukee, and lured residents of that heavily German-populated city to Grafton with promises of fun for children and athletic competitions for adults. Though confounded by the situation, some Grafton officials tried to make the best of the problem. In a show of good will, the fire department band occasionally entertained the big city visitors with German oom-pa-pas.

George Froboese, the Midwestern gau leader, denied accusations that Camp Hindenburg was a paramilitary training camp. Federation president Bernard Hoffman was skeptical. A heavy presence of OD guards and uniformed teenagers marching in formation was all the proof he needed. Something nefarious must be going on inside the private grounds. If not, why did the Bund need swastika-clad OD protection? Grafton had an excellent police force for such purposes. ". . . [I]f these Nazis want to wear uniforms and carry arms," he told a reporter, "let them join the United States Army and Navy."[2]

"Legally a city, Fort Beulah was a comfortable village of old red brick, old granite workshops, and houses of white clapboards or gray shingles, with a few smug little modern bungalows, yellow or seal brown," Nobel Prize–winning author Sinclair Lewis wrote in his 1935 novel *It Can't Happen Here*. "It was a downy town, a drowsy town, a town of security and tradition, which still believed in Thanksgiving, Fourth of July, Memorial Day, and to which May Day was not an occasion for labor parades but for distributing small baskets of flowers."[3]

It Can't Happen Here, Lewis's novel of creeping fascism taking hold in late 1930s America when a totalitarian fanatic is elected president, was meant as a cautionary tale. His descriptions in the book of a small New Hampshire village with a pedigree dating back to pre-Revolutionary America might have well applied to Southbury, Connecticut, a rural town with striking similarity to the fictional Fort Beulah.

All resemblance between fiction and fact ended on the page. When fascist reality loomed over Southbury, the citizens of this rock-ribbed New England town united to stop the Bundists from taking root in their community.

It began on October 1, 1937 when one Wolfgang T. Jung bought land in the Kettletown district of Southbury from its owners, Frederick T. Andrews and Garfield Morrison.[4] On the surface, the transaction was innocuous and merited no attention. Five and a half weeks later the truth behind the sale began to emerge. Typically Southbury Sundays were quiet; on November 7 a sizeable contingent of men, women, and children were seen on the property clearing brush, as though preparing the land for some future construction. In the afternoon four men from the crew drove to nearby South Britain to buy food for their hungry coworkers.[5]

In a small town like Southbury, a large group of strangers descending en masse to clear out a newly sold wooded property was a peculiar sight. It didn't take long for the truth to emerge. Carl Nicolay, a district organizer for the Eastern gau, told a reporter for the *Waterbury Republican* that the 187 acres of undeveloped land was the future site of Camp General von Steuben. The camp was to be a home away from home for Bund Youth Movement members living in the Bronx, New York's Westchester County, and the entire state of Connecticut. "We want to get the German-American boys and girls away from the city streets and undesirable environments and bring them up in wholesome surroundings," Nicolay said. Camp von Steuben was to be the largest such Bund facility in the country.

What they did not count on was pushback.

Within days after the news broke that the notorious German-American Bund now owned this land and were planning to descend en masse on their quiet town, the people of Southbury took action. A town meeting was announced for Tuesday, November 23. The agenda would focus on one piece of business: the formation of a new commission to reconsider zoning laws within Southbury's borders.[6]

Mailboxes throughout Southbury were stuffed with a magazine article, "An American Fuhrer Organizes an Army." The piece, published by *American Magazine*, was a contentious interview with Fritz Kuhn. The mass mailing was from an anonymous person or group named The Kettletowners, after the Kettletown area of Southbury where the property was located.[7] The handwritten cover letter boldly challenged readers: "Every Citizen and Resident of Southbury ATTENTION! The attached article describes an organization which purposes to overrun *YOUR* town. Please read it and then decide whether or not you want the swastika and goose step thrust upon you, whether your want your land values depressed." It closed with a call to attend the upcoming town meeting "and do your civic duty."[8] It was later revealed that this mailing was the work of Basil Bass, a New York attorney with a summer home about a mile from the proposed camp.[9]

On Sunday, November 19, Southbury's two major houses of worship were packed. Reverend Felix A. Manley, pastor of the Southbury Federated Church, and Reverend M. Edgar N. Lindsay of the South Britain

Congregational Church both delivered impassioned sermons, warning their congregants of the danger of the Nazi menace right in their own backyard. With a nod to the upcoming Thanksgiving holiday later in the week, Manley dubbed his sermon "Thanksgiving by Thanksliving." He decried the underbelly of fascism in the United States as represented by the Bund. America, Manley said, is "not a picnic ground in which un-American inhabitants can tear down what has been built so slowly and at such cost."[10] Lindsay's sermon, a fiery denunciation of Hitler and Kuhn, compared Nazi Germany and the Bund to Biblical interpretations of the anti-Christ.[11] American Legionnaires, Veterans of Foreign Wars, and the Sons of Union Veterans of the Civil War from throughout Southbury and surrounding towns got involved, writing various resolutions condemning the planned Bund camp.[12]

Given that the meeting was on a Tuesday afternoon, turnout was impressive. The public meeting was originally planned for the Southbury town hall. Over two hundred people tried to get in, many more than officials had anticipated. A quick decision was made to move the proceedings to Reverend Lindsay's South Britain Congregational Church, which could handle the sizeable audience.[13]

Official business, the creation of a zoning committee to oversee any property development in Southbury, was quick. No questions were raised or taken specifically addressing the German-American Bund though it was obvious the committee's mission was to shut down Camp von Steuben before the first brick was laid. The assembly dismissed after the formal agenda was completed but the afternoon was far from over. Reverend Lindsay asked people to stay at the church for an impromptu town meeting. Given that the majority of residents had plenty to say about the Bund, this invitation was well received.

Two resolutions were offered. The first, delivered by Jennie Hinman, an elderly resident who called herself "the town's oldest taxpayer," decried "organizations that fly foreign flags on American soil." The resolution had to be amended, given that on Armistice Day the American Stars and Stripes was often displayed side by side with the banners of other Allied nations. A second resolution condemning the very idea of Bund camps was put to vote by George Holmes, a veteran of the Great War.

After the two motions were passed with great enthusiasm, Reverend Lindsay offered a prayer, appealing for "courage to battle un-Christian movements." The meeting closed with a rousing chorus of "The Star Spangled Banner."[14]

Lindsay received supportive letters and telegrams from around the country. One correspondence came from Mountain Home, a government hospital for wounded veterans in Tennessee. Its author George Chase, a former Navy man, wrote on behalf of "some twenty five men here, mostly cripples and wrecks of 1918. . . . they unanimously unite with me in sympathizeing [sic] with and commending the good people of Southbury in any action they take to crush in its infancy this menace to the inailonable [sic] rights of all mankind."[15]

Another letter, composed on stationery from New York's Grand Hotel Victoria, was far more compelling. Its author detailed a personal horror story of Nazi Germany. His father, a Protestant minister, was thrown into a concentration camp, used for medical experiments, and died after two weeks. The writer's mother was also arrested and held in an undisclosed prison. She was released on the verge of death after three days. German doctors refused to treat the woman, but a sympathetic Jewish physician came in secret at great personal risk. She was beyond help, the writer told Lindsay and died about a week later. "My two sisters, 15 and 17 years old, were taken by the Stormtrooper Officers barracks to satisfy their degenerate bestial desires," the author continued. "Such news you could never get outside of Germany. But it is true."

After escaping from a Czech labor camp, the writer made it to the United States, married, had a child, and opened his own business. "But here in this beuatiful [sic] country the evil Nazis are strong too," the letter continued. He was forced to join the Bund and pay a business protection fee of five dollars per week.

"Fritz Kuhn-Hoch Officer of the German-American Bund . . . has a long criminal record in Germany," he wrote. "From rape to murder, like the majority of the Hitler leaders. Every German knows it to be true. But all these records are wiped out."

He closed with an ominous note. "I could go on and tell you lots more, but it is too dangerous. . . . Warn your friends in other parts of your State Conn. not to let the Nazis gain a foothold. It will mean the beginning of the end. The Nazis are stronger than your police. Because they do not abide by civilized law."

Lindsay had no way of knowing whether or not his correspondent's tale was true. But he took seriously the man's PS: "Please do not mention my name to anybody—my life wouldn't last long." The clergyman obliterated the author's signature with a heavy black pen.[16] A similar letter from another German refugee so disturbed Lindsay that he destroyed the document after reading it.

On November 28, a Sunday afternoon, Kuhn's national publicity director Gerhard Wilhelm Kunze went to Southbury on behalf of the Bund and Camp von Steuben to make a personal appeal, meeting with Reverend Lindsay and attorney Pat Ewing at the pastor's home. For two hours Kunze pled his case. The camp would be a boon to Southbury, a place where good people would gather on the weekends. And there would be widespread support. All blond-haired and blue-eyed people understood the importance of the Bund's philosophies and the struggle of the Aryan race.

As if on cue, Lindsay's three young daughters Lois, Joan, and Carol came running through the room, a tow-headed trio of blond-haired, blue-eyed youngsters. The reverend delighted in the irony with a hearty laughter, shutting down his visitor's assertions.[17]

Regardless, the Bund moved forward, the people of Southbury and their resolutions be damned. On Sunday, December 5, Gustav Korn and Richard Koehler, two New York Bundists, were seen clearing brush on the Kettletown property. Alrick E. Nelson, a Connecticut grand juror, backed up by a small army of policemen, stormed the site. The duo was arrested, hauled off to jail, and released on a bond of seventy-five dollars. Their crime: the two Bundists "did with force and arms do manual labor, the day being Sunday." Korn and Koehler were guilty of violating dusty "Blue Law" statutes that still remained on Connecticut state books.[18]

In the wake of this unusual arrest Harold Hicock, the judge overseeing the case, received an anonymous letter from a man claiming to be a neighbor of Koehler. The writer urged Judge Hicock to look into the status of the Bundist's citizenship. "He has a large Swasteka [sic] flag draped in his store here but no signs of our beautiful AMERICAN flag. If he and such men like he, like Hilter [sic] and his Swastika why not send them back to Germany where they can have their fill of him. This country is good enough for us without all the isims of foreign dictators." The letter was signed "AN AMERICAN PATRIOT."[19]

On December 14, the new Zoning Code for Southbury was approved by a vote of 142 for to 91 opposed.[20] Its powers were far reaching. The Kettletown property was rezoned "as a purely farming and residential district which cannot be used for recreational camping or drilling purposes." Any "military training or drilling with or without arms except by the regular armed forces of the United States" was prohibited, and violation would be subject to a fine of $250. Albert Aston, an attorney who served as the committee chairman, insisted the rules were adopted to maintain the natural beauty and historical nature of an age-old colonial New England town.[21] The law also allowed for inspection and examination of any building as the commission saw fit. Not everyone in Southbury was happy with this new policy, with some objecting that the statute was unconstitutional. "The code is a step from democracy to Hitlerism, the very Hitlerism we are trying to drive out," complained one resident.[22]

There still remained the matter of Korn and Koehler. Their trial was held December 27. In front of a packed courtroom of fifty people—some Southbury residents and others New York Bund members—Judge Hicock dismissed the case after Alrick Nelson, the grand juror, decided to drop all charges. "Our objective has been accomplished," Nelson told the court. Korn and Koehler, who had no legal representation, left the courtroom in an entourage led by Duncan C. Folger of the New York Westchester County Bund chapter.

Heated shouting matches broke out in the hallways outside the courtroom between Kuhn loyalists and Southbury citizens. "You have been 100 percent propagandized by the Jews," Folger sneered. He told war veteran George Holmes to concentrate on the real enemies of the United States: the Communist Party and the labor faction Congress of Industrial Organizations (CIO), an organization Folger claimed was filled with Reds.

As for the Kettletown property, Folger said the Bund would look over the new regulations before making any decisions on what to do with the land. However, for the time being there would be no action taken to "get around" the law.[23]

In New York, Kuhn declared the Southbury real estate would be sold to Father Divine, and the Bund would build its camp elsewhere in Connecticut. Neither threat came to pass.[24] For all intents and purposes, the fight was over. Eventually Jung sold the property to George W. Munk, former leader of the Bund's Stamford, Connecticut division. The price was cheap by any standard, with the total cost listed as "one dollar and other valuable considerations." Just what those considerations were was not stated.[25]

The push back against the Bund in Southbury was a national news story in newspapers, radio, and "The March of Time" newsreel, which was shown in theaters coast to coast. Newsreel producers and cameramen came to town to film their version of the Battle of Southbury, with speeches and events reenacted by principal players.[26]

"This is just a 'sleepy little country town' as the reporters characterized it," read the *Southbury Town Report* of 1937, "but it seems we know when to wake up."[27]

Grafton and Southbury weren't the only ones fighting back. In August 1937 United States Attorney General Homer Cummings made loud and official noise declaring an FBI probe into Bund camps. These facilities, he said, could be fronts for Nazi activities and hotbeds for German spies. In the name of the American citizenry, the Department of Justice would uncover exactly what Bundists were doing behind their rural swastikaed gates. Kuhn publicly welcomed the investigations, declaring his group had nothing to hide.

Privately, Kuhn left nothing to chance. His subordinates were schooled in stock answers to investigators' questions.[28] Claiming that he had repeatedly asked the FBI to investigate the camps, Kuhn fired off strict guidelines to all Bundists on how to cooperate with any government inquiry. Only unit leaders had permission to speak with outsiders. "Frivolous conversations with unknown persons are to be avoided," Kuhn wrote in "Bund Command #13," noting that "a number of secret service people have been ordered to sound out [our] members and collect information." People purporting to be investigators must be asked for identification papers. "We are an American organization and everything we do is within the law and is good for the U.S.A.," Kuhn insisted. Though the Bund was neither funded by nor officially connected with the German government, they were, the *Bundesführer* explained, "endeavoring to obtain, by lawful means, an influence in the legislation" for German-Americans. "[W]e oppose Marxism without compromises of any kind, and we are especially opposed to Communism and its Jewish Leader."

If investigators asked about the OD, it must be stressed that these squadrons were a "patriotic group." No figures were to be given about the size of Bund membership. And under no circumstances was President Roosevelt to be "personally attacked by any speech or address."[29]

Summer ended. Fall came and went. The nation shut down as usual for the last two weeks of December for Christmas and New Year's. On January

5, 1938, Cummings released his findings in a fourteen-volume report, *Nazi Camps in the United States.*

The verdict: the German-American Bund was guilty only of producing unpopular speech. No matter how noxious their activities, Fritz Kuhn and the German-American Bund were constitutionally free and clear. "It is possible that some members [of the Bund] have taken the oath of allegiance [to the United States] with a mental reservation in renouncing all allegiance to their former country," the report noted. However this was not a crime.

No further investigation was warranted, Cummings said. Fritz Kuhn had beat the Feds at their own game.[30]

For the time being, at least.

This brush with government authorities made Kuhn cautiously creative. Displaying the NSDAP banner was clearly risky business and an open invitation for accusations against Bundists of disloyalty to the United States. A new flag was conjured up to represent the German-American Bund exclusively. It was centered by a swastika thrusting upward in a three-dimensional tower that bore an odd resemblance to the Chrysler Building; and anchored by a half-circle base with the initials *AV* for the organization's German name *Amerikadeutscher Volksbund.* This symbol was a study in mustard yellow and black, centered against a field of red and white that clearly resembled the German Iron Cross.[31] "The Bund flag is to be carried on the pole by the [OD] in place of the German Reich flag," Kuhn stated. "When marching on the street or in halls this flag will also be carried by the [OD]. The Bund flag is the banner of our movement. In the future the [OD] will only carry the American and Bund flag. As heretofore, the Swastika will be used for decoration in halls [next to the American flag]. The Swastika will also remain in our camps."[32]

10

New Moon and Red Cloud

IN PERHAPS THE MOST improbable action within the Bund's brief history was the organization's outreach to Native Americans. This potential alliance was not meant to be a benevolent union of two beleaguered peoples joined in a mutual battle. Rather, it was driven by a combination of faux admiration, exploitation, and outright graft by the Bund.

Respect for Native American culture was a small thread within the overall Nazi world, fostered by Hitler and his love for the novels of Karl May, a nineteenth-century German novelist who specialized in fanciful tales of the American West. The *Führer* was enamored with two of May's recurring characters: Old Shatterhand, a stoic German who traversed the old West; and his Indian sidekick, Winnetou. Though obviously by NSDAP perspectives Native Americans had none of the superior racial qualities of Aryans, as drawn through May's imagination these dark-skinned people possessed a stoic presence and cunning, coupled with superb fighting skills—qualities Hitler felt should be the embodiment of every man within the Third Reich.[1]

From the dawn of European settlement in North America, ill treatment of the continent's indigenous people was a scar on the land. By the early twentieth century, the majority of Native Americans had been shoved onto stark reservations, stripped of their culture and their dignity. The Indian Citizenship Act of 1924 provided that all Native Americans were now recognized Americans with all rights and privileges associated with such status. This law changed little when it came to how Native Americans were treated. Pushback was inevitable. In 1934 Joseph Bruner, a full-blooded descendent of the Creek tribe, founded the American Indian Federation (AIF).

Bruner had a three-fold mission: to repeal the Indian Reorganization Act, which returned land to individual tribes while encouraging development of their own constitutions; to close down the government's Bureau of Indian Affairs; and to eliminate John Collier from his position as the United States Indian Commissioner. These goals were sound on the surface, but the AIF operated outside the fringes of mainstream thought. Bruner, unlike the majority of Native Americans, was a wealthy man. He'd made his fortune in oil and real estate, giving him a personal interest in opposing the free return of land by the government to Indian tribes. Anyone who disagreed with Bruner was labeled as a communist, with Collier as the top Bolshie. The anti-Roosevelt, anti-New Deal stance of the AIF put the organization at odds with the majority of other Native Americans.[2] The AIF distributed literature with a strong anti-Semitic bent. One pamphlet, called "Communism with the Mask Off" was the reprint of a speech delivered by Joseph Goebbels at the 1935 NSDAP Nuremburg Rally.

Alice Lee Jemison, a New York state resident with a Seneca mother and Cherokee father, was another loud voice within the AIF. Married/divorced/married to different men with the same surname, Jemison brought an unusual résumé to her role as AIF activist. At various times she worked as a housekeeper, theater usher, seamstress, nurse, beautician, and secretary to Ray Jimerson, president of the Seneca Nation.[3] In 1930, two Seneca women were charged with murdering the wife of Henri Marchand, a renowned French sculptor based in Buffalo. Jemison wrote a blazing series of newspaper articles on the case, which led to a brief career as a syndicated columnist.[4]

She possessed a shrill but effective voice both as writer and speaker, honing her talents with intense Red baiting hatred aimed at Collier and the Indian Bureau. As for Roosevelt, Jemison declared the President and his New Deal as a "financial boondoggle, communist-inspired and anti-Christian." In August 1936 she spoke at the American National Conference in Asheville, North Carolina. This gathering, a veritable conclave of extremist groups, allowed Jemison to share the stage with William Dudley Pelley of the Silver Shirts and a few unnamed Bundists. Native Americans sporting swastika armbands worked the audience, handing out pro-Nazi pamphlets. From there it was off to an AIF conference in Salt Lake City, Utah, where Bundists turned out to hear Jemison fire off one of her popular tirades.

Her anticommunist presentations were embedded with pointed attacks on Jews. This captured the attention of Henry Allen, a Bundist with unique ties to other North American fascists. At various times Allen lent support to the Gold Shirts, an anti-Semitic, anti-Red faction operating in Mexico; provided Yaqui Indians with Nazi propaganda; ran guns across the Mexican-United States border; and helped organize Gold Shirt confederates in the United States. This pedigree made Allen a good partner for Jemison. Together they spread fascism and raised cash on the lecture circuit through Oklahoma.

Native Americans, while not viewed as racially pure, were a unique market for Bundist manipulation. With this in mind, Allen traveled to Chicago, where Kuhn was to deliver a speech. Given Jemison's fiery popularity in the American southwest, plus their mutual political and social interests, Allen suggested to the *Bundesführer* that he should consider opening Bund appeal to Indian interests.

Kuhn seized on the idea. Articles appeared in the pages of the *Deutscher Weckruf und Beobachter* under patronizing headlines like "Our Indian Wards and their Guardian." The *Bundesführer* wrote about Native Americans of "a Christian Nation . . . being forced into a program of anti-Christian Communism." Pro-Indian lines were occasionally laced into Kuhn's speeches as well.[5] Gerhard Wilhelm Kunze once defended the Bund as a group not inspired by NSDAP, but age-old traditions of Native Americans. Objecting to accusations that the Bund formal dress was inspired by Nazi garb, he declared "They are American uniforms. The swastika is not foreign but one hundred per cent American. The Indians always used it."[6]

The *Bundesführer* developed a partnership with an Indian leader who went by the name Chief New Moon. New Moon was the stage persona of Thomas Dixon, a writer for anti-Semitic and anti-black publications. As a full-blooded Cherokee, Dixon was exactly what Kuhn needed for Bund promotion.[7] He crisscrossed the country, warning Native American groups about communist saturation within the Indian Bureau and secret Jewish cabals determined to bring down the United States government.[8] Blessed with slick black hair, high cheekbones, and a stoic presence, Dixon had the Noble Savage look necessary to pull off the charade. Dixon's compensation was paltry, ten to twelve dollars a week at best. And there was no guarantee he would always collect his salary. Often when he demanded his money, Kuhn would brush Dixon off with empty assurances of "Tomorrow, come tomorrow."[9]

Another Native American Bund recruit was Elwood A. Towner, a Hupa tribe member and attorney from northeast Oregon. Towner, a staunch anti-communist and vehemently opposed to the Roosevelt Administration, Collier, and the Indian Reform Act, was attracted to the Bund by Frederick G. Collett, an ex-minister and former missionary to Native Americans. Collett ran a group called Indians of California, an organization for raising funds to help Native Americans with legal claims against the United States government. Members were often invited to anti-Indian Bureau meetings held in the offices of the Bund's Los Angeles headquarters.

In the summer of 1939 Collett asked Towner to speak to a group of fifty Indians of California members, a request that was eagerly accepted. Towner adopted the stage name of "Red Cloud," donned full Indian regalia and swastika armband, and wrapped a Bund message in what he thought was Native American–friendly guise. In his speech, delivered July 9, 1939, Towner blamed government treatment of Indians on Jews, whom he called "chuck-na-gin," a supposed Indian word for "children of Satan." The Indians must unite with good Gentile Christians to fight the communist-infested Roosevelt administration, which was rife with what he called "the forces of evil—the reds, pinks, and Jews." Towner told his audience that the United States government was run by Jews. He emphasized a favorite bund talking point, that President Roosevelt was in reality a secret Jew whose true name was "Rosenfelt." Native Americans, he concluded, would be wise to adopt the principles of Nazism. For all his bluster, Towner aka Red Cloud made little impact on the group, who wasn't buying what he had to say.

As it was, Collett's altruistic fund-raising on behalf of the Indians of California and Native American causes was filled with as much veracity as Towner's pretense as an authentic Indian chief. Money Collett raked in from Native American charities and their benefactors was ultimately filtered via clever bookkeeping into Bund bank accounts.[10]

11

Disturbances

As EDITOR OF *DEUTSCHER Weckruf und Beobachter* Walter Kappe pulled no punches. The paper was as lavish in its praise for Hitler and Nazi Germany as it was disdainful of Jews and other Aryan foes. Early on, during his work as a propagandist for The Friends, Kappe made clear how he felt about German-Americans who rejected the NSDAP cause. "You are nothing," he wrote. "You are too narrow to conceive what it means to be German; too cowardly to take advantage of your rights as Americans. You have become slaves and vassals of those who spread hatred against the country of your birth." He demanded change of such weak-willed men, "for the roots of our strength lie in the homeland."[1] If anything, Kappe was even more loyal to Germany than Kuhn, which led to one of the Bund's bigger rifts.

Kapp was at constant odds with Kuhn. He accused the *Bundesführer* of skimming eight hundred dollars of funds designated for "The Golden Book" in order to pay for round-trip tickets for both Kuhn and Elsa during the 1936 Olympic journey.[2] He also derided Kuhn's belief that the Bund should be a more Americanized organization. Things turned uglier in February 1937. Kuhn grew convinced that Kappe, who refused to become a naturalized American citizen, was feeding information about the Bund to the German consulate in a twisted plot to overthrow the *Bundesführer*. At Kuhn's orders, a group of OD men grabbed Kappe and hustled him out of the *Deutscher Weckruf und Beobachter* offices like a common criminal.

In June Kappe headed back home to Germany with his wife and two children via the S.S. *St. Louis*, a ship that later earned infamy of its own in the so-called "voyage of the damned," when in 1939, more than nine hundred Jewish refugees aboard the ship were denied entry to Cuba, the United States, and Canada. The *St. Louis* returned to Europe, where many of its passengers were sucked into the Nazi death machine they had so desperately tried to escape.[3]

Kappe's successor was Severin Winterscheidt, a polemicist with unshakeable disdain for America. Winterscheidt referred to the United States as a "degenerate nation."[4] His credentials as a Bundist were strong. Before taking on the role of editor, he worked as unit leader in Nassau County and the Bronx, and then traveled the country giving speeches and training in NSDAP principles on behalf of the organization.[5] Under his editorial direction, the *Deutscher Weckruf und Beobachter* thrived. Winterscheidt was as strong an anti-Semite as any other Bundist, but he was an equal opportunity hater. One of his articles in *Deutscher Weckruf und Beobachter* engaged in a savage attack on Catholicism, while giving high praise to the Hitler government for its crackdown on priests and their "immorality."[6]

"Immorality" was something in which Winterscheidt had a certain expertise. His often uncontrollable libido leaned toward perverse forms of pleasure. He once was arrested for indecent exposure in New York's Penn Station, an offense that got him thirty days behind bars. Winterscheidt became an American citizen in June 1938. That same month he was caught molesting a little girl. This time Winterscheidt received a three-year sentence.[7]

In fall of 1937, as the mayoral election heated up between the incumbent Mayor Fiorello LaGuardia and his Democratic rival Jeremiah T. Mahoney, LaGuardia had a severe monkey wrench thrown into his campaign. The Bund was granted a parade permit for a march through Manhattan streets. This authorization was given by the police department but it was LaGuardia who was slammed by the backlash. Forces backing Mahoney seized on the issue. One clout-filled judge accused LaGuardia of cynically allowing the parade to go forward, with plans to inflate his image as a fearless politician by forcing the Bund to call it off at the last minute. Anti-LaGuardia newspapers pulled out their best indignation, accusing the mayor of being a Nazi sympathizer. Not everyone was buying it. *The Jewish Daily Forward*, perhaps the most influential Jewish newspaper in New York if not the country, defended LaGuardia and suggested that unscrupulous political interests were exploiting the situation for political gain.

LaGuardia, a staunch free speech advocate, could not in good conscience forbid the Bundists from the right to assembly guaranteed by the Constitution. Instead, he worked loopholes. Rather than withdraw the parade permit, LaGuardia used the powers of his office to restrict the parade route to a limited number of streets. Furthermore, Bundists could not sing *"Horst Wessel Lied"* or any other song during the march, and uniforms were forbidden.

A pamphlet from an unknown group was circulated, declaring that LaGuardia held more pride in his heritage as a Jew on his mother's side rather than his Italian half. While this had potential to infuriate Italian voters, LaGuardia had nothing to worry about. He won reelection by comfortable leads with Jewish and Italian New Yorkers, earning more than sixty percent of ballots from both camps.[8]

LaGuardia learned his lesson. When an opportunity later arrived for the mayor to take more direct action against Fritz Kuhn and the German-American Bund, he seized on it.

On April 20, 1938, a rally was held at the Yorkville Casino in honor of Hitler's forty-ninth birthday. The casino, a combination meeting hall and social center at 210 East Eighty-Sixth Street, was packed with a capacity crowd of thirty-five hundred people. OD men wearing gray shirts and sporting ominous blackjacks on their belts, stood guard along the aisles.

There was good reason for the heavy OD security. Outside the casino protestors gathered en masse. Two anti-Nazi groups, the German-American Workers Club and the Young Patriots of the United States, marched back and forth, holding picket signs and throwing jeers.[9] One protestor held a sign reading "Mankind Should Not Be Crucified On The Swastika."[10] Beyond these two organizations was a good-sized mob of unaffiliated protestors, all eager to see the meeting shut down. A paltry force of just two dozen cops was there to run interference should the volatile combination of protestors and Bundists boil over into an ugly street brawl.[11]

Unbeknownst to any of the demonstrators on the street, police officers, or the Bundists, about one hundred clandestine men slipped into the auditorium. They grouped together in twos and threes, taking seats throughout the hall, waiting for the evening's program to begin.[12]

Gustave Elmer opened the evening, thanking everyone for attending.[13]

Joining him on the speaker's platform was Otto Wegener, one of many Bund propagandists, and Elsa Kuhn as stand-in for her husband. In his speech Wegener threw heaping praise on the German *Führer* for his successful annexation of Austria.[14] Now, he declared, President Roosevelt and Secretary of State Hull must accept Hitler's New Order within Europe.[15]

Wegener was interrupted by a loud cry in the audience. "Is this an American or German meeting?" someone shouted.

The unexpected interruption came from Jean Mathias, a thirty-nine-year-old veteran of the Great War. He stood in defiance, ready for whatever may come.

Reaction was instantaneous. A Bundist sitting behind Mathias threw a hefty punch. OD men jumped in, some ripping off their Sam Browne belts to inflict extra damage with the heavy belt buckles.[16]

As the melee heated up the one hundred covert interlopers, most of them American Jewish war veterans, stood up, thrust blue American Legionnaires caps on their heads, and went to battle.[17] They slugged it out with bare fists as OD squads put their blackjacks to business. Someone crashed a chair against Mathias's head.

The Jewish veterans, outnumbered thirty-five to one by OD men, were shoved out the casino doors. The vets, many with bloodied faces, stumbled to safety. Sidewalk protestors were enflamed by the sight. They attempted to take the hall, while twenty-four cops tried to keep the mob at bay. It was a policeman's worst nightmare about to come true, a full-scale riot threatening to take over the Yorkville streets. Fifty additional policemen were called to the scene. Somehow the mob was wrangled. Only four arrests were made.[18] Ten injuries were reported.[19]

One of the arrested street brawlers was Otto Geissler, a seventeen-year-old German citizen and Bund member. He was hauled before Judge Mathew Troy in New York's felony court. The young Bundist was unable to afford an attorney of his own, so the court appointed counsel: Joseph Ellison. Two of the Jewish war vets testified they saw Geissler bearing a dagger on his belt. Ellison argued that the knife was merely ceremonial, and besides, the two arresting officers had confiscated the offending item without any objection from his client. Troy agreed. The case was dismissed.

Ellison and Geissler were photographed shaking hands. Attorney and client both had broad smiles. At first glance, the photo might have been taken at a Boy Scout meeting, with Ellison as adult leader congratulating

Geissler on receiving a merit badge. Closer examination showed Ellison wore a business suit but Geissler was decked out in full Nazi military regalia, complete with a double lighting bolt, the symbol of Hitler's SS goon squads stitched on his cap.

The picture was published in newspapers throughout the country. Many noted that the young Nazi's court-appointed defender was Jewish.[20]

New York, with its large Jewish population was a crucible for Bundists and their enemies. This was something not limited solely to the Big Apple but extended through the Midwest and on to California.

Hermann Schwinn, an ex-insurance agent, couldn't have been a better choice to lead the Bund's Western District, headquartered in Los Angeles.[21] Schwinn was a German-born naturalized American citizen as was his close friend Kuhn. But unlike the *Bundesführer* with his corpulent physique, Schwinn cut a dashing figure in his Bund uniform. Slim and fit, with a neatly trimmed pencil mustache, Schwinn held a passing resemblance to Claude Rains's character Inspector Renault in the movie *Casablanca*. Yet while Renault ultimately renounces the Nazi-loyal French Vichy government to join forces with Humphrey Bogart's anti-fascist Rick Blaine, Schwinn was a stalwart Bundist, holding fast to Nazi philosophies. Among Schwinn's credentials were letters praising his activities, signed by no less than Adolf Hitler.[22] He also emulated *Der Führer*'s SS guards, keeping a vicious German Shepherd by his side. Schwinn relished telling friends that the dog, named Lump—a German word for "rogue"—was trained to sink his fangs into any Jew within the canine's reach.[23]

The Western District's *Deutsches Haus*, was a gathering place for Los Angelinos of German heritage and an obvious front for German-American Bund activities. Located at 634 West 15th Street, *Deutsches Haus* ("German House") literally was built as a house, and was then remodeled for multifaceted use. Part of the building served as a restaurant and old-fashioned German *bierwirtschaft*, or beer pub. An enormous skylight diffused natural light over a hall where Bundists gathered for meetings, informational bull sessions, and entertainment. The hall doubled as a movie theater, regularly screening anti-Semitic propaganda films like *Kosher Slaughter*.[24] Facing the street was the Aryan Bookstore, a shop specializing in German and English language books and other reading material promoting Nazi causes and anti-Semitism. Hitler's *Mein Kampf* was an obvious bestseller, as was Henry Ford's *The International Jew*, and the perennially popular anti-Semitic remnant of Tsarist Russia that was a purported—and utterly fictional—Jewish plan for world domination, *The Protocols of the Learned Elders of Zion*. Other materials for sale included Father Coughlin's weekly newspaper *Social Justice*, the Bund's *Deutscher Weckruf und Beobachter*, Elizabeth Dilling's anti-Semitic and racially charged anti-Communist book *The Red Menace*, and something titled *Jews, Jews, Jews*.[25]

Young and old came to *Deutsches Haus* meetings. One attendee was an alienated, acne-scarred, wart-faced teenager named Charles Bukowski. Years before earning literary fame for his frank depictions of L.A.'s Skid Row, the future poet/novelist was a regular at Bundist gatherings. Born August 16, 1920 in Andernach, Germany, Bukowski immigrated with his parents to Baltimore in 1923. Seven years later, the family resettled in South Los Angeles.[26] Bukowski's mother Kate, like many expatriates, felt Hitler was a compelling leader, a person who cared deeply for fellow Germans and what she called "all of us working class." The admiration inspired her son. As a teenager Bukowski attended Bund meetings on his own.[27]

During adolescence Bukowski's face broke out with severe acne, boils, and warts. Though his countenance didn't fit with Aryan ideals of beauty by a long shot, Bukowski found refuge and excitement in Nazism. In his 1982 novel, the nakedly autobiographical *Ham on Rye*, Bukowski recalled with a certain affection his days as a Bundist hanger-on. ". . . I had not desire to go to war to protect the life I had or what future I might have," writes Bukowski's alter ego, Hank Chianski. "I had no Freedom. I had nothing. With Hitler around, maybe I'd even get a piece of ass now and then and more than a dollar a week allowance . . . Also, having been born in Germany, there was a natural loyalty and I didn't like to see the whole German nation, the people, depicted everywhere as monsters and idiots."[28] Years later, Bukowski spoke candidly with his friend and biographer Ben Pleasants about life as a Bundist. "We went down into a cellar. They had this great big American flag there. They had all these chairs. It was an upper middle class house. Very large. The speaker [Schwinn] had his desk on stage. We all stood up to pledge allegiance to the flag. . . . Then he started talking about the Communist menace. How we had to fight force with force. These guys were ready."[29]

That they were. They spread their message in meetings in private homes and rented spaces. The Bund's Western division stretched its reach south toward San Diego and north to San Francisco; crossing the California border into Portland, Oregon; farther north to Spokane and Seattle, Washington; and east into Salt Lake City, Utah; and pockets of independent Bund groups and sympathizers emerging throughout the district.[30] They held rallies and marches, churned out newspapers, and infiltrated businesses where they could. Some enterprising Bundists found confederates within the *Los Angeles Times* printing plant. Anti-Semitic literature was secretly stuffed into newspapers as they came off the presses, then delivered throughout the California southland to the dismay of many and delight of others.[31]

In spring of 1938, Schwinn planned a convention of Western affiliates on April 30 at San Francisco's California Hall. The building, also known as the German House or the German-American Hall, had Teutonic *Rathaus* architecture similar to the town halls found in older German cities. Built in 1912 at 625 Polk Street, California Hall was an imposing landmark in the heart of the city's German-American community.[32]

The Hearst-owned *Call-Bulletin* dubbed the rally as an invasion of "Hitlerites."[33] On Friday, May 20, ten days before the rally, the San Francisco Labor Council passed a protest resolution that was sent to newspapers throughout the region.[34]

Public opposition be damned: the rally went on as scheduled, with some one thousand enthusiastic supporters packing California Hall. Stressing his beloved theme of Jewish Communist influence, Schwinn proclaimed that the Roosevelt administration was rife with "pink and red Jews." Not until this specter was removed, he charged, would America's woes be resolved.

Schwinn's speech brought inspirational cheers throughout the hall, but the surrounding neighborhood was a different story. Three thousand protestors—three for every one Bundist soaking in Schwinn's words—swarmed the streets. Many waved signs reading "Drive the Nazis out of town." The more rambunctious hurled rocks through hall windows, raining showers of glass in their wake.[35]

12

Hollywood

LOS ANGELES PROVIDED THE Bund with a considerable target for their activities: Hollywood and the movie industry. In the 1930s, a large number of the city's Jewish citizens worked in the film colony as actors, directors, producers, writers, cinematographers, and other aspects of the industry. It was no secret, of course, that many immigrant Jews of the early twentieth century were pioneers of the fledgling movie business in a time when "the pictures" were considered a novelty entertainment without much of a future. As film historian Neil Gabler noted, Jewish entrepreneurs ". . . had a special compatibility with the industry, one that gave them certain advantages . . . [H]aving come primarily from fashion and retail, they understood public taste and were masters at gauging market swings, at merchandising . . . [A]s immigrants themselves, they had a peculiar sensitivity to the dreams and aspirations of other immigrants and working-class families, two overlapping groups that made up a significant portion of the early moviegoing audience."[1]

Regardless of their strength in numbers, Jewish executives and talent often masked their backgrounds to avoid anti-Semitism. Names were changed to sound more "American": the Polish-born immigrant Schmuel Gelbfisz Americanized his name to "Samuel Goldfish" upon becoming a garment worker, then switched to the less-ethnic sounding moniker "Samuel Gold-wyn" when he entered the film industry. Lazar Meir, an immigrant Jew from Minsk who worked in his family's scrap metal business, became Louis B. Mayer. A group of Russian immigrant brothers—Harry (Hirsz), Albert (Aaron), Sam (Szmul), and Jack (Itzhak) Wonskolaser—got started in the business showing movies to miners in rural Pennsylvania; along the way they changed their family name to "Warner" and ultimately created their own studio.

Mayer became a Hollywood powerhouse, merging two Jewish-owned production companies—Metro Pictures founded by Marcus Loew, and Samuel Goldwyn's Goldwyn Pictures Corporation—into the legendary dream factory, Metro-Goldwyn-Mayer. Largely credited with developing Hollywood's "star system," MGM's talent pool boasted a brilliant array of actors, directors, and other creative talents throughout the 1930s and 1940s. Actors in the studio stable included Greta Garbo, Clark Gable, Jean Harlow, Mickey Rooney, Judy Garland, Norma Shearer, Joan Crawford, and the Marx Brothers; films were guided by directors Mervyn LeRoy, George Cukor, Victor Fleming, and Vincente Minnelli; producer Irving Thalberg (another leading member of Hollywood's Jewish community) was praised for genius acumen. The list of movies produced by and released through MGM reads like an encyclopedia of classic cinema: *The Wizard of Oz*, *Gone With the Wind*, *Anna Christie*, *A Night at the Opera*, *The Good Earth*, and many lavish, brightly colored musicals. Under Mayer's leadership everyday dramas and comedies portrayed an idealized America, free of any ethnicity or religious faith other than generic Christian backgrounds, perhaps best exemplified by the *Andy Hardy* series.

They had a profound impact on American culture, but the Jewish studio bosses still couldn't overcome the anti-Semitism that prevailed in southern California. It was a force stronger than even Mayer's legendary power. When his children, along with those of fellow movie mogul, Paramount co-founder Jesse Lasky, were denied admittance to an exclusive private school thanks to unwritten but hard-fast policies to maintain a Jew-free educational environment, Mayer implored gossip diva Hedda Hopper to intercede on his behalf. Thanks to her *Los Angeles Times* column Hopper was just as feared throughout Hollywood as Mayer. Given an item of juicy note—often provided by studio execs like Mayer—Hopper could change the destiny of any film star. Knowing that she was friendly with the school's headmistress, Mayer implored Hopper for help. "Can you tell [her] how important I am?" he asked. But Hopper's much-lauded tabloid brawn was not enough to eradicate deeply rooted prejudices and her intercession was fruitless. There was no way to deliver the news other than bluntly: "They will not take Jews," Hopper told Mayer.[2]

There were rumored ties between the German-American Bund and behind-the-scenes Hollywood professionals, a development that certainly was recognized by Jewish talent. "I see Bund members dropping down my chimney," Groucho Marx—originally Julius Henry Marx of New York City's Jewish immigrant class—jokingly wrote to a friend.[3] But the sardonic wisecrack was based in reality. A group billing itself as the Hollywood Actors and Technicians Committee on Unemployment circulated an inflammatory handbill to colleagues throughout the film colony. "*UNEMPLOYMENT* in the Motion Picture Industry is reaching TREMENDOUS PROPORTIONS," blared the missive. "Not more than 50% of the capacity personnel is working today . . . These American workers are DEMANDING TO KNOW the true reasons for this *ALARMING CONDITION* whereby their families are kept on the verge of *STARVATION*, while the JEWISH MONOPOLY of the Motion Picture Industry, BRAZENLY DISCHARGES NON-JEWISH MEN AND WOMEN, and replaces them with refugee JEWS from Europe." The flyer strongly urged confrontation with "the Jew Motion Picture Producers . . . the Jew-controlled publicity staffs of the Studios . . . the Jew Motion Picture Publications . . . the Jew writers of the ANTI-American propaganda pictures . . . the Jew actors themselves." The dodger's anonymous author also claimed that "American" workers were being tossed out in favor of Jews "thrown out of Europe; and to antagonize FRIENDLY, ANTI-JEWISH Governments in Stirring up INTERNATIONAL WAR for Jewish Vengeance and Profit."[4]

The whispers of Bundists within their midst, to say nothing of public activities by Schwinn and his minions, did not go unnoticed. A small group of film industry talent—both Jew and Gentile—banded together in July 1936 to form the Hollywood League Against Nazism, which soon took on the less cumbersome name the Hollywood Anti-Nazi League. Founders included writers Donald Ogden Stewart, who served as chairman, and Dorothy Parker, director Fritz Lang (himself a Jewish refugee from Nazi Germany), actor Frederic March, and composer Oscar Hammerstein. At its height, membership was estimated between four to five thousand people. Members came from all levels of the movie business ranging from stagehands and technical people, to actors, directors, writers, and some studio power brokers. The league published newsletters: *The Anti-Nazi News: A Journal in Defense of American Democracy* and *Hollywood Now*, both of which denounced fascism and Nazi elements in the film industry, the rest of the country and abroad; and also hosted a twice-weekly radio program.[5]

On October 20, 1936, the group held a massive gathering at L.A.'s Shrine Auditorium, denouncing "Hitlerism in America." Reverend L. M. Birkhead, a prominent Unitarian Universalist minister from Kansas City, who claimed to have spoken with "every Nazi Jew-baiting and Anti-Democratic Leader in America," was a featured speaker, along with pop-eyed comedian Eddie Cantor—born Isidore Iskowitz to Russian-Jewish immigrants—and Broadway producer Gifford Cochran.[6] Other events followed, including a speech at the Los Angeles Philharmonic by civil rights pioneer W. E. B. DuBois, who related what he saw during his visit through Nazi Germany.[7]

(Gradually the Hollywood Anti-Nazi League shifted focus, embarking on various liberal causes beyond speaking against fascism. This led to charges that the group was a Communist front, investigations by the FBI, and blacklisting of numerous members during the Hollywood witch hunts of the 1940s and 1950s.)

The Anti-Nazi League's organizational skills were put to the test—and succeeded—in November 1938 when German film artist Leni Riefenstahl arrived in the United States for a national tour. Riefenstahl was renowned—and infamous—for *Triumph of the Will*, her 1935 documentary of Germany's Sixth Nazi Party Congress and Nuremburg Rally. Given complete access to the event, Riefenstahl had made a film that was groundbreaking in cinematic technique and a masterpiece of propaganda, portraying Hitler as a near-mythical conqueror, a demigod who literally descended from the clouds via airplane.

On the evening of November 9, 1938, Nazi factions throughout Germany ran organized riots aimed specifically at the Jews. Jewish shops and homes were destroyed, synagogues were torched, thirty-thousand plus Jews were arrested, and at least ninety were known to be murdered. The NSDAP-sanctioned nightmare became known as *Kristallnacht*, the so-called "Night of the Broken Glass." Riefenstahl was crossing the Atlantic on the night of attack and later claimed to have no knowledge of the rampage. In her self-serving autobiography Riefenstahl wrote, "Aboard ship we read American newspapers that printed a lot of nonsense about Germany, stories I thought had to be libel. We had been reading only old papers . . . [and] we couldn't know anything about the dreadful events of *Kristallnacht*." Upon her arrival in New York, Riefenstahl refused to accept headlines of the shocking brutality back home. "[H]ad I believed the press reports I never would have set foot on American soil," she contended.

Regardless, Riefenstahl began her cross-country American tour in New York, "carefree and unaware." She toured Radio City Music Hall in what she thought was a "delightful" start to her American journey. Riefenstahl's time in New York proved to be the exception. ". . . I had no inkling of what was brewing for me (in America)," she later said.[8] Riefenstahl claimed that during her Radio City visit she met with King Vidor, director of such humanist classics as *The Crowd* and *Our Daily Bread*, though Vidor denied the story. At best, he later told an interviewer, he sent Riefenstahl what he termed were "professional congratulations" after seeing *Olympia* during a trip through Europe.[9]

Next was Chicago, where Riefenstahl met with Avery Brundage. Brundage held her in the highest regard. *Olympia*, Riefenstahl's artistic rendering of the 1936 Berlin games was another masterpiece, a documentary that effectively changed how sports were portrayed on film for generations of cinema and television professionals. Yet for all its international acclaim, *Olympia*'s inclusion of Adolf Hitler got the film banned in several American cities. Brundage was outraged, regarding this prohibition as an insult to the entire Olympic movement. He had previously addressed a New York rally—where many Bundists were in the audience—angrily denouncing what Brundage felt was a conspiracy against Riefenstahl's film. Their meeting in Chicago was a homecoming between two good friends with mutual interests.

While in the Windy City, Riefenstahl also received a personal invitation from Henry Ford to tour his Michigan automobile plants. "When we left," Riefenstahl recalled, "Ford said to me, 'When you see the Führer after your return, tell him that I admire him and I am looking forward to meeting him at the coming Party rally in Nuremberg'."[10] Ford had good reason to send his compliments to Hitler. Earlier that year, on July 30 the German Counsel in Cleveland presented Ford the Grand Service Cross of the Supreme Order of the German Eagle in recognition of the automaker's seventy-fifth birthday. This was the highest honor Nazi Germany bestowed on foreigners and Ford was the first American to receive the award.[11] The only other person to receive this medal was aviator Charles Lindbergh, a man with unique ties of his own to Hitler and the Nazi war machine.

When Riefenstahl was in New York, Walter Winchell added to his anti-Nazi slanguage, dubbing the beautiful celebrity "as pretty as a swastika."[12] Once she reached California in the last week of November, rhetoric heated up considerably and most of Riefenstahl's industry peers turned their backs on Hitler's documentarian. Protests greeted her every move. The Anti-Nazi League dogged her throughout the visit, posting signs on the streets, handing out flyers, and taking out newspaper advertisements proudly declaring, "There is no place in Hollywood for Leni Riefenstahl."

She did find some refuge. Riefenstahl spent a few days at the Palm Springs villa of one supporter; others, as she later wrote, "begged me to stay on. The [Anti Nazi] League, they said, represented only a minority and I had lots of friends here."

One of the "friends" who welcomed Riefenstahl was a beloved figure throughout the world, a congenial, family oriented movie mogul—and long whispered to be a closet anti-Semite: Walt Disney. He gave Riefenstahl a personally guided tour of his studio, taking particular joy in showing her the ongoing work for what was to become *Fantasia*. During their meetings Disney suggested a viewing of *Olympia* in his private screening room, a flattering proposition Riefenstahl relished. Disney's invitation was a powerful repudiation of the Hollywood elite shunning her.

Yet it was not to be. A few days later Riefenstahl was shocked when the offer was withdrawn. It wasn't the glorification of naked human bodies filling *Olympia*'s opening scenes to which the prudish Disney objected. Rather, he was uneasy that word of the screening would filter out of his fortress, then wind through Hollywood rumor circuits and beyond, ultimately causing considerable damage to his stellar reputation. This was a financial gamble Disney could not afford to make. The economic backlash at the box office could be disastrous should the public discover Hitler's filmmaker was in any way associated with his studio. "No one will know about it," Riefenstahl implored. "My projectionists are unionized," replied the notoriously antilabor Disney. Art was art, but business was the catalyst that made it possible.

"Three months later, after leaving America, I found out from the American press how powerful the Anti-Nazi League was," the still embittered Riefenstahl recalled decades later. "Walt Disney was forced to make a statement to the effect that when I had visited him he hadn't known who I was."[13]

Disney's repudiation of Riefenstahl wasn't enough to counter whispers of his own anti-Semitism. Art Babbitt (née Arthur Harold Babitsky) was a top animator at the studio. His distinguished credits include the development of Mickey Mouse's canine pal Goofy, and animating Geppetto in *Pinocchio*, the Wicked Queen in *Snow White*, and the Stork in *Dumbo*. He and

Disney had a strong disliking for one another. Babbitt felt Disney was a skinflint with both pay and screen credits. (Babbitt later became a leader in the infamous 1941 animators' strike against the studio.) Conversely, Babbitt's personal life incurred the wrath of his employer. While recognized as one of the most talented men in the business, Babbitt also had a well-earned reputation as a lothario. The notoriously puritanical Disney disdained Babbitt's roving eye and aversion to marriage. This contempt reached its pinnacle when Babbitt had an affair with the most virginal of Disney images, Snow White. Marjorie Belcher was a talented, strikingly beautiful woman, whose physical grace made her the ideal human model for *Snow White* character animators and a delectable sex partner for Babbitt. Tension between employer and employee was eased somewhat after Babbitt and Belcher married, albeit their mutual loathing remained. (The Babbit-Belcher marriage lasted from 1937 to 1940; Belcher later married dancer/choreographer Gower Champion, in what became a legendary show business coupling.)[14]

Babbitt had other outside interests besides women. Los Angeles Bund activities were no secret, of course, so he decided to learn more about the movement. "Nobody asked me to go, but I did out of curiosity," Babbitt told an interviewer. "They were open meetings, anybody could attend, and I wanted to see what was going on for myself." It wasn't what Babbitt saw that made an impact; it was *who* he saw that really stunned him. "On more than one occasion I observed Walt Disney and [Disney's lawyer] Gunther Lessing," Babbitt claimed, "along with a lot of other prominent Nazi-afflicted personalities." If Babbitt's accounts are to be believed, Disney was a regular at public Bund gatherings. It seems unlikely, given Disney's caution with Riefenstahl; after all, he was a recognizable figure with a sterling reputation as a family-oriented filmmaker. It's doubtful that someone of Disney's stature would risk everything to attend meetings where Nazi ideals were trumpeted. Still, Babbitt insisted, "Disney was going to meetings all the time." Babbitt continued his freelance undercover work, getting himself invited to the homes of disgruntled Hollywood personalities whom he claimed were active American Nazis. Yet in discussing his days as an infiltrator, Babbitt wouldn't name names, other than Disney's.[15]

PART IV

Golems

"If somebody's lights had to be put out, you just put them out, that's all."

—Mickey Cohen[1]

13

The Legend of the Golem

MUCH LIKE THE MYSTICAL clay from which it was molded, the legend of the Golem shifts and changes shape throughout Jewish history. Its best-known incarnation is the Golem created by Rabbi Loew of sixteenth-century Prague. This tale begins when anti-Semites attack the Jews of their city with violent rage. The rabbi, desperate to help his people, chooses an extraordinary means of revenge: he forms a clay behemoth as protector of Prague's Jews. Different aspects of how the manlike figure comes to life are told. In one version, Rabbi Loew puts a slip of paper with mystical words in the Golem's mouth; a variant on this plasters the paper on the Golem's forehead. Either way, once the words are applied, the Golem rises up, large, strong, hulking, and ready for action.

The Golem attacks with no mercy, systematically cracking the skulls and breaking the bones of his foes. He is a borderline creature who straddles a realm between the righteous and the dangerous. Eventually, when the Golem's assaults are veering out of control, Rabbi Loew calls him back and removes the mystical words to end the violence.

But as he recedes back to his underworld, the Golem is remembered with a certain degree of awe and respect. For all his faults, he is a stalwart antihero protecting his Jewish brethren against anti-Semitic aggressors.

With the rise of Fritz Kuhn and the German-American Bund, the Golem transmigrated into a splintered brute of many forms. He had names like Meyer "Little Man" Lansky, Abner "Longy" Zwillman, Benjamin "Bugsy" Siegel, and Meyer "Mickey" Cohen. He hired the toughest of thugs with the hardest of baseball bats and the strongest of fists to help beat down a

twentieth-century American version of medieval Prague's Jew haters. These
men had no qualms about using their unique and diverse talents to hammer
back at the Bundists wherever they gathered, just as the Golem did when
lurking through the dark streets of Prague some four centuries before. In
some cases their actions were requested. Other times they were self-appointed.
Often it was a combination of the two, with respected figures turning a blind
eye to the violent response of their back-alley avengers.

Though almost universally looked down on by their co-religionists for the
disgrace and dishonor Jewish gangsters brought to their people—via loan
sharking, extortion, theft, labor racketeering, illegal gambling, prostitution,
shakedowns, drug trafficking, and other crimes; crimes often underscored by
murder of the most brutal fashion—like the Golem of Prague Lansky, Zwillman, Siegel, Cohen, and others earned a certain degree of gratitude within
the Jewish community. There were times when well-applied sins could be
seen as virtues.

14

Little Man

BENJAMIN SUCHOWLJANSKY, A DEEPLY religious man and loving grandfather, often told his beloved grandson Meyer stories of their hometown Grodno and its Jewish history. For centuries, Grodno, located on the eastern edge of the vast Russian empire (what is now modern Belarus) was a dichotomy for members of its small, closely knit Jewish population, which dates back to 1389. Jews were expelled from the city in 1495, but allowed to return just eight years later. Cries of "blood libel!" and accusations of Christian children ritually murdered rocked Grodno with violent reprisals against its Jews in 1790 and 1820. And yet, Grodno's Jewish community thrived. It grew into a center of learning, bolstered by the modest wealth of its successful merchants. At the close of the nineteenth century, some 25,000 of the city's 46,871 citizens were Jews. One would think Grodno was a Jewish paradise within a historically anti-Semitic country.[1]

But Russia being Russia, the serenity was at best temporary. Pogroms, the state-sponsored terrorism of Mother Russia's Jews, were periodic specters in Grodno, as they were throughout the rest of the country. Tsar Nicolas I, who reigned from 1825 to 1855, was, in Grandpa Benjamin's restrained words, a "dreadful anti-Semitic despot." His laughing Cossacks forced Jews from their homes, burned their holy books, killed their men, raped their women, and ripped children from families. Things improved under Alexander II, who was, Benjamin told little Meyer, "a good man."[2] While popular with his people, underground revolutionaries sought to remove the Tsar from his throne through any means necessary. On March 13, 1881, bomb-throwing insurrectionists succeeded. In the wake of Alexander's assassination his son

Alexander III unleashed a hell storm. Cossacks ran wild through Jewish villages and towns in a bloody frenzy of murder and destruction. Jews were forbidden from buying farmland or attending university; and were forced to carry identification marking them as Jews. After the 1894 death of Alexander III, there was no improvement under his son, Tsar Nicolas II. The terror only increased.[3]

One night, probably sometime in 1906, a secret meeting was held at Benjamin Suchowljansky's home. Four-year-old Meyer, who was supposed to be asleep, lurked outside the room, watching and listening as a strange man berated the gathering. "Jews!" he roared. "Why do you just sit around like stupid sheep and allow them to come and kill you, steal your money, kill your sons, and rape your daughters. Aren't you ashamed? You must stand up and fight," he continued. ". . . I have been a soldier in the Turkish army. I was taught to fight. A Jew can fight. I will teach you how. We have no arms, but it doesn't matter. We can use sticks and stones. Even if you're going to die, at least do it with honor. Fight back!"

Older people dismissed this soldier as a dangerous crank. Young people rallied to his words. Guns, forbidden to Jews under Russian law, were secretly stockpiled. Weapons were crafted from iron bars and wooden sticks. Covert paramilitary training was held deep in the forests near Grodno.

A sympathetic Christian leaked word to Grodno's Jewish community that a new pogrom was coming. Homes were boarded up. Valuables were stashed in secret caches within the woods. Meyer sensed the tension and excitement in the air, but Benjamin kept his grandson safe in the house. The elder Suchowljansky now saw the light. These fighting young men were exactly the right measure necessary to combat Cossack thugs eye for eye and tooth for tooth. If I were not so old, Benjamin told Meyer, I would join their ranks.

In advance of this new wave of terror, a police inspector in charge of organizing pogroms for the region made a scouting trip to Grodno. The Jewish avengers met in secret, agreed the man must be eliminated, and plotted their revenge. Their coordination was perfect. The official was killed, but no trace of his assassins was found.

The anonymous soldier who urged the Jewish fighters of Grodno into action made a powerful impact on four-year-old Meyer Suchowljansky. Decades later Meyer Lansky née Meyer Suchowljansky fondly recalled that initial meeting at Grandfather Benjamin's home and the rallying cry of the nameless man. "That speech . . . burned into my memory . . . ," Lansky told

Israeli journalist Uri Dan. "I carried this soldier's words with me when I finally traveled with my mother to America . . . I remember every single word and exactly how he sounded . . . They were like flaming arrows in my head. That's why I always fought back, and why I started my own gang of fellow Jews to protect ourselves."[4]

Meyer Lansky is a legendary figure in the annals of American organized crime. He rose to prominence during the 1920s in the cutthroat bootlegging business. When the Volstead Act was repealed and booze was again a legal commodity, Lansky turned his business interests to casino operations. Though ostensibly this was a mostly legitimate enterprise, the operation required a hefty payroll of law enforcement officials and politicians looking the other way from Lansky's proscribed methods of business. It was a multistate empire, with casinos in Hot Springs, Arkansas, New Orleans, and South Beach, Florida.

Lansky's journey to America began in 1909 when his father Max left Grodno for New York City. Like many Jewish immigrants fleeing from the oppression of Russia and Eastern Europe, Max was determined to forge a better life for his family in the Promised Land of America. He broke nonstop sweat working as a pants presser in Brooklyn's Brownsville neighborhood. Within two years Max earned enough money to book passage for his wife Yetta, eight-year-old Meyer, and his other son, six-year-old Jacob. Meyer's birthday was originally listed as August 28, 1902, a date that he later changed to July 4. It seemed fitting that his new birthday would be forever connected to the birthday of his new homeland. Meyer Suchowljansky was reborn as a full-fledged American.[5] In a few years the family name would be shortened and Americanized, jettisoning the hard consonants of "Suchowljansky" for the less unwieldy "Lansky," a surname that still retained strong Jewish flavor.[6]

Max relocated from Brooklyn to New York's Lower East Side, the Manhattan ghetto teeming with Yiddish *landsmen*.[7] Immigrants from Russia and Eastern Europe, Italy, Sicily, and Ireland were stuffed into rickety tenement buildings. Yetta did her best to keep a proper Jewish home. The tiny oven of the cramped Lansky apartment was not large enough to cook the Sabbath dinner of cholent, a traditional Jewish stew that was the delicacy of every mother in the ghetto. Meyer was assigned the important task of bringing the Lansky cholent dish to a neighborhood baker, who charged Jewish families five cents to use his oven for cooking their Friday night meals.

Young Lansky took great pride in this task. "It made me feel a man—responsible," he recalled.

His route to the bakery took him along Delancy Street, the Irish quarter of the Lower East Side ghetto and a hub for curbside casinos. Lansky's attention jumped from Sabbath meal to the many Irishmen, Italians, and fellow Jews hunched over the sidewalk, a pile of loose change and bills in front of them and fists held aloft rattling a pair of dice. The crap games and the apparent ease it took for winners to rake in quick cash proved to be too tempting for the impressionable boy. "With the five cents my mother had carefully horded during the week, I decided to try to win a fortune," he said. To no surprise, he was an easy mark. The family nickel was gone in one quick roll of the dice. Mortified but honest, Lansky returned to the apartment, told his mother what happened, and was ripped to the core when Yetta burst into tears. "I think maybe that was the worst moment of my life," Lansky said. "[W]hat troubled me more than anything else was the fact that I had lost that money. My cheeks burned with the thought that I had been a loser, and that night before I went to bed I swore to myself that one day I would be a winner—I would beat them all."

Becoming that kind of champion required the kind of education not found in the New York public school system. He hung out on Delancey Street, closely watching every move of the sidewalk crap games. Quiet observation paid off: within a few weeks, Lansky could single out the setup guys, their bosses, and the powerhouses bankrolling all operations. He learned how suckers were drawn in and fleeced of a hard workweek's pay. Other boys could spend time in Hebrew school; just a year shy of bar mitzvah age, Lansky preferred a *cheder* of the streets.

Having soaked in the rules, nuances, and tricks of the game, Lansky decided to risk another Sabbath dinner. He sat in on a game one Friday, watched for a little while, then threw down his nickel for the next roll. "That was one of the most fateful moments of my life," he recalled. "My timing was perfect but my hands trembled so much that I thought I was going to drop the cholent dish. But I won. I knew I would."

Lansky learned one of the key lessons of his life that day: think slowly, plan ahead, don't be greedy, rake in your winnings, and step away. Foolish gamblers were the losers; smart and thoughtful players won the games. "It was a golden moment," he said. "The winners are those who control the game, the professionals who know what they're doing. All the rest are suckers."[8]

The Lower East Side was a sort of human version of the cholent, a real-life stew of ethnicities and religions crammed together in the space of few blocks. Pushcart vendors sold food, rags, and pots. Pimps peddled women to the poor of the neighborhood and wealthy slummers from Uptown. Weaving through the streets were Orthodox Jews who looked like they never left their small Eastern European villages. Long black coats and black hats, beards, and side curls bouncing off their ears, books tucked under their arms, deep in thought, trying to ignore the chaos of the streets. They stuck out with their Old World ways and strict religious practices. They also did not put up a fight, making handy quarry for punks in search of easy marks. Jewish shops routinely were robbed. Irish and Italian hoodlums grabbed learned rabbis by their beards, a humiliation of both person and faith. Jewish youngsters were forced by bullies to drop their pants and display their boyish foreskin-free penises.

Lansky, now fourteen and bar mitzvahed, was considered a man in the eyes of the Jewish world. And still, he faithfully fulfilled his weekly childhood task, carrying his mother's cholent back and forth from the bakery.

It made him an obvious target for gangs on a Jew hunt. On this day half a dozen of the Irish bruisers stood in Lansky's path. They were in their late teens, and towering large over the diminutive Jewish adolescent. Taunts flew thick and furious. "What are you carrying there, Jew boy?" the top thug demanded, pointing to the cholent. "Have you got the body of a Christian baby there to suck out its blood? Are you going to make matzos with its flesh?"

Bringing up the ancient blood libel was just the beginning. The leader whipped out a blade. "Take down his trousers!" he spat to his underlings. "We'll see if he's cut properly, and if he isn't maybe we can help him lose a little more."

A ghost from Grodno called out to Lansky. A Jew can fight! Fight back!

The older boy never saw it coming.

Lansky was small for his age, but filled out with sinew and muscle. He raised the cholent, still piping hot from the bakery, as high as he could, then ploughed it hard into his tormentor's face. The cholent dish broke up, shards ripping into Irish flesh, hot meat and vegetable and crust and gravy flying. The older boy, a mess of scorching food and streaming blood, fell to the street, howling as his head smashed into the curb.

Lansky wasn't done. He grabbed the bully's knife and hurled himself into the other gang members. Lansky was all fists and feet, slashing with the knife, hitting, kicking, and then biting. His body was a fighting machine.

One boy had his leg slashed. Another had a cut in his back. Their leader moaned and gripped his mangled face. By now the melee was public news up and down the street. Lansky was knocked around, but not beaten. Slightly dazed, his clothes ripped to pieces, and blood dripping down his face, he still had presence of mind to split the scene as police arrived. He disappeared into the thick sea of people always on Delancey Street, running as fast as his skinny legs could take him.

When he got back home Yetta was stunned. Her little Meyer, her beloved elder son, was a bloody mess. He had no cholent dish.

Meyer retreated to his small room in the Lansky family apartment. He opened up a secret hiding place, counted out some of his gambling winnings, and went back to his mother. He handed the money to Yetta.

"I want you to go and buy some food for our cholent," he told her. And then he went to the kitchen sink to wash up.

Yetta did not question her son where he got such money. The Sabbath dinner was served and consumed in utter silence.[9]

Jews needed to stick together in this hardscrabble arena and Lansky built up a gang of tough-minded and strong-fisted friends. Benjamin Siegel, a fellow Jew from the neighborhood, was a seeming mirror opposite of Meyer. Where Lansky was quiet and thoughtful, Siegel was brash and outgoing. Though both could handle themselves on mean ghetto streets, Lansky used violence as last resort. Siegel, marked with a hair-trigger temper, was fast on the draw. Tall and handsome, Siegel could be charming one minute and terrifying the next. Some said he was crazy as a bedbug, and dubbed him with the cockeyed nickname "Bugsy." Lansky was small and slow to show anger, but backed his even disposition with muscle and fighting skills that surprised anyone on the receiving end of his punch.[10] He was respected and feared, with a presence that in later years earned him the moniker "Little Man."

One cold January day, as freshly fallen snow turned to sludge on the dirty pavements, Lansky found himself alone. He was on the wrong part of Hester

Street, a main thoroughfare used by tenement Jews, Italians, and Irish alike. A gang of Sicilian toughs, a few years older and with more brute force, saw this solitary, undersized Yid and seized the opportunity for some vigorous Jew baiting.

Their leader was a swarthy kid. Through his thick Sicilian accent he growled out an ultimatum. "If you wanna keep alive, Jew boy," he told Lansky, "you gotta pay us five cents a week protection money."

Lansky considered the situation briefly, looking at the aggressor and his six associates. Finally, he gave a reasoned response.

"Go fuck yourself," he told the Sicilian.

It should have been an opening salvo for another bloody street brawl. Instead the Sicilian teen, Salvatore Lucania, admired Lanksy's gutsy response, taking an instant liking to the little Jew. In the course of a few months the two became fast friends. By 1931, Lansky and Lucania—popularly known as Charlie "Lucky" Luciano—had changed the face of American organized crime.[11]

By all appearances, Lansky became a successful businessman, running an empire that brought in millions of dollars annually. In later years the FBI secretly taped Lansky telling his wife that the enterprise he built with Luciano and others was ". . . bigger than U.S. Steel." The line was a screenwriter's dream; it was repeated in *The Godfather II* by the Lansky-inspired character of Hyman Roth.[12]

But Lansky achieved his success through ugly means, making him a pariah with his people. The Jewish outlaw represented a *shanda*—something of deep shame—in the respectful order of Jewish traditions. To follow Torah was everything, and at the heart of Torah was to work honestly. The commandants decreed one shall not steal nor kill. A story is often told of the great Jewish sage Rabbi Hillel explaining the meaning of Torah as, "what is hateful unto you, don't do unto your neighbor. The rest is commentary."[13]

To make it in America meant to work hard, enter a house of study, and bring no shame to either family or fellow Jews. Some chroniclers of the early twentieth-century ghettos chose to deny the criminal element entirely. Irving Howe, in *World of Our Fathers*, his seemingly definitive study of the Eastern European immigrants and their families, never once mentions Lansky, Siegel, or the Brooklyn Jewish hit squad known as "Murder, Inc."

Max I. Dimont's highly acclaimed *Jews, God and History* is outlandish in the assertion that American urban slums "did not breed crime."[14]

To official keepers of Jewish Word and The Law, a gangster emerging from their midst represented moral and ethical failures in the three thousand plus years' continuum of The People of the Book.

So it was a great surprise when—by Lanksy's account—the great Rabbi Stephen S. Wise approached the notorious Meyer Lansky with a unique request.

Rabbi Wise was a revered figure in both Jewish and Gentile circles. A Hungarian immigrant, he founded the Jewish Institute of Religion, a training institution for rabbinical students of Reform Judaism. With Supreme Court Justice Louis Brandeis, Wise was a key leader in the American Zionist movement. And with the rise of Hitler in the 1920s, Rabbi Wise was one of the first public figures to denounce the Nazi movement within Germany, a cause he championed throughout the 1930s and into the war years. He was one of the founders of the World Jewish Congress, an organization built to bring attention to and combat the evil of Nazism.[15]

As Lansky told the story, Rabbi Wise sent word asking the gangster "to do something about this dangerous trend."[16] Wise's appeal was followed by that of another large figure in the Jewish community, Judge Nathan Perlman. Perlman was a powerhouse in New York Republican politics. He served in the United States Congress in the 1920s; became a New York City magistrate in 1935; and in 1936 was appointed by Mayor Fiorello LaGuardia to the Court of Special Sessions of the City of New York.[17] Like Rabbi Wise, Judge Perlman was a leading figure in American Jewish causes, including the National Jewish Congress.

Contacting one of organized crime's kingpins was seemingly unthinkable—and certainly a dangerous move, both personally and politically to such men whose reputations were impeccable. But attention, they felt, must be paid to Fritz Kuhn and the German-American Bund. The threat of Nazism must not thrive in America.[18] Seemingly Wise himself addressed the difficult ethics of the situation in a sermon first published in 1920: "The basis of the ideal of Americanism is the duty of each to all and the responsibility of all to each."[19] Now, it appeared, Perlman was asking Lansky to be a part of that responsibility Wise spoke of.

A clandestine sit-down was held between the judge and the mob boss. "Nazism is flourishing in the United States," Perlman said. "The Bund members are not ashamed to have their meetings in the most public places."

Then, as Lansky told the tale, Judge Perlman crossed into extralegal terrain.

"We Jews should be more militant," he said. Such actions required Jewish men of special abilities. "Meyer," Perlman continued, "we want you to take action against these Nazi sympathizers. We'll put money and legal assistance at your disposal, whatever you need. Can you organize the militant part for us?"

Lansky was impressed that his services were sought by a man of Perlman's distinction. Without hesitation he agreed to help address the Bund, but declined any support proffered by Wise and Perlman. "I'll fight these Nazis with my own resources," Lansky said. "I don't need your cash."

Lansky did have one stipulation. Inevitably Jewish mobsters brawling with German-American Bundists would attract attention from the press. Given the stories of anti-Semitic Nazi thuggery oozing out of Germany, Jews fighting American brown shirts was a juicy story any newspaperman would love to get his ink stained hands into. "[A]fter we go into action," he told the judge, "you'll try to make sure the Jewish press doesn't criticize me."[20]

Lansky was a man of honor who agreed to do the work out of a sense of duty to his Jewish brothers and sisters. "My conviction that a Jew should lead a normal life and a proud life stayed with me all the days of my childhood," Lansky told Uri Dan. "I am not and never pretended to be an Orthodox Jew—I don't go around with a yarmulke on my head. But I've been ready at any time in my life to defend myself against insults to Jews or to me as a Jew."[21]

Perlman agreed to see what he could do about the Jewish newspapers. The judge had one final request: under no circumstances were any of the Bundists to be killed by Lansky's men. Beatings and broken bones were acceptable, but murder was off limits. Lansky was disinclined to this limitation, but agreed to follow the judge's insistence.[22]

The pact was now sealed. Lansky began his work.

Initially Lansky relied on the muscle within his organization to carry out the action. But he was surprised when men from all walks of life, young and old, and most assuredly not part of the criminal world, came forth to volunteer their services. Under normal circumstances, Lansky would have been suspicious of outsiders asking to be part of his operations. In the case of the Bundist attack squads, all such qualms were put to the side. The "civilians" were welcomed into the fold and with Bugsy Siegel's assistance Lansky held training sessions specifically tailored for Bundist bashing. "We taught them how to use their fists and handle themselves in fights," Lansky recalled, "and we didn't behave like gents."

And so it began. "We knew how to handle them, me and my friends," Lansky related. At times he forsook his daily duties overseeing gambling, the numbers rackets, and other elements of his criminal outfit. Rather, Lansky went into the field, a general organizing his troops, planning attacks, and throwing his share of punches during the brawls. It was dirty, sometimes dangerous work, and a job Lansky relished. "I must say I enjoyed beating up those Nazis," he told Uri Dan.

Some of Lansky's colleagues from the Italian side of the organization offered to lend their expertise to the proceedings. Lansky politely turned them down. "[A]s a matter of pride I wouldn't accept," Lansky said. This was strictly Jewish business. "[T]he main point," he said, "was just to teach them that Jews couldn't be kicked around."[23]

In other words, in the long ago echoes from Grodno, a Jew can fight.

Lansky's posh Manhattan apartment was in the same building as that of Walter Winchell's. A hot tip crossed Winchell's desk: Fritz Kuhn was to deliver a speech to a throng in Yorkville. The source was a good one, providing Winchell with the exact address for the meeting, information dutifully passed along to Lansky. As much as he enjoyed baiting Fritz Kuhn via the airwaves and in his column, Winchell well understood that his words could not deliver the same kind impact as those of the talented hands of his neighbor and associates.[24]

On the night of Kuhn's speech a squad of fifteen soldiers rendezvoused in Yorkville. Inside a meeting hall several hundred Bundists listened to fiery words delivered by speakers on a dais festooned with swastika flags and images of Hitler. On the surface, Lansky's men were considerably outnumbered. But Little Man didn't get to the top by underestimating his talent or the odds in any operation.[25]

At the signal, Lanksy's fighters went into action. Some threw firecrackers in the hall, starting mini-explosions that signaled the beginning of physical pyrotechnics.[26] Fists flew, chairs cracked across heads, and a few brown-shirted bodies crashed through windows. Other Bundists fled the scene. According to Lansky, a few of them "were out of action for months." His men were efficient.

After the dust settled and the blood was mopped up, Lansky called Winchell. The operation was a success, Lansky told him, although the columnist got one small item wrong. Normally Winchell was impeccable with details but in this case his source had provided him with the wrong address. Fortunately Lansky had resources that Winchell did not and the mistake was easily corrected.

The professional handiwork at the Yorkville melee apparently impressed Lansky's secret partners. Word filtered back to Little Man. Lansky claimed for a fact that "the judge and Rabbi Wise were pleased with us."

While Lansky held up his end of the bargain, Perlman either could not or simply did not attempt to do the same. Battles with the Bundists were strong fodder for Jewish newspapers. Lansky was heartily condemned for his brute force. Violent public free-for-alls, editorialists harrumphed, were not something good Jews should be engaged in. *Morgen Journal*, one of the most influential of the bunch, denounced the "mob of Lansky and Bugsy Siegel." Ironically, Lansky noted, "It was the first time I was ever publicly mentioned as a gangster."

The stories crossed over from the small Yiddish newspapers to New York's major dailies and radio stations. Lansky appealed to his friends in the mainstream press, asking them to stop referring to him as a criminal. It was a fruitless request. Why, reporters asked him, should they not call Lansky, Siegel, and others "gangsters" when that was how they were being treated in the Jewish media? "I had no answer to that one," Lansky said.

Pressure mounted for the public beatings to stop. "[I]nfluential political people in the Jewish community . . . objected to our direct action program," Lansky said. All Jewish mobsters, such the violent boys of Brooklyn's "Murder, Inc."—which included the likes of such notorious killers as Louis "Lepke" Buchalter, Abe Reles, and Jacob "Gurrah" Shapiro—were being lumped together with Lansky. "Of course there were criminals, but I had nothing to do with that kind of criminal violence," Lansky claimed. He suspected that in some select places within the country, people were lumping Murder, Inc., Siegel, Lansky, and others into the same category, the deeply rooted prejudices of "polite" Gentile America. ". . . I do believe some circles in America wanted to create the impression that all Jews were criminals," he said. "It was another form of anti-Semitism."

Rabbi Wise sent word that the actions must cease and desist. Perhaps the pressure from his peers was too acute, for now the rabbi decided it was against Jewish moral code to respond to problems through violent action. "I tried to argue," Lansky said, "but if leaders like Rabbi Wise decided it was wrong, I had to respect their wishes.

"Yes, it was violence," Lansky said in retrospect. "We wanted to teach them a lesson. We wanted to show them that Jews would not always sit back and accept insults."[27]

A Jew can fight. Lansky was the biggest name of the criminal world to take on the Bundists. And though he voluntarily stopped, others gladly picked up the torch of the baseball bat and continued the offensive.

15

King of Newark

IN 1919, NEWARK'S THIRD Ward was a compact version of New York's Lower East Side, a chockablock amalgamation of Jewish immigrants struggling to get by. Shopkeepers and peddlers operating horse-driven carts sold goods up and down busy Springfield Avenue. A miasma of fruits and vegetables, fresh meat, and sweat hung in the air. The back-throated syllables of Yiddish were the standard *lingua franca*.

And like the New York ghetto streets, Springfield Avenue was a prime target for outsiders looking to entertain themselves with a hearty afternoon of Jew bashing. Irish hooligans made sport of the old rebbes, grabbing a beard here, seizing a yalmukah there, and firing anti-Semitic slurs at everyone. Men, women, and children, it didn't really matter. A Jew was a Jew was a Jew.

Things changed. One day some thugs came for their usual afternoon of random intimidating. A cry went through the neighborhood: *"Reef der Langer! Reef der Langer!"*

"Call the Tall One!"

From out of nowhere he came. He was a tower of muscle, this Tall One, a looming six feet, two inches, and still a teenager. He was backed up by his usual crew, a gang dubbed the Happy Ramblers. And ramble they did. Irish mugs were schooled with Jewish fists, hearty punches right to the solar plexus. The interlopers were given their due.

Der Langer was a hero in the ward, a tough guy who looked out for everyone. He refused to accept any compensation for his work. Fighting the enemy was a duty, albeit one he thoroughly enjoyed.

Der Langer's moniker gradually transformed into American vernacular as "Longy."[1] By the time he reached his early twenties, Abner "Longy" Zwillman was one of the most powerful gangsters in the United States.

Abner Zwillman was born on June 27, 1904, in Newark's Jewish ghetto, the son of Russian Jewish immigrants.[2] His father Abraham was a threadbare chicken farmer. Peddling chickens out of a street cart could only stretch a family budget so far in a household with three girls and four boys. "All I remember," Zwillman said, "is that as kids my brothers, sisters, and I were always hungry."[3] At age twelve, Zwillman went to work as an errand boy for Third Ward boss, Alderman Morris L. Skolnik. The ward office was a place for political dealings of all sorts, legal and otherwise. Panderers, pimps and their employees, assorted gamblers, and other shady figures were regular denizens of the place, making for a lively and sometimes dangerous ambience. Young Zwillman did what he was told, kept his mouth shut, and studied just how this world operated.

His formal education ended in 1918 with the death of his father. Zwillman, now fourteen years old and just shy of his eighth grade graduation, was thrust into manhood. He must leave school and work. It was a story played out in countless ways throughout the ethnic ghettos of the American urban landscape.

Zwillman closed his father's chicken business, quit his ward errand boy job, and became a fruit and vegetable man, complete with rented cart and horse, selling his wares in Newark's wealthier neighborhoods. The housewives purchased not just food but also the illegal lottery tickets Zwillman vended on the sly. Running numbers paid better than hawking apples and lettuce.

At sixteen Zwillman was making good coin, building a loyal organization with his Happy Ramblers, and providing muscle where needed to help out the neighbors. As a nascent businessman he learned how to invest. Paying off cops to look the other way from his numbers rackets was a necessary business expense.[4]

Then came the one-two punch of the Volstead Act and the Eighteenth Amendment. As it was for so many of his underworld peers, the onset of Prohibition was a bountiful present from the United States government to Longy, the perfectly wrapped gift that would keep on giving for years to come.

In 1923, Zwillman invested in a fleet of trucks and developed a thriving business hauling booze for assorted bootleggers. Not bad for a kid of just nineteen. Word on the street was Zwillman's drivers were armed and had no qualms about pulling triggers. Longy's tough-guy reputation was well-known. Rivals in the business never dared to mess with his shipments. Who needed trouble when there were plenty of other opportunities to make money in the bootleg economy?

Leo Kaplus, a thug of some renown along Newark's "Bootlegger's Row," was the exception. He applied his brand of violent intimidation to the Zwillman crew, intrusions Longy took personally. He confronted Kaplus face-to-face.

According to the FBI, Longy shot Kaplus in the leg. But there's another account of the story, one that's much more brutal. In this telling Zwillman aims his gun at Kaplus's manhood, pulls the trigger, and sends a bullet straight into his rival's testicles.[5] Regardless of which version is true, Longy made his bones shooting Kaplus. The FBI noted, "As a result of the shooting, other Newark mobsters took particular note of ZWILLMAN . . ."

Within two years Longy was one of east coast's biggest bootleggers. Interference from the law was minimal since Newark's cops, judges, and elected officials were part and parcel of the Zwillman payroll. His whiskey-running operation flowed rich with cash, profits that soared even higher when Zwillman opened his own wildcat breweries in 1927.[6]

As the controlling mobster of New Jersey, Zwillman acquired a set of colleagues that reads like a who's who of the underworld: New York mobsters Lansky, Luciano, Siegel, Frank Costello, and Murder, Inc.'s Louis "Lepke" Buchalter; Atlantic City boss Enoch "Nucky" Johnson; and kingpins of the Midwest including the biggest of them all, Chicago's Al "Scarface" Capone.[7] When two rival brewers Max Hassel and Max Greenberg secretly plotted to kill Zwillman for control of New Jersey, their bodies turned up as a bloody mess in some anonymous hotel suite. The murders were never solved but their territories opened up. Zwillman soon had complete control over all New Jersey liquor distribution.[8]

Despite his roguish good looks Zwillman wasn't much of a ladies' man. His few flirtations and romances over the years never amounted to much. This changed one night in 1930 when he saw Howard Hughes's movie war epic *Hell's Angels* at Newark's Adams Theater. The screening was accompanied by some vaudeville acts, including a publicity performance by one of the film's featured players, a blonde teenager with hair one of Zwillman's friends described as "the color of eggnog." Longy watched from backstage as the young woman struggled her way through an act that generated more pity than applause. Eyes almost in tears, she hustled off stage, took a look at Zwillman, and snapped, "What the fuck are you doing back here, mister?"

The street-hardened gangster was instantly smitten. He took the girl under his wing, taught her how to dress, how to move, and how to interact with a crowd. A pair of veteran Broadway scribes was hired to write her a new act. Reporters were coerced into pitching the right questions. When asked about her fetching hair color, she fired back the Zwillman-coached answer.

"Look," she said, "I guarantee the color of my hair is real. One hundred percent platinum."

The ploy worked. Zwillman's protégé and eventual mistress Jean Harlow—"The Platinum Blonde"—became a smash hit. Longy pressured Hughes into providing her better pictures, fatter paychecks, and ultimately a movie career that transformed this skinny teenager into a Hollywood icon.[9]

Zwillman delighted in the ensuing romance. He showered Harlow with pricey jewelry and the fanciest of roadsters.[10] One evening, while dining with fellow gangsters at the Ambassador Hotel in Los Angeles, Zwillman revealed the secret of Harlow's trademark coiffure. He showed his dinner companions a locket containing a curl of dark brown hair. It was, Zwillman informed his friends, a snippet from Harlow's nether regions. Her signature color, it seemed, was not a natural look.[11]

As a city teeming with both native and immigrant Germans, Zwillman's hometown was a hotbed for Nazi sympathizers and Bundist endeavors. Newark's German Jews, who'd preceded their Eastern European immigrant brethren to America by a generation or two, were torn. They initially ignored the rise of Hitler and his popularity among fellow German-Americans, hoping the embrace of National Socialism was just an ugly but passing fad.[12]

In fact Newark's chapter of the Friends of New Germany was one of the largest in the country. They held late-night meetings and rallies in the

heavily Jewish Third Ward, much to the consternation of the neighborhood. The men at these events wore full Nazi regalia, as if they had just
stepped across the ocean from Berlin to Newark. Reaction was inevitable.
Protestors swarmed outside meeting halls, jeering the brown shirts inside.

Public berating only encouraged pro-Nazi factions to ramp up their rhetoric and actions. Some 400 supporters gathered at an April 1933 pro-Hitler
rally in nearby Irvington, New Jersey. The crowd included forty-five German
crew members of the *Hamburg*, a ship that traveled between Germany and
New Jersey as part of the Hamburg-America Line. Members of the local
Communist Party swarmed outside hurling both words and rocks at the attendees.

The April soiree was a warm-up for a bigger rally, scheduled for September of that year at *Schwabenhalle*, a meeting place run by Newark's German
community. Swastika-emblazoned posters brazenly appeared on trees near
Jewish businesses. Speakers for the event, ostensibly designed to honor
German president von Hindenburg's eighty-fifth birthday, included Fritz
Gissibl, Newark's Friends chief Albert Schley, and Dr. Hans Borchers, German consul general of New York.[13]

Reef der Langer.

Longy Zwillman may have been a nationally respected figure of organized crime, a man watched closely by the FBI, and a movie star's sugar
daddy, but he still was a Third Ward Jewish kid who wasn't going to watch
idly as anti-Semites stomped through his Newark neighborhood. As Zwillman saw it, the Nazi situation was not something that could be easily neutralized by Reds using airborne rocks. No, this required a more disciplined
brand of ferocity.

Reef Nat Arno.

Arno was born Sidney Abramowitz on April 1, 1910 to Romanian Jewish
immigrants. A year after his bar mitzvah, he dropped out of school for the
kind of education found in the sweaty confines of Newark's seedy boxing
gyms. During the day he sparred with club fighters. At night he took the
fisticuffs into the streets, honing his skills anywhere he could. Arno dreamed
of a career in prizefighting but according to New Jersey law, a boxer couldn't
turn pro until age fifteen. When that milestone arrived Arno gave himself a
birthday present by making the official move from amateur to full-fledged
professional. He was something of a prodigy in the fight game, taking four
knockout wins with his first seven bouts.

But the action in Newark wasn't enough to satisfy this spirited kid. He split town in January 1926, hitchhiking his way down the eastern seaboard to Florida, where he established himself as a scrappy up-and-comer with a strong knockout punch. In just over a year Arno traded blows in forty-one fights, winning thirty-six and the other matches ending in draws. He returned to Newark in February 1927, where he proceeded to win another forty-eight fights.[14] Over the course of his boxing career Arno pounded away in 121 matches, with only eleven loses.[15]

Arno was strong and talented, but prizefighting in the Jersey circuit did not earn much of a living. Some nights the winner of a match ended up with a paltry $125. Other bouts were for tangible prizes, and in the long run these paid a little better. A fighter who got a gold watch for his efforts could hock his reward at the local pawnshop for a slightly larger purse of two hundred bucks.

Clearly the fight game was not enough to pay the bills. Arno needed to supplement his income. But the Depression was on and jobs were scarce. Fortunately, a man with Arno's skill set had the right qualifications for a position in Zwillman's Third Ward Gang. The Jewish boxer joined the Jewish gangster as a paid enforcer. You don't want to buy Zwillman's booze? *Bam!* You haven't paid Zwillman protection fees? *Bam!* You don't do whatever Zwillman wants? *Bam! Bam! Bam!*[16]

He was an impressive employee. And just the kind of front man Zwillman needed for his Nazi fighting operations.

Unlike Lansky, who enjoyed getting Nazi dirt under his fingernails, Zwillman preferred to stay in the background. It was not a micromanaged operation but one Zwillman backed up with all the tools in his arsenal. Key to this was Zwillman's tight relationship with Newark's police department. When they received tips about pro-Nazi meetings, the information went straight to Zwillman. Cops then conveniently steered clear of the area.[17] Zwillman and Arno pulled together a ragtag unit of golems, many of whom like Arno were ex-pugilists working for the Third Ward Gang as enforcers, bodyguards, and other capacities within the organization. They included the likes of tough guys such as Benny Levine, Lou Halper, Abie Bain, Al Fisher, Moe Fisher, Max "Puddy" Hinkes, and Hymie "The Weasel" Kugel.

The resulting fights inevitably resulted in injuries for some of the avengers, ranging from cuts and bruises to broken bones. Longy provided his underlings with an underworld benefits package, delivering quick cash when necessary to cover any medical expenses as a result of injury during melees.[18]

Breaking up regular meetings was a simple task. But careful planning was paramount for Arno's men to make any kind of impact—both symbolically and physically—at the September *Schwabenhalle* meeting. They prepared in secret. An army of boxers marching through town wielding metal clubs certainly would have been a dead giveaway to any Nazi en route to the *Schwabenhalle*. Weapons had to be at the ready, but hidden from any possible discovery. Consequently, lead pipes were concealed in newspaper camouflage and stashed in a nearby alley.

Some three hundred Friends, many in uniform, packed the hall. A token police unit manned the entrance doors on the street, seemingly there to provide a sense of safety. Like it or not, the cops had to be there regardless, though Longy owned them. This was the United States, after all, and an anti-Semitic pro-fascist had the right to speak his mind, no matter whom he might offend.

At the appointed time, Arno flung stink bombs through a window on the second floor. The air turned putrid, and choking American Nazis swarmed for the exit.

Now for step two.

Arno's man Kugel was stationed near the police guard. As Nazis spilled from the front door, lungs on fire, wheezing, coughing, Kugel grabbed the eye-blink moment of opportunity. He let out a yelp. "Look!" he screamed at the confused policemen. "Look what they did to me!"

The cops darted toward Kugel leaving Nazis unprotected and vulnerable. Arno's boys moved in, swinging lead pipes without mercy. Kugel disappeared in the chaos. The mission was a success.

Undeterred, The Friends scheduled a second rally at the *Schwabenhalle* for October 16. They would not back down, especially to a wild band of thuggish Jews. Some eight hundred Nazis and their sympathizers were coming in from throughout the tristate area just for the event. Two hundred policemen were brought in as protection, even though the cops were on Longy's payroll. The potential for mass chaos and rioting was not something that could be easily ignored. Certainly the brown shirts needed assistance that night, for protestors came out in full force. By one estimate more than two thousand anti-Nazis surrounded the hall, easily outnumbering those inside by more than two to one.

This time Arno secreted a ladder behind the building for easier access to the second-floor auditorium. As the standing-room-only crowd soaked in a speech by New York chapter head Fritz Griebel, Arno and one of his men scrambled up to the window. As Griebel's words reached a fiery peak, the stink bombs flew.[19]

Again Nazis poured into the street. Max "Puddy" Hinkes, one of Arno's best punchers, lovingly recalled the event years later. Hinkes was another Jewish kid from the Newark ghetto. His mother was president of the local synagogue sisterhood, an important position within the temple hierarchy. Puddy was well qualified as a defender of his people. Like Longy, he'd busted Irish skulls whenever the thugs descended onto Springfield Avenue merchants. And like Arno, he translated this talent for violence into the boxing ring for a minor career as a prizefighter. When he wasn't in the ring himself, Puddy enjoyed a good night at the fights, cheering on his pals while puffing furiously on a beloved Havana cigar. One night, while a fellow Jewish boxer slugged it out in the ring, Puddy found himself sitting behind a rambunctious anti-Semite. "Hit that Jew!" the fan screamed. "Kill him!" Puddy wasn't having any of it. He tapped the man on the shoulder. When the guy turned around, Puddy furiously shoved his lit cigar straight into the loudmouth's eye.[20]

Hinkes felt similar emotions on that riotous October night. "As they came out of the room, running from the horrible odor of the stink bombs, and running down the steps to go into the street to escape, our boys were waiting with bats and iron bars," he recalled. "It was like running a gauntlet. Our boys were lined up on both sides and we started hitting, aiming for their heads or any other part of their bodies, with our bats and irons.

"The Nazis were screaming blue murder. This was one of the most happy moments of my life. It was too bad we didn't kill them all."[21]

The ensuing free-for-all lasted well into the night. Those not throwing punches hurled chants. Cries of "Down with Hitler's gang!" rang through autumn air. The overwhelmed police force finally resorted to tear gas in hopes of ending the riot. Friends leaders were spirited away by automobiles reserved for just such an emergency.

Seven men were arrested for disorderly conduct. Six of them were Third Ward Gang associates, who ultimately faced a Zwillman-owned judge. Their sentences amounted to perfunctory wrist slaps.

The next day tabloids throughout New York City breathlessly detailed the violence and its aftermath, and implicated Longy as the brains behind it all. The New York *Daily Mirror* reported Zwillman was in the thick of the battle, calling out strategy to his men from the safety of an armored car. Longy personally phoned *Mirror* editors to set the record straight. Two days later they graciously printed a retraction, stating that their source for the story admitted he was in error. One didn't mess with Longy Zwillman.

The Newark papers paid more respect to their local boss. A gaggle of ink stained New Jersey wretches met at the Newark Police Department on the morning after the riot and listened to Zwillman's cool alibi. Longy insisted that he'd spent the previous evening at Dinty Moore's, the popular Times Square restaurant on West Forty-Sixth Street, some seventeen miles from the scene.[22]

Regardless of who pulled the unseen strings, Zwillman's pugilist militia was a hit with the public. They received support from the Newark chapter of Jewish War Veterans (JWV), which nicknamed Arno's group The Minutemen, after the famed militia of the American Revolution. The more polite bureaucrats running the national JWV frowned on this advocacy. They issued a resolution denouncing Arno and his men, with the edict that no JWV chapters should be associated with such untoward behavior. Members of the Newark JWV had to follow orders, but lent support on the sly wherever they could. Athletes from the Newark Young Men's Hebrew Club also volunteered, and their fighting skills were welcomed into the fold. Even a local pharmacist pitched in, using his knowledge of chemical combinations to manufacture stink bombs for Minutemen raids.[23]

The work continued. The Minutemen staged commando attacks on Bund meetings throughout Newark, inflicting damage any way they could. "In [some] places we couldn't get inside," Hinkes later said, "so we smashed windows and destroyed their cars, which were parked outside." Desperate Bundists pleaded with Newark authorities to put a stop to the violence, but Zwillman still ran the law. Though police officers did have to show up for the bigger events, regular Bund meetings were generally cop-free zones. As Hinkes simply put it, ". . . the police favored us."[24]

Not all encounters were riots. On April 16, 1938, Bundist second-in-command Gerhard Kunze delivered an address to his Newark stalwarts. Arno attended as well, standing in the back with some of his men, but did nothing to disturb the speaker. Perhaps Kunze knew better than to provoke a Minuteman; he never mentioned the words "Jew" or "Jewish" in his speech, instead using the standard anti-Semitic code phrases about communists and the "anti-German" media as well-understood surrogates.

Arno's presence was merely a front. While Kunze was speaking to his minions, a group of Minutemen found his automobile, bribed a garage attendant to keep his mouth shut, and then proceeded to get creative with the carburetor wiring. Off waiting in the wings was a carload of Minutemen, wielding rubber-coated iron bars and eagerly waiting for Kunze to return to his car. Despite the bribe and accompanying threats, the parking attendant slipped word to Kunze and his OD men as they entered the garage. Kunze was prepared for just such an emergency, for one of his guards was also a nimble-fingered mechanic. The soldier quickly worked his magic, and the group sped away, taking a different route than the Minutemen were expecting. When Arno's boys realized what was going on, they pulled a hard U-turn and renewed pursuit. From out of nowhere a woman leaped in front of the car. "No!" she screamed at the Minutemen. "You stay here!" They tried to pull the human shield off the hood, but she was unstoppable, a Bundist wildcat, all arms and legs thrashing away for the cause. Kunze made a safe escape.[25]

Harold "Kayo" Konigsberg, a bloodthirsty hit man who first joined the underworld as Zwillman's bodyguard and personal chauffeur, waxed nostalgic about his own work fighting the bundists. "[Longy] used to send us in to disrupt these guys—and I mean *disrupt* them," he recalled. "Once a week, he organized fifty, sometimes a hundred of us and gave everybody a hundred dollars apiece. There were boys from Jersey and some of Meyer's kids from the Lower East Side, and all of them doing it were Jews. We were instructed to break legs, arms, shoulders. We were instructed never to hit them in the head, sometimes they got hit in the head." Kayo and his confederates never told the Bundists of their religious heritage. "The only thing we told them was with a baseball bat," he said.[26]

Judd Teller, a reporter for a Yiddish-language newspaper, eloquently described a Zwillman strike on a Bundist meeting as something akin to "the night when God struck all the firstborn in Egypt." Terrified brown shirts leaped from fire escapes as gangsters wailed away inside the hall, wrenching arms, breaking teeth, smashing jaws, plowing in noses. And then it was over. "Like commandos," Teller wrote, "they were gone before the police arrived."[27]

16

The West Coast Racketeer

BEYOND THE EAST COAST were plenty of Jewish mobsters, eager to take up the cause as well. A new Golem emerged from the seamy dark side of Los Angeles. When Bundists and their sympathizers spoke, Mickey Cohen answered as a Defender of His People.

Born on September 4, 1913, in Brooklyn, last child in a brood of five, Cohen was dubbed Meyer Harris Cohen by his immigrant parents, Jewish refugees fleeing Kiev. Cohen's father Max passed away when Meyer was just two months old.[1] Shortly after his death, Max's widow Fanny struck out with her youngest child for a new life in the growing suburban city sprawl of Los Angeles, settling in the Jewish ghetto of Boyle Heights. The sun and space seemingly offered a different environment from the rough Brooklyn streets, but as a youngster Cohen was drawn to the underworld. His older brothers Harry and Louis ran a family pharmacy; at age six Mickey helped out with the covert distillery hidden in a back room. Three years later he was delivery boy, hauling illegal hooch to thirsty customers. Now a second grade dropout and seasoned criminal, Cohen graduated to attempted robbery, leading a gang of punks in an attack on a Hollywood picture palace, the Columbia Theater. While his ruffian colleagues tried to make off with the cash, Cohen provided protective muscle with a mean baseball bat. The failed heist took a lot of *chutzpah*, something this skinny little kid had in spades.[2]

Like Jews of so many generations, Cohen learned the hard lessons of anti-Semitism early on. Hustling papers at L.A.'s Coliseum and Olympic

Auditorium, he grew accustomed to slurs like "Jew bastard!" Not one to take such taunting without action, Cohen replied with his fists. Back on his home turf, in a neighborhood that included a growing Mexican and Italian population, the same fighting spirit went into action when Cohen or any of his pals got pegged with words like "kike" "spic," or "wop."[3]

Desperate to avoid family shame, Cohen's older brother Sam—the honorable member of the family—tried enrolling young Meyer into Hebrew school. In his first half an hour as a *yeshiva boucher*, Cohen was permanently kicked out after punching another kid in the mouth. Juvenile reform school was next, but it did no good. Cohen's mother often found bulging ill-gotten bankrolls brazenly filling her baby's pants pockets. His scrappy talents as a street slugger led the teenaged Cohen to amateur—and illegal—boxing in fight clubs throughout the city's toughest neighborhoods: Compton, Watts, East Los Angeles, and elsewhere.[4]

Living at home was no longer an option, so at age fifteen Mickey split Los Angeles for Cleveland. Sam Cohen had relocated to Ohio for a government job; again he made a valiant attempt to get his kid brother on the straight and narrow. Mickey was given a job by a ladies' dress manufacturer. The boss took a shine to his new employee, and helped Cohen further his fledgling boxing career. He joined the Midwest fight club circuit, fighting amateur bouts throughout the region.[5] Mickey turned pro on April 30, 1930 when he faced Patsy Farr in a featherweight match. It took just four rounds for the tough little Jew from L.A. to take down Farr.[6] Not bad for a diminutive kid who topped out at five foot, three inches and at ninety pounds was no weakling.[7] And like many Jewish boxers Cohen proudly wore a Star of David embroidered on his boxing trunks.[8]

At the end of his fighting career in 1933, Cohen's ring nickname was "Gangster Mickey Cohen." By this time Cohen was in with Lou Rothkof, one of the so-called "Cleveland Four," a quartet of Jewish mobsters that also included Morris Kleinman, Sam Tucker, and was overseen by Morris "Moe" Dalitz. They were a powerful bunch, lording over considerable gambling interests throughout the region, and maintaining solid business relations with East Coast boss Charles "Lucky" Luciano.[9]

But Cleveland was small potatoes and Cohen longed for bigger stuff. He headed to the crime capital of the Midwest, Chicago, and through a fortuitous gun battle managed to impress the top man himself, Al Capone.

Though Capone's heyday was in decline now that the Roaring Twenties had stopped roaring, Cohen still swooned to be in the presence of the great Scarface. "I walked into his office kind of awed," Cohen fondly recalled, ". . . and he did something which was a very big thing for me—he kind of held my head and kissed me on both cheeks."[10]

Being in Capone's good graces didn't last long. Though Cohen was initially a loyal soldier in Capone's army, success got to his head. He opened up an unauthorized crap game, was told to shut it down, and refused. A few dodged bullets later and unexpected heat from the usually affable Chicago police force, Cohen finally got the message and left the Windy City.[11]

He went back to Cleveland for a time, and then returned to his L.A. hometown. Finally Cohen found his niche, landing a job as mobster-in-training to a Jewish gangster with panache and national recognition: Benjamin "Bugsy" Siegel, Meyer Lansky's old friend and partner, who had relocated to Los Angeles to oversee organized crime's westward interests.[12]

Siegel's mobster credentials were legendary, but lesser known was the flashy gangster's devotion to his own Jewish heritage. Like many underworld figures, Siegel, a married man with two daughters, enjoyed extramarital dalliances. One of his paramours, Countess Dorothy di Frasso—the former Dorothy Caldwell Taylor, heir to a leather goods fortune courtesy of her wealthy father—was wed to Count Dentice di Frasso, a minor Italian nobleman who, like Siegel, held liberal views on marital fidelity. In 1936, Siegel and his countess lover went on an Italian sojourn to her husband's swanky Villa Madama, a secluded estate just outside of Rome. Their visit, while certainly not without romance, was a business trip. The countess was peddling "Atomite," an experimental explosive with a powerful kick. Using her husband's connections, di Frasso convinced Benito Mussolini that Atomite was Italy's ticket to battlefield dominance. Impressed by the countess's pitch, Il Duce dipped into the national coffers, shelling out forty grand to the countess for expenses so she could demonstrate Atomite on Italian soil.[13] Siegel—who'd seen his share of bombings in the underworld—witnessed the stuff in action and was duly impressed. As di Frasso's traveling companion, he hid his mobster status with the unlikely guise of an English baronet, "Sir Bart."[14]

Atomite proved to be a big bust. It failed to ignite during di Frasso's presentation, instead emitting only a few pathetic smoke plumes. Mussolini was infuriated and the countess found herself in an awkward international position. Meanwhile, Siegel nearly set off an explosion that would have changed world history.

While strolling through the grounds of Villa Madama, Siegel spied his lover chatting with another houseguest: Hitler's second-in-command, Hermann Göring. Alongside Göring was Joseph Goebbels, head of the Nazi propaganda machine. That night, alone with the countess, Siegel dropped his noble facade for New York mobster lingo. "Look, Dottie," he snarled, "I saw you talking to that fat bastard Göring. Why did you let them come to our building?"

Di Frasso demurred, explaining she'd known the Nazi official via social connections. And surely she couldn't tell a man of Göring's stature to get lost.

Social protocol had no place in Siegel's inflamed Jewish passion. He wanted to kill the two Nazi big shots right then and there. In Siegel's eyes, whacking Goebbels or Göring wasn't different from any mob hit he'd done in the past. "I'm going to kill him, and that dirty Goebbels too," Siegel told the countess. "It's an easy setup the way they're walking around here."

Di Frasso pleaded with her lover to reconsider. Should Siegel take out two of the German Reich's top men at her husband's villa—which was on Mussolini's turf—the repercussions could get very ugly very quickly. Undoubtedly the count would face execution. Siegel cooled off and thus history was forever sealed.[15]

Back home, the same anti-Semitism permeating the legitimate world was widespread in the Los Angeles underground prowled by Siegel and his protégé. In his autobiography Cohen described the mob as "an organization," rather than a criminal operation. It was strictly business, albeit one operated by thugs with guns. And—just as it was in so many other organizations—Jews remained outcasts. Sure, Cohen pointed out, Jews had their place in the "business." But "being Jews, Benny [Siegel] and me and even Meyer [Lansky] couldn't be a real part and parcel . . ."[16]

Not being fully accepted in his chosen profession didn't diminish Cohen's self-respect. Blessed with a hearty Jewish name and a certain pride at being an outsider amidst outsiders, Cohen took on anti-Semitism with the stuff he learned as a kid fighting Jew haters in the streets: good old-fashioned brute force. And the German-American Bund offered Cohen a bountiful channel to vent his inflamed Jewish passions.

The strong Bund presence in California naturally influenced others with similar inclinations. One such personality was Robert Noble, a dishonorably discharged Navy man who worked on the fringes of Hollywood. Noble was in the radio business, where he acquired considerable skills as a public speaker, then jumped into the "Ham and Egg Movement," a dubious pension scheme percolating through California politics in the 1930s.

Noble's next career move was sparked by a close reading of Hitler's *Mein Kampf*. He found the *Führer*'s screed a revelation, praising it as "idealistic" and filled with "marvelous thoughts." Inspired, Noble developed the Friends of Progress with the assistance of his partner in anti-Semitic activities, Ellis Jones. The duo held meetings in downtown L.A. at the Embassy Auditorium at the corner of 9th and Grand, where California Bundists, happy to soak in and spread Friends of Progress ideas to their peers, made up a considerable part of the audience.[17]

Noble got plenty of attention not only from the Bundists and their sympathizers, but also from L.A.'s finest. He and Jones were often arrested for various charges related to their activities. One night it was their misfortune to be locked up at the same time as Cohen, who was being held on what Mickey termed "some roust."

Despite his notoriety, Cohen had a certain charm and was well liked by some elements within L.A.'s police force. Thanks to his friends among the boys in blue, Cohen's usual extended stay setup was sweet: a nice bed and food catered in from the famed Brown Derby restaurant on Wilshire Boulevard. On this occasion, upon learning Noble and Jones were also in the jail, Cohen's instincts kicked in. As Cohen put it, these guys were "real rabble rousing anti-Jew Nazi bastards" and he wanted to give them what they had coming. "I'd like to lay my hands on that son of a bitch Noble," Cohen told the jailers. "Can you make some arrangements?" The guards, themselves no great lovers of Noble and Jones, happily obliged their prisoner. "Arrangements" were made. The two men were transferred to a holding pen where Cohen was patiently waiting.

The cell was easy real estate to navigate. Cohn sat in the front on a bench, head ostensibly buried in a newspaper. Noble and Jones sat at the far end, doing their best to keep a healthy distance from their cellmate. By Cohen's account, the "weasel bastards . . . must have known or somebody must have told them don't go near me, because they were trying to squeeze as far away as they could from me."

Finally the time came. The newspaper was dropped and Cohen went into action, wailing on Noble and Jones with unmitigated glee. "I grabbed them both," Cohen gloated in his autobiography, "and I started bouncing their heads together. With the two of them, you'd think they'd put up a fight, but they didn't do nothing."

Cohen was unrelenting. The two men screamed like a pair of wounded animals in the last throes of a savage attack. It sounded like a jail riot of the highest order. Cohen was effective.

Having done his damndest, Cohen returned to his seat, picked up his newspaper, and nonchalantly resumed reading. When guards came back, they were greeted with an astounding scene. Mickey Cohen, notorious mobster, quietly reading a newspaper. Two bloodied American Nazis, clinging to cell bars, screaming, "Why did ya throw us in with an animal, with a crazy man?"

The chief in charge, a man named Bright, apparently didn't know about the arrangement between his cops and Cohen. He demanded some answers.

"What are ya asking me for?" Cohen replied innocently. "I'm sitting here reading the newspaper. Them two guys got in a fight with each other. I don't know what happened, I didn't want to mix in with them."[18]

It was as bold-faced and brazen a lie as ever told in the confines of a jail cell. But what could Bright do? A pair of incendiary admirers of Hitler turned to bloody pulp in some fashion or other, whimpering for retribution. A career criminal reading a newspaper. It was the word of Noble and Jones against Cohen. Which unsavory character should he believe?

The jailhouse beating earned Cohen a stellar reputation throughout the Los Angeles Jewish community as something of a heroic antihero. Calls came in from screenwriters asking for Cohen's help weeding out Bundists in their midst. He happily obliged.[19]

Cohen alleged that an unnamed judge also tapped his services. Legal niceties were one thing, but the judge knew that Bundists, while entitled to their First Amendment rights, sometimes required extralegal treatment. Cohen rose to the occasion, bringing a gang of associates to a Bund meeting where the jailhouse melee was repeated. "[We] grabbed everything in sight," Cohen wrote. "All of their bullshit signs . . . and smacked the shit out of them, broke them up as best we could.

"Nobody could pay me for this work. It was my patriotic duty. There ain't no amount of money to buy them kind of things."[20]

17

The Chicago Avenger

IT WASN'T JUST THE big names of the Jewish underworld who rose to the occasion: criminal golems of the small-time variety were plentiful, penny-ante tough guys looking to smash in Bundist heads wherever and whenever they could. In Chicago's immigrant Jewish ghettos along the storied Maxwell Street marketplace, a scrappy kid named Jacob Rubenstein joined up with another street tough named Barnet Rosofsky. Rosofsky, born in 1909, was just fourteen when his old man was murdered, victim of a holdup at the family's grocery store.[1] Bad as this was, Rubenstein's life was far more harrowing. He was two years younger than Rosofsky, born in 1911 to Joseph and Fanny Rubenstein, Russian and Polish immigrants respectively. The Rubensteins came to Chicago in 1905, where Joseph worked intermittently as a carpenter. There were eight children in the family, Jacob being the fifth born. Joseph was rarely home, preferring to spend his pitiful wages on liquor and whores. As it was, thanks to his uncontrollable temper he rarely had money since he was usually fired or quit a job before he was paid. His anger boiled over at home, beating his wife without mercy and smacking his children around for any infraction. Yet the man was a real dichotomy. He didn't think his children needed schooling beyond the eighth grade, but somehow could scramble together enough money for a private tutor so his sons could get a rudimentary Jewish education.

At various points in their combative marriage Fanny filed assault-and-battery charges against her husband. Finally, ten years after Jacob's birth, she decided she'd had enough. She left Joseph, but was unable to take care of eight children on her own. As it was, Fanny's own state of mind was fragile.

Like her husband, she abused the children both emotionally and physically, having convinced herself that her four sons and four daughters were incestuously coupling. Mercifully, the Jewish Home Finding Society of Chicago stepped in and put the children in foster care.

By his eleventh birthday, Jacob was barely attending school. He preferred the world on the streets, where life was a constant hustle. Having inherited his father's explosive temper, Jacob learned to use his fists. He and Rosofsky became friends, united in Chicago's rough ghettos by the ugly slams life doled out to the boys.

The teenage duo got hired as delivery boys for one of the Windy City's most successful entrepreneurs. They carried sealed envelopes from one place of business to another, and did not ask any questions. Standard payment was a buck an envelope, nice pay for a pair of Jewish street kids, courtesy of their boss, Al Capone.[2]

Both Rosofsky and Rubenstein were handy with their fists—it was a necessity for survival on Chicago's West Side—but the elder boy figured out there had to be safer ways to channel that energy. Like many Jewish boys of his generation, he took to the boxing clubs. Rosofsky proved to be a real talent in the Golden Gloves circuit. He turned pro, drained his name of its Jewish ethnicity for the more Celtic-sounding "Barney Ross," and in 1933 slugged his way to a world championship in the lightweight division. By the mid-1930s he also won the junior welterweight and welterweight titles, making Ross one of those rare boxers who reigned as champion in three different weight classifications.[3]

Rubenstein went the other direction. He left his job on the fringes of the Capone Outfit for the semi-straight life of a city factotum. At various times Rubenstein worked as a peanut vendor at ball games, sold racetrack tip sheets, flowers, chocolate, costume jewelry, and newspaper subscriptions. On the sly he scalped tickets to sporting events, hawked "hot" sheet music published by firms with no interest in honoring copyright laws, and sold chances to suckers in punchboard gambling schemes. Rubenstein worked out his vocal chords as a singing waiter—badly—and then translated his street skills into a brief career as a nightclub bouncer.[4]

He had a certain wanderlust. In 1933, Rubenstein moved to California, shacking up at various times in Los Angeles and San Francisco. He learned to control his hot temper, became a dapper dresser, and inevitably a ladies man. For a while he ran around with Virginia Belasco, granddaughter of famed Jewish Broadway impresario David Belasco.

In 1937 he returned to Chicago. His father was no longer a part of his life, and Fanny was confined to a mental hospital in suburban Elgin. Rubenstein hustled jobs here and there, then found employment as a labor organizer for the Scrap Iron and Junk Handlers Union.[5]

Rubenstein was not a religious man, but carried a certain pride in his Jewish heritage. He burned deep with hatred toward any anti-Semitic taunts. His younger brother Earl recalled Jacob often would come home giddy with excitement—and sometimes blood on his clothes—after pounding away at random Jew haters. Sometimes he used his fists, other times he wielded whatever he could grab as a handy bludgeon.[6]

He reconnected with his old street pal Ross, becoming part of a loosely knit gang of Jews who hung out in the Lawndale Poolroom and Restaurant on Chicago's West Side. A new facet of Rubenstein's personality was beginning to emerge. He banged heads with some college kids who insulted an African-American piano player. When he saw a man attacking an elderly woman, Rubenstein put a stop to it. He now was a man who would literally fight for his ideas of social justice, albeit with blind rage and over-the-top violence. "[He was] somewhat overbearing regarding the rights and feelings of others," one friend politely recalled.[7]

Chicago's German-American Bund presence was extensive. In 1938, Fritz Kuhn declared there were between four to six thousand members in Illinois, with another one thousand across the border in Wisconsin.[8] Trustees of the Germania Club, described as "one of Chicago's leading German social organizations," were mortified when they realized their meeting hall had been rented for a bund meeting, where a top official in the organization spoke to an enthusiastic audience about the evils of Jewish influence. A fight broke out when one young attendee refused to salute the swastika flag. The story made the papers, much to the embarrassment of club officials. "The Germania Club should not be used as a battleground for the advancement of any 'ism' but Americanism," declared one trustee.[9] The ban did not last long. Within a year the Bund was back. Kuhn and Chicago leader Dr. Otto Willumheit, joined by Midwest leader George Froboese, were guests of honor at a Germania Club Bundist dance, attended by four hundred partiers. The soiree came to an end when two stink bombs were tossed by anonymous foes into the hall.[10]

At Riverview, the legendary amusement park on the city's northwest side, protestors assailed management after they rented facilities to the Bund for a German folk festival in July 1938. Kuhn and Froboese were the headline speakers.[11] Two weeks later, the duo were again the guests of honor, this time at a Bund picnic held in a forest preserve in northwest suburban Park Ridge. Two banners draped the gates to the park: the American Stars and Strips and the Bundist flag emblazoned with a swastika. Young men and women marched in formation, much to the *Bundesführer*'s delight. "It is our privilege and duty," Froboese told the approving crowd, "to oppose anti-German propaganda by Jewish capitalists. The Jews are taking over Washington. Let the reporters of our so-called free press go back and tell their Jewish publishers it takes more courage to be a Nazi than a cowardly sucker who kowtows to those in authority."[12]

Rubenstein and his friends felt duty bound as Jews to take action. The Lawndale Poolroom was an informal headquarters where the gang plotted their attacks. One member of the bunch, future Illinois state senator Ira Colitz, recalled the boys would hang out in the pool hall or Dave Miller's Restaurant, waiting for their sources to report where Bundists were meeting. After the anticipated phone call came in, the pack rose to the occasion. Rubenstein, another member recalled, particularly enjoyed "cracking a few heads" here and there.[13] Barney Ross, by now an international figure, was part of the pool hall regulars. "It's quite probable," wrote Ross's biographer Douglas Century, "that he was one of the leaders." Certainly the talents of a three-time world boxing champion would have been welcomed in any anti-Bund fighting fracas.[14]

Rubenstein had a divided personality: he was a good citizen with blunt ideas of justice, tempered by a hair-trigger temper and thuggish personality. During World War II, while a private in the Air Force, he pummeled a sergeant who dared to call Rubenstein a "Jew bastard."[15] After returning to civilian life, Rubenstein moved to Dallas, Texas and worked on the fringes of legitimate society, operating two-bit strip clubs and burlesque houses. Over time his Jewish name watered down into the more Gentile-sounding "Jack Ruby."

For countless generations of Jews throughout the centuries, the ten days between Rosh Hashanah (the Jewish New Year) and Yom Kippur (the Day of Atonement) have been known as "the Days of Awe." It is said that on Rosh Hashanah God writes one's destiny for the upcoming year into the Book of Life.

But this judgment can be modified. Through prayers and confession of sin on Yom Kippur, an appeal is made to the Eternal asking for forgiveness and to not make one's fate too harsh. In mob movie vernacular, it's akin to the closing of *The Godfather* when Sal Tessio, played by Jewish actor Abe Vigoda, pleads with Corleone family lawyer Tom Hagen to "get me off the hook."

As Lansky, Cohen, and others openly admitted, they were not pious men. And yet, no matter how far they delved into the underworld, they still felt that spark of Jewishness. In their realm where the worst of human sins was a standard part of business operations, perhaps deep in those secret places of the soul they sought their own brand of atonement, seeking forgiveness from a Higher Authority by defending their fellow Jews and annihilating the Jew-vanquished Swastika Nation dreams of the German-American Bund.

PART V

Girlfriends

"...in my opinion, [Fritz Kuhn] is a mixture of Charlie McCarthy and Dizzy Dean."

—Roy P. Monahan, Representative of the Disabled War Veterans testifying to congressional subcommittee, September 15, 1938[1]

18

On the Town

IT'S A TYPICAL NOCTURNAL swing around Manhattan's chi-chi club circuit. Start with drinks at Leon & Eddie's. Then rendezvous at a hotel bar, maybe the Waldorf or the Biltmore. See a floorshow parading gorgeous girls bedecked with feathers and spangles in just a whisper of a costume. A sizzling time for the swells packed into rooms with smoke, booze, and the hottest of jazz blasted out by the biggest of bands. High-class decadence New York style, circa late 1930s.

And in the midst of the action, sporting a snappy outfit, pouring rivers of premium champagne to the reverberation of endless cork pops, proffering substantial tips to attentive waiters, and with his latest blonde or brunette cutie snug on his arm: *Bundesführer* Fritz Kuhn.[1]

It was often reported that Kuhn lived in Yorkville near the German-American Bund national headquarters. Rather, his home was a simple four-room apartment on the top floor of a three-story building at 33–42 73rd Street in the Queens neighborhood of Jackson Heights. His wife Elsa was often seen walking down the street or going to the grocery store, greeting people in English just as broken by German as her husband's. For unknown reasons, the Kuhn's teenage daughter Waltraut went to live in Germany after her graduation from P.S. 109. Her younger brother Walter was a regular playmate with other nine- and ten-year-olds on the block. Once a woman found her grandson engaged in childhood games with some schoolmates. One boy salted his language with a hearty string of playground curse words. The culprit, she learned, was Walter Kuhn, and the irony of the situation was that the youngsters were playing in a basement beneath the home of a Jewish kid.

Everyone on the block knew exactly who this family was. Living on the same street as the notorious Fritz Kuhn certainly had its downsides. His neighbors sometimes received phone calls from a nameless individual. "Are you American?" the anonymous caller would ask. "Then watch out for Fritz Kuhn." Kuhn's telephone itself was first listed under Elsa's name, and then was pulled from the phone book. An unknown Bundist then provided his name as a beard for the Kuhns' telephone number.

Yet the *Bundesführer*'s presence, stomached as it was, did provide the block with a dubious sense of safety. A twenty-four hour police guard was assigned to protect Kuhn's building. It was a thankless shift, manned by twelve cops reluctantly handling the chores in two-hour shifts. They were a necessity, however, since anti-Nazi protestors came from time to time upsetting the otherwise quiet normality of the community. And no one wanted to take a chance on public demonstrations erupting into violence throughout the neighborhood.[2]

Fritz Kuhn was a long way away from those days as a lowly chemist in Ford's realm, dreaming at night for an empire of his own. He'd traveled from Germany to Mexico to Detroit, taking his wife and children with him from place to place; and now, here they were, an American family living in the shadow of the greatest city of the world.

But Kuhn was rarely at home. He was an important man, overseeing businesses and divisions of a great movement, traveling the country to make speeches, and pushing back against enemies, real and perceived. Official duties were only part of what kept him away from the Queens domicile. Gone were the days of minor flirtations and broom closet romances at Henry Ford Hospital. Fritz Kuhn was not only *Bundesführer*, but also a bon vivant of the most flagrant order.

His romantic dalliances were an open secret throughout New York's nightclub world. A syndicated AP article, "Glamour Girls and Boys of Gotham Have Busy Nights" noted that among the many highbrows, glittering social jewels, theater personalities, and other regular denizens prowling the Big Apple's ritzy jazz and liquor joints, one could readily find Kuhn on a barstool canoodling with a girlfriend.[3]

Any Bundist worth his swastika would have been shocked beyond measure dare he plunge into those lower depths and bear witness to Kuhn's decadency. The great Fritz Kuhn stamping his feet, a wide grin on his face, gulping down champagne to the swinging sounds of his favorite pop hit,

"The Flat Foot Floogie (With a Floy Floy)."[4] The song, composed in 1938 by the African-American songwriter team of Bulee "Slim" Gaillard and Leroy Elliott "Slam" Stewart—Slim and Slam—was a hit from coast to coast. Its bouncy melody and infectious lyrics were seemingly nonsense words, a song anyone could enjoy, even a *bundesführer*. The reality behind the song was much more entertaining. Slim and Slam filled their lyrics with massaged-over ribald expressions laced into catchy phrasing. "Floogie" was toned down from the term "floozie," slang for a prostitute. "Floy floy" was code for a rip-roaring venereal disease.[5] Exactly the kind of music banned from Germany and denounced by one writer for the Bund newspaper as, "These jungle dances and the assortment of noises which go along with them."[6]

And so it went, night after night. Sometimes in clubs. Other times in secret rendezvous. But always the same: Fritz Kuhn, *Bundesführer* by day and nightclubbing womanizer when the sun went down.

The Stork Club. Table 50. A typical evening, or so it appeared, as Walter Winchell held his nightly court, eyeballing the crowd for potential column items.

He saw something strange. Improbable and out of place. No, it couldn't be . . . but it was.

Fritz Kuhn in a one-man Bundist invasion of Winchell's beloved Stork Club.

Kuhn saw Winchell staring in his direction. The two locked eyes. And then Kuhn blinked. He stood up, and in a haze of alcohol and anger exited Winchell's kingdom.

Once Kuhn was gone Winchell repaired to the men's room, blood boiling. He took his ever-present pistol out of his pocket and removed the bullets. In the wake of Kuhn's departure, the columnist did not trust himself to hold back from doing something regrettable.[7]

He did not write a word about the incident. That changed a few weeks later when another newspaper scooped him with a photograph of Kuhn and his latest paramour. Winchell fired back in a strangely subdued response.

"Yesterday's papers revealed Fritz Kuhn, the leader of the Ratzis has a new blonde," Winchell wrote. "This column could have had that 'story' several weeks ago when they both were at the Stork Club.

"Now it is no secret that no love is lost between this column and Fritz

Kuhn," he continued. "In fact we can't think of anyone we loathe more. But scoop the town that he was towning with a new woman? What good would that do? Break Mrs. Kuhn's heart?"[8]

In a backhanded way Winchell was being kind, but there was no need to protect Elsa Kuhn. She was used to her dual role as loyalist to her husband's greater cause and long-suffering wife. In 1936, while accompanying her husband to the Berlin Olympics, Elsa wrote a scathing letter to a "Mr. R____," whose spouse apparently had been Kuhn's secretary in Detroit. It was not the first time Elsa confronted the man over his wife's indiscretions.

"Once again I write you in good intention," Elsa said. "All I want is to ask you to get your wife back and help me to wipe out this dirty matter." She icily pointed out that there were children who could be hurt and, "[m]y husband has no money to support your wife . . . The whole branch of the Bund at Detroit stands behind me. There will be a great scandal."

Pointing out that Bund members were "not so dumb," Elsa maintained that she, as the wronged woman, "protected your wife in order to prevent any dirty talking." A repentant Kuhn promised Elsa and his children that the affair was over. As viewed through Elsa Kuhn's cynical eyes, it was obvious the entire peccadillo was a crime by Mrs. R____, as well as Mr. R____, who could not control his wife's indiscretions.

"This is the truth," Elsa concluded. "Now act like a German man of honor on behalf of the movement."[9]

19

The Edict

ATTORNEY GENERAL HOMER CUMMINGS'S investigation into the network of Bund camps wasn't the only governmental consideration given to the organization in the fall of 1937. Overseas, Kuhn was upsetting bureaucrats of all stripes. His pretensions as Hitler's ally in America were troubling and potentially troublesome. In September Prentiss B. Gilbert—the temporary American *chargé d'affaires* after Ambassador William Dodd stepped down from his post for health and political reasons—attended the 1937 Nazi Party rally, where he and other foreign diplomats were treated to the ominous display of German military power. The sky was filled with airplanes flying in the formation of an epic swastika.[1]

In October Gilbert was sent by the State Department to the German Foreign Ministry. Relations between the United States and Nazi Germany were prickly enough. Fritz Kuhn and the Bund made the relationship more problematic. Americans were unsettled with uniformed men goose-stepping in the streets of New York, Chicago, and Los Angeles; or young people gathered for pro-Hitler activities at secretive retreats. There was a growing belief in some circles that the Bund was forming German colonies in the United States and taking direct orders from the NSDAP government. Kuhn, in his march toward an American Swastika Nation, did nothing to discourage these impressions.

Hans Freytag, the senior counselor to the Reich's *Auslands-Organisation,* an office handling foreign affairs, agreed with Gilbert's assessment. On October 11, 1937, Freytag released an official statement denouncing any relationship, real or implied, between the Third Reich government and the German-American Bund. The Bund, in Freytag's opinion, had to go.

Hans Dieckhoff, Germany's ambassador to America, was of a similar mind-set. He cared little for Fritz Kuhn's grandstanding, which did nothing to improve the Reich's image with Americans. Nor were they popular with German counsel generals in New York and Chicago. In November Dieckhoff sent a report to his higher-ups, writing of the Bund, "Nothing has resulted in so much hostility toward us in the last few months as the stupid and noisy activities of a handful of German-Americans."

On January 7, 1938, two days after Attorney General Cummins released his embarrassing findings that Bund camps were not NSDAP-affiliated, Dieckhoff delivered a new report to his superiors, giving an overview of Germans in America. He felt that German-Americans were disparate, more American than Teutonic and perhaps only one-third of an estimated population of twelve to fifteen million had a comprehensive understanding of the mother tongue. As for the Bund, they were doing nothing to foster a love for the Fatherland amidst their fellow German-Americans. For all his talk of devotion to his adopted country, Kuhn had done little to convince anyone beyond his followers that the German-American Bund was a patriotic society for United States citizens of Teutonic background. With Nazi-styled uniforms and substantial displays of the swastika, the group was alienating their countrymen in America. The hyphen in "German-American Bund" might as well be a subtraction symbol of "American" from "German" for all the good Kuhn was doing on the Fatherland's behalf.

Dieckhoff concluded that working with the Bund was not in the best interest of the German Reich. Any official connection between the NSDAP government and the Bund should be officially *verboten*. On February 28, Dieckhoff met with United States Secretary of State Cordell Hull. While the ambassador insisted he hoped the two countries could maintain a congenial relationship through cultural exchanges, the NSDAP would not interfere with the United States government and certainly had no ties to organizations like the German-American Bund. For the time being, Hull in Washington and Gilbert back in Germany were pleased.

In the wake of Dieckhoff's actions, Kuhn displayed a cool demeanor. He maintained publicly that the German-American Bund was strictly an American organization of its own making. "We take orders from no one, German or otherwise," was his official response.[2]

But in reality Kuhn was stunned. A rejection by the NSDAP was impossible, a mistake or misunderstanding that had to be corrected. The *Bundesführer* issued a secret memo to his top brass. "During the month of March, I shall be travelling," he wrote. "The Unit Leaders are to treat this confidentially."[3] Ostensibly Kuhn was making a trip to Belgium to attend an anticommunist conference. In reality, he planned to make a personal appeal to German officials.[4] Upon his arrival in Brussels, Kuhn rented an automobile—a Ford—and hightailed it to Berlin.

Kuhn hoped to meet with Werner Lorenz, the SS man in charge of the *Hauptamt Volksdeutsche Mittelstelle* (HVM), or Welfare Office for Ethnic Germans. The HVM was yet another office in the endless Nazi bureaucracy, this one aimed to help Germans living outside the Fatherland. Lorenz refused to meet with Kuhn, instead sending his flunky Fritz Wiedemann.

Wiedemann informed Kuhn that their meeting was to explain the relationship between the NSDAP and the German-American Bund, nothing more, nothing less. For once, Kuhn, who introduced himself to Wiedemann as "an American citizen," left his braggadocio at the door. "I have the feeling that Reich German officials are opposed to the Bund," he told Wiedemann. "I wish to remove the obstacles, the causes of which are unknown and incomprehensible to me." The new edicts from Dieckhoff on behalf of the German government were, Kuhn pleaded, "tantamount to the destruction of the Bund."

Kuhn insisted he'd always listened to decrees from Berlin and was willing—he claimed—to dissolve the Bund if that was the wish of the NSDAP government. But doing so would demand a heavy price. If the Reich insisted on ostracizing the Bund, Germany risked alienating all German-Americans. What's more, Kuhn felt wounded by the actions. "There is no ground for action against me personally," he concluded. "I have never claimed to have a second conversation with the Führer in Berchtesgaden or even to have received instructions from him."

The appeal was futile. Wiedemann informed the *Bundesführer* that, given Kuhn was an American citizen, the German government had neither official interest in him, nor any instructions to be taken back to membership. The Bund had done nothing to enhance Germany's image in the United States, but rather brewed uneasy tensions between the two countries. What's more, Kuhn's reputation as an aggrandizing loudmouth wasn't winning him any respect from the German High Command.

Kuhn was infuriated. "We desire friendly relations with Reich-German officials, but the desire to understand us is lacking," he spat out.

Wiedemann dismissed Kuhn's rage with a cool response. "The latter remark is a serious accusation, which I reject and which, besides, does not tally with the facts." The meeting was over. The *Bundesführer* was told to go back to the United States, and once there to stay within the letter of American law.[5]

The defeat was humiliating. But given the secrecy of the meeting, Kuhn was able to twist Wiedemann's pronouncements with a positive spin upon his return to New York.

In early May Kuhn issued an official statement to the Bundists. He declared himself "strengthened" for having witnessed the annexation of Austria by Germany during his trip abroad, a triumphant move by Hitler, which Kuhn said magnified the beauty and strength of "our country."

Nothing was revealed of his humiliating tête-à-tête with Wiedemann. But clues to its significance were wrapped within new diktats he now demanded of Bund membership.

"It is about time to make several changes," he said, "but these will not undermine the principles of the movement." He called these changes "expansions of the movement," by which "the Bund stands or falls!" Foremost among these was a reinforcement of the idea that United States citizenship was mandatory to be a Bundist. Though always a prerequisite to join, the policy now would be more strictly enforced. Henceforth, all Bund applications must have a prospective member's United States citizenship certificate number, plus the date, town, and court where the oath of allegiance was taken.

Most telling was his pronouncement that "no official connections are to be maintained with German consulates or other German representatives," although such officials would still be invited to "important occasions which express unity with the old home land," including German Day festivities and Hitler's birthday celebrations.

His own position was unchanged and what was expected of members remained solid. "I therefore demand," he concluded, "the unselfish support of each Bund member for the strict carrying out of the Leadership Principles within the laws of the land as the only essential guarantee of the striking force of our movement."[6]

Kuhn also delivered what he said was a message for American Jews he had been asked to give on behalf of their brethren in Germany. Flanked by two OD men, he told reporters, "I talked with lots and lots of Jews in Germany and they all told me this: 'Tell Jews in America to let us alone. We're all right.'" Given Field Marshall Herman Göring's freshly adopted declaration that all existing Jewish property rights must be stripped from their owners, Kuhn's follow-up statement sealed the veracity of his message. "Thousands of Jews are returning to Germany and I was really surprised to see how many Jewish stores were open."[7]

Other changes were made in coming months to emphasize the Bundist loyalty to the United States. One of the more dramatic was the dropping of "*Sieg Heil!*" at meetings and public gatherings. The stiff-armed, palm-down salute stayed intact, but now was accompanied by the words "Free America!" It was notable that this new battle cry had a similar rhythmic cadence as "*Sieg Heil.*"[8]

Kuhn's trip overseas was not a complete loss, at least as far as his personal life was concerned. In February, while traveling to Belgium on the ocean liner *Westernland* for his mission to Berlin, he mingled with fellow passengers. One traveler in particular caught Kuhn's attention, a plump blond married woman from Los Angeles, Florence Camp. Seemingly a golden angel.

Kuhn was not one to let political troubles stand in the way of personal conquests.[9]

20

The Golden Angel and Miss America

KUHN WAS LOVE-STRUCK BY Florence Camp, who had been separated from her husband Charles for eighteen months. During their voyage on the *Westernland* he showered her with silly love letters, meant for her eyes only. The shipboard romance blossomed into a full-blown affair after both returned to the United States. Camp reunited with Kuhn for a romantic dinner at Baltimore's Biltmore Hotel on May 5, and then the *Bundesführer* whisked his new beloved to what he perhaps thought was an idyllic getaway resort: the Bund's Camp Nordland in Andover, New Jersey.

Their whirlwind affair sped up.

In early July Camp made a stop in Reno, Nevada, quickie divorce center of America, and got her walking papers. It was back to her home in Los Angeles.

Kuhn could not live without the woman he called "his golden angel." The mash notes continued to arrive. And then money.

The *Bundesführer* told his new love that the Bund needed her furniture, though why is not clear. Regardless, he sent Camp money to move her chairs, tables, and other accoutrements to New York. The furniture traveled cross country, and then halfway back when more money was provided to send Camp's belongings to Cleveland. In the meantime Kuhn pelted her with endless marriage proposals, claiming his marriage to Elsa was over. Soon after Camp's divorce was final, he presented her with a sparkling rock of an engagement ring. Kuhn squired his Golden Angel around New York. For all intents and purposes, from spring of 1938 until spring of 1939 when the romance fizzled, Florence Camp was in line to be the next Mrs. Fritz Julius Kuhn.[1]

What the matronly Florence Camp did not realize was she was part of a harem. While being wined and dined in Manhattan nightclubs, Kuhn was cheating on his paramour with another woman.

Kuhn would come to learn that hell hath no fury like a scorned Golden Angel.

Camp's rival Virginia Cogswell, another sizeable blonde, was in a certain sense a perfect match for the *Bundesführer*. Both personalities fueled their enormous egos with fame and notoriety built on illusion, exaggeration, and outright lies.

Cogswell was something of a celebrity in her own right, mostly for her well-publicized string of ten marriages and nine divorces. Her first round at the altar was at the tender age of sixteen. By her thirtieth birthday her unofficial name could have read: "Virginia Overshiner-Patterson-Stark-Blank-Seegar-Gilbert-Kahn-Cogswell." Two additional surnames, Raymond and Kaplan, were still to come. In a syndicated self-composed story, "How to Hold a Husband," Cogswell wrote: "[P]ersonally, I consider myself an authority on the subject [of marriage] because if I do not know what to do to hold a husband, I at least know (and when I say 'know' I mean really—from experience) most of the things not to do." Ultimately, she gave would-be brides the cockeyed conclusion that: "(t)he best way to hold a husband is either (1) not at all, or (2) have him married to somebody else," or (3) fasten him to a large piece of flypaper and hang him up over the mantel.

"Take your pick."[2]

Cogswell's other claim to fame was her reign as Miss America of 1925, a sparkling tiara she earned after her stint as Miss Georgia. Her proclaimed former status as *the* national beauty queen was widely accepted by newspapers of the 1930s, as well as in FBI reports on Fritz Kuhn, and in histories of the German-American Bund.

There is one problem with Cogswell's Miss America story. It's not true.

It is possible Cogswell could have won a local beauty pageant in the Peach State, but there is no official record of Miss Georgia winners prior to 1936. Not until 1953 was a Miss Georgia, Neva Jane Langley, official crowned as America's greatest sweetheart.[3]

The official Miss America of 1925 was Fay Lanphier of Oakland, California. There is no mention of Cogswell—under any of her surnames—in the exhaustive database of the Miss America Pageant. It is possible Cogswell was crowned as "Miss America" in a copycat pageant staged outside of Atlantic City, New Jersey, home to the official extravaganza. This was not unheard of during the Roaring Twenties. However, no queen of a rogue beauty competition has ever been venerated as the real deal.[4] Regardless, after Cogswell's association with Kuhn became public her fabricated claim to the certified title was universally accepted as fact.

Cogswell met Kuhn shortly after her divorce from Arthur Cogswell, an artist with a few ex-wives of his own. These former spouses were not a happy sisterhood, given Cogswell's meager alimony payments. Some of Arthur's exes stalked him in public, creating unhappy street theater with their animated demands for money owed. When this didn't produce intended results, some ex-wives stormed the bastille of Arthur and Virginia's apartment. "I was afraid to go out, [but] it was nerve-wracking to stay in," Virginia recalled. Virginia grew isolated from friends until she finally had enough. "Arthur, what you need is not a wife but a bodyguard," she told him. It was off to divorce court, where Cogswells Mr. and Mrs. were rendered asunder.[5]

Virginia was on the rebound when she landed with the *Bundesführer*. Cogswell later claimed not to know who Kuhn was upon their initial meeting. Nevertheless, as with so many of the previous men in her life, Cogswell fell quick and hard in love. The two spent stolen hours in passionate soirees, swigging champagne and sharing kisses in nightclubs and hotel rooms. Once again, Elsa was a negligible factor in Kuhn's personal life. He was smitten by Overshiner-Patterson-Stark-Blank-Seegar-Gilbert-Kahn-Cogswell, proposing "hundreds of times," according to Cogswell. "I probably would have married him," she said, "if he hadn't been so fanatical."[6]

Kuhn presented Cogswell a unique gift: an autographed photo of himself, standing tall at a podium, dressed in his German military uniform, and his right arm extended in a Nazi salute. He inscribed it "Love for my darling Virginia."[7] But in spite of all the sweet talk, the couple's romantic evenings often ended up in ugly fights. "Nothing was right to Fritz," Cogswell said, "except Hitler." What's more, Kuhn forced himself on his new lover as a Pygmalion to Cogswell's Galatea. "He wanted to change . . . my friends, my habits, and me," she recalled. In the course of a whirlwind six-month romance, Cogswell—who was not a woman of diminutive size—dropped a quick fifteen pounds from stress. By fall of 1938, she was desperate to end the relationship but saw no way out.[8]

A savior came in the form of Richard Rollins, a former sociology student turned undercover man for Senator Dickstein's House Committee on Un-American Activities. Rollins was a freelance agent running a government-backed fishing expedition in an attempt to nail Kuhn on anything remotely illegal. As part of his covert activities, Rollins took to tailing the *Bundesführer* during his rollicking nights on the town. Rollins secretly connected with Cogswell, appealing to her sense of patriotic duty. Remuneration would not be great, just fifty dollars a week, but what Cogswell could do for her country by helping to get the goods on Kuhn was worth far more than any paycheck could provide.

Cogswell bought Rollins's jingoistic line and agreed to let him record the secret trysts, provided one condition was met. She was seeing Dr. Francis La Sorsa, a physician treating her for a nervous condition. Six months with Kuhn only amplified her mental trauma. Someone had to pay Cogswell's medical expenses. Rollins agreed to pick up the tab for these bills and the operation began.

Kuhn would only consent to rendezvous at hotels rather than his lover's apartment, claiming Cogswell's flat was "too public a place and there are always Jews around." This phobia was a perfect opportunity for Rollins and Cogswell to set up a ruse. The newly christened counter agent was installed in a hotel on West Twenty-Third Street, she in one room, Rollins and his recording equipment in the room next door. A microphone was concealed within Cogswell's telephone, its wire intertwining with the telephone cord as camouflage. The line led to the floor, then under a rug, out a hole to the hallway, snaking tight and unnoticed along the wall into Rollins's room, where it connected to a recording device that captured conversations onto steel disks. A state-of-the-art prewar snooping system.

A scenario was created by Rollins that Cogswell played to the letter. With her handler listening in, Cogswell telephoned Kuhn, telling him that she needed money as a result of her move to the hotel. When the *Bundesführer* balked, she threatened to hawk her personal diary to *The New York Post*. Potential ramifications were considerable. Kuhn readily acquiesced and agreed to bring the needed funds to the new love nest. Cogswell's threat also turned Kuhn preemptively romantic: she received a box of roses prior to his arrival.

That night Rollins listened as Kuhn knocked on Cogswell's door, a clumsy secret code of one long rap on the door, followed by two short knocks. The first words from his lips were as equal in sincerity as the roses. "Hello, dar-ling," he exclaimed.

From there Kuhn quickly descended into paranoia. He looked under the bed and behind curtains for recording devices. "What do you expect to find?" Rollins heard Cogswell say. "There's nothing under the rug or be-hind the curtains."

Kuhn brushed off her objections with a reasonable explanation. When-ever he was somewhere he'd never been before, all obvious spots must be scrutinized to make sure the room was secure. It was vital that no one know what Fritz Kuhn did behind closed doors.

Bed, curtains, and rug were clean. It never occurred to him to look at the telephone.

While Cogswell remained cool under pressure, Kuhn was a wreck. He threatened suicide should his mistress double-cross him. He received word via an anonymous telegram from a source in Washington, D.C., that Cog-swell was not to be trusted. No, she falsely reassured him. There was no truth to the telegram. Clearly the sender had some personal issues. Kuhn had noth-ing to worry about and yes, she would not show anyone the autographed pic-ture he'd given her. Cogswell proved to be an actress of some ability in spite of her nerves.

Kuhn went off into a rant on his enemies, promising to destroy these "American gangsters." His most colorful threats were reserved for Winchell. "If it the last thing I do," he spat through his thick accent, "I have him rubbed out."

Over the next few months, Cogswell used her well-honed wiles at Kuhn's expense. He detailed wild plots of Bundist glory, claiming he had spies work-ing deep undercover in the Brooklyn Navy Yard. Fires would soon sweep through ships, effectively rendering them useless. He claimed to operate two chemical manufacturing plants outside of Newark and Chicago, enormous facilities capable of building powerful weapons. The manufacturing plants also turned a tidy profit. "I can make more money with my chemical labora-tories than with the Bund," Kuhn insisted.

The pressure to maintain a cool facade while extracting potentially use-ful information took its toll on Cogswell's mental and physical health. At one point Rollins consulted Cogswell's physician, Dr. La Sorsa, who reassured him that despite Cogswell's nervous condition and "fluttery heart," there was nothing seriously wrong with her. Rollins's Mati Hari continued her work.[9]

The recording sessions continued throughout the fall of 1938, but Rollins came up empty every time. There was no wrongdoing he could pin on Kuhn, other than a lot of overblown bragging.

Cogswell and Kuhn continued their affair throughout the operation, which intrigued the feds on a salacious level. One FBI memo, noting that the recordings "indicated some startling sex relationship," described the content as "quite spicy."[10]

One night Rollins listened in as Kuhn made a disturbing overture to Cogswell. The *Bundesführer* took out a razor and made a cut into his own flesh, claiming he felt no pain when the blade dipped into his skin. Now it was Cogswell's turn. Kuhn asked to carve a swastika in the cleavage between his lover's breasts.

This unexpected dive into sadomasochism was too much for Cogswell's handler. Rollins decided to blow the whole operation before Kuhn went too far in this bloody sexual foray. He held back at the last minute when it became clear Cogswell had finessed the situation, deftly turning down Kuhn's depraved overtures.

On another afternoon, long before Kuhn's expected evening arrival, Rollins let himself into Cogswell's room. Virginia was not at home, though one of her girlfriends was in the flat. Suddenly there was an unexpected knock at the door: one long, two short. Kuhn's secret code. It appeared the *Bundesführer* wanted to surprise his beloved.

In classic cloak and dagger B-movie fashion, Rollins quickly explained the situation to his spy's friend, demanded her cooperation, and leaped into the closet. The young woman agreed to help, then removed the key from its lock, lest Kuhn tried to open the closet door. Safely ensconced amidst Cogswell's dresses and skirts, Rollins pressed his ear to the door. He had a hunch something might happen. Kuhn was cautious around strangers, but when it came to women he was insatiable and often careless.

Rollins's instinct was on target. Once Kuhn realized that he and Cogswell's friend were alone, his womanizing nature kicked in. The *Bundesführer* initially revealed nothing to the woman but a few minutes later he offered to reveal a great deal more than Rollins could have expected. Kuhn convinced Cogswell's friend that the two of them could have a high time of it playing a few rounds of strip poker. Inside the closet Rollins nearly broke out laughing. He held his hand over his mouth, stifling snickers while on the other side of the door clothes were shed hand by hand, card by card.

Various garments piled on the floor. Kuhn and his new would-be con-quest were relishing the game. Then the inevitable happened. A click at the front door. Cogswell's key turning in the lock. The surprise of three par-ties, two of them uncovered in every sense of the term. A fourth party lis-tening from behind a door to the farce outside. Kuhn dropped down his cards, grabbed up his drawers, and fled. Cogswell's girlfriend, freed of a few items of clothing, got a different sort of dressing down.

Delusions of grandeur and "spicy" adventures aside, the operation was turning up nothing. Rollins was convinced there had to be more. "These sidelights were wonderful indices to the character of Hitler's American en-voy but they didn't solve the problem of how to give Kuhn a one-way ride to Sing Sing."

Rollins was dead wrong about Kuhn as an NSDAP proxy for the United States. Yet his feeling that Cogswell would somehow be his conduit to nail-ing Fritz Kuhn proved to be on the money both figuratively and literally.

Throughout his investigation, Rollins picked up the tab on Cogswell's med-ical bills with Dr. La Sorsa. It was a fair tradeoff, considering she had been putting herself on the line. But doctors cost money and Cogswell had been seeing La Sorsa for some time. Out of curiosity, Rollins asked Virginia how she managed to afford expensive medical bills before he had stepped in.

Her reply was unforced and natural, as though Rollins asked the stupid-est question of all time. "Why, Fritz, of course," she replied.

A spark went off in Rollins's mind. He made an appointment with La Sorsa.

The good doctor was no fool. He had his suspicions all along why Cog-swell suffered from a nervous condition and why Rollins was now his patient's benefactor. La Sorsa was no fan of Kuhn, the German-American Bund, or Hitler, and was quite happy to tell Rollins all that he knew about his patient and her lover.

Prior to Rollins, Kuhn was Cogswell's medical benefactor, having paid all her bills in cash, cold untraceable cash. But one session in September 1938 stood out in particular.

La Sorsa explained Kuhn loved to brag about his importance, claiming that he never had to pay taxes. After all, he was the American *Bundesführer* and was beholden to no one in the United States government.

The doctor continued with this mother lode of a story. "Any way, one night—I think he was a little drunk—after a long lecture, he pulled out his check book, and wrote a sixty-dollar check for one of my bills. When I got home, I began thinking about that check. There was something very funny about it—it was drawn against the Bund's bank account."

La Sorsa showed Rollins a copy of the bill and Photostat of the check. The payment, made on September 13, 1938, covered eight visits for Cogswell, four night calls and four day calls.

The check number was 246 and was made out to Dr. Francis P. La Sorsa, M.D. Beneath Kuhn's signature was the name of the account from which the funds were drawn: "German-American Bund."

Rollins stared at the Photostat, holding it delicately in his fingers.

Bundesführer Fritz Kuhn, charged with absolute control over the German-American Bund through its autocratic Leadership Principle, was funding private romances using the money provided by his membership for official Bund business. It was a clear-cut case of embezzlement.[11]

At long last. A smoking gun, personally loaded by the *Bundesführer* himself.

PART VI

George Washington's Birthday

"What would George Washington think . . . and DO, were he alive today?"

—JAMES WHEELER-HILL, NATIONAL SECRETARY OF THE GERMAN-AMERICAN BUND, MADISON SQUARE GARDEN, FEBRUARY 20, 1939[1]

21

Madison Square Garden

ON FEBRUARY 10, 1939, Winchell's column contained this item of note: "The Ratzis are going to celebrate George Washington's Birthday at Madison Square Garden—claiming G.W. to be the nation's Fritz Kuhn. There must be some mistake. Don't they mean Benedict Arnold?"[1]

The German-American Bund George Washington's Birthday rally on February 20 was ostensibly designed to honor the country's founding father, a man Kuhn declared was America's "first fascist" and believed democracy was an unsound form of government.[2] The rally was to be Kuhn's shining moment, an elaborate pageant and vivid showcase of all he had built in just three years. There would be food, music, and speeches representing Bundists from coast to coast. A capacity crowd of twenty thousand would be packed into the arena. Three thousand OD men would be a mighty show of force. The Youth Movement members would be a vision of the future. Kuhn's dream of a Swastika Nation would be on display for the whole world, right in the heart of what the Berlin press called the "Semitized metropolis of New York."[3]

As part of their agreement to rent Madison Square Garden, which in 1939 was the third incarnation of the famed arena, located at Eighth Avenue between Forty-Ninth and Fiftieth streets, Kuhn accepted demands by booking manager Major Harold Dibbles that no signs bearing anti-Semitic sentiments be displayed. Similarly, no anti-Semitic speeches were to be delivered. Once the papers were signed, all promises were sent packing. Enormous American flags and the swastika-emblazoned banner of the German-American Bund hung behind the speaker's podium, flanking a thirty-foot picture of the presumed honoree of the evening. Other signs ringed the hall beneath its balconies. "Wake Up America—Smash Jewish Communism." "Stop Jewish Domination of Christian America." "1,000,000 Bund Members by 1940."[4] Interspersed between these banners were standard arena signs advertising shaving products and an upcoming boxing match.[5] Madison Square Garden officials decided to avoid confrontation and let the propaganda stay in place. It was safe to assume that speeches for the evening would have similar anti-Jewish and pro-Nazi themes as well.[6]

Before anyone could enter the Garden, the police bomb squad combed the arena from top to bottom, under every seat, between every rafter, inside every pipe. A letter delivered to the mayor's office the previous Wednesday promised that a trio of time-activated devices would explode during the event if the city didn't put an end to the Bund's plans. LaGuardia refused to let any threat stop the rally, no matter how noxious the Bundists were. ". . . [I]f we are for free speech we have to be for free speech for everybody and that includes Nazis," he declared. Anonymous bomb threats didn't bother him. "If they bomb it," LaGuardia said, "we'll catch the bombers."[7]

Protestors and lots of them were guaranteed for the eight o'clock rally. Police Commissioner Lewis J. Valentine understood this and was taking no chances. Both Valentine and Acting Mayor Newbold Morris were on the scene to assure New Yorkers no nonsense would be tolerated. Mayor LaGuardia was out of town, but Morris was a worthy surrogate. Officers arrived four hours early to set up blockades in key geographic areas around the arena, from Seventh to Tenth avenues, Forty-Eighth to Fifty-First streets. Seventeen hundred policemen were on the scene with twelve hundred on the streets, including horse-mounted patrols; another five hundred were stationed throughout the arena, watching every hall and every doorway. One hundred and fifty of the insiders were waiting in the basement along with thirty-five firefighters equipped with heavy-duty water hoses should a riot break out.[8] A truck, equipped with four loudspeakers, was at the ready should any orders need to be given in the midst of street cacophony.[9] All told, this was the largest show of police protection for any event up to that time in the history of New York City.[10]

A police captain inspecting the security inside walked up and down the aisles of the arena. He noticed a man standing along a section reserved for members of the press. The lone figure's hands were shoved deep into his coat pockets. He continually stared at his feet, and periodically let out a sigh. "Move along, buddy," the captain told this man. "It's OK," the man replied. "It's OK." He showed a gold badge, revealing his identity as a plain-clothes detective. Russell Maloney, a writer covering the rally for *The New Yorker*, noted that the man was "a Jew," though how he established that was not clear. Satisfied, the captain continued his inspection. Every five yards he would stop in front of similarly dressed men who also displayed their badges. The ethnicities of these plainclothesmen went unreported.

One cop seemed to be rehearsing phrases should there be trouble. He kept muttering to no one in particular, "Ah, get along there. Break it up!" Periodically he gave his opinion of the people he had to guard tonight. "Those god-damned Dutchmen," he spat out.[11]

Negotiating Manhattan traffic is always a frustrating experience, but on this night it was positively nightmarish. Cars and buses were diverted in the city blocks surrounding Madison Square Garden, a move made to accommodate the many pedestrians—both Bundists and protestors—streaming to the arena. From six to midnight, no vehicles would be able to get through the choked streets.[12]

Tickets for the rally were a dollar and ten cents for a seat on the main floor, and forty cents for balcony. Most of the attendees purchased these in advance, though tickets were also for sale in the lobby. This was a moot point. Police were under orders not to allow entry to Madison Square Garden to anyone without a ticket or legitimate press pass. That didn't stop anyone besides Bundists from trying to get into the rally. Some would-be interlopers forged police credentials. Other people claimed to be running errands into the arena.[13]

Fights were expected but the first real problem came from an unexpected source. Around 6:30 an automobile accident sparked a crowd of rubberneckers, all straining for a glimpse of the smash-up. It was a minor incident, as inconsequential as any other fender bender might be on a typical February night.

And then the floodgates opened.

First came members of the Socialist Workers party, a group of Trotskyites who promised to bring some fifty thousand strong to the event. At best, however, these demonstrators appeared to be a crowd of no more than twenty-five to thirty men and women. The comrades, gripping concealed banners beneath their coats, tried their best to get to the Bundists but were easily stopped when policemen locked arms at the front line.

A fluid scene with all varieties of humanity added to the growing sea of demonstrators. If Kuhn's goal was to unite New Yorkers on this night, he certainly succeeded, although the teeming masses were not his dreamed for multitude of Aryan fascists but an ethnic and political hodgepodge determined to grind down the German-American Bund.

Signs dotted the crowd. "Smash Anti-Semitism" read one. "Drive the Nazis Out of New York" said another.

A group of war veterans, wrapped in the Stars and Stripes and determined to enter the arena, were held off by police mounts. Another flag bearer, beefy and leading a gang of his own, was stopped by the police. He clearly meant business of some sort, for the cops confiscated his flag and sent him packing.

Not all protestors were part of a mob, organized or otherwise. One lone figure in a mackinaw coat wandered in and out of the action, crying to anyone within earshot, "What for is democracy?"

Louis F. Costuma, chief inspector for the police department, hit on an idea to divert some of the protestors. He closed down traffic along Fifty-First Street, essentially turning it into a "free-speech zone" where people could gather at a relatively safe distance from police lines. "Several of them seemed to want to talk," Costuma said, "so we thought we'd let them."

Costuma assessed the burgeoning crowd at 100,000 anti-Nazis. Valentine put the figure at ten times less. With the Garden's location so close to the theater district he speculated many people in the area where there to see shows. "They didn't come to see this thing," Valentine proclaimed. But given that Monday theaters are traditionally dark on Broadway it's unlikely the commissioner's estimation was correct. Regardless, just a few hours before the rally was to begin streets surrounding the Garden were overstuffed with thousands of anti-Bund protestors.[14]

Inside the arena, eager Bundists took their seats. Some clutched newly purchased souvenirs: buttons, pennants, pamphlets, books. *The New Yorker*'s Maloney captured a verbal snapshot of the audience for his readers. "Imagine a huge assembly of German bakers, butchers, waiters, garage mechanics, maids, governesses, and cooks, all dressed in their Sunday clothes and in a holiday mood," he wrote. "That was the civilian membership of the German-American Bund at the Garden." As for uniformed members, some OD men wore shabby or ill fitting garb while others looked military snappy. Unit leaders carried large flashlights on their hips. Should the lights go out, the torches would be needed. Additionally, the heavy-duty quality of the flashlights could also make for a useful bludgeon should a situation call for it.[15]

A cab pulled up in front of the Madison Square Garden entrance. Out stepped Joseph Goldstein, a former New York magistrate, with a summons in hand for the arrest of Fritz Kuhn. Goldstein had filed a libel suit against *Der Bundesführer* at a Brooklyn courthouse. He had previously tried to deliver the legal papers to Kuhn at the German-American Bund's Yorkville headquarters, but for unknown reasons was unable to complete the mission. Kuhn's grandstanding at the George Washington's Birthday Rally seemed like an opportune time to make a new move.

Apparently Chief Inspector Costuma knew this was coming. As Goldstein tried to march toward the door, firm in step and determined in mission, Costuma put a quick end to the showboating.

"I told you you couldn't do that here," he informed Goldstein.

Goldstein fired back that he was an American citizen. Though he had no ticket to the rally, he had every intention of purchasing one. Once inside, Goldstein would then present Kuhn with the summons. How could he do this now that his legal rights were being infringed? Goldstein demanded. Regardless, Costuma's men quietly moved the indignant ex-judge from the entrance and told him to vamoose. No summons would be served tonight.

At 8:00, just as the program was beginning inside the Garden, a ghostly voice decrying the rally echoed above the packed streets exhorting Bundists to "Be American. Stay at home."

The disembodied sound cast an eerie presence over an already tense situation. Officers narrowed their search for the mysterious orator to a rooming house window overlooking Forty-Ninth Street and Eighth Avenue. A phalanx of cops coupled with members of the police bomb squad, unsure of what they might find, stormed the room. James Pyke, acting lieutenant of the division, was ready for anything—except what he found. The simple flat contained a record player rigged up to a loudspeaker, with a twenty-inch recorded disk spinning on its turntable. A timing device attached to the machine had set the recording off at 7:55 P.M. Pyke also found a receipt showing that two dollars was paid for a five-dollar weekly rental by a duo with the given names Karl Flieger and Murray Wein. It was not known if these were aliases.[16]

22

The Rally

THE PROGRAM INSIDE THE Garden opened with a rendition of "The Star Spangled Banner" led by singer Margarete Rittershaus. A color guard of OD men and Youth Movement members presented the American and German-American Bund flags. Next was the opening address from James Wheeler-Hill, national secretary of the Bund. He was introduced by Reverend Sigmund von Bosse, a clergyman from Roxborough, Pennsylvania, and member of the Philadelphia General Conference of the Lutheran Church.[1] As the first person to speak from the dais, von Bosse had the unique privilege of setting the tone for the evening. He did not fail in this task, preaching, "if Washington were alive today, he would be a friend of Adolf Hitler, just as he was of Frederick the Great." Von Bosse's speech utilized code phrases easily understood by his audience, warning of dangers posed by "internationalist serpents of intrigue."[2]

In his keynote Wheeler-Hill liberally quoted from President Washington's farewell address to the nation, using it as a touchstone for Bundist ideas. The United States was falling away from the greatness of its Constitution so wisely laid out by the Founding Fathers. Wheeler-Hill decried what he saw as class warfare, moral decay, and the burgeoning national debt, blasting away with uncompromising take-no-prisoners language of a loyal American nationalist. It was a bold challenge of a speech, deeply chauvinistic to the core and tinged with an "us versus them" extremism aimed not at uniting America, but with the divisive brashness utilized by countless self-declared "patriotic" demagogues and figureheads throughout the country's history.

"Never were such admonitions more timely than TODAY!" he thundered. "Reviewing the state of the Nation today, in the light of this historic observation: WHAT DO WE FIND? A nation of TRUE Americans? UNITED? . . . in a noble common cause? PATRIOTIC? . . . The CONSTITUTION . . . has it been free from attack? ARE we avoiding public debt?" He pondered what President Washington might say to restore the will of "loyal and law-abiding people, the true Christian Americans." The speech concluded with a powerful challenge for the assembled "to restore America to the true Americans and to the ideals and principles given expression in the great farewell address of George Washington."

For all of Wheeler-Hill's jingoistic bluster, laced within his speech was the subtle hint of a different nationalist agenda. He opened with the greeting, "My fellow Christian Americans." Further into his keynote, Wheeler-Hill decried Roosevelt's Secretary of the Interior Harold Ickes as "dictatorial" for his "irresponsible attacks on German leaders and Germany." His restrained words were a mere prologue to the less artful diatribes to come.[3]

Outside the Garden, at around 8:40, an orchestra emerged from the Longacre Theatre on Forty-Eighth Street between Broadway and Eighth Avenue, where the backstage musical *I Must Love Someone* was playing. The musicians struck up the show's theme song, then were joined by the production's male chorus, who served up a harmonious rendition of "The Star-Spangled Banner."[4]

Wheeler was followed by Rudolf Markmann, leader of the Eastern gau, who decried "every crack-pot and bankrupt lawyer" who believed the country must be saved from the Nazi organization that was the German-American Bund. "We have never claimed to be and are not 'Nazis,'" Markmann said, noting that *Der Führer* himself "proclaimed to the world many times that National Socialism is not for export!!"

He bellowed to the receptive audience that, "in the course of tonight's speeches we will have the opportunity to tell of a particular race of people which has more and proven qualities in the game of overthrowing established governments." That race was, of course, the Jews and their "hate campaign" against the Bund predecessor, the Friends of New Germany, and other German-American organizations.[5]

Midwestern gau leader George Froboese pushed themes of Jewish world domination in a speech spiked with familiar canards that were twisted with crisp originality. "Jewish preaching" drove class warfare in America, using ideas "prepared by the oriental cunning of the Jew Karl Marx-Mordecai!" White Americans and their labor unions were "exploited . . . by Jewish-International moneyed interests" and "debased and misused by Jewish agitators." Froboese spoke again of the 1933 boycott against the Friends, "instigated for the sake of some of the four million Jews living in America, [and] has been definitely detrimental to the welfare of a hundred and fifteen million White and Colored American Citizens," a hyperbolic rant of disingenuous inclusiveness. He denounced wealthy financier and presidential consultant Barnard Baruch as "the Jew Barney Baruch, often called the unofficial President of the United States," and other influential American Jews, including Secretary of the Treasury Henry Morgenthau Jr. and journalist Walter Lippmann. To roaring approval, Froboese cited words of Father Coughlin, the Royal Oak, Michigan priest and Bundist favorite, whose national weekly radio addresses blazed with anti-Semitic fever. Froboese brought down the house with a rousing conclusion, calling on the audience "to join with us in the battle for a socially-just, economically really stabilized, financially independent, Jew-free America!"[6]

Banding in the press box with her newspaper peers covering the rally was syndicated columnist Dorothy Thompson, one of the country's best journalists, and like Winchell an early and outspoken voice keen to the rise of Nazism. During the late 1920s and early 1930s she worked as German correspondent for the *New York Post*. This gave Thompson the rare distinction of not only having access to Hitler in the infancy of the Third Reich, but also the honor of being the first foreign journalist thrown out of Germany. The NSDAP government expelled her for vivid and unflattering depictions of Hitler and his *Volk*. Her portrait of the *Führer* published in *Harper's Magazine* was sharply honed example of Thompson's anti-Nazi stance. "He is formless, almost faceless, a man whose countenance is a caricature, a man whose framework seems cartilaginous, without bones," Thompson wrote.

"He is inconsequent and voluble, ill poised, and insecure. He is the very prototype of the little man."[7]

Thompson, wandering the arena halls before the rally commenced, was belted with déjà vu. It was as though somehow she had been transported from a stadium in Manhattan back to the streets of Nazi Germany. On this night Madison Square Garden was filled, she said, with "the same scenes I witnessed in Berlin seven years ago." Arena hallways, where on normal nights hockey or fight fans could buy their hot dogs and beer, were now lined with tables hawking Bundist propaganda, pro-Nazi Germany literature, and books including *Mein Kampf.* Also prominent were copies of Father Coughlin's publication *Social Justice.* Thompson was no fan of Coughlin's. Just a few months earlier she demanded the Federal Communications Commission look into the clergyman's harsh abuses of the public airways. "The tie-up between the Coughlinites and the German-American Bund is perfectly clear . . . if you read their common literature," she wrote to a friend. "They are working both sides of the same street . . ."

On the night of the rally, Thompson was to deliver a speech at the nearby Hotel Astor. Yet she could not resist making a brief stop at the Garden, with every intent to create a scene.[8] Despite the intense security, her press pass allowed her *carte blanche* entrance into the Garden. Thompson laughed loudly at each new speaker, making sure that everyone within earshot and then some would hear the cackling. *The New Yorker*'s Russell Maloney, who was standing close to Thompson, described her laughter as "high-pitched, forced, and rather meaningless." But the laughter was not intended for Maloney or any of the other journalists. Thompson's loud snickers were aimed specifically at every single Bundist. She continued for a solid ten minutes, doing everything she could to infuriate her targets on stage and in the audience.

Thompson's catcalling finally pushed exasperation levels beyond their limit. A cry went up among the audience: "Throw her out!" Some policemen tried to move her away, including the cop who'd cursed "those goddamned Dutchmen."[9]

It was widely reported that OD men took Thompson away. In reality she left on her own volition, albeit with a squadron of Kuhn's guards watching her every move and policemen eyeballing everything in toto. Thompson refused to let anyone else have the last say. "Bunk!" she hollered on her decampment. "Bunk, bunk, bunk! *Mein Kampf,* word for word!" Thompson continued the laughter, kidding policemen, "Oh, boys, come *on!*"[10] For their part, the cops appeared to be sympathetic to Thompson. "We didn't do nothing to her," Maloney's cop said.[11]

"I laughed for a purpose," Thompson said the next day. "I laughed because I wanted to demonstrate how perfectly absurd all this defense of 'free speech' is in connection with movements and organizations like this one."[12]

Winchell praised her actions. "Dorothy Thompson is our nominee for Pulitzer honors," he wrote. "She performed a disinterested service by being heaved out of Madison Square Garden Monday night during the Bund demonstration of how to bite the hand that feeds you. Miss Thompson laughed at the idiocies."[13] In another column, he noted that Thompson "was thrown out of Germany, so what's news in the Ratzis throwing her out of Madison Square Garden?"[14]

Next up was Hermann Schwinn, the West Coast leader. Based in Los Angeles, Schwinn was the appropriate choice to rail on Jewish control of Hollywood, the newspaper industry, and radio. He ripped out expected talking points, ending with a mini-masterpiece of an anti-Semitic run-on sentence: "Everything inimical to those Nations which have freed themselves of alien domination is 'News,' to be played up and twisted to fan the flames of hate in the hearts of Americans, whereas the Menace of Anti-National, God-Hating Jewish-Bolshevism is deliberately minimized!"[15]

Outside the Garden, at around 9:30 a group estimated around five hundred tried to break through the police lines. Mounted cops intervened. This action meant nothing to the more zealous protestors. Peter Saunders, "a Negro" noted *The New York Times,* lunged at Patrolman Harold Lee, trying to throw the man off his horse. Saunders managed to grip the horse's bridle and pulled hard, injuring the animal's mouth. As Lee came off his mount, Sanders managed to get in another shot, connecting his fist to the policeman's jaw. He was the only known person that night to attack both man and beast.[16]

Gerhard Wilhelm Kunze, the national public relations director and Kuhn's unofficial second-in-command, spoke on the importance of race and the dangers of mixing Aryan blood with inferior ethnicities. He decried interracial sexual unions as unnatural, asserting that "some artificial 'standard Human Race,' is Madness and Blasphemy!" The United States, he said, "[is] the product of a particular Racial Group, the ARYAN!" This was not some sort of "race-hatred," he insisted, but "Race-Recognition and the Will to the Preservation of our Own!"

And just who was responsible for the plague of racial muddle and destruction of American culture? "The only true Internationalist, the only ever-homeless Parasite, racially so mixed and consequently torn within himself as to be at home to a degree everywhere and truly at home nowhere is the Jew!" He pointed out that lawmakers throughout American history had banned interracial marriage, set up "Jim Crow" laws, and other legislation "to instinctively protect the Aryan Character of our Nation!" Now, Kunze declared, it was time for the United States government "to awake to the fact that the Jew is an Alien, in Body, Mind and Soul, as ANY other Non-Aryan, and that he is a thousand times more dangerous to us than all others by reason of his parasitic nature!"

He concluded with a rabid defense of both the Nazi swastika and the stiff-armed fascist salute as vital to Aryans and "White Gentiles" around the world and especially in the United States. "There is no symbol better suited to unite the hundred million White Americans," he swore, "none which will more definitely divide friend from foe, as the reaction of any red Jew upon coming face to face with it will prove to anyone!"[17]

And then, at last, it was time for the address by their national leader, the great *Bundesführer* Fritz Kuhn.

Kuhn's speech was a verbal symphony played through his thick German accent, a melodious sound to the ears of his audience. The address opened through introductions of themes well known and much loved by his listeners: the persecution of German-Americans by conniving Jewish sorcerers, money-mad leeches throughout all elements of society. "For they have shown great ability in making white appear black and are proving themselves master magicians in slowly but surely converting the American commonwealth to a closed Jewish cooperation," he intoned. The speech developed with flourish, emphasizing the glory of Germans, German-Americans, and the German-American Bund. Throughout the movement, he infused familiar motifs with pungent modifiers like: "the slimey conspirators who would change this glorious republic into the inferno of a bolshevist Paradise" and "the grip of the palsied hand of Jewish Communism in our schools, our universities, our very homes."[18] Other familiar notes were instant crowd pleasers. Kuhn's referred to President Roosevelt as "Rosenfeld" and Manhattan D.A. Thomas Dewey as "Thomas 'Jewey.'" The city's half-Jewish/half-Catholic mayor became "Jew *lumpen* LaGuardia"[19]

He built into his main allegro, tying the Bund to Washington's ideals and the great elements of human events usurped by Jews throughout the generations. "Whenever a Jew appears in history," Kuhn said, "he is worked up by his fellows into a 'Personality,' who 'overshadows' the white man who really accomplishes the things for which the Jew takes credit."

Kuhn delved into a litany of Jewish expropriation within his adopted homeland. Benedict Arnold, the great traitor of the American Revolution, was assisted by a Jew. Haym Salomon's financial assistance to the colonial government and the war against the British was pure mythology. Jews were held in contempt by Union General Ulysses S. Grant during the Civil War. Jewish carpetbaggers sweeping through the postwar South, exploited newly freed blacks with promises of "a white woman for a sweetheart." So horrific were the evils of Jewish induced miscegenation Kuhn said, that, "The details of this reign of terror are not fit to be told in public."

The lust for money by Jews foisted the nation into a bloody world war. The extended tentacles of "Barney" Baruch's financial control gripped labor, business, and the government. And of course this cabal of Jews, from the secret Jewish president in the White House to Jews lurking in every corner of the country, was dead-set on repressing German-Americans.[20]

The words poured from Kuhn's mouth. *Der Bundesführer* was in full glory.

Despite all precautions, errant anti-Bundists managed to slip past the tight cordon surrounding Madison Square Garden. One such miscreant was Isadore Greenbaum, a twenty-six-year-old unemployed plumber's assistant from Brooklyn. Greenbaum was a former merchant marine who witnessed the impact of Hitler firsthand during a voyage to Germany in 1933.[21] Dressed in a blue suit, he was nondescript, just another young man in the audience, watching speeches.[22]

Kuhn was wrapping up into a furious anti-Semitic crescendo.

Greenbaum seethed. And then he acted.

Oblivious to the OD guards, he charged toward Kuhn. Podium micro-phones amplified the sounds of his feet on the stage. The OD swarmed him with everything they had, subduing Greenbaum with effective punches and stomps. It was an uncanny replication of Nazi street thuggery, a pack of uniformed men blasting away with fists and boots on a lone Jewish victim. The audience shouted their approval at this unexpected development, a physical Jew bashing that intensified and underscored everything the Wash-ington's Birthday celebration really stood for.[23]

Greenbaum's pants were ripped from his legs. Mercifully police pulled Greenbaum loose, probably saving him from serious injury. Once in cus-tody Greenbaum fought back against the arresting officers. No one, not Nazi thugs, not New York cops, would stop him from giving Kuhn what he deserved. Greenbaum was hauled off to the police station, and charged with disorderly conduct.[24]

Rattled, yet overall unperturbed Kuhn delivered his rousing finish, call-ing for an America ruled by white Gentiles, labor unions free from Jewish communists, a "[t]horough cleaning of the Hollywood film industries of all alien, subversive activities," the "[c]essation of all abuse of freedom of the pulpit, press, radio and stage," and most importantly, a return to the policies of George Washington, free of any foreign influences.

"This is our program," he concluded. "Take it or leave it. If you approve and wish to make your influence felt—for alone you are powerless—the Bund is open to you, provided you are sincere, of good character, of Aryan (White Gentile) Stock, and an American Citizen imbued with patriotic zeal! Therefore: Join!" (parenthesis in original)[25]

The audience clamored as one massive body, right arms thrust forward as they joined Kuhn in the Bundist slogan. "Free America! Free America! Free America!"

It was Kuhn's moment at last, a triumph of his will. Nothing could stop him. Nothing.

And then, at 11:15 p.m., it was over. No longer under the safety of police lines, the once-proud OD men buttoned up their thick overcoats against the night air, a two-fold necessity—it kept out the cold while hiding their uniforms.[26]

Bundists were escorted through police lines along Fifty-Second Street, presumably to return to their homes in Yorkville, Brooklyn, the Bronx, and
beyond. Egressing twenty thousand Nazi sympathizers was no easy task.
Demonstrators lined the police blockade, still ready for battle, still hurling
catcalls and jeers. More enthusiastic members of the protestors managed to
get in a few final punches at Bundists as a denouement for the evening.[27]

Inside Madison Square Garden workmen scraped away what remained
of the rally. George Washington, American flags, and anti-Semitic banners
came down. Policemen who had survived a tense shift finally could relax. One
officer complained that his feet were killing him. "Take it easy . . . ," a fellow
cop replied. "Them god-damn square-heads will be home in bed in half an
hour."[28]

At midnight the streets surrounding Madison Square Garden were relatively empty, serene in comparison to the fracases of just a few hours earlier.
It was as though the rally never happened in the first place.

All told there were just thirteen arrests for disorderly conduct in the streets.
The perpetrators were hauled off to night court, where their guilty verdicts
received negligible punishments, a simple series of suspended sentences or
fines ranging from two dollars to ten dollars. A few of the arrestees were
deferred to other courts.

Casualties were negligible as well. Four policemen and four protestors
had minor injuries, while a fifth policeman who was knocked to the ground
by a horse refused treatment. One Bundist with some scratches to his forehead was taken care of at a nearby hospital.[29]

At his arraignment, with his wife and sixteen-month-old son sitting in the
spectator's gallery, Isadore Greenbaum remained defiant and cocksure, telling the judge, "I went down to the Garden without any intention of interrupting, but being that they talked so much against my religion and there
was so much persecution I lost my head and I felt it was my duty to talk."

The magistrate would have none of it. "Don't you realize that innocent
people might have been killed?" he asked with rhetorical flourish.

"Do you realize that plenty of Jewish people might be killed with their
persecution up there?" Greenbaum snapped back.

The judge handed down a sentence of twenty-five dollars or ten days in jail. Greenbaum's friends threw resources together and paid his fine.[30]

Six years later, now a chief petty officer and photographer for the U.S. Navy, Greenbaum happily recalled the story for the military newspaper *Stars and Stripes*. "Gee, what would you have done if you were in my place listening to that s.o.b. hollering against the government and publicly kissing Hitler's behind—while thousands cheered?

"Well, I did it."[31]

23

Reactions

BERLIN'S RESPONSE TO THE rally was muted under official channels but grist for the mills in their tightly controlled press. Both the Nazi government and the NSDAP released a statement disavowing any connection to Fritz Kuhn and the German-American Bund. This would be contrary to the state policy of interfering "with the internal affairs of another nation." It was well known that Germany stood firm in its mandate that National Socialism was not an "export commodity." While this was true in February 1939, six and a half months later Germany's invasion of Poland effectively ended that political philosophy.

That said, C. Brooks Peters, the German correspondent for *The New York Times*, reported, "Official quarters admit 'natural sympathy'" for the Bundists, " 'honest Americans' who recognize this 'threat' of Jewry and communism to their nation and who, as patriotic citizens, are militantly determined to do something about it." Another obvious point NSDAP officials emphasized to Peters was that Americans of German heritage certainly looked at their native country with pride, just as citizens of French, English, "or any other ancestry would feel well disposed toward the land of their forefathers."

The German newspapers were not as polite. They screamed about the record number of police at the rally.[1] One headline blared "Jewish Terror in New York." Stories emphasized protestors and melees outside the Garden and their "challenge to Germandom in America." *Der Angriff*, a government-sponsored tabloid brainchild of propaganda minister Joseph Goebbels, decried the mass protests as "a new attempt of Jewry to express its hate and revenge." What happened in New York, the article stated, was shocking and an outrage to Germans, as well as to citizens of "all civilized nations."

Valentine dismissed the German reaction in a razor-sharp comeback. "I am not worried about irresponsible statements of irresponsible governments."

LaGuardia also would have none of the Nazi outrage. The city of New York had provided considerable protection so Fritz Kuhn could exercise his first amendment rights to a peaceful gathering. Would a group opposed to Hitler and the Nazi government have been allowed to hold a massive rally in Berlin? Of course not. "I will never do anything in any way resembling what they are doing over there," the mayor avowed. By providing freedom of speech rights to the German-American Bund in one of New York's crown jewels was a clear example of what LaGuardia called "a contrast between the way we do things here and the way they do things there."[2]

Mike Jacobs, a honcho at Madison Square Garden, wanted no repeat of the Bund rally, which resulted in a threatened boycott by other potential renters. "There are two versions of how Madison Sq. Garden will try to melt the boycott—the result of allowing the Bund to meet there, despite contract violations," Winchell reported. "(1) The Garden will never permit them to meet there again; (2) Mike Jacobs will mediate with both sides for permitting the boycotters to hold Americanism meetings (rent free) every time the Communists, Fascists, et al foul the air there." (parenthesis in original)[3]

On February 22, 1939, in camaraderie with their New York brethren, Bundists in Los Angeles gathered at *Deutsches Haus* for their own Washington's birthday celebration. It was an exclusive event, with OD guards stationed proudly at the front door, uniforms cleaned and pressed for the occasion. The regulation look didn't last long. Protestors jammed Fifteenth Street, wielding eggs, vegetables, and other projectiles. The foodstuffs were put to good use, hurtling through the air and spattering any Bundist within range. OD men abandoned stoic posing for undignified duck and cover maneuvers. Wiping sloppy yolks and eggshells from their brown shirts, they retreated to safer ground, assisting latecomers through the volleys and into a side door. Once safely ensconced, three hundred Bundists sat enraptured during speeches linking Washingtonian ideals to Hitler's New Order. A slight miasma of vegetables and raw eggs lingered in the air.[4]

———

Given his devotion to the First Amendment, LaGuardia developed a creative law aimed to at the very least tamp down any future demonstrations. One week after the rally, on February 27, the mayor sent out a strict and unbending edict to "owners and places of public assembly"—such as Madison Square Garden—"that under no circumstances are such places to be leased for occasional use with the permission to the lessees to provide their ushers." Those in charge of arenas and rental halls would now be responsible for all safety and "only duly licensed special policemen may be used." Such guards would solely be authorized by Police Commissioner Valentine, "and wear only such uniforms as have had the previous approval of the commissioner." Exceptions to these rules would be allowed only for "recognized fraternal, veteran and religious organizations."

At no point were the German-American Bund and the OD guards mentioned, but the message was clear. It was a legal crackdown *The New York Times* called "an ingenious new formula" to prevent another large-scale conclave of brown shirted thugs emulating Nazi Germany's SS squadrons.[5]

Leaders from New York's religious and political worlds decided to hold a rally of their own, emphasizing the true meaning of America as opposed to Fritz Kuhn's swastika-framed ideologies. On the night of Friday, March 3, the interfaith nonpartisan "Council Against Intolerance in America" welcomed a capacity audience of thirty-five hundred at Carnegie Hall. A sound system was set up outside so the overflow crowd could hear the proceedings. Radio station WMCA broadcast the rally for supportive listeners in their homes.

Only thirty police officers were utilized for token security, a chasm of a difference from the Washington's Birthday rally. In contrast to the three thousand OD men, this rally's color guard was five Boy Scouts, including a Jewish boy whose parents were Russian immigrants, a German-Jewish refuge who had arrived in the United States just ten days prior, and boys of Scottish, Swedish, and Italian heritage. These choices were a deliberate thumb in the eye to the Bundist version of "Americanism."

Clergy of many denominations and political dignitaries sat on the speakers' platform beneath the Stars and Stripes and a banner bearing the theme of the rally: "Intolerance is un-American." Those who could not be there sent messages of support, including Governor Herman Lehman, Senator

Robert Wagner, Rabbi Stephen S. Wise, president of the New York State
Federation of Labor, George Meany, and the German-born conductor of the
New York Symphony Orchestra, Walter Damrosch. Damrosch had been a
scheduled speaker but came down with a bad case of laryngitis. A statement
was read on his behalf, affirming that he was just one of many German-
Americans who abhorred Fritz Kuhn, the German-American Bund, and all
they stood for.

Congressman Bruce Barton told the audience that he had gotten letters
urging him not to speak at this rally lest he risk voter backlash. He ignored
these warnings, declaring that the real political danger to America was blind
acceptance that fascism and communism were superior to democracy. Walter White, secretary of New York's NAACP, said he spoke on behalf of the
city's population of twelve million black citizens. "We denounce the brazen
attempt of Fritz Kuhn and his cohorts because we do not want to see other
minorities suffer as we have suffered," he said. George Gordon Battle, a
powerful New York attorney, Tammany Hall politician, and chairman of
the evening asked for a voice vote from his audience, requesting that any
meeting with people wearing paramilitary uniforms—such as the OD—
should be banned in the city. He was answered with a powerful cheer.

The Bundist's provocateur Dorothy Thompson had her say as well. De-
mocracies throughout the world were being challenged by the Nazi menace,
she said, a threat that must be stopped in its totalitarian tracks.

Mayor LaGuardia, a latecomer arriving about halfway through the rally,
was given a rouser of a standing ovation. He applauded this meeting of "respectable, law-abiding Americans." In comparison, the Madison Square
Garden rally was nothing more than an "exhibition of international coo-
ties." There would be no threat of Nazism in New York City, he declared,
"not as long as I'm mayor."

LaGuardia pointed out another dignitary sitting on the dais, his opponent in the previous mayoral contest Jeremiah T. Mahoney. "There you
have a living example of what democracy means," LaGuardia joked. "You
see, I didn't shoot my opponent."

In what was both a contradictory show of egalitarianism as well as a deliberate insult, William B. Herlands, New York's commissioner of investigation, had extended an invitation to the "Intolerance is un-American" rally
to *Bundesführer* Fritz Kuhn. Kuhn hinted that he might show up, although
he was reluctant to do so. Besides, he had good reason to stay away. "Those

people are nine-tenth Jews and the others are Communists," he told Herlands. "They won't allow me to talk anyway. We don't consider them worthwhile. They don't represent New York and they want us there to make a laugh, that's all." If Kuhn did indeed show up, he did not make himself known.

New York's District Attorney Thomas E. Dewey was another dignitary unable to attend. In his message to the gathering, Dewey described the Bundists as "disciples of bigotry" who libeled the memory of George Washington when they referred to him as "an eighteenth-century Nazi." "Let them have their stupid say, protected by police who have not the slightest sympathy with what they say, but only in their right to say it," Dewey's message read.[6]

Like it or not, Fritz Kuhn had the freedom to say whatever he wanted no matter how noxious his words. There had to be another way to silence the *Bundesführer* and cut the German-American Bund off at its head.

Such things required careful planning. And Fiorello LaGuardia hadn't become mayor of the world's greatest city by making rash decisions.

PART VII

Cracks in the Madhouse

"Funny thing working on a case like this for so long. Something like spending a great deal of time going through a madhouse. You see these Nazis operating here, and you think of all those in Germany, you can't help feeling somehow that they're, well, absolutely insane."

—EDWARD G. ROBINSON AS FBI AGENT ED RENARD IN THE WARNER BROTHERS PRODUCTION *CONFESSIONS OF A NAZI SPY*, 1939

24

Legalities

NEW YORK DISTRICT ATTORNEY Thomas E. Dewey was summoned to Mayor LaGuardia's office.

Kuhn's First Amendment rights could not be questioned. A new tactic was needed to go after the German-American Bund. As an elected official and prosecutor respectively, LaGuardia and Dewey didn't have the unfettered public platform of a Walter Winchell. Nor could they operate using the extreme methods of a Meyer Lansky. Congressman Dickstein had the ability as a legislator to form investigative committees, but that was a political tool afforded a man of higher office. As mayor of New York City, the largest metropolis in the world, LaGuardia had to fairly apply the law to all citizens, a fact he made clear through official statements.

What happened behind closed doors was another matter.

What LaGuardia and Dewey needed was a legal means to shut Fritz Kuhn down permanently. Their answer was found in one of the Federal government's most successful convictions. As the Roaring Twenties roared down, the Feds bypassed filing any criminal charges on Al Capone over his violent business methods in Chicago. Instead Scarface was nailed in 1931 on tax evasion, effectively knocking down his criminal career to a whimpering conclusion. If the tax codes could bring down a powerful figure like Capone, surely there must be an angle within existing tax laws to stop the *Bundesführer*. Therein lay their hook.

As a business making more than ten thousand dollars annually, the bund was required by Depression-era emergency tax relief laws to pay one-tenth of one percent of all income. Additionally, they were required to fork over two percent tax on all items sold, including membership dues, pamphlets, newspapers, buttons, uniforms, and other ephemera. Back taxes might be owed on a mountain of paraphernalia. All this amounted to earnings by the Bund overall and via their incorporated business divisions, A.V. Publishing Corporation, the German American-Business League, and the German-American Front, Inc., among others.

This added up to considerable tax dollars. Perhaps the Bund was hiding something, perhaps not. Dewey's office issued ten subpoenas.

On Monday, February 27, one week after the Madison Square Garden rally, bundists at the Yorkville headquarters were startled by a banging on their doors. A squadron of New York police detectives and plainclothes officers, armed with legal papers in hand and led by Commissioner of Investigation William Herlands, stormed in demanding all membership rolls, subscription lists to the *Deutscher Weckruf und Beobachter*, bank accounts and statements, and canceled checks. The Bund books were to be checked for any possible tax violations, a routine process by federal law.

There was nothing to be found. Herlands and his men were told that all official records were kept not in the Yorkville headquarters but at an office in Manhattan's financial district. Every Bundist present claimed not to know the address of this mysterious second office.

Next on Dewey's list was a subpoena for the Bund's national secretary, James Wheeler-Hill. He was booked but would not cooperate, giving simple yes or no answers to some questions, and refusing to answer others. Wheeler-Hill offered up only one tidbit: contradicting what personnel at the Yorkville office said, all Bund tax records were not at a mysterious office in lower Manhattan. Rather, they were in Kuhn's possession, and the *Bundesführer* was away on business in the nation's capital.

Wheeler-Hill's claim was only believed in part. Kuhn may be holding the books, but nobody in Dewey's office was buying the Washington, D.C. alibi. Agents were dispatched for a thorough scouring of Yorkville and Kuhn's neighborhood in Queens. Nothing. Three days later Kuhn showed up at the Bund headquarters, and was served a subpoena for appearance at a grand jury investigation.

Herlands issued a perfunctory official statement. "This is a routine investigation," he told the press, "conducted in cooperation with City Treasurer [Almerindo] Portfolio for tax purposes."[1] Over the next few weeks Kuhn spoke behind closed doors to investigators of the Special Tax Emergency

Investigation team, a group concocted by LaGuardia and Dewey to put a heavy squeeze on the Bund.

As always, Kuhn was defiant and undeterred. On April 21 he staged a party commemorating Hitler's April 20 birthday. This rally for the faithful, held at a large Bronx meeting hall, attracted some eight hundred Bundists. OD men, one hundred in full regalia and thirty in street clothes, stood guard. Outside there was a heavy presence of New York's finest. Neither side, it seemed, wanted a repeat of the Washington's Birthday Rally near-riots.

None of the speakers at this birthday rally lashed out at enemies with the standard vitriolic Jew baiting. Instead Christianity and its redemptive promise was emphasized, though the words of Jesus were warped beyond recognition through the Bund's fascist perspective. At the end of the evening Kuhn read a telegram, sent to the *Führer* on behalf of all Bundists: "To the greatest German, the liberator and protector of the Reich, Adolf Hitler, who showed to all Aryan people the way to freedom, on his fiftieth birthday: victory and hail." Whether or not Hitler received or even knew of these warm wishes is unknown.[2]

Herlands dug deep into the seized Bund records. Sales tax on items sold at the Washington's Birthday Rally and assessments of the group's organizational corporations were parsed and divvied into every number the Special Tax Emergency Investigation team accountants could crunch.

While Kuhn kept up his bold front, behind closed doors he was in panic. Bund accountants were ordered to balance the books and pay off any debts. Financial coffers within Bund bank accounts withered.[3]

The initial raid in March was a mere warm-up. On Tuesday, May 2, Dewey dispatched a new squad of officers to the Yorkville headquarters, armed with a subpoena giving authority to look for material that would indicate "certain alleged grand larcenies in substantial amounts." Fritz Kuhn was not in the office, but James Wheeler-Hill was and did nothing to impede the investigation. Official papers germane to the case were seized, as per the district attorney's orders.[4]

Two days later Peter E. Lockwood, an assistant DA in Dewey's office, received a blistering phone call. On the other end of the receiver was Fritz Kuhn, furious not only about what he felt was an unauthorized search; he also claimed that his personal desk had been rifled through by Dewey's goons, who helped themselves to $1,380 found in one of the drawers. The *Bundesführer* told Lockwood that he had been in California at the time of the raid. Lockwood laughed off Kuhn's accusations. If the *Bundesführer* was convinced any representative of the district attorney had stolen money from the Bund office, then he was welcome to file formal charges.[5]

On May 11, newspapers throughout the city published a juicy photograph, a candid picture snapped at the New York's World's Fair on May 3, the night after the Yorkville raid when Kuhn claimed he had been in California. The image showed the *Bundesführer* in hat and coat, cigarette in one hand and a plump blonde on his arm. She was wearing a fur coat and flowery hat. The look on Kuhn's face resembled the horror of a proverbial rabbit caught in headlights before being smashed by a car. A photo caption in the New York *Daily News* read, "How About It, Herr Kuhn?"

Kuhn's story changed. Yes, he had been in California on May 1. He had flown back to New York on May 2 and was indeed at the World's Fair the evening of May 3. His companion? He refused to give her name, though it wasn't hard to pin her as Florence Camp. Kuhn explained that this mysterious woman, "charming and wonderful," was his soon-to-be spouse. He would be divorcing Elsa and marrying his new partner in about a month, once "certain legal actions are ended."[6]

The *Bundesführer*'s troubles compounded when his former Munich employer Reinhold Spitz emerged. Now a refugee in America running from the Jewish persecution of the Third Reich, Spitz realized that the young thief he once spared was leading a Nazi movement within the United States. Spitz would not let Kuhn off so easy this time. He swore an affidavit with the United States Attorney's office in New York, and then met with the FBI. Kuhn had lied about his convictions and jail time back home in Germany when he applied for United States citizenship in 1934, Spitz told the agents.[7] Though his story was confidential, someone leaked word to an organization with the awkward name of The Non-Sectarian Anti-Nazi League to Champion Human Rights. They passed along the information to a reporter at *The New York Times* and the bombshell hit the streets.[8]

LaGuardia was concerned that the *Bundesführer* might try to bolt back to the Fatherland. Carl Nicolay, a top Bundist, had slipped onto a German-bound ship on April 6 to escape a potential subpoena. With the legal pressures mounting, it was conceivable Kuhn would follow Nicolay's lead. Herlands passed information he'd received to LaGuardia, reporting that

Kuhn, Gerhard Wilhelm Kunze, the Bund publicity director, and Fritz Schwiering, head of the publishing division, all had applied for renewal of their United States passports shortly after Nicolay's disappearance. The mayor took no chances. He sent a telegram to Secretary of State Cordell Hull explaining the situation. The New York investigation was close to completion. Kuhn was within the government's grasp, and no chances should be taken. Hull agreed. Bureaucratic stopgaps were implemented, freezing the passport requests for all three men.[9]

Though Kuhn had not been seen in public for days, a reporter went to the Yorkville headquarters, hoping to get some kind of statement out of the *Bundesführer*. He was rebuffed at the office by someone calling himself "Mr. Kunzler—never mind the first name." Kuhn, the spokesman said, had no intention of leaving the country. "We are paying no attention to the action of the mayor," Kunzler concluded. "It is just another of his attempts to harass Mr. Kuhn. We're quite used to that. Good day." With that, the reporter was summarily dismissed.[10] Shortly thereafter Kunze made a public statement, explaining that he had only applied for a passport renewal and assumed his colleagues had done the same. He was just as dismissive of any government actions as was the shadowy Mr. Kunzler. "There are more of the same tricks we're getting used to," he said. "We're not worried by things like that."[11]

The atmosphere at City Hall was tense. On May 17, Herlands provided the mayor with a forty-two-page report on potential Bund tax violations, more than two score charges and all misdemeanors. If convicted, each count had a potential sentence of six months to three years. Multiply that times forty-plus, and Kuhn could be put out of business.[12]

In addition to Kuhn and Wheeler-Hill, the report urged for the arrest of Max Rapp, Bund treasurer; William Leudtke, secretary and general manager of the German-American Business League, a Bund corporation; Max Buchte, a tailor who provided the OD with uniforms; and Karl Kienzler and Fred Hackl, two men who operated Bund-backed businesses. The list originally called for eight people to be detained but Richard Mettin, who also served as a Bund treasurer, died from blood poisoning days before Herlands presented the mayor with his findings.

It was also revealed that Fritz Schwiering had beaten Cordell Hull to the punch, having fled back to Germany on May 3 after sneaking aboard the S. S. *Hamburg* without a passport.[13]

The study was passed along to Dewey. "These facts are submitted to you for such prosecutive action . . . as you deem appropriate," LaGuardia wrote in a cover letter.[14]

LaGuardia and Herlands believed they had a solid case based on sales tax charges alone. Dewey felt otherwise. Misdemeanors were trifling matters. The district attorney wanted a big conviction. With a little more digging, Dewey believed, something felonious was bound to be uncovered.

Kuhn emerged from seclusion on May 18, holding court with reporters at the Yorkville headquarters. He all but dared the chief inspector and the mayor to arrest him personally. "I'm not running away from the Jew Herlands and that little Red, LaGuardia," the *Bundesführer* declared. Late that afternoon a representative from Dewey's office paid a visit. The man bore a "John Doe" grand jury subpoena in hand, a legal tool used to get statements from witnesses who may be unknown to the Court but have specific information about a case in question.[15]

Dewey's man fired a series of questions at Kuhn. The answers were terse.

"Will you answer the subpoena on Monday?"

"I shall."

"Will you waive immunity in order to give your testimony?"

"I shall."

"Do you care to make any statement in connection with the service of the grand jury subpoena on you?"

Here Kuhn hesitated. "No," he said, adding "(t)here was no need to serve a subpoena on me. I would have appeared before the grand jurors without a subpoena, had they asked me. This whole thing will end merely in a subpoena having been served on me. That's all it amounts to."[16]

"Here I've been waiting all day to be arrested and all they do is hand me a subpoena," Kuhn laughed. "And you can bet I'm the John Doe." The *Bundesführer* was still indignant over the investigation of the Bund office during his faux California sojourn *cum* frolic at the World's Fair. "I am thinking of writing to the governor and asking Dewey's removal because he broke the law," Kuhn told reporters. This threat was noted by the New York *Daily News* with the wry conclusion, "Dewey was not advised immediately, and there was no telling how alarmed he might be."[17]

On the day before the hearing, Kuhn rallied the faithful at Camp Siegfried on the retreat's summer season opening day. The eager crowd of some three thousand (including about three hundred OD guards) soaked in Kuhn's provocations. The Bund, he declared, was "waking up" the country, leading the charge against the Red menace and "the big men of this country are now coming into the battle against communism." Another speaker, Wilhelm Kunzer, a leader in the Youth Movement, made an appeal for Bundists to provide the organization with more money. Fighting for justice within the corrupt United States legal system was impossible, he said, "unless you have the money with which to fight for it."[18] Throughout the camp grounds American flags flapped in the breeze alongside swastikaed Bundist banners.

The next morning Kuhn and Wheeler-Hill breezed through a phalanx of reporters, photographers, and newsreel cameras as they entered the New York Criminals Courts building. Both men wore light gray suits and smiles. No, Kuhn told the media throng, he had not spoken with Dewey, no other members of the Bund were subpoenaed, and he had no idea what was about to happen.

Once past this media gauntlet, the duo was escorted to an office on the sixth floor where Frank Severance, an assistant DA, greeted them. He presented each of them with a waiver of immunity agreement. By signing the document, Severance explained, anything said in their grand jury testimony could be used against them in any future court case.[19]

Just the week before Kuhn gave the blunt public response "I shall" when asked if he would testify without immunity. Now, with the reality of a legal document before him, everything changed. "I'll testify," Kuhn told Severance, "but I won't sign." When told that was not an option, Kuhn left the building, grumbling to himself about being used as a "John Doe."[20] Wheeler-Hill left as well.[21]

Later that afternoon Wheeler-Hill returned, alone. This time he agreed to testify before the grand jury.

That afternoon Kuhn told his side of the story to the press. "We waited around there to be called for testimony," he maintained. The *Bundesführer* claimed that there were no waivers of immunity offered by investigators. Rather, after coming to the courthouse, Severance told him that testimony would be taken at a future hearing.

"But did you know," asked one reporter, "Wheeler-Hill went back to the grand jury room in the afternoon?"

Yes, Kuhn said, and was aware that his colleague provided testimony.

"Did he sign a waiver of immunity . . . ," the newsman asked.

"I have not seen him since," was the terse response.[22]

The interview was over. The case was not.

On the afternoon of Thursday, May 25, the New York County Grand Jury released an indictment for the arrest of Fritz Kuhn, charging him with twelve counts of grand larceny and forgery for embezzling $14,548.59 from the German-American Bund bank accounts. Issuing a summons was a simple matter of court paperwork. It would take a little more time to bring in Kuhn.

25

Arrest

LATE THAT AFTERNOON, AT 5:45 P.M., New York detective James Cashman popped some change into a gas station pay telephone at in Krumsville, Pennsylviana, a little town off Route 22 just over one hundred miles from Manhattan. While his companions Detective James Canovan and Detective Joseph Norbury filled their automobile gas tank, Cashman dialed a number and then listened carefully to instructions given by the man on the other end of the line. The detective hung up the receiver, went back to Canovan and Norbury, spoke with them for a moment, and then the three men walked into a diner next to the gas station.[1]

This was the culmination of a long day for the trio. Early in the morning the three men got in an automobile and, as per Dewey's orders, followed Fritz Kuhn's every move to three separate locations. At each stop, Kuhn picked up a piece of luggage and put it in his car.

There were three other Bundists accompanying Kuhn: Gustave Elmer, Gerhardt Wilhelm Kunze, and Thomas Dixon, aka "Chief New Moon." The quartet headed west out of town and out of state, unaware of the car following them mile after mile.

Upon arrival at the Krumsville gas station, Kuhn collected three trunks waiting for him at the establishment. The region was a hotbed for Pennsylvania Bundists and sympathizers; it's conceivable Kuhn arranged for friends to deliver the trunks ahead of his arrival. Kuhn, Elmer, Kunze, and Dixon sat down for dinner at a café next to the filling station. Canovan and Norbury waited, while Cashman received orders from New York: arrest Fritz Kuhn. Only when he telephoned Dewey did the detective learn that an indictment on criminal charges was handed down almost three hours earlier, and that Judge Cornelius F. Collins had issued a bench warrant for Kuhn's arrest.[2]

The trio of detectives approached Kuhn as he was placing the three trunks into his automobile, and told him he was under arrest.

"Where are you from?" Kuhn asked.

"New York," Cashman said.

"Do you know what state you are in now?" Kuhn replied.

"Yes," said Norbury, "Pennsylvania."

Kuhn laughed at the detectives, telling them they had no authority outside of New York. The situation was quickly rectified when Pennsylvania State Troopers were called to make the arrest.[3] The *Bundesführer* claimed that he was not running from the law, but on his way to speaking engagements in Chicago and Milwaukee. Elmer, Kunze, and Dixon were let go. Kuhn was taken to the State Police station in nearby Hamburg, where he agreed to be extradited back to New York.[4] ". . . [I]f I don't go back without extradition, maybe it would look as though I was running away," he said.[5] The *Bundesführer* had just one request. He needed a safety pin for a temporary mending of a hole in his pants.[6]

Did Dewey think Fritz Kuhn was on the lam when the detectives arrested him?

"It looks very much like it," Dewey said. "The indictment shows that Kuhn is just a common thief." [7]

Back in New York the next morning Kuhn was put through the requisite drill: lineup, fingerprinting, mugshot. He cooperated throughout the process but held clear disdain for the cops shuttling him from room to room. Once booking was completed, Kuhn was led to a police wagon that would take him to the courthouse for arraignment. A strange smile was plastered on the *Bundesführer*'s face.

A few gawkers waited outside, curious to see the infamous prisoner. "Hey, Fritz!" one man yelled in immaculate German. "How's Hitler doing?"

Kuhn's smile snapped into a glower at the man's taunt. The *Bundesführer* entered the van and arrived at the courthouse free from hecklers.[8]

Kuhn was antsy before the court proceedings began, drubbing a heavy tattoo on the Bible used for swearing in witnesses. The charges were read: grand larceny in the first and second degree, forgery in the second degree. Then, the inevitable question: what was the accused's plea?[9]

"Not guilty," Kuhn replied, voice loud and clear.

A representative from the district attorney's office asked for bail of five thousand dollars. Kuhn had not contested extradition from Pennsylvania, he explained, and thus the district attorney was willing to given the *Bundesführer* a break. The judge was more cynical. "If it was left to me I would not have fixed it so low," he said. Regardless, bond was held at five grand. Now came the matter of payment.

Bail bondsmen, usually wont to take on even the most desperate of clients, wouldn't touch him. Kuhn was locked up in the Tombs with no apparent way out.[10] He spent the afternoon in utter humiliation. Other prisoners threw catcalls and insults at the *Bundesführer*. Lunch, a meager offering of potatoes and bread, was capped with a main course of fish, a food Kuhn disdained in particular.[11]

At four o'clock two people, a burly man and a dark-haired woman entered the Tombs asking if Kuhn had made bail. No, they were told. The couple, who did not provide their names, left the building.

Thirty minutes passed. Vahan H. Kalenderian, an attorney representing Kuhn, and Gustave Elmer appeared at the jail with cash in hand—lots of cash. Most of the bail money was in five- and ten-dollar bills.

"Was this money raised by contributions?" they were asked.

"No," Elmer said, "someone was kind enou—"

The lawyer stopped Elmer short and advised him to keep his mouth shut. Elmer complied.

The money had to be counted. It also had to be checked to assure none of it was counterfeited cash. The numerous bills added up and all were legitimate. Kuhn was released.[12]

On Lafayette Street outside the Tombs there was a car waiting. The dark-haired woman got out, while the stocky man remained at the wheel, motor running. She walked down the street as Kuhn, Elmer, and Kalenderian got in the car. The driver sidled down the street to the corner, and the mystery woman got in.

Maritime police, immigration officials, and federal agents were stationed at the West Forty-Sixth Street Pier, where the passenger ship *Bremen* was preparing for its voyage back to Germany. When pressed by reporters, none of the thirty-five men assigned to watch the ship would say if their presence had anything to do with Kuhn making bail.[13]

Members of the German-American Bund wanted answers over their leader's public disgrace. In his *Bund Command* #22, issued on June 1, Kuhn delivered what they expected, a fiery denunciation of his mounting troubles. "Jewish adversaries" were on the ropes Kuhn declared, thanks to the "enlightenment work" of the Bund. But his enemies were insatiable in their lust to bring down Kuhn, and would stop at nothing in this quest. "[F]inally the Jewish-controlled District Attorney, Thomas Dewey, New York County, proceeded to take gangster methods and without warrant illegally broke into my office and into the private dwellings of two Bund officers and confiscated all books and other things in the hope of finding something which he could use against us and especially against me," the *Bundesführer* wrote. Dewey, Kuhn insisted, "indulges in the hope that the Bund could be destroyed by bagging me." He dismissed the district attorney as nothing more than an ambitious politician with his eyes on the White House. "[T]hrough doing away with the Bund, [he] thinks he can win for himself the Jewish votes for the presidential election." Kuhn blamed "the Jewish controlled press . . . attempting to discredit me before my own members."

He dismissed accusations of womanizing forthright, claiming he was a loyal husband to Elsa. "I furthermore emphasize," he wrote, "that I never, either here or in Germany, committed an unlawful deed."[14]

Kuhn refused to back down. He headed to Wisconsin to give the speech postponed by his Pennsylvania arrest. He first spoke at a rally in Milwaukee, maneuvering past protestors to greet an audience of one thousand followers. Chief New Moon also spoke.[15] Arriving in Grafton via the Milwaukee train, the *Bundesführer* was then greeted by more enthusiastic supporters. They marched to Camp Hindenberg in a route that deliberately passed Schurz Park. As angry members of the Wisconsin Federation of German-American Societies looked on, Kuhn and his Bundists sang a rousing chorus of *"Horst Wessel Lied."*[16]

His troubles compounded. The June issue of a ten-cent monthly magazine *Click* (released in mid-May) published a photograph of what was alleged to be Kuhn's office at one of the Bund camps, though which one was not disclosed. The desk could be that of any slovenly businessman with its clutter of documents, a whiskey bottle, and spittoon. But among the papers was a map of the United States dotted with swastikas, each representing one of the Bund camps; a study in black and white of Kuhn's Swastika Nation. An enormous swastika hung over the desk. To the right were various pictures of

Bund leaders, including Kuhn delivering an impassioned address. On the right were other photographs: a snarling Hitler, beneath him a headshot of Kuhn, and under the *Bundesführer* was a picture of the Italian dictator Benito Mussolini.

Most notable was the scruffy object beneath Kuhn's desk chair: the American Stars and Stripes. In the *Bundesführer's* office the United States flag, which Bundists claimed to honor and revere, was nothing more than a throw rug muddied with dirty footprints and significant symbolic weight.[17]

Damage control was swift and predicable. The official response, as printed in *Deutscher Weckruf und Beobachter* on May 18, claimed the picture was a complete fraud perpetrated by "The Jews" in their never-ending smear campaign to "lie the German-American Bund out of business . . ." by appealing to "human knavery." The anonymous author decried the recent disclosure of Kuhn's criminal past by Reinhold Spitz as "phoney [sic]." The article managed to work in a slam against perennial enemy "Walter Winchel [sic] (whatever his other name may be)" and derided LaGuardia. (Parenthesis in original.)

It ended with another appeal for Bundists to dig deep into their wallets. "[T]his is an opportunity for patriots to show their sincerety [sic] in the cause the Bund espouses by sending in their contribution to carry on a fight to a finish."[18]

At a meeting in the Bronx, held in late June, Kuhn made a triumphant entrance to a crowd of five hundred people. Flanked by OD men, he strode down the middle aisle while the audience shouted and cheered. Waiting for him on stage were his staunch lieutenants James Wheeler-Hill and Gerhard Wilhelm Kunze. George A. Van Nosdall, leader of the Bund-sympathetic group Crusaders for Americanism turned on a small phonograph and played "The Star-Spangled Banner." When the National Anthem came to an end, Van Nosdall stood on the speaker's platform, thrust out his right arm, and shouted the Bundist salute "Free America!" The audience responded in kind, voices ringing throughout the meeting hall. Kunze gave a short speech, denouncing Jews and the government "persecution" of the *Bundesführer*. And then it was time for the man himself to speak.

Van Nosdall introduced Kuhn. "You know I look upon Hitler as the greatest man since the time of Christ. I now present . . . the greatest living Christian American in the country—our own Fritz Kuhn . . ."

The crowd rose as one in a powerful show of support, a standing ovation coupled with the stiff-armed salute. Kuhn took his place before the crowd, and looked them over. It was Madison Square Garden all over again, though on a smaller scale and under dire circumstances. Neither fact seemed to bother Kuhn.

"De Joos, they are persecuting me again," he declared in a voice filled with anger and defiance. "Eleven times I have been to court and eleven times I have returned a free man. But I am glad to see that Ameri(c)a is waking up. Ve shall have it yet—a Free Ameri(c)a."

Van Nosdall put on another record, the Nazi anthem *"Horst Wessel Lied."* Kuhn was rewarded with a second standing ovation. Again, arms shot out to hail their falsely accused leader. "Free America! Free America! Free America!"[19]

The nonstop appeal to membership was effective. At a July Bundist convention in Yorkville Kuhn was easily reelected as *Bundesführer.* The Leadership Principle, giving him absolute control of all the organization's finances, remained unaltered.[20]

26

Confessions of a Nazi Spy

FRITZ KUHN WAS MANY unsavory things, but being a spy for Nazi Germany was not among these. There were many reasons for this. As a self-aggrandizing egomaniac, he lacked the subtle smoothness needed for undercover work. Some rank-and-file members may have been involved in covert activities, feeding back information to confederates in Germany, but none of this would have been sanctioned by the *Bundesführer*. Certainly there were Nazi spies working undercover in the United States, and undoubtedly more than a few might have attended Bund meetings or had some vestigial connection to the group via friends or family members. But as various Reich bureaucrats from Hitler on down demonstrated, they wanted nothing to do with the Bund other than use them to spread generic Nazi propaganda. The reality was that the NSDAP High Command kept their distance from Kuhn and the German-American Bund.

But given all the scrutiny he was now facing through Dewey's investigations and other government heat, Kuhn's unsavory public image was further compounded on May 6 when the anti-Bund motion picture *Confessions of a Nazi Spy* opened at theaters across the country.

In the late 1930s, Hollywood producers were beginning to develop a stronger focus on Nazi Germany. Americans knew a lot about the people running the Reich, the elaborate uniforms, goose-stepping and stiff-armed salutes, violent methods of law enforcement, the sometimes menacing accents of its thugs and commanders, all orchestrated by the maniacal evil oozing from the top man, *Führer* Adolf Hitler. Nazis were living clichés and stereotypes, ready-made stuff for movie villains of all varieties. Hollywood

honcho Jack Warner, head of Warner Brothers studios, decided to take on
the Nazi menace via the cinema in the same way his studio went after organized crime. Among other film genres Warner Brothers specialized in gritty
portraits of the criminal underworld, including *Little Caesar* that made a
star out of Edward G. Robinson, and *The Public Enemy*, which did the same
for James Cagney.

The studio had a solid record opposing Nazism. In 1934, after a gang of
Nazi thugs savagely murdered Joe Kauffman, a Jewish representative for the
studio, Warner Brothers became the first American movie company to shut
down its German offices.[1] This was a risky financial move as Germany was
still a strong market for Hollywood product during the early 1930s. But in
this fight, money was no object to the brothers Warner who generously do-
nated to the Hollywood Anti-Nazi League and hosted fundraisers for the
group. Studio bosses also "encouraged" employees to make donations, using
non-too-subtle pressure in this effort.[2]

In 1938, as German Jews were forced to register their property, carry
identification cards, and endure the horrors of *Kristallnacht*, Warners made
a bold move that surprised many of their movie studio peers by producing
a film damning Nazism both home and abroad. *Confessions of a Nazi Spy*,
released in 1939, was loosely based on the writings of Leon G. Turrou, a
former FBI agent who rooted out Nazi spies in the public and private sector.
His exploits, detailed in the pages of *The New York Post* and a book published
by Random House, *The Nazi Spy Conspiracy in America*, ultimately lost him
his position at the secretive agency. Salvation came from Hollywood, when
Warner Brothers bought the rights to Turrou's story.

The film's director, Anatole Litvak, a Russian-born Jew and member of
the Hollywood Anti-Nazi League, had helmed a few films in Germany during the early 1930s, then fled to Hollywood in the wake of Hitler's ascension
to power. Edward G. Robinson was cast as G-Man Ed Renard. Known as
one of Hollywood's premier movie gangsters for his iconic performance in
the title role of 1931's *Little Caesar*, Robinson was a Jewish immigrant from
Romania. The "G" in his professional name came from his original surname, "Goldenberg." Robinson referred to the middle initial as "my private
treaty with my past . . . [I]n my deepest heart, I am, and have always been
Emanuel Goldenberg."[3] He actively lobbied for the role, telling producer
Hal Wallis, "I want to do [the film] for my people."[4]

Confessions of a Nazi Spy was the first Hollywood feature to use the word

"Nazi" in its title, breaking an unspoken taboo. People throughout the film industry were impressed. At one meeting of the Hollywood Anti-Nazi League Groucho Marx offered a toast to Warner Brothers, declaring them "the only studio with guts."[5]

The plot revolves around German émigré Dr. Karl Kassell, played with cold efficiency by Paul Lukas. Kassell recruits disaffected Americans and Germans to steal military information from factories and shipyards. Through the efforts of G-Man Ed Renard (Robinson), the Nazi spy ring is smashed and Kassell runs back to his native Germany. *Confessions* developed in a semi-documentary style similar to *March of Time* newsreels, complete with a forthright narrator. The film included scenes pirated from *Triumph of the Will*, contextually changing Riefenstahl's work into anti-Hitler agitprop. Footage from actual Bund meetings was also incorporated.[6] Warners took considerable artistic license when it linked the German-American Bund to the Third Reich; in reality, of course, Hitler dismissed the Bund as ineffectual to his goals. But the film's portrayal of Bund meetings was accurate, right down to the Sam Browne belts and heated rhetoric.

Coming off the heels of a sensational book, and featuring top Hollywood talent, the film attracted much attention during production—including an avalanche of angry responses from factions opposed to the film. Robinson was a specific target. "I . . . received obscene letters and phone calls threatening me and my family with death," he wrote in his autobiography. The studio took these threats seriously, providing Robinson and his family with extra security. ". . . [W]hile I tried lightheartedly to dismiss the whole thing," Robinson said, "I was worried." The protection also proved to be something of an annoyance. "Going to the bathroom is probably one of the most difficult maneuvers when you are under security," he noted.[7] In the wake of these threats other people working on the film slept at the studio during production. Another incident caused some concern when a camera boom unexpectedly collapsed near Litvak. Had he been stuck, the heavy machinery surely would have caused serious injury or death. Some within the production speculated this was no accident but sabotage by Bund members working at the studio.[8]

Precautions taken during production were repeated on opening night, albeit some of the safety measures sounded like good old-fashioned public relations stunts. The actual film print was brought to the screening by armored car. Plainclothes security guards were stationed throughout the theater should there be any disturbances. Yet fears real, imagined, and possibly manufactured did have impact: few stars showed up to the premiere. One journalist claimed word was sent out by studio chieftains to their talent "that it might not be good policy to be photographed at the preview or reported among the audience."

Like the film itself, advertising campaigns were bold. One poster declared *Confessions* was "the picture that calls a swastika *A Swastika!*"[9] In some markets flyers, seemingly produced by the German-American Bund, were distributed to potential filmgoers. The inflammatory documents declared, "Hitler and the Third Reich will take serious reprisals against you if you see this picture when Adolf Hitler realizes his inevitable destiny over America." This "propaganda" turned out to be a creative hoax conjured up by one theater chain's enterprising public relations department. Another movie house distributed cards emblazoned with a swastika and "Heil Hitler!" On the other side was information on where and when audiences could check out *Confessions*.

The film did reasonably well at the box office upon its release, even in cities with heavy German populations and a known Bund presence. *Confessions* was well received by critics, earning overall positive reviews in newspapers across the country.[10] Edwin Schallert, writing in the *Los Angeles Times*, called the film, ". . . a unique screen event and one that may exert a far-reaching influence for the cause of Americanism as preached in the cinema."[11] Further praise came from the prestigious National Board of Review of Motion Pictures, which declared *Confessions of a Nazi Spy* one of the best films of the year.[12]

One reviewer, however, pulled no punches in his disdain for the movie. A writer for *Deutscher Weckruf und Beobachter* listed the film's credits as: "produced by Jew Jack Warner, story by Jew Milton Krims, acted by Jew Emmanuel Goldenberg (Edward Robinson), Communist supporter of Leon Trotsky, acted by Francis Lederer, Communist 'peace' advocate; directed by Jew Anatole Litvak, sponsor of Communist Hollywood Anti-Nazi League, technical advisor Jew Rabbi Herman Lissauer, founder of Communist 'Liberal Forum,' historical director Jew Leon Turrou . . .'"[13] More direct action in criticism came from German immigrant Arthur Wolter, a naturalized American citizen who penned the column *"Wir Amerikaner"* ("We Americans") for *Deutscher Weckruf und Beobachter*. Wolter, who lived in Hundington, Pennsylvania, was so insulted by *Confessions* that he and his wife Marie stormed out of the theater halfway through the picture and demanded their money back.[14]

Kuhn, of course, was outraged and decided to make an example of Warner Brothers. He filed suit, demanding a temporary injunction to have *Confessions* pulled from theaters, plus five million dollars for libel. Going against a major film studio and its army of lawyers was a losing battle. Kuhn's attorney quickly found himself mired beyond his capabilities. And ultimately the action was meaningless. Within a few months, Kuhn's lawsuit would be quietly dismissed and forgotten in light of the *Bundesführer*'s other legal troubles.[15]

Kuhn and his loyalists couldn't stop the might and money of Warner Brothers, but lower rungs of Hollywood presented potentially better opportunities for retaliation. The so-called "Poverty Row" studios, such as Republic, Monogram, and Grand National, were reliable low-budget film factories, churning out a steady stream of predictable fare for theaters across the country. The movies were usually workmanlike and a staple of Depression-era entertainment, with crime pictures, comedies, Westerns, and action-adventure serials as the stock in trade. Generally speaking, Poverty Row productions were shown at theaters scattered throughout small town America or neighborhood movie houses in larger cities. Often these films played as double features, with the bill changing several times a week. Sometimes theaters supplemented on-screen entertainment with promotions like free dishes or "Bingo Night."[16]

In 1939, Ben Judell, a seasoned veteran of Poverty Row, founded Producers Distribution Corporation (PDC). The company's first production was an anti-Nazi film with the sizzling title *Hitler: Beast of Berlin*. This rousing tale of brave Germans risking their lives to battle Hitler and his fascist regime in the Fatherland was directed by Sam Newfield, an efficient artisan whose Hollywood career began in silent films, stretched throughout sound movies, and into broadcast television. It was a modest programmer, with a low-key $100,000 budget, a mere pittance in terms of major studios, but good enough for PDC. Also known as *Hell's Devils* and *Goose Step*, (the title of the Shepard Traube novel on which *Beast* was based) the supporting cast included struggling actor Alan Ladd. A few years before, he emerged as a leading man in such big studio films as *This Gun for Hire*, *The Blue Dahlia*, and *Shane*.

Unlike their counterparts in the moneyed world of MGM or Warner Brothers, PDC had no phalanx of security guarding the studio lots twenty-four hours a day. Such luxuries simply were unaffordable along Poverty Row. When word hit the street that an anti-Hitler film was being produced by PDC, Bundists acted accordingly. Late one night, a group of them broke into the studio lot, found the sets for *Hitler: Beast of Berlin*, and destroyed everything in sight. What the saboteurs didn't count on was the scrappiness and survival instincts inherent within low-budget Hollywood. The sets were rebuilt, the cast and crew thrashed their way throughout their back lot Berlin, and the film was released—and ironically suffered at the box office for "anti-German" sentiments.

Because Poverty Row pictures were shown at independent movie houses rather than through major theater chains, they were not subject to the same standards of exhibition as *Confessions of a Nazi Spy*. Across the country theater managers with an eye on box office receipts chose not to screen the film at their theaters when some German-Americans angrily protested the movie. Censoring committees throughout the country sided with audiences. The New York State Censor Board initially banned the film as "inhuman, sacrilegious and tended to incite crime." However, when the title was changed to the presumably less inflammatory *Beast of Berlin*, the film was deemed suitable for theaters.[17] In Chicago, the city censor board decided the film was "propaganda against the German government." Police Commissioner James Allman agreed and the movie was banned, although the Chicago Civil Liberties Committee protested. Judell, a small-timer lacking the clout of any Warner sibling, had no recourse.[18]

27

Hindenburg Park

HERMANN SCHWINN AND HIS minions were a determined lot, eyes ever set on the destiny of their California foothold in Fritz Kuhn's Swastika Nation. Jewish hoodlums, outspoken moviemakers, and the egg-throwing protestors at *Deutsches Haus* at their Washington's Birthday celebration were not enough to stop the Bund in Southern California. Schwinn planned a monumental celebration at Hindenburg Park, a beautifully landscaped recreational area located in Los Angeles's La Crescenta neighborhood.

Ostensibly funded by the "German-American League," a Bund front, Hindenburg Park was anchored by a statue of its namesake, Paul von Hindenburg.[1] The late German president held a special place in the hearts of Bundists. It was by his decision in January 1933 that Adolf Hitler became German chancellor. One month later Hindenburg's "Reichstag Fire Decree" suspended basic civil liberties throughout the country, including such democratic ideas as freedom of the press, freedom to organize and assemble, and privacy of postal, telegraphic, and telephonic communications. Upon Hindenburg's death in 1934, it was a short step from suspending civil liberties to Hitler's dictatorship and the Nuremburg Laws.

The park, located at the corner of Honolulu and Dunsmore Avenues, offered German-Americans a sunny alternative to *Deutsches Haus*. A brochure described the area as "Your Ideal Picnic Grounds," and that it certainly was. Families spent afternoons there, idyllic young lovers strolled through the winding paths, children played in the fields. It was a place for outdoor concerts and a hearty annual Oktoberfest celebration, replete with foaming mugs of beer, Wiener schnitzels, music, and dancing. A utopian ideal of a park, created by and exclusively for people of modern Teutonic mind. Here a German-American could speak openly of wonderful changes being instituted by the National Socialists in the Fatherland.[2] Hindenburg Park was, by all Bundist standards, a marvelous location for the rally.

The event was set for April 30, 1939, ten days after *Der Führer*'s fiftieth birthday. An array of magnificent activities was in store: a grand military band concert, folk dancing, a gymnastic exhibition, and "Games for Young and Old." Admission was a reasonable twenty-five cents, with children admitted free.

The featured speakers were Kuhn, Schwinn, and Arno Risse, a Schwinn lieutenant. Flyers distributed throughout L.A.'s German enclaves promised a "Giant Pro-American Rally and May Day Festival" that would "Expose The Real Enemies of Our United States."[3] Another advertisement for the event declared the Bund as "A militant American Organization for Flag and Constitution and For a Truly Free America."

Two days before the rally Kuhn arrived from New York via airplane, a considerable extravagance in an era when major movie stars regularly traveled from Hollywood to New York by rail. His accommodations were another luxury: a room at the illustrious Biltmore Hotel, which in 1939 was home to the annual Academy Awards ceremony. Once ensconced in his sumptuous quarters, Kuhn met a reporter from the *Los Angeles Times*. He emphasized throughout the interview that the German-American Bund was devoted to the philosophies of America's Founding Fathers. "If we could follow the ideas of George Washington—that would be perfect," Kuhn said. Claiming that Jewish elements held sixty-two percent of the highest positions in the federal government, he elaborated on this theme. ". . . the Jews have plotted to get hold of almost everything, especially in New York and Hollywood," he declared. "What would George Washington think of that?"

Yet the anonymous individual who wrote the story for the *Los Angeles Times* couldn't help but ridicule the *Bundesführer*, using mocking transliteration that turned Kuhn's thick accent into a cartoon. "Jews" became "Chews," George Washington became "Chorge Vashindon." Journalistic standards fell to the wayside; it was a lampooning of the first order.[4]

The southern California weather cooperated nicely that Sunday; it couldn't have been a better day for an outdoor rally. OD men, replete in crisp uniforms of black pants, ties, caps, and armbands, patrolled the area. The hearty aroma of German ales mingled with smells of sausages and sauerkraut. Families and friends gathered for musical performances. Swastikas, commanding respect from all who viewed them, were prominently displayed throughout the grounds.

That morning, somewhere in the Los Angeles region, a small airplane was packed with a unique cargo. The plane took to the skies.

It was a great day for Schwinn. Taking his place at the speaker's podium, standing before a crowd of two thousand attendees, he read from a telegram sent on behalf of the Bund to President Franklin Delano Roosevelt. The boldly worded missive urged Roosevelt to "do everything in your power to quarantine the United States against alien influences which are at work to drag the nation into war." "Alien influences," obviously, were the Jewish element Bundists believed were rife within Roosevelt's administration.

Finally it was time for the great leader to speak. Kuhn took the stage, a line of twelve honor guards stoically framing him on the podium. "The time is past when we must ask for our rights," he thundered. "We now demand them. We're not trying to overthrow the United States, but to give Americans of German descent a true understanding of current problems."[5]

Unlike the New York Washington's Birthday rally, tickets were sold to the general public. One uninvited outsider was Elizabeth Barber, who paid her twenty-five-cent entry fee and now repeatedly interrupted Kuhn's speech, decrying his version of "Americanism" and demanding that he speak "the truth."

Barber—who was alternately labeled by newspapers as "an insignificant American housewife"[6] and "a Hollywood housewife"—was easily shouted down.[7] Protective Bundists encircled her, determined the *Bundesführer* would have no interruptions. Taunts of "Go back to Moscow!" were hurled. Barber refused to surrender, and calmly recited selections from the Declaration of Independence and the United States Constitution. Kuhn continued speaking, unperturbed by his heckler's taunts.[8]

Another sound joined Barber's catcalling. Overhead, approaching from the south, was the buzzing engine of a small airplane. The plane descended in a low swoop just above the rally and its pilot released a rain of paper.

Fluttering down over the crowd were thousands of copies of a flyer resembling an FBI "Wanted" poster.[9] Two unflattering portraits of Hitler—one in profile, the other in quarter turn to the camera—were printed below enormous block letters reading:

WANTED FOR KIDNAPPING
ADOLF HITLER
alias Adolf Schucklgruber
alias Der Fuehrer
alias Adolf Schicklgruber

There was a detailed and most disparaging description of the great Nazi leader. "Claims to be German, which he speaks badly, but is really Austrian," the flyer stated. "Has hallucinations of greatness, modestly refers to himself as 'Little John the Baptist' and sometimes even as God. Warning: It is dangerous to mention 'democracy' in his presence."

Among the crimes for which Hitler was "indicted by world opinion" were "murder, and kidnapping with intent to kill. He is holding sixty-five million people in bondage in Germany, and many more millions in Austria and Czescho-slovakia." [sic] The flyer was issued by Leni Riefenstahl's old nemesis, the Hollywood Anti-Nazi League "for the Defense of American Democracy."[10]

Naturally, the handbill did not settle well with the crowd. The plane ascended back into sky, leaving an angry serenade of angry boos and catcalls in its wake.

Interlopers on the ground and from the air were not enough to spoil the rally. Unperturbed by any of this, Kuhn returned to his speech.[11]

The next evening at the Hollywood Bowl, just a short drive from Hindenburg Park, there was another rally, this one sponsored by the American Legion. Twenty-five thousand people jammed the seats, many of them war veterans, ROTC units, and Boy Scouts. The evening, titled "Stand by America," included speeches by religious leaders of all faiths and denominations. Rabbi Edgar F. Magnin—grandson of the department store magnate I. (Issac) Magnin—told the crowd, "We are here to rededicate and reconsecrate ourselves to the principles of American government." Radio and music star Rudy Vallee, backed by a fifty-member orchestra, joyously sang "God Bless America," by Irving Berlin (née Israel Baline, a Russian immigrant and Jewish cantor's son). Fireworks were timed with the National Anthem, "The Star Spangled Banner," simulating "bombs bursting in air." A spotlight then shone on an enormous American flag suspended above the Bowl, bringing lyrics to life with "proof through the night that our flag was still there."

The featured speaker was Congressman Martin Dies Jr., the flamboyant Texas chairman of the House Committee Investigating Un-American Activities. His oratory gifts were on fire, holding the crowd under a patriotic spell. "We should say to subversive groups," he declared, "'if you believe in other philosophies, the only honest and decent thing for you to do is catch the first boat for some place else!'" As the reporter for the *Los Angeles Times* noted, "this remark caused one of the most spontaneous outbursts of cheering during the evening."[12]

Edward Kunkel, owner of the Forest Club—a drinking establishment in Webster, Massachusetts, a small town in the northeast corner of the state just a few miles from the Connecticut border—was getting ready to shut down for the night. It was Sunday, July 16, around half past midnight. Last call had been sounded and the regulars were heading out the door. But as people were leaving, a new party walked in. They were loud, boisterous, filled with self-importance and perhaps too much to drink. One of the party, a pudgy man with thick glasses, wobbled to the men's room. The rest of the group sat down and demanded to be served.

"You know who that is?" one man yelled. Kunkel didn't know who was using his bathroom, didn't care, and made his feelings clear. Regardless, the man continued. "That's Fritz Kuhn and he's the leader of the German-American Bund."

So what, Kunkel replied. Bar's closed. Russ Martin, bartender and amateur boxer, looked at Kunkel. Neither man wanted any trouble from these drunks.[13]

An altercation ensued. Kuhn grabbed someone by his hat and tried to pull it down over the man's ears.

By now Police Officer Henry "Buck" Plasse, a no-nonsense cop used to dealing with inebriated barflies, was on the scene. When he tried to arrest Kuhn, the *Bundesführer* turned belligerent. Two more officers, Richard Healy and Justin Herideen, jumped into the fray. Kuhn was finally subdued and hauled to jail, where he was charged with public drunkenness and public profanity.[14] He was released on a fifty-four-dollar bail. Police Chief John Templeman had little regard for the accused. "He was just another wise guy who thought this was a hick town and he could stage one of them beer hall putsch things and be the dictator in it."[15]

All in all, just another weekend drunk arrest in Webster, with a bit of a Nazi flourish to it. No one in town had any idea what they were in for.

By Monday night Kunkel was tired of answering the telephone. Calls came in from all over the country. Was it true that the notorious Fritz Kuhn was arrested at the Forest Club? And was Count Anastas Vonsiatsky really with him?

The count was something of a local fixture in nearby Thomson, Connecticut. A leader of the White Russians who'd slugged it out in Moscow streets with Bolsheviks, Vonsiatsky was now a well-to-do supporter of all things fascist. The weekend of the altercation Kuhn and his colleagues were honored guests at Vonsiatsky's country mansion to discuss mutual interests. Rumor was that the mad Russian was also among those arrested and reporters were desperate to confirm the story was true. Kunkel informed all media that the count had not been in his establishment during the altercation.[16]

Judge Louis O. Rieutord, the magistrate with the dubious honor of hearing the case, refused to make any deals with Kuhn's lawyer, H. V. Kalenderian. A full trial would be held, unless the *Bundesführer* agreed to plead guilty as charged. Kuhn, who had bigger legal problems on his mind, accepted to the judge's request. The sentence amounted to a five-dollar fine for profanity and no penalty for drunkenness.

Outside the courthouse was a jeering crowd of five hundred people, every one of them eager to get a glimpse of the notorious Fritz Kuhn. Extra police were called in to help with crowd control. The local newspaper, *The Webster Times*, printed a special edition with a screaming front-page headline announcing Kuhn's guilt.[17] Other newspapers were out in force, including a staff reporter from *The New York Times*. RKO sent a newsreel camera crew for their Pathé News division.[18]

Kuhn issued a statement, read to the press by Gustave Elmer. At no time, the *Bundesführer* insisted, did he act ". . . boisterously and directed no profanity at any person.

"In consideration of the decided hostility shown by the arresting officer, and of the prejudicial atmosphere created before the trial, I pleaded guilty to the charges of drunkenness and profanity as the best means of avoiding a theatrical performance."

Nonsense, retorted Templeman. Plasse was as trustworthy as they came and the charges he filed could be "fully proved." Furthermore, the backup officers, as well as two eyewitnesses, could back up Plasse's story. Templeman also shot down the rumors that Vonsiatsky was involved in the altercation. The count's only involvement was to play dinner host to the *Bundesführer* and a few friends.

When the trial ended Kuhn had one more encounter with Officer Plasse. "If I had been in civilian clothes when you said what you said," the policeman told the *Bundesführer*, "I would have fixed you up so that your mother would not know you."[19]

Unfortunately, the remarks made by Kuhn in the early morning hours of July 16 that earned such a threat have been lost to history.

PART VIII

Trials

"It is perfectly clear to me that no means will be eschewed by our opponents to eliminate me . . . I am being persecuted and defamed because I am the leader of the German-American Bund."

—*BUNDESFÜHRER* FRITZ KUHN
PREPARED STATEMENT ISSUED TO THE PRESS, JUNE 1939[1]

28

Un-American Activities

THE INQUISITION OF FRITZ Kuhn by the House Committee on Un-American Activities began on Wednesday, August 16. The witness dispensed with his usual public uniform, trading in military jacket and Sam Browne belt for a neutral suit and tie. Rhea Whitley, counsel to the committee, threw preliminary questions at Kuhn. Gone was the *Bundesführer*'s usual braggadocio, though his dexterous approach to truth was still in play. Witness Kuhn spoke of his days in Germany, speaking briefly of upbringing, military service, education—and no, he was never once arrested for any crimes of any sort. To his Bundists Kuhn had bragged about charging into the *Bürgerbräukeller* alongside Adolf Hitler during the Beer Hall Putsch. Now he denied even being in Germany when the failed coup took place.[1]

Kuhn's answers were often peppered with the ambiguous phrase "to the best of my knowledge." Early on the testimony turned tedious, as Bundist bureaucracy was laid out. Divisions, dues, membership levels—on and on it went. Kuhn claimed that the German-American Bund wasn't one hundred percent German; in fact, he stated, many Irish immigrants were part of the Bund's auxiliary unit, the Prospective Citizens League. In addition to teaching German and American history at Bund meetings, Kuhn insisted, Irish history was also part of the education.[2]

Time and again he ran away from previous public statements. Kuhn recalculated membership numbers with clumsy runaround answers.[3] He denied having authority over all Bund camps, claiming that his relationship to the retreats had undergone a transformation.[4]

Kuhn's great moment of triumph, his 1936 meeting with Hitler, was now dismissed by the *Bundesführer* as a ten-minute trifle of little consequence. The *Bundesführer* insisted his audience with the *Führer* amounted to nothing but chitchat over the Olympic Games. Neither the inquisitors nor the witness brought up Hitler's words often repeated by Kuhn: "Go over there and continue the fight."

Kuhn was shown picture after picture of the German-American Bund marching and posing under swastika banners, annual yearbooks festooned with swastika photographs, and the Washington's Birthday Madison Square Garden rally.

"That swastika is the emblem of the modern German government, is it not?" asked Alabama representative Joe Starnes. No, Kuhn replied, it is not. Starnes was incredulous. "When was it first used?" he demanded.

"It was used four thousand years ago."

When pressed further on the issue, Kuhn declared that the Nazi swastika was "an entirely different swastika." What he meant by this was never explored by the committee.

But they continued to press the issue. When asked if there were any swastikas displayed at the Madison Square Garden rally in February, Kuhn avoided the question. "We did not have any German flag there," he said. No German flag, to be sure, but on that night Madison Square Garden had been the epitome of his Swastika Nation. The twisted cross could be found everywhere. On the German-American Bund banners flanking George Washington. On pennants, pins, and uniforms of rally participants. Emblazoned on armbands worn by audience members. Festooning the expansive variety mementos, books, and other propaganda hawked at souvenir tables throughout the Garden.

He was shown photographs of the camps, photographs of rallies, and photographs of himself, all with prominent swastikas. This meant nothing to Kuhn. He pointed out that one could easily find the American flag in any of these pictures.[5]

Dies kept pace with Kuhn in a game of semantic tag, trying to catch the *Bundesführer* on the Bund's swastika fetish. Kuhn made clumsy steps when pressed on Hitler's SS as inspiration and model for the Bund's guardsman. The OD marched in formation, Dies noted. Did they also wear a distinctive uniform?

"We have a uniform; yes," Kuhn said.

Was the Nazi swastika part of this uniform? Dies asked.

No. The OD wore an emblem distinctive to the bund.

What was this symbol exactly?

Kuhn gave a rapturous description. "It is the sun with the rays of the sun."

Congressman Starnes, as exasperated as Dies was by Kuhn's nomenclature dodges, would have none of it and cut into the questioning. "In other words, it is the flaming swastika?"

The witness buckled in a rare moment of capitulation. Yes, a swastika.

Kuhn was shown photographs of Bund events at camps and in meeting halls where a swastika was always part of the décor. In one picture, taken at Camp Siegfried, Kuhn stood alongside the German national flag with its prominent black swastika. Another photograph of a Camp Siegfried Fourth of July rally featured Kuhn speaking to an audience, estimated at ten thousand strong, a German flag with blatant swastika flapping in the breeze. Neither image showed any evidence of an American flag on display. In both cases Kuhn blamed the photographer, whom he declared might have been an undercover agent for the government.[6]

Kuhn's verbal tap dance continued late into the morning. At one point he tried to turn questions around onto the inquisitors. When Starnes asked if Hitler was against Communism, Kuhn fired back, "Yes. Aren't you against the Communists?" Starnes ignored the wisecrack, and pressed forward, asking if Hitler was anti-Semitic.

"Aren't you anti-Semitic?" Kuhn sneered.

"I am asking you the question," Starnes said. "Is not Mr. Hitler anti-Semitic?"

Kuhn remained cool. "I suppose so, from what I hear."[7]

Hearings resumed the next day, with similar results. Questions from the committee. Roundabout answer from Kuhn. Follow-up question. Evasive answer. Dodge. Weave. Duck. Kuhn was pressed on the Youth Movement, family camps, the OD, membership, the Friends of New Germany and its former leaders, relationships with similarly-minded American organizations such as the Silver Shirts and the Christian Front, and the various business divisions of the Bund.

On the afternoon of the second day Rhea Whitley, the committee counsel, grew frustrated with Kuhn's verbal subterfuges. Time after time Kuhn claimed he could not remember a name of someone or if a specific person was involved in the Bund in some way. He insisted he could not remember who provided Nazi propaganda for the Bund newspaper. "You have a very poor memory for names, Mr. Kuhn," Whitley observed.

"Well, is that a question, or is that a speech?" Kuhn asked.

"No; that is a comment," was Whitley's dry response.

Kuhn fired the words back. "That is a comment."[8]

At times the tense exchanges between the witness and the committee members turned comic. Dies pushed Kuhn on the nature of his relationship with Gunther Orgell, a German national who provided Nazi propaganda for distribution through Bund bookstores and in the pages of the *Deutscher Weckruf und Beobachter*. Kuhn grew playful in describing his relationship with Orgell, refusing to admit where the two men met. He clearly was enjoying this banter with Congressman Dies.

"What has been the occasion of his visits to your office; in connection with your business?" asked Dies.

Kuhn replied that Orgell came neither for personal business nor Bund-related business.

"He would just come to you to say 'Howdy'?" Dies asked.

"Howdy do," Kuhn shot back.

"How do you do?"

"Yes; that's the way they would say it in Texas. How do they say it in Alabama?"

If Dies was annoyed, he didn't let it show.[9]

It took two days and little was obtained. On Thursday afternoon, Dies adjourned the hearings for the day, announcing that another witness would be heard.

"Am I released?" Kuhn asked.

Yes, he was told.

"Then I don't have to come anymore?"

No.

"It is a pleasure, gentlemen."[10]

And with his mocking farewell, Fritz Kuhn left the congressional chambers.

Speculation ran in some circles that in the wake of his testimony Kuhn intended to flee back to Germany, just as others before him. Kuhn sneered at the notion. "So Mr. Dies is worrying about me," he told a reporter at the Yorkville headquarters. "He thinks I am running away. I would not run away from a thousand Dies. I like it here very much. I would not feel at home on the *Bremen* or any other ship. I will be at this office tomorrow and the day after and the day after that."[11]

On Friday, August 18, Helen Vooros, former member of the *Mädchenschaft* and friend of the Youth Movement martyr Tillie Koch, testified before the Committee. Now unfettered by the harsh supervision of Youth Movement leaders, she unspooled a story detailing a darker side.

She contradicted Kuhn's benign assessment of camp life as a healthy combination of pastoral tranquility and robust activity. Congressmen listened as she unfolded her story of autocratic and sometimes sadistic leadership forcing campers on midnight hikes through jagged brush; of allegiance sworn to Adolf Hitler and the swastika rather than Roosevelt and the American flag; and anti-Semitic propaganda served up like daily bread with morning breakfast.

Her testimony then took a hard-core descent into darker aspects of the Youth Movement as promulgated and encouraged by leadership from the top down. In halting language Vooros recounted a meeting she had with Frederick Vandenberg, an adult leader from the South Brooklyn Bund branch. At the time she thought the appointment would be a standard meet-and-greet session provided by an authority figure to one of his campers. Instead, Vooros was an unhappy and unsettled recipient of Vandenberg's sexual overtures.

Vooros was filled with shock and appalled by what she believed to be inappropriate behavior. She ran to Theodore Dinkelacker, head of the Youth Movement, to report this amorous confrontation. Dinkelacker's response oozed with knowing sarcasm. "He said, what was the matter, and couldn't I take it," Vooros told the committee. "I did not know what he meant by it."

Vooros quickly found out what Dinkelacker was talking about when she went for summer recreation at Camp Nordland. She lasted only three days. Vooros quickly realized her peers were engaging in physical activities beyond swimming and hiking. A modest girl of limited social experience, Vooros told the committee that Camp Nordland was rampant with "immorality."

Vooros wanted nothing to do with the Youth Movement's hedonistic after-hours activities. Hoping to find some female compassion for the situation, she went to Ereka Hagebusch, one of the adult leaders for the girl's camp.

Hagebusch told the frightened girl to keep her mouth shut.

Two days later Ernest Weida, another adult leader, confronted Vooros. "[H]e said I took everything the wrong way," Vooros testified. The clandestine nightly activities at Camp Nordland, Weida told her, were "nothing compared to what it might look like."

Vooros learned exactly what Weida's snide remark meant when she went to Camp Siegfried. "On the second day I was there, I saw immorality going on between the boys and girls, and nothing was said about it." The sexual relations were quietly championed by camp leaders. Yes, there were separate tents for adolescent boys and adolescent girls, Vooros explained. But these were maybe ten to twenty feet apart, easy boundaries for horny teenagers to cross.

Some parents got wind of the escapades and came to check out the situation for themselves. "They saw the boys and girls there together, doing things that they should not be doing," Vooros said. The situation was brought up with Vandenberg, now running activities at Camp Siegfried.

During a meeting with the teenaged campers he addressed the issue. Vooros recounted that Vandenberg ". . . said that the boys and girls should go somewhere where people did not see them and should hide it better." Hormonal lust was a matter of "natural instincts" to be encouraged.[12]

The cavalier attitude by adult leaders toward all things sexual between campers wasn't a matter of turning a blind eye to illicit behavior. Rather, it was the Bund's unspoken version of Germany's official Baby Policy. Teenagers in Hitler Youth and League of German Girls were encouraged by the Nazi government to reproduce, and often. A boom of Aryan babies was an investment in the future of the Third Reich. Goebbels infused adolescent-aimed movies, newspapers, and magazines with something he dubbed "healthy eroticism." Male and female campgrounds were placed in close proximity to each another. From there, human nature and teenage hormones were left to their own devices. One sixteen-year-old wrote to her mother, "[t]here are 48 girls in our labor camp. Near us is a boys' camp. We see the boys very often, and mend their clothing as well as spend the evenings with them. A funny thing: of these 48 girls, 35 are pregnant. And, still funnier, I'm one of the 35 . . ."[13]

Sexual intrigue within the Bund Youth Movement was not limited to carnal entertainments between teenaged peers. During the ocean voyage en route to Germany for the conclave with Hitler Youth peers, Vooros discovered why Dinkelacker was so cavalier when she complained about Vanderberg's sexual overtures. The adult leader was caught in a shipboard liaison with a seventeen-year-old girl. Scandal was tamped down when Youth Movement chaperones enforced a strict code of silence on their charges. Hedwig Klapprott, the wife of August Klapprott—a close confederate to the *Bundesführer* and head of the New Jersey Bund—called a special meeting. What went on between Dinkelacker and the young woman was a private affair.

Vooros felt otherwise. She told Hedwig that as Youth Movement leader, Dinkelacker was supposed to be a role model, someone they looked up to. Bedding down one of his charges, the naïve girl said, was just not nice.

Mrs. Klapprott regarded Vooros for a moment, and then repeated her order in no uncertain terms. Circumstances were what they were and the young people were to keep their collective mouths shut. End of story.

Vooros had other ideas. She snuck into the room of the young paramour and drenched the bed with a pitcher of water. When the deed was discovered Dinkelacker's teenage lover confronted Vooros, demanding answers. The answer was succinct. With a soaked mattress, the promiscuous adolescent would now have a good excuse to find other sleeping arrangements.[14]

"The children will benefit by this training indoors and outdoors and will learn to understand the true meaning of our cause . . . ," Dinkelacker had once told parents. Vooros's tales of physical abuse, indoctrination as propagandists, and the encouraged forays into sexual "immorality" by Youth Movement members and the adults who watched over gave an unsettling portrait of the Bundist camps.

There was nothing left to say. The witness was dismissed by the committee.

29

The People v. Fritz Kuhn

WINCHELL WAS OUTRAGED BY what he perceived as a legal system gone soft on the *Bundesführer*. In a column item labeled "Sudden Thought for District Attorney Dewey of New York," he blasted the city's prosecutor as spineless. He spared no anger or verbal expression denouncing Kuhn's speech in Wisconsin "insulting President Roosevelt and praising Hitler, etc. . . . Who gives the Kuhn-Kluxer the permission to leave jurisdiction of the court—and why isn't he dumped in a cell for disturbing the peace?"

The columnist then noted the Richard Rollins operation with Virginia Cogswell the previous fall. "The proper authorities have 120 recordings of Kuhn's voice (and that of a certain woman, last-initial'd "C") giving a touching summary of his activities between October 1938 and January 1939." Winchell showed particular glee for his prodigious talent to incense the *Bundesführer*, quoting his cameo appearance in the Cogswell recordings from the lips of an angry Fritz Kuhn: "If Volter Vinchell does not stop writing about me, I rub him out."[1]

Three weeks after Winchell threw his verbal stink bomb at the prosecutor's office, Dewey took action. On September 30, Kuhn's bond was hiked ten times the original five thousand dollars to fifty grand by Judge Collins. "We are convinced that the defendant doesn't intend to be present for the trial," Assistant District Attorney Milton Schilback told the judge. The information was based on the strength of what was called an "authentic report," though the nature of that document was not made public. Kuhn was immediately taken into custody.[2] An appeal was made to throw out the decision, but was turned down by New York Supreme Court Justice Aaron J.

Levy.³ For now, it was back to the Manhattan House of Detention—better known as the Tombs.

Warden William A. Adams made it clear that Kuhn was no longer a *bundesführer* inside the facility, but should expect the same treatment as any other prisoner: housed in a sparse cell, and fed commonplace meals of soup, meat, potatoes, bread, and water. Kuhn's only luxury would be extras such as cigarettes or playing cards bought at the prison commissary should he have money to pay for these items.⁴

Incarceration did not change Fritz Kuhn, who used his time behind bars to try a little extortion. One failed attempt to fleece a Philadelphia Bundist was intercepted by the FBI. "As you know (?) I have been put in jail by the Jews," Kuhn wrote his would-be victim. "I will make you Fuehrer (Leader) of the Gestapo here in this part of the country if you send me 3,000. If not I will report you to my friend Adolph. Ask your employer or friends how you (can) rush me money." (parenthesis in original)

The note closed, "Heil Hitler."⁵

In a move designed to save his client, Kuhn's lead defense attorney Peter L. F. Sabbatino argued before Judge Saul S. Streit of the New York City Court of General Sessions that Dewey's seizure of Bundist accounting books was unlawful and thus could not be used in the upcoming trial. Herman J. Mc-Carthy, Dewey's surrogate and lead prosecutor, offered a counter position, arguing that the Bund had supplied Dewey's office with these records after a subpoena was issued. Handing over the books gave implied consent that the Bund had no legitimate objection to prosecution using their bookkeeping as material evidence against Kuhn. Judge Steit sided with the prosecution, ruling that, according to the New York State Constitution, even if documents were improperly seized according to law, they still could be used in court should they demonstrate any pattern of illegal activity.⁶

The trial was to be heard in the courtroom of Judge James Garrett Wallace, known around legal circles as "The Singing Judge." This had nothing to do with his jurisdictive responsibilities. Rather, Wallace was famous for belting out songs in his fine tenor voice at dinner parties and soirées of all sorts. In the late 1910s, as a young assistant in the New York District Attorney's office, Wallace entertained fellow lawyers at Bar Association functions. He cowrote a musical with fellow public attorney Newman Levy, *May*

It Please the Court, a comic revue based on their professional experiences.[7]
But Wallace, who was considered a tough and fair-minded magistrate by his
peers, was in no mood for turning the high-profile Kuhn trial into courtroom burlesque.

Sabbatino made desperate last-ditch efforts to save his client from going
to trial. First he appealed to Judge Wallace for a postponement and change
in venue, claiming it was impossible for Kuhn to get a fair trial in New York
City. He also implored the judge to consider possible prejudices against
Kuhn given that President Roosevelt had "shown hostility toward Germany."
Furthermore, Sabbatino declared "it is common knowledge that the present
sympathies in this country preponderate in favor of the so-called Allies and
against Germany." Both motions were denied.[8]

On Tuesday, November 8, the day before the trial was to begin, Sabbatino stood before New York Supreme Court Justice Isidor Wasservogel,
once again arguing for a change in venue and indefinite postponement. His
reasoning was the same as with Judge Wallace: given all the negative opinion
in both the general public and the press against his client, it was impossible
for Kuhn to receive a fair trial anywhere in the state of New York. A few
hours of contemplation later, Judge Wasservogel turned Sabbatino down flat.
Next Sabbatino went to Judge William Allen, a colleague of Judge Wallace's
in the General Sessions Court, again asking for an order of postponement,
with the demand that Dewey show cause why the trial should not be held off.
Kuhn personally put in an affidavit, with the same argument that receiving
a fair trial in New York City was impossible.[9]

Judge Allen concurred with Judge Wasservogel. On Wednesday, November 9, rather than celebrating his alleged participation with Hitler on
the sixteenth anniversary of the Beer Hall Putsch, Fritz Kuhn sat in a Manhattan courtroom. *The People v. Fritz Kuhn* was under way.

Judge Wallace opened the trial with a no-nonsense statement to potential
jurors. Fritz Kuhn was not on trial for his political viewpoints and public
actions. The only thing to be taken into consideration was any evidence pertaining to the charges against him: four counts of grand larceny in the first
degree and four counts of grand larceny in the second degree for diversion
of Bund money for personal or unauthorized use, and two counts of forgery
in the third degree for falsifying entries in Bund account books.

Sabbatino grilled potential jurors over any conceivable prejudices they might have against his client. He paid special attention to men with traditionally Jewish surnames, eliminating twelve such candidates through peremptory challenge. The men were dismissed without question. Sabbatino invoked the tactic eight more times, burning through his legal limit. McCarthy requested only five peremptory challenges.

One of the excused jurors, Lewis B. Rigger, told Sabbatino that he had no feelings one way or the other about the word *"Führer."*

"Do you mean that you like Adolf Hitler?" asked the defense.

"No, I do not," Rigger snapped back.

Judge Wallace jumped in. "We can take it for granted," he instructed Sabbatino, "that he doesn't like a hair on Hitler's head."

Sabbatino pressed on. "What do you think about the Bund and Kuhn?" he asked.

"You want me to be truthful? I have no use for them."

The courtroom erupted in laughter over the verbal give-and-take. Kuhn, a stoic presence at the defense table throughout jury selection, managed to work up a bitter smile.

Robert Jordon, a New York business executive, told the attorneys point blank that he considered the Bund to be an "un-American" group but felt he could put his feelings aside to give the accused a fair hearing. Surprisingly, he was empaneled.[10]

Other jurors included a sales engineer, a bank official, a hotel manager, a superintendent of a steamship company, a motor company officer, a banker, an insurance man, a retired economist, and three trust company employees. Two alternates were also selected, an artist and an electrical engineer.[11]

The fourteen were all white males and all Gentiles. Sabbatino served up a straight-faced claim that an all-Jewish jury would have been perfect for his client. "Jews have been persecuted for centuries," he told unbelieving reporters. "They know what persecution is and are tolerant." Given defense's efforts to purge Jews from the jury box, it's difficult to ponder the thought process driving Sabbatino's absurd theory.[12]

Opening statements began on Friday, November 10. McCarthy immediately dived into the prurient elements of the case. There was no interest by the State over Kuhn's involvement with either Florence Camp or Virginia

Cogswell, the prosecutor explained. Rather the two women were being brought into the mix to prove Kuhn had used Bund money to fund private interests, and then lied about it. His paramours were merely components within the charges. Camp, he said, was not simply a Kuhn acquaintance or an outsider sympathetic to Bund causes. "We will show," McCarthy told the jury, "in [Kuhn's] own handwriting, that she was more than a casual friend, and that his interest in her was keenly sentimental."

For his part, Sabbatino told the jury that Kuhn was nothing more than a victim of Thomas Dewey's ambition, that the prosecution was using the case for "political motives." Furthermore, given that under the Leadership Principle Kuhn had complete control of all organization funds, providing money for his extramarital affairs fell well within the Bund constitution and hence no crime had been committed.

The first witness called to the stand by prosecution was James Wheeler-Hill. As national secretary of the Bund it was his duty to handle all financial records and other responsibilities as stated in the group's constitution. Under McCarthy's questioning, Wheeler-Hill admitted that he had no training in the job. Records? He never kept records.[13] Either Wheeler-Hill was lying or just plain inept. According to Section Three of the Bundist constitution, "Duties and Powers of the National Secretary," he had to keep a repository of all correspondence and documents, and work with the national treasurer to "attest to all signatures of the National Leader on any instruments for the disbursement of Monies of the Bund."[14]

Next up was Gustave Elmer, the ex-bartender turned Bund organizer from Hoboken, New Jersey. McCarthy pressed him on Kuhn's alleged abuse of the Leadership Principle. Under the laws of the Bund, McCarthy asked the witness, could the *Bundesführer* use the organization's money for his dalliances?

Elmer, who started off as a reluctant witness, erupted in anger. "I said to spend it for a woman is not right, to spend it for a woman should not be done."

When McCarthy tried to push the issue further Sabbatino jumped in, demanding Judge Wallace declare a mistrial. Wallace ordered the jury into their cloisters so the two attorneys could slug it out. For fifteen minutes defense and prosecution argued fine points of the law with the judge. Sabbatino hammered home that his client was not on trial for being a lothario. McCarthy, he argued, was "trying to paint my client as a gay boy."

Wallace sternly disagreed. "This man isn't on trial either as a gay boy or a sad boy. Let's get on with it."[15]

Periodically Kuhn would focus a hard stare in particular on one reporter covering the trial, his long-running nemesis Walter Winchell.[16]

Kuhn's day in court was a cornucopia of salacious joy spilling out of Winchell's typewriter. He reveled with over-the-top zeal in every last tidbit that could be squeezed out of the proceedings. Winchell treated *The People v. Fritz Kuhn* not as a criminal trial but as comic theater. Rather than his usual venue of his column, Winchell lampooned the proceedings in a series of separate *Daily Mirror* stories.

His first piece, published on November 11, led off under bold type: "Winchell in Bunderland." "The People vs. Fritz Kuhn is the official title of the melodrama now being staged in Judge James Garrett Wallace's court," read the lead. The story ripped out in short paragraph bursts, each one sharpened with stiletto syllables and scalpel sarcasm. Sabbatino was dubbed "Kuhn's kapable kounsel," who was overruled "more often than any husband is by any mother-in-law." "The early session disclosed that Kuhn's middle initial is 'J,'" Winchell noted. Though it was public knowledge the defendant's middle name was Julius, the columnist had other ideas for what the letter represented. ". . . [T]he 'J' couldn't possibly stand for Jehovah or Jeeves. It could be for Julius as in Caesar, Jesse as in James, Jake as in Jerk or Jack as in donkey."

Winchell noted that during a bench discussion, ". . . Fritz got bored and began flirting with us!!! He turned on his charm and gave us a Casaba melon grin. A concrete example of hate at first sight."[17]

Day after day Winchell pounded out the taunts. One headline read, "Da Ist Wieder Der Vinchell!" The subhead provided a handy translation: "If you're inquisitive, this means idiomatically, 'Here's that man Winchell again.'" The story was credited to "Herr Winchell."[18] Another story "Unser Volter's Veenchill-View," took an alphabetic swipe at the initials of the NSDAP with a byline reading "By Herr Vinchell, N.Y.D.C.C*" The asterisk led readers to the bottom of the story for the playful explanation of "New York Drama Critics Circle."[19]

No detail was too small for Winchell's zings. "Fritz keeps a lemon drop in his kisser," Winchell noted one day. "Poor little lemon drop!"[20]

When West Coast gau leader Hermann Schwinn took the stand,

Winchell remarked how calm and collected the man initially seemed under prosecutor's questioning. As the defense cross-examination escalated into harder edges, Winchell told readers that Schwinn's ". . . temperature lifted high and his color made him look like an over-rouged chorus boy." Winchell noted that Schwinn was the first Bund witness who did not speak with a German-inflected dialect. "He has a dialect in his brain, however."[21]

At one point a gleeful Winchell picked up on a delicious irony. "Haw! The prosecutor accidentally called Kuhn 'Kohn!'"[22]

Sabbatino called on James Wheeler-Hill to underscore the basic tenet of the Leadership Principle. Yes, Wheeler-Hill said, the *Bundesführer* was supreme ruler and thus could use funds as he saw fit. On cross-examination, McCarthy demanded Wheeler-Hill elaborate the point. The witness showed a line in the Bundist Constitution: "[The] Office of National Leader renders the final decision in all matters pertaining to the Movement and has the absolute power of ownership over the Bund, its monetary or other property and its policies . . ."[23]

Judge Wallace jumped in.

". . . [Y]ou say he can do anything he wants with the money?"

"He can do anything absolutely," Wheeler-Hill replied.

"Do anything?"

"Yes, sir."

Wallace ramped up the questions. "He can use it to buy a race horse?"

"Yes."

"He can use it to buy a cargo of liquor?"

"Yes, sir."

"Throw it down the sewer?"

"Absolutely."

Again Sabbatino was furious with the judge's one-liners and blasted Wallace. ". . . Your Honor's cross-examination of this witness has created the inference you do not believe this witness."

Another defense motion for mistrial, like all the others, was denied.[24]

McCarthy pressed his case on Kuhn's diversion of Bund money to pay for his romances. Seventy-nine separate checks drawn from the Bundist treasury were presented as evidence Kuhn was diverting funds for his personal use. One check, made out for $567.76 covered Camp's relocation costs for a move from Los Angeles to New York. A second check for $151.26 covered her move from New York to Cleveland. Three telegrams sent to Camp were also introduced to the court, each one signed "love and kisses."

Throughout the presentation Kuhn sank low into his chair, as though he wished the floor would open up and take him far away from the courtroom.[25]

The *Bundesführer*'s dalliances underwent further scrutiny when Dr. La Sorsa, Virginia Cogswell's physician, was called to the witness stand. McCarthy introduced another check, this one for five hundred dollars made out to "Cash." Dr. La Sorsa identified it as the payment to cover Cogswell's medical bills written by Kuhn from Bundist accounts.[26]

The undercover work by Richard Rollins now proved its worth. The check was clear-cut proof that Kuhn was using Bund money for personal expenses. As an added but legally negligible bonus, this evidence gave a sexual zing to reporters who were looking for a sensational angle to juice up their stories.

Yet when it came to Kuhn's peccadillos, the best stuff for hungry newsmen was still to come.

One day Sabbatino made seven appeals for a mistrial. Five of the charges were in response to Judge Wallace's questioning from the bench of defense witnesses.

In each case the request was denied. Frustrated by Wallace's continued rebuffs Sabbatino made an exasperated appeal. "[T]hree times on this record Your Honor has reflected on my understanding of English," he said.

Wallace was infuriated. "I make no such reflection. You seem deliberately to attempt to misunderstand."

An angry Sabbatino cackled in frustration. "I am without resources to defend myself," he said.

"You're defending yourself beautifully. Now sit down," the judge replied.

Sabbatino refused, and demanded yet another mistrial. Wallace denied the request and again ordered the defense attorney to take his seat.

"I take an exception," Sabbatino said.

"You always have an exception. Sit down." The verbal duel ended.[27]

A good chunk of the prosecution's case was based on money Kuhn allegedly misappropriated in the wake of previous legal action in Riverhead, a Long Island community not far from Camp Siegfried. A year and a half earlier, in July 1938, six members of the German-American Settlement League, one of the Bund's subsidiary corporations, were brought to trial for violating an obscure state law requiring that any group requiring a loyalty oath by its fellows provide a membership list to the New York Secretary of State's office. Though the law was in flagrant violation of the First Amendment, legal authorities viewed the case as a method to chip away at the Bund's hold in Long Island.[28]

The Riverhead prosecution hinged its case on the testimony of one "Willy Karl Friedrich Von Mach Brandt," a twenty-six-year-old German immigrant who used the ham-fisted alias allegedly to protect the identities of family members back in Germany, including his father who'd served as an ambassador. For his part, Brandt was a dubious witness. He testified that upon joining the Bund he took an oath pledging allegiance to Adolf Hitler and fidelity to "those put in charge by him and well known to me." When asked who gave him the oath and if there were any other Bundists at the ceremony, Brandt could not provide a single name.

On May 5, about two months before the Riverhead trial began, Brandt was picked up by police for swiping a five hundred dollar ring. Compounding his criminal act, Brandt was in the country illegally, having overstayed his visa. To their credit, the Bund had ejected Brandt from the organization for not being an American citizen and joining under a phony name.

Ultimately Brandt's testimony mattered little. What really won the case for the prosecution was a parade of defense witnesses who could have stepped out of the pages of a Bund yearbook. One man wore a swastika lapel pin while giving his testimony. An elderly Bund sympathizer, born in the U.S. in the post–Civil War era, declared that German–Americans were treated far worse in the U.S. than Jews in Germany, based on what she'd seen firsthand on a recent trip to the Fatherland. Another witness for the defense, also American born, ranted about centuries-old Jewish oppression of Christianity. When asked if he was anti-Jewish as opposed to anti-Semitic, the witness replied, "There are some good Semites." However, he had yet to meet a Jew that he could call "good" in any way, shape, or form.

For his part, Kuhn—who attended the trial with an unknown pretty blonde woman—confronted Judge L. Baron Hill outside the courtroom, demanding a mistrial. "The guy," Kuhn declared in his broken accent, "he lie."

"Who says he lies?" the judge asked.

"I do."

Kuhn's standing amongst the Bundist minions meant nothing to Judge Hill. If Brandt was indeed committing perjury, he told Kuhn, "then go out and testify on the witness stand." The *Bundesführer* backed down.

On July 12, the Riverhead case went to the jury, all of whom were German-born naturalized American citizens. It took them just two minutes to reach their verdict: the German-American Settlement League was guilty as charged. A fine of ten thousand dollars was imposed and the so-called "Riverhead Six" were each sentenced to one year's jail time. Sentences were suspended, though Ernest Mueller, head of the Brooklyn Bund, was sent to jail for nineteen days.

Kuhn wasted no time to exploit the situation. That night he was at the Yorkville Turnhalle, railing against the "Jewish plot" behind the Riverhead trial.[29] On July 21, the *Deutscher Weckruf und Beobachter* published a full-page appeal, headlined "Help! Help!"

Money was needed, Kuhn told his readers, to overturn the verdict. He argued—correctly—that the Bund was convicted solely on the testimony of a witness of dubious merit.

This appeal was perfectly sensible to any solid constitutionalist. Had any other group used this wording in a *New York Times* or *Chicago Daily Tribune* advertisement, public sentiment would have fallen on the side of the wrongfully convicted. Yet one item in the *Deutscher Weckruf und Beobachter* ad clearly separated Kuhn from other victims of the judicial system. He compared his unfavorable verdict to that of another German target of the American courts: the late Bruno Hauptmann, who'd been executed three years earlier for the kidnapping/murder of the infant Charles Lindbergh.[30]

The Riverhead conviction was overturned three months later in a Brooklyn appeals court. In his ruling in favor of the Bund, Judge George H. Taylor declared, "You can't convict them because they are strange people."[31]

In the interim between the Riverhead conviction and successful appeal, cash poured into the Bund coffers. Money over which *Bundesführer* Fritz Kuhn held total control.

Now the Riverhead trial was coming back to haunt him. Three attorneys, William I. Karle, Joseph Lonardo, and James D. C. Murray, hired by Fritz

Kuhn to appeal the decision, were brought to the stand. Karle and Lonardo both testified that they had been unceremoniously dumped from Kuhn's Riverhead defense, never received promised fees, and were now suing the Bund for money owed. "Both were excited and voluble witnesses," noted *The New York Times.*

Murray's testimony was much more damning. He'd previously helped Kuhn on other legal issues for a fee of one thousand dollars. When Kuhn asked for assistance with the Riverhead case, Murray agreed to help. The two settled on a flat fee of five hundred dollars for services rendered. Yet each time the attorney set up a meeting, Kuhn would cancel or break the appointment. Murray decided enough was enough. He sent a letter to Kuhn on July 2, 1938, announcing that he was withdrawing from the case and sent a bill of $250 for services rendered. There was, Murray told the court, no response to this letter.[32]

Other lawyers and court watchers might have wondered about the legal and business acumen of Karle, Lonardo, and Murray. None of them worked out a formal contract with Kuhn, instead relying solely on oral agreements with their infamous client. As Lonardo explained from the witness stand, when he told Kuhn that they should seal their arrangement in writing, the *Bundesführer* was outraged. "I'm afraid you don't understand who you're dealing with," Kuhn told him. "My word is my bond."

Of Kuhn, Lonardo told the court—twice, "I like him personally."[33]

The prosecution received a major and unexpected blow in its case thanks to an error by Benjamin Blattner, an accountant with the D.A.'s office.

A lynchpin in Dewey's case against Kuhn was that the *Bundesführer* stole $5,614 and change from the Bund coffers. This original 4,000 plus figure should have been only $674. However, the books showed that $3,678 was missing, plus Murray's $500, the $717 used for Florence Camp's cross-country moves, and Virginia Cogswell's $60 doctor's bill. Furthermore, a receipt for $3,678, previously unaccounted for by the D.A.'s office, unexpectedly showed up without explanation. Additionally, there was a general disbursement from the Bund bank account of $11,215, which included the Riverhead defense fund. There was no distinction in how this money was used. There should have been $4,024. On October 24, 1938 there was only $745, which could possibly explain away the $3,600 plus discrepancy. In his defense, Kuhn claimed that his bookkeeping was incomplete and in poor condition, thereby making it impossible to tell exactly how much was missing from the treasury.

It appeared that the only thing Kuhn might be guilty of was keeping poor financial records.

Sabbatino was furious. He asked that the Bundists be allowed to let their own accountants comb over the books, which Judge Wallace granted.[34] The trial was recessed for the day and Bund records were examined at the courthouse. Kuhn was in the room while the moneymen went through his sloppy notes and scribbles. He answered all question posed, while nervously chain-smoking and pacing up and down the room throughout the ordeal.[35]

When court went back into session, Judge Wallace granted Sabbatino unexpected permission to question Blattner regarding two counts against Kuhn brought up during closed-door grand jury hearings but not at the public trial. Under oath, it was revealed Blattner's total was $8,907 and change misappropriated by Kuhn. Wheeler-Hill's grand jury testimony proved that $7,000 of this figure never existed. Further questioning by Sabbatino uncovered that Blattner had assumed that the money was deposited in a Bund bank account. The government's star financial witness had presumed without any evidence that such a financial transaction explained any bookkeeping discrepancy.

For once Judge Wallace sided with the defense, admonishing the prosecution that, "lacking proof that the money was improperly spent, there was left a large amount not proved as larceny 'beyond a reasonable doubt.'"[36]

Between Blattner's foul ups, the Bund's poor record keeping, and Judge Wallace's unexpected sympathy for the defense, Fritz Kuhn could breathe a little easier. For the moment, at least.

The revelation affirmed one of Sabbatino's solid beliefs, that the mayor, Dewey, and other top honchos collaborated behind closed doors to destroy Fritz Kuhn for their own political gain. LaGuardia had a city to run and a partisan machine to maintain. Nailing the notorious Fritz Kuhn would improve his standings in voter's eyes. Dewey had made a failed but popular run for New York State governor the previous year, and now was being talked in some circles as a potential presidential candidate in 1940. In a country paying close attention to Hitler's Reich and any possible connection to the

German-American Bund, bringing down the *Bundesführer* and smashing his organization could go a long way to improve and solidify the public images of both men.

With this in mind, Sabbatino fearlessly plunged into a chancy legal move. Mayor Fiorello LaGuardia and District Attorney Thomas Dewey, and other city officials should be called as witnesses for the defense. It was an unorthodox strategy filled with great risks. If he could plant the seed of reasonable doubt in the jurors' minds, Sabbatino could prove there was a conspiracy in higher circles to bring down his client via extralegal means. But should the tactic go wrong on any point, the case would implode through disastrous self-sabotage.

And so it did. Sabbatino's dangerous ploy collapsed the moment Mayor LaGuardia was called to the witness stand. Over Sabbatino's objections, Judge Wallace cut off questioning and dismissed the first high-powered witness before defense counsel could ask a single question. Mayor LaGuardia—ever the showman—gave a comic bow to defense, jury, and judge.

It was just the beginning. In rapid succession the judge denied Sabbatino's call for testimony from Police Commissioner Valentine or City Treasurer Portfolio.

One big name remained. To everyone's great surprise, Judge Wallace allowed that Dewey could be called as a defense witness.

On November 17, the day scheduled for this noteworthy courtroom action, a few Bundists were brought to the stand by the defense, squeezed into the schedule in anticipation of the district attorney's later arrival. Sabbatino used these witnesses, ranging from rank and file to higher-ups, to bolster the position that under the German-American Bund constitution, their Leadership Principle permitted Kuhn to use any organization funds as he saw fit. Each witness attested to the correctness of Kuhn's word as final pronouncement. One dues-paying member told the court that he saw this element of Bundist law as an "advanced form of democracy."

As George Forboese, the Midwestern leader, was about to testify under McCarthy's cross-examination, there was a sudden break in the action. The doors at the back of the courtroom opened. A lone figure walked into the gallery, a sly smile playing about his mustachioed lips, hands nonchalantly held in his coat pockets as though he hadn't a care in the world.

District Attorney Thomas Dewey entered the courtroom.

Sabbatino motioned that Froboese's testimony be suspended for the time being and Dewey be questioned by defense.

Dewey waved his hand toward the magistrate. "No, no, Your Honor, please do not let me interrupt," he said.

Wallace disagreed. He cut off the district attorney's little show and ordered him to take the stand. The smile disappeared from Dewey's face.

For the first time that day, Sabbatino seemed to have control over his unconventional strategy. He was determined in his mission and not about to put up with any displays of wry humor from the bemused witness.

"Mr. Dewey," he opened, "you have heard of Fritz Kuhn before today?"

Dewey replied in the affirmative.

"When did you first hear of him?"

Dewey maintained his cool attitude. "Oh, within the past few years when people, when the Bund was started. I don't recall when."

Sabbatino would have none of it. "You have heard of him from the public press?"

Again the affirmative answer.

"Prior to May 2, 1939, did you have a personal animus against this defendant?"

Wallace stopped the proceedings. "What is the object of this query?" he demanded. "Is it your intention to show that there was some illegal seizure of documents? Is that the idea?"

"No," Sabbatino replied, "that is not the purpose of this questioning." The judge allowed defense to resume.

The witness began his answer. "I should say in answer to your question . . ."

Sabbatino, his voice filled with scorn, rebuffed Dewey's obvious amusement. "Well, can I have a yes or no answer to that," he demanded. Defense turned to Judge Wallace with the curt explanation that he wanted a concise understanding of Dewey's overall feelings toward Kuhn.

"I will allow the district attorney to answer that more fully than a yes or no if he wants to," the judge said.

For once, it seemed, Sabbatino understood that he should pull back, telling the judge he would "respectfully" accept the witness's answer.

Dewey completed his response. Having never met Kuhn it would be impossible to hold any individual feelings against the *Bundesführer* one way or other. "On the other hand," he continued, "I must say that I regarded him as a nuisance to the community and probably a threat to civil liberties and the proper preservation of the American system if he should become more important than he was."

Sabbatino pounced. "As a matter of fact," he said, "you have got a very strong hatred against the German-American Bund. I think you can answer that yes or no."

Again, Wallace denied defense a straight-up one-word answer. Dewey responded in full form, telling Sabbatino that "hatred" was the wrong word to describe his feelings. "[I]t is really merely contempt," he said.

Sabbatino was clearly frustrated, a man caught in a trap of his own devising. He fired back with a rhetorical question. "Well, you call it contempt?"

"I should say, if you were willing to use the word 'contempt,' my answer is that I definitely had it, contempt."

Wallace stopped the proceedings, instructing the jury that they were to ignore Dewey's opinion of the Bund and Fritz Kuhn. Once more the judge asked Sabbatino where defense was taking this line of questions. It was his contention, Sabbatino said, to establish Dewey and others based their prosecution of Kuhn on nothing more than "feelings of hostility." Exasperated, Wallace demanded Sabbatino explain why this was necessary. In a long-winded response, defense wound out an intricate theory of a plot to destroy Kuhn that could have been hatched in the district attorney's office. In essence Dewey created an environment within his staff where any possible way to bring down Kuhn would be acceptable. The end result, Sabbatino claimed, was that ". . . evidence has been distorted and records have disappeared."

The court allowed for it and Sabbatino surged forward. He questioned Dewey about a speech he'd given in Riverhead in the wake of the Bund's legal issues following their July 1938 rally. "Do you recall attacking the German-American Bund in that address?"

McCarthy jumped in with an objection. Dewey waved him off. "Please," he said with unruffled assurance, "I will take care of myself." Dewey hadn't risen to the top of his game by being a fool. He smiled at the jury, many of whom were smiling themselves. Turning back to counsel, he told Sabbatino, "If you want to know what I said about the German-American Bund, I would be delighted to repeat it under oath."

Sabbatino ignored the wisecrack and reworded his question, asking if the witness ever referred to the Bund when giving a political speech. Dewey

explained that during his Riverhead talk he had congratulated the local
D.A. for enforcing statutes.

From there, Sabbatino laid out a convoluted line of questioning, grilling
Dewey on timelines of his investigation of Kuhn the previous May. Dewey
was impenetrable, sticking to his contention that no prejudices were nur-
tured against Kuhn within the district attorney's office.

Dewey's testimony carried into the next morning. Sabbatino introduced
a letter sent on May 22 from LaGuardia to Dewey, which included an editorial cartoon from an Oregon newspaper. The drawing depicted Dewey
tugging on Kuhn from one side and LaGuardia on the other, with a caption
reading, "I saw him first." A note on the clipping in LaGuardia's handwriting read, "Dear Tom, you can have him." A note back from Dewey, dated
June 7, read "Dear Fiorello . . . Many thanks for the gift. I don't want him
either. I guess the ashcan is the best place for him."

Sabbatino switched the line of questioning. Had Dewey been involved in
preparing any witnesses for this trial? Wallace disavowed the question. Defense tried follow up after follow up, but again was shot down by the judge
each time.

Sabbatino had one last desperate attempt to show prejudice against his
client from the top-down command within the D.A.'s office labyrinthine
structure. Was Dewey widely quoted in New York newspapers as calling
Kuhn nothing more than "a common thief"? McCarthy objected; Wallace
ordered the jury to ignore the exchange.

Sabbatino was a beaten man. Dewey was quickly cross-examined by his
employee McCarthy and with precision and accuracy turned Sabbatino's
strategy on its head. "I should say that I have a prejudice against the German-
American Bund," Dewey concluded, "and I have not use for it, but that has
nothing to do with the performance of my duties." If this animus was a factor in prosecuting Fritz Kuhn, Dewey told the court, then "I should be removed from this office." With that, Thomas Dewey was excused from the
stand.[37]

The next government official to face off with Sabbatino was Commissioner
of Investigation Herlands, who testified that he had looked into the Bund's
taxes following a discussion with LaGuardia.

Sabbatino thought he'd found solid evidence to support his conspiracy theory and started to press the point. Again Judge Wallace cut him off. Exactly where was this line of questioning going? Once more, Sabbatino said he was attempting to uncover a scheme developed by Dewey to bring down Fritz Kuhn. The judge dismissed the defense's argument as "far fetched," but Sabbatino persisted. Hadn't Blattner's admission of faulty accounting shown something was amiss? Couldn't this be a hard look into deliberate mishandling by the D.A.'s office as part of some overall machination?

"I will not permit further testimony on that line," Judge Wallace snapped, "and if you persist after I have ruled I will take appropriate action."

Sabbatino remained feisty. He accused Wallace of trying to "intimidate counsel following the age-old custom of performing his duty to see that a defendant gets a fair trial from everyone."

Wallace looked at Sabbatino with smoldering anger. "That remark is contemptuous and I'll take action on it at a proper time."

Sabbatino apologized to the court, adding with perhaps a subtle hint of sarcasm that he was "endeavoring to be respectful at all times."

"Your statement is on the record," Wallace replied.

The trial dismissed for the weekend. The next witness would have to wait a few more days to give his testimony.[38]

On Tuesday, November 21, came the moment every courtroom watcher and reporter was waiting for. *Bundesführer* Fritz Kuhn was called to the stand.

Gone was the towering leader of the Washington's Birthday Rally nine months ago. The confrontational jokester from the August congressional hearings was at bay. Fritz Kuhn was now a subdued man, voice uncharacteristically quiet.

He began with a brief autobiography: married, two children, came to America and worked at Ford Motors as a chemist, became Bund leader in 1936. When asked by Sabbatino if since ascending to the Bund's top commander Kuhn had always enforced the Leadership Principle, the answer was barely audible.

"I have," he said.

Once the Bund membership handed over complete control of all finances to the *Bundesführer*, Kuhn explained, he could then use the money "as I saw fit."

From there, defense entered a new legal minefield. Kuhn had to justify his financial assistance to Florence Camp. Yes, he had met her while traveling to Belgium in 1938. Yes, he'd written a check on the Bund account for $565.76 to pay for her moving expenses from Los Angeles to Cleveland. And yes, he did have "a liking for Mrs. Camp."

Kuhn explained that Camp was interested in Bund activities and wanted to be part of the women's division. She later paid back the loan with cash. Likewise, her move from Cleveland to New York was settled when Camp gave Kuhn $200 in cash, money provided before he cut a check for $151.26 for other Bund business. What happened to the balance of that $200 was not said.

And, Kuhn emphasized, even if Camp hadn't recompensed the loans, it didn't matter. As *Bundesführer*, he could spend the Bund money however he saw fit.

Next up was Murray and the Riverhead case. As Kuhn detailed it, Murray's fee was $5,000, of which he received $1,000 "for about twenty minutes in the courtroom." When Kuhn learned that Murray planned to subcontract the case to other attorneys, he decided to withhold the rest of the payment.

"Simple people that we are, we thought that if Mr. Murray is going to hire a lawyer to represent us, we might hire one for ourselves," he told the court. As for Karle and Lonardo, Kuhn stated he'd written out a check to himself, cashed it, then sent the money to the two attorneys via his subordinate William Leudtke, national secretary of the Bund.

On and on it went, with Kuhn patiently answering Sabbatino's questions. Murray's payment was made on July 8, but recorded as July 28. This was, he explained, a result of hodgepodge bookkeeping methods. Kuhn would mark down various payments on scraps of paper over the course of days or weeks, then put all the disbursements into the accounting books on a single day. Other deposits and payments might be written down in the margins of his ledgers, rather than in the proper columns.

Sabbatino went to the heart of the case.

"Did you steal a single cent of defense fund money?"

"I did not."

"Did you use every cent for purposes you thought you had a right to use them for?"

"Yes, I did."

"Did you intend to steal when you drew the check for Mrs. Camp?"

"No. I drew from my own account." The $60 he used for Dr. La Sorsa was also drawn from his personal account, Kuhn told the court.[39]

This was clear-cut perjury. Dr. La Sorsa's Photostat of the check procured during Richard Rollins's undercover investigation proved this money had been drawn from the German-American Bund checking account.[40]

Kuhn's testimony grew laborious as he detailed various check stubs, deposits, and withdrawals. Judge Wallace attempted to follow the convoluted trail, writing down each figure on a yellow legal pad. Some jurors followed suit, scribbling numbers on the backs of envelopes. When Kuhn finally concluded his mathematical journey, the judge wearily told him, "We'll take your word for it."

The day ended with a lengthy list of investigations and inquiries made about the Bund overall and the *Bundesführer* personally. Kuhn gave another perjurous statement, telling the court that he "never before was charged with a crime."

It would appear Fritz Kuhn explained himself. McCarthy had other ideas.

The prosecution hit hard and fast the next day. Kuhn could not provide a straight answer when asked about the source of the thirteen hundred plus in cash he claimed was stolen from his desk by the D.A.'s office. The *Bundesführer* conflicted himself over both the source and recipient of another five hundred dollar check. Throughout McCarthy's questioning, Kuhn maintained his unusual subdued voice.

McCarthy focused on the relationship with Florence Camp. Was there a marriage proposal made to her? Kuhn flatly denied it.

Prosecution had been waiting for this moment.

McCarthy introduced three letters to the court written by "Fritz" to his "Darling." His contention was these documents were necessary to show why Kuhn provided Bund money for his lover's needs. Wallace allowed it, but advised jurors that Kuhn was being charged with larceny and not adultery.

The first was short and quick, written to Camp while she and Kuhn were aboard the *Westernland*. Before McCarthy began to read, Kuhn confirmed the penmanship was indeed his.

"Florence—I am terrible in love with you [sic] I beg you to become my beloved wife. I will always be real true to you and I will love you forever. I can be [sic] without you any more because I realize haven [sic] did send you and I never will forget you."

"Do you still deny that you proposed marriage to Florence Camp?" Mc-Carthy asked.

Kuhn's face was deep crimson.

"It was after a party. It was only in fun," he replied.

Judge Wallace leaped into the fray. "What were your relations with Mrs. Camp? Was she your mistress?"

Kuhn's subdued tones found sudden strength. The answer was loud, forceful, and rippling with anger. "She certainly was not," he spat back.

McCarthy introduced two more letters, one dated May 20, 1938 and the other June 11, 1938. They were classic mash notes, stuffed with passionate and starry-eyed romantic embellishment worthy of a schoolboy in the sweet agony of young love, penned in broken English, and tinged with occasional dips into anti-Semitic paranoia. "So you have gained 15 lbs—do I love that?" he wrote on May 20. "Yes, sweetheart, I like it, of course it makes not difference [sic] to me how heavy you are and how you look—I love you and that is all." He effusively thanked Camp for the birthday present of a wrist-watch. "I have no words—I just cried as I got it." Asking about the status of her ongoing divorce, Kuhn tenderly referred to Camp as "my soul—my wife and my everything."

Kuhn boasted that "the Jews" were afraid of him. Calling Camp his "Golden Angel," Kuhn closed his letter, "I kiss you until you tell me to stop—I kiss your hands and everything."

The June 11 letter contained more of the same. Kuhn piled on amorous hyperboles, discussed possible marriage plans, and playfully asked Camp, "what does your family say that you are going to Marry Public Enemy Number One, as the Jewish papers call me today." Much of the letter to "my beloved darling wife" crowed over his victory against anti-Bund forces at a rally in Schenectady, New York. "[T]he C.I.O., the Jews and the Communists had a meeting and decided that Kuhn can't come to Schenectady and if he comes they will try to kill him," he wrote. He bragged of a mob riot determined to stop him as streets overflowed with thousands of protestors.

The scene, as recounted by Kuhn, grew dangerous. "There was a shot fired which of course missed me but went through the window of my car." After the rally Kuhn received a police escort out of town, "but our meeting was great success."

Kuhn closed with, "I am kissing you and take you in my arms—always yours forever—Fritz."

McCarthy was just warming up. There were eight more letters to go. Wallace called the two attorneys to a conference at the bench. Rather than subject the courtroom to more of Kuhn's purple prose, the remaining letters should be put aside. McCarthy was instructed to ask the defendant questions based on content. Both counsels agreed. Without objection McCarthy continued his humiliating line of questioning to the cowed defendant.

"Did you tell Mrs. Camp that September 24 should be your wedding day?"

"Yes."

"Did you tell her you were ready to go to Mexico and had the travelers checks prepared?"

"Yes."

"Were you lying to her when you told her that?"

"Yes."

"Did you tell her you were going to resign from the Bund?"

Kuhn perjured himself again, claiming he'd tried to relinquish his position numerous times, but his membership "wouldn't let me."

McCarthy returned to the romance. "In a letter dated June 14, 1939, did you tell her 'my divorce papers will be sent to you in a few days'?"

"Yes."

"Did you say to her in that letter that everybody in the Bund office had cold feet?"

"Yes."

"When I asked you the same questions this morning you said you hadn't told her any of these things. Where you lying then?"

"Yes. I found out Mrs. Camp is not the fine lady I thought she was."

And exactly how did Kuhn come to this conclusion? "When the letters went into evidence . . ."

McCarthy produced a glittering jewel of a ring. Was this purchased by Kuhn for $240 under the name "Frank Karsten," a man whose address just happened to be the same as the Bund's Yorkville headquarters? While Kuhn admitted to having purchased the ring using that pseudonym, he said it only cost $200, and was intended for Elsa Kuhn. This ring, Kuhn claimed, was paid for with personal funds and not Bund money.

Next McCarthy showed Kuhn page after page of a lengthy phone bill charged to the Bund for calls from New York to Camp's Los Angeles home.

The prosecutor was relentless, a legal jackhammer that showed no signs of stopping. There was plenty to be broken down in Kuhn's illicit liaisons.

Once more Judge Wallace reminded the jury that anything emerging from the letters or other documents related to Kuhn's love life was intended to establish whether or not to they should believe the witness's testimony. Aside from this, Kuhn's love letters had "no value here as literature or anything else."

What did matter was Section 1306 of the Penal Code, which the judge read aloud.

"Upon an indictment for larceny, it is a sufficient defense that property was appropriated openly and avowedly under a claim of title preferred in good faith, even though such claim is untenable."

The rest of the afternoon was anticlimactic. Kuhn was asked about a liquor license for Camp Siegfried, paid to an unknown Brooklyn liquor salesman. Expenditures were $500 for a license that normally cost only $150. And to compound the issue, the camp never received the license.

The questioning was completed. Kuhn was dismissed. Unlike his congressional testimony in August, Kuhn made no sarcastic exit from the witness stand.

The courtroom drama closed for the day. Tomorrow was Thanksgiving. The holiday would be a brief one-day respite for defendant, counsels, judge, and jury.[41]

Court reconvened on Friday, November 24 with Florence Camp taking the stand. Her testimony was a stark contrast to the comic soap opera provided by her former lover. Camp gave a brief recounting of her romantic entanglements with *Bundesführer* Kuhn, beginning with their meeting aboard the *Westernland*. She detailed how Kuhn paid to move her furniture first from Los Angeles to New York, then from New York to Cleveland. She returned the money in three chunks for a total of $550. No, she told McCarthy, she never gave Kuhn a lump sum amount of $565 and change as Kuhn claimed.

The ring Kuhn claimed to have purchased for Elsa was immediately identified by Camp. It was, she said, a gift the *Bundesführer* "gave me for an engagement ring" after her quickie Reno divorce was finalized.

McCarthy tried to pin Camp to Bund activities. Was she a sympathizer or had she ever given money to the organization?

"Never."

Was she ever a member of the woman's division?

"Never."

McCarthy made the point that Camp's testimony contradicted Kuhn's story on two key issues. During a July Bund meeting in Astoria, as the scandal was unfolding, Kuhn told his followers he'd given Camp a loan because of her sympathy to their cause and that the money had been paid back. Additionally, Kuhn claimed that on July 27 he deposited into Bund accounts what supposedly was Camp's repayment; this contradicted her statement that she'd paid back part of the money on July 31 and was unsure about other transaction dates.

In his cross-examination Sabbatino pulled an interesting tidbit from the witness. Following her affair with Kuhn, Camp moved to Miami Beach. Prosecutor McCarthy traveled to Florida twice to get information from her; there were later follow-up interviews in Miami with Camp, conducted by Arthur Robertson, an investigator with Dewey's office. Robertson, the witness explained, spent a little over a month in Florida to discuss the case with her. Prior to Kuhn's trial, she was brought to New York City by the D.A.'s office, and lodged with all expenses paid at a pair of luxurious hotels, first at the Brevoort and then the Berkshire. From there she was moved to a comfortable home in Great Neck, the posh Long Island community where F. Scott Fitzgerald set *The Great Gatsby*. Sabbatino hoped to prove that in the quest to bring down Fritz Kuhn, the prosecution was happy to spare no expense for their witness, and all on the taxpayers' dime.

Camp was dismissed.

And then defense found an unlikely ally in the courtroom.

The intricacies, confusing threads, and creative accounting methods within *The People v. Fritz Kuhn* often seemed ancillary to the cast of characters and salacious details within the courtroom drama. Though Wallace at times appeared to favor the prosecution through his own line of questions, he was a fair-minded magistrate. While he disbelieved Sabbatino's conspiracy theories, he agreed that five of the ten charges against Kuhn should be thrown out.

Two of the dropped charges were the result of Blattner's errors. An agreement was reached between both counselors that other charges would be submitted to the jury as either larceny or embezzlement. With larceny,

Kuhn was a common thief stealing from the Bund treasury. The second option was stronger for the prosecution. The legal definition of embezzlement zeroed in on fraudulent conversion of property or money by someone to whom it is entrusted. Wallace reasoned that the Leadership Principle as outlined in the Bund constitution, coupled with Kuhn's own testimony, did not give him overwhelming authority to use money as he pleased. In essence, Wallace ruled, Kuhn was a trustee of the Bund treasury and thus had the obligation to oversee his responsibilities with wisdom that should come with leadership.

Wallace kept in place the two second-degree larceny and third-degree forgery charges regarding James Murray's testimony that he never was paid for his legal services.[42]

All that remained was summations. From there, Kuhn's fate would be in the hands of twelve jurors.

Before summations commenced, Sabbatino again demanded a mistrial. His client had been all but found guilty and sentenced by the news media, not in the courtroom. Judge Wallace, while denying Sabbatino's request, had some empathy with defense when it came to coverage of *The People v. Fritz Kuhn*. Newspaper reporters, Wallace declared, had skewed their stories to readers with less intelligence than "a moron." "I wish I had the power an English judge has, for I would cheerfully jail some of the editors and writers," he said.

Sabbatino began his summation with a condemnation of Fritz Kuhn, insisting he was not about to "magnify the importance of my client." Kuhn was an ineffective leader of a deplorable movement. However, this did not make him a criminal. Political persecution by Dewey's office was the motivation behind the indictments, not Kuhn's messy financial books. As for the libidinous notes to Florence Camp, these were mere props to tickle the fancy of reporters looking to sell papers. Camp, he told the jury, was manipulated by McCarthy, "the handsomest man in New York and one with brains as well."

Kuhn's romance with Florence Camp should have no bearing on the jury's verdict, he said. "My client is not the first man, even though married, to fall in love with another woman. Not to magnify his importance, even the great Caesar fell in love with Cleopatra."

McCarthy, handsome, brainy, and a historical nitpicker, threw in a wry retort. "You mean Marc Anthony?"

"No," Sabbatino shot back. "I mean Julius Caesar. Cleopatra had a child by him. Marc played second fiddle." And Caesar wasn't the only emperor to find romance beyond the marital bed. Had not Napoleon romped with Marie Walewska whilst still married to Josephine?

As for the claims by Murray over the missing five hundred dollars, Sabbatino insisted Kuhn kept records of the transaction. Seizure of the Bund books was despotism by authorities.

Fritz Kuhn, Sabbatino said, was a legal kinsman to Albert Dreyfus, the Jewish French artillery officer wrongly convicted of treason by an anti-Semitic judicial system. Like Dreyfus, Kuhn was a "victim of political persecution." If the *Bundesführer* objected to the comparison with a wrongly convicted Jewish soldier, he gave no indication.

Sabbatino ended with the words of French philosopher Voltaire who, like Kuhn, was a notorious anti-Semite. Paraphrasing Voltaire's famous dictum on the right to free speech, Sabbatino declared, "I utterly detest what you stand for but will fight to the death for your right to say it."[43]

McCarthy took his place before the jury, telling them that this case should be decided on the facts, plain and simple. Pointing an accusatory finger at the defendant, McCarthy declared, "Fritz Kuhn has a pathological condition for not telling the truth." He fired off a long list of lies Kuhn delivered in August to the Dies Committee, and then on the witness stand. For two and a half hours McCarthy poured it on. He wrapped up with a sarcastic sneer directed at the *Bundesführer*. ". . . [T]his poor innocent flower," McCarthy sneered, "was the victim."

Kuhn merely looked at his fingernails, as if he had nothing more to worry about than an errant hangnail.[44]

Before final instructions, Judge Wallace sent out the jury to face down both lawyers one last time. Once the jury was gone, Sabbatino again moved for a mistrial. He fired one reason after another. The prosecution's summation, calling Kuhn's defense nothing but a fabrication, was in Sabbatino's words, an "unfair and dastardly attack." It was, Sabbatino thundered, the "most vicious I ever heard in twenty-three years of service as a lawyer."

"I've heard a good deal worse in my twenty-five years around here," was Wallace's dry response.

Sabbatino continued, unbowed and unbroken. Words fell upon words, his tongue tangled up in a torrent of motions and demands. Wallace could take no more. "You're utterly lacking in self-control, and you're trying to work yourself into a lather. You'd better calm down," he ordered counsel.

Shortly after eleven A.M. Judge Wallace called back the jury and commenced with his instructions. The task took one hour and twenty-five minutes.

"Take this case and decide it on the law," Judge Wallace concluded. "Do not be concerned about who your verdict hits or who it helps."

And with that, twelve men were sent to a sequestered room where they would decide on Kuhn's guilt or innocence.[45]

Hours of deliberation dragged. McCarthy paced up and down the hall outside the courtroom. Kuhn remained at the defense table with his attorney, enjoying a sandwich. At nine o'clock tension ratcheted up when word came from the jury room. No, it was not a verdict. The jury needed a re-reading of the instructions Judge Wallace gave regarding the charges involving Kuhn's financial matters with Florence Camp. The response was straightforward: If the twelve men believed the Leadership Principle gave Kuhn the right to do as he pleased with the Bund treasury, and if they believed his claim that he took Bund money as debt owed on a drawing account, the defendant must be found not guilty.

Another thirty minutes went by. Then the announcement came. After eight and a half hours of deliberation, a verdict was reached in the case of *The People v. Fritz Kuhn*.

Court reconvened. Judge Wallace asked the jury foreman for the final decision. Kuhn stood military straight, hands pressed against the seam of his pants, eyes fixed and unblinking.

The verdict was read.

Guilty of larceny in the first degree and guilty of larceny in the second degree for diverting Bund money to pay for Camp's cross-country moves. Guilty of larceny in the second degree for appropriating five hundred dollars of Bund money intended to pay attorney James Murray. Guilty on two charges of forgery in the third degree for falsifying Bund account books to hide the money diverted from Murray's payment.

There was no emotion on Kuhn's face. The index finger of his left hand danced nervously along the seam of his pants.

For the five counts the *Bundesführer* could spend up to thirty years in prison.

A bailiff led Kuhn through a door separated from the courtroom by a wire screen. The door led to a bridge separating the courtroom from the Tombs.

The passageway was commonly known as the Bridge of Sighs.[46]

News of the verdict quickly hit the streets. In Yorkville, the lights at the German-American Bund headquarters remained on. No one answered reporters' repeated knocks on the door. Whoever might be inside was sealed from the outside world.[47]

On Wednesday, December 6, Kuhn, furiously working on a wad of gum in his mouth, was led back into Judge Wallace's courtroom for sentencing. Chomping halted as he stood before the court. Did he have anything to say in his favor before the decision was handed down? "Nothing," was the barely audible answer.

It was Sabbatino's turn. He pleaded with Judge Wallace that his client should not be considered as a notorious public figure, but as any other ordinary man convicted of the same crimes. Wallace agreed. Fritz Kuhn was, he said, ". . . an ordinary small-time forger and thief." The sentence would reflect only these crimes, not ". . . his disseminations of any gospels of hate or anything of that sort."

For the two counts of diverting Bund money to Florence Camp, suspended sentence. For the remaining count of larceny and two counts of forgery, two and a half to five years for each offense, with sentences to be served concurrently. Eligible for parole after two-thirds of time served. The prisoner was marshaled back to his cell to await transportation to Sing Sing, New York State's infamous maximum-security prison, home to the hardest of hard-core criminals.

But Wallace wasn't done. Looking directly at Kuhn's allies in the courtroom, Gerhard Wilhelm Kunze, James Wheeler-Hill, William Leudtke, and Gustave Elmer, Wallace addressed the quartet, denouncing "this small fry aggregation of busboys, locker-room attendants, bartenders and other small fry." The Bund, he declared, "would not amount to anything if other rabble rousers did not attack Kuhn and Kuhn did not attack other rabble rousers. The newspapers cast a big shadow over the whole screen and built his type up. They get an exaggerated importance in everybody's mind, including their own." The press had turned this trial into a mockery, a full-blown media circus. Walter Winchell in particular was singled out. If the judge's condemnation bothered the columnist—unlikely given Winchell's oversized ego—it received no mention in "On Broadway" or elsewhere in the *Daily Mirror*.

Next up on the judge's hit list was Defense Attorney Sabbatino, damning him with faint praise. He commended Sabbatino for defending a publicly unpopular client in a case that brought the attorney much public denouncement and the recipient of many abusive letters. That said, Sabbatino's many calls for mistrial and histrionic conduct throughout the proceedings went beyond the bounds of courtroom protocol. Sanctions would be handed out within a week, the judge promised, after "calm and cool" reflection. "In view of the fact that you did come forward to represent an unpopular client, that fact weighs heavily with me in considering your temperamental qualities," he told counsel.

Kuhn's supporters left the courthouse, led by *Bundesführer* heir apparent Kunze, and refused to comment at the barrage of questions flung at them. They returned to Bund headquarters. Once again the door was locked tight.[48]

30

The Encounter

AFTER SENTENCING A HANDCUFFED Fritz Kuhn, wearing a simple gray suit and hat under a brown overcoat, was led from the Tombs to a waiting car. Surrounding Kuhn and his jailers were an estimated one hundred plus newspaper reporters, photographers, and a few newsreel cameramen, each one of them eager for some sensational words to emerge from the disgraced *Bundesführer.* Just a few months before he would have relished the chance to play with members of what he saw as a Jew-controlled media. Now all Kuhn would give reporters was a cold and artless smile, coupled with the occasional "yes" or "no" to the cacophony of questions flying at him from every direction.

The prisoner was taken to Grand Central Terminal, commonly known as Grand Central Station. At 10:15 he and a police escort took their seats on a train bound for Ossining, the "Albany Special." There was nothing more to do but wait for the scheduled 10:30 departure.[1]

On this day an elderly man of seventy-six was also in Grand Central, the largest, most expansive train station in the world, a place considered a miniature city within a major metropolis, a cavernous building where thousands of people passed through every day. The man's visit to the train station was strictly business. He was waiting in the freight office for delivery of a new automobile. It seemed as unlikely a task as it was absurd given the man's age and stature. He was an important tycoon, a man whose prowess for mechanical ingenuity, engineering genius, and unparalleled business sense made him one of the most influential and powerful figures in modern history. Surely by firing a snap of the fingers at a personal assistant he could have remained in a comfortable hotel room while some flunky picked up the automobile. A person of his standing need not waste time puttering around in some cold, anonymous railway freight office waiting to sign for the delivery of an automobile like he was a run-of-the-mill, everyday commoner.[2]

And yet there he was.

While waiting for his delivery the man strolled with precision from the freight office into the train terminal where the Albany Special was waiting to depart.

Somewhere between his 10:15 arrival at Grand Central and the scheduled departure to Sing Sing at 10:30, Fritz Kuhn's former employer Henry Ford found time to leave the freight office, make his way through a sprawling building to one specific terminal, walk up to the train waiting to depart, look into the passenger car, and regard his former worker, the now-convicted and disgraced *Bundesführer*, Fritz Julius Kuhn.

No words were exchanged between the two men.[3]

When later asked by a *Detroit Times* reporter about the curious visit, Ford replied that he "chanced to be in the station." What went unexplained was why such a powerful man would interrupt his regular business schedule for an unceremonious audience to a disgraced ex-employee en route to prison.[4]

An inevitable question gnaws at the troubled legacy of Henry Ford. Did he help fund Fritz Kuhn and the German-American Bund? Rumors persisted of a link between the two men. The December 1936 *New York Times* caught wind of an exchange between Samuel Untermyer, the Jewish activist attorney, and Ernest G. Liebold, Ford's right-hand man, attorney, designated mouthpiece, and fellow anti-Semite. Telegraphing Henry Ford directly, Untermyer demanded to know why the likes of Fritz Kuhn was on the payroll of Ford Motors. Though Kuhn was fully engaged as *Bundesführer*, he remained listed as an employee of the company. It was Liebold who huffed back Ford's cold, enigmatic, and official response. "Inasmuch as Mr. Ford has always extended to Ford employees the fullest freedom of any coercion with respect to their views on political, religious or social activities, they cannot be reproved by us for exercising such liberties," he wrote.[5] A month later on January 16, 1937, Kuhn officially resigned from Ford, explaining to his former employer that he was now living in New York and working as head of the Bund. With that he turned over his employee identification badge and ended all official ties with the company.[6]

Rudolph Heupel, a Bundist who also worked for the Ford empire, told one reporter that higher-ups at the company were happy with Kuhn and his work with the Bund. "[T]hey know that Herr Ford is a militant Jew-hater," Heupel said of his employers. Given the well-known sentiments of Ford, Liebold, and the thuggish head of Ford security, Harry Bennett, Heupel's remarks had merit. Clearly this assertion touched too many wrong nerves. Pressure was applied from unknown parties and Heupel was persuaded to recant the statement.[7]

There is no paper trail or other solid evidence proving Henry Ford helped fund Fritz Kuhn or the German-American Bund. But the encounter at Grand Central between the auto magnate and his former employee on December 6, 1939 lingers in the mind. Perhaps, as Ford told the *Detroit Times* reporter, it was sheer coincidence that he happened to be in the train station while Kuhn waited to be taken to Sing Sing.

Yet it remains a mystery as to why, with just a short window of time, Henry Ford would go out of his way just to gaze at Fritz Kuhn for a few fleeting moments.

31

Prison

As Sing Sing Convict Number 97363, Kuhn was initially placed into protective custody for his own good. Any prisoner looking for some glory among his fellow inmates could make a name for himself with a violent takedown of the notorious Fritz Kuhn. A segregated cell had a plus side; it was more comfortable than anything holding the general population and all Kuhn had to do was keep his quarters clean. The tradeoff was ceaseless, endless boredom. 97363 could not go use the exercise yard, play on prison football or baseball teams, or watch movies. He was assigned no job within the institution.[1]

Though disgraced and exiled, Kuhn was a political prisoner in the eyes of his devoted followers. Letters poured into Sing Sing for 97363, sending him good wishes for Christmas. One form letter, addressed to "our revered leader, Fritz Kuhn" was filled with signatures from still-loyal supporters. The Youth Movement sent their good wishes. One creative Bundist provided Kuhn with a poem. Another individual offered a business opportunity for the jailed *Bundesführer*, suggesting the two make a start of in the world of horse racing.

There were detractors. One letter came from a disillusioned Bundist, furious with Kuhn for bringing disgrace onto the entire organization through his carnal urges and perjurous actions. The writer had some sympathy for Kuhn for his "involuntary vacation in the Jew state prison," but all compassion ended there. Throughout the letter the writer castigated Kuhn for his affair with Cogswell, "a nine times divorced woman (five times because of adultery and three of these with a Jew) . . . To the joy of Israel we have ourselves exposed the Bund. The contemptual manner in which you have betrayed the trust of the thousands of sacrificing Germans in this country defies any description." The writer closed with perhaps the ultimate insult to his disgraced leader. "You always were as eager to quote Martin Luther that the Jew is the master of lies. The Jews in this respect have nothing on you. Your tempestuous bragging has cost us the good will of our new home country. You think the Jews are the only people who are glad you're in prison. Just remember that you are getting all you deserve."[2]

On December 14, Peter Sabbatino once more faced Judge Wallace. As promised, Kuhn's defense attorney was being sanctioned for his courtroom behavior.

"If this were an ordinary case, I'd give you thirty days in jail," Wallace told Sabbatino.

The attorney was contrite. "It was a very trying case," he said. "Colleagues of mine . . . told me I made a mistake in defending Kuhn, and I believe that is true."

Wallace dismissed these assertions, stating that Kuhn had every right to be defended. "You should be commended for taking that case," he told Sabbatino.

"I am not going to impose a penalty on you," Judge Wallace concluded. "I'm going to let the spirit of Christmas permeate my feelings."

"I am sorry for everything I did," Sabbatino said. "I always had respect for Your Honor."[3]

The *Bundesführer* was no more, but the Bund shouldered on. Hard decisions had to be made for the future of the movement, a process that began on the day after Kuhn's convictions. To outsiders, the Bund was united in support for their *Bundesführer*, a man considered now as a political prisoner and victim of Jewish persecution. But within Kuhn's trusted inner circle, a new order took drastic action. Kunze, often considered Kuhn's second-in-command, called together Schwinn, Klapprott, Luedtke, Elmer, and Wheeler-Hill for a clandestine top-secret meeting that amounted to a coup within the badly broken organization. He issued a series of edicts to the assembly. For all intents and purposes, Kunze was now top man. Fritz Kuhn was ousted from both his leadership position and the Bund itself.

And though by Kunze's secret decree the *Bundesführer* was now persona non grata, Kuhn's sentence would be appealed. To that end, cash needed be raised. Lots of cash.[4]

Donations poured in. Yet bills went unpaid. Rather, in the midst of financial crisis Kunze and his associates continued to draw full-time paychecks. Many of them were seen driving sporty new automobiles.

As the debts mounted, rank-and-file grew suspicious about how their contributions were being used. One of the *Bundesführer*'s old loyalists decried the obvious graft. "These guys are lining their pockets while Kuhn rots in prison," he grumbled. Kunze was no fool. He deferred all questions over spending to a special committee overseen by OD men. Objections disappeared. Bund leaders continued living the highlife.

Sabbatino, faithful counsel as he was, was fighting through the court system to overturn Kuhn's sentence. Kunze brought in a new lawyer, Wilbur Keegan, who was sympathetic to the Bund's overall philosophies and objectives. On January 29, 1940, Keegan informed Sabbatino that his services as Kuhn's attorney would no longer be required.

Kunze dispensed the long-suffering Elsa Kuhn with a nominal amount of money for her service to the organization, a token gesture that was symbolic rather than substantive.

She was furious with her husband's successor. Elsa wrote letter after letter to the withering local Bund units across the country, begging for assistance and asserting that Kunze had no intention of helping to free her husband. Word inevitably trickled back to Kunze, who went into damage control mode. Kunze dismissed as nonsense any accusation that he was seizing power in the wake of Kuhn's conviction. He decried these "recent rumors" as "monstrous insults of persons who are still seeking means to destroy the movement. Every comrade, especially if he is an OD Man, knows what the propagator of such murderous stories deserves."

If Kunze had learned anything from his predecessor, it was how to manipulate and bury the truth. In March he issued a formal statement: an appeal of the *People v. Fritz Kuhn* had burned through ten thousand dollars of Bund money. Furthermore, Kunze said, the *Bundesführer* had resigned from his position on February 22. The German-American Bund was now under the command of the *Bund Führer*—the new preferred term as dictated by its holder, Gerhard Wilhelm Kunze.[5]

Meanwhile, Kuhn languished in prison.

PART IX

The Fall of the German-American Bund

"We must carry on, comrades."

—Acting bund leader George Froboese

Bund Command, Number L December 2, 1941[1]

32

Honored Guests

PERHAPS AS A RESPONSE to Helen Vooros's testimony the Newark *Star-Ledger* investigated possible sexual mischief at Camp Nordland. Klapprott was furious, and would not stand for it. Wilbur Keegan tried to smooth things over, informing the publisher that in exchange for more favorable stories about Camp Nordland, the Bund would not file any libel suits. The offer was turned down flat. Klapprott sued for $1.9 million. In turn, the attorney for the *Star-Ledger* suggested the paper would start printing stories about connections between Nazi Germany and the Bundists should the suit go forward. Klapprott and Keegan blinked. On the day of the trial, neither man showed up to court and the case was dismissed.[1]

A meeting of the minds—of sorts—was held on August 18, 1940 when honored guests bedecked in white robes arrived at Camp Nordland. Two groups with mutual interests, the German-American Bund and the Ku Klux Klan, were having a get-together. One estimate suggested thirty-five hundred people were in attendance.[2] Another put the rate much lower, with perhaps only one thousand present, and just one hundred of them Klan members.[3]

A squadron of two score and ten OD men escorted twenty-four white-sheeted Klan dignitaries around the grounds. Inside Camp Nordland, all seemed serene.

But growing fissures among the Bundists were in strong evidence. A sign posted on the entrance read "We reserve the right to refuse admittance to anyone and eject anyone we find undesirable."[4]

It would appear Kunze was serious in his behind the scenes machinations to eliminate what veneration he could for the *Bundesführer*. More OD men with brass knuckles on their fists guarded the entrance. An estimated one thousand anti-Bund/anti-Klan protestors demonstrated outside camp grounds. Picketers were standard fare for any Bund rally, and given the two groups meeting inside Camp Nordland, no one was surprised by it. The OD men were on hand for something else entirely.

Twenty-three Bundists from New York came to the rally with one goal in mind: expose Kunze and Klapprott as traitors to the movement, two men with a secret plan to grab power while the *Bundesführer* rotted in a prison cell.[5] The men tried to pass around literature bearing the bold headline "Appeal to the Friends of Fritz Kuhn."[6]

The inevitable fight ensued. Stories differ as to how many Kuhn supporters were arrested for disorderly conduct, six by one account and nine by another.[7] Regardless, the arrestees were all charged with disorderly conduct and fined ten dollars each. The Kuhn loyalists didn't take any of this lightly. They later sued Klapprott for assault. He was arrested and released after paying one hundred dollars bail. Two of Klapprott's colleagues were taken into custody with him, and also released on one hundred dollars bail each.

No Bund rally was complete without speeches, and today that task belonged to honored guests. A contingent of six men and seven women, bedecked in their white robe finery, sat on the speakers platform with Reverend Edward E. Young, a Baptist preacher who doubled as a Klan accountant.[8] Young, who also held the title of "Grand Giant of the New Jersey Realm of the Klan," stressed the familiar Aryan nationalist themes that were standard fare in both Bund and Klan rallies. The song "God Bless America" should be on everyone's boycott list, he said, because its author, Irving Berlin, was a Jew.[9]

Edward James Smythe, who served as go-between for the Bund and Klan so this conclave could take place, claimed in his speech that he'd worked for three years with Kuhn to bring together a summit between these two like-minded groups, declaring this task was his "patriotic duty." In words that must have grated in Kunze's and Klapprott's guts, Smythe waxed poetic over his imprisoned friend. "Dear Fritz is not in our midst today; God bless him. His only crime was in trying to bring friendship between the United States and the German dominion. The heart of every Christian is with you, Fritz, my friend, I shall always remember our pleasant associations."

August Klapprott followed Smythe. He provided a warm welcome to

Arthur Bell, Grand Dragon of the New Jersey Klan, emphasizing the shared values of all in attendance. "The principles of the Bund and the principles of the Klan are the same," Klapprott declared through his thick German accent.[10] The Klan, he continued, was not an anti-Semitic organization lest anyone miss the point.[11]

Klapprott exchanged a warm handshake with his honored guest.[12] Bell, a lawyer by trade, treated the audience to a speech filled with the usual canards. His accusations that Jews were trying to shove America into war drew sizeable applause.[13]

The evening was capped by a wedding of a Klansman and Klanswoman in a ceremony held beneath a burning fifty-foot cross. From outside the camp one person was heard to shout "Put Hitler on that cross!"[14]

Though Fritz Kuhn was behind bars and the Bund was in deep financial straits, the congressional investigation continued. Kunze was called before the Dies Committee on Tuesday, October 1, 1940. His demeanor was much different from Kuhn's. The *Bundesführer*, with well-honed oratory skills, was able to hold his own with his inquisitors through verbal games, misleading answers, and at times sheer buffoonery. Kunze was a mirror opposite, a man playing it close to the vest as though he had something to hide. His sentences were stiff, formal, and enigmatic. Often he would remain silent and not answer a question. At one point Alabaman congressman Joe Starnes remarked, "I don't want to be discourteous to you but your answers are too involved and they are not responsive, sufficiently responsive."[15]

Klapprott was on the next day. He was questioned on the Klan rally. ". . . I figured Camp Nordland was hit hard by all this propaganda against the place and the boys from the newspapers did their best to chase the people away and, of course, I welcomed the idea . . ." of what he called "an Americanization rally."[16] Klapprott insisted he would be happy to rent Camp Nordland to any group of loyal Americans. New Jersey congressman J. Parnell Thomas jumped in. Would the witness be willing to rent the facilities to a group of, say, Jewish war veterans?

"Yes," Klapprott said. "And when I say 'yes' I mean it."[17]

The Bundist chiefs were undercut on October fourth when Richard W. Werner, a former OD man who had split from the Bund, provided damning testimony to the committee. Werner had been part of the action at the

Yorkville Casino riot and testified that other OD men stuck metal shards within their belts to inflict more severe damage during fights. Marksmanship was an important part of secret OD training in preparation for *Der Tag*, "The Day"—which, as explained by Werner, would be the bund's "overthrow of this Government and the establishing of a government like they have in Germany." According to the witness, OD men were told by Bund leaders that *Der Tag* would begin on the direct order of Adolph Hitler. Blood would flow in the streets, capitalism would be destroyed, and National Socialism would reign supreme. As for Kuhn's testimony before the committee the previous year, Werner said it was common knowledge within the Bund that what the *Bundesführer* had to say was a series of lies and falsehoods. The attitude within the ranks, Werner said, was simply "Just forget about it."[18]

Joseph Matthews, an investigator for the committee, asked Werner why he willingly agreed to testify openly about the secretive OD operations. "My sole reason and my sole ambition is that all my former friends get wise to the German-American Bund and think it over," he replied. "They know they are making a living over here and making a better living than they would in Germany; and to forget about the things the bund is standing for and just be real Americans."

At the end of Werner's testimony, Congressman Starnes thanked the turncoat OD man for his bravery and candor. "We hope that you will become a good American citizen," he told Werner.

"I will try my best," Werner said. "I will try to make up for what I was doing that was wrong."[19]

33

Dissolution

BUND FÜHRER KUNZE REMAINED defiant, issuing order after order to his remaining loyal followers. But rather than strengthen the Bund, Kunze's demands led to more fracture within what was already a badly broken group.

He forbade remaining members of the Prospective Citizens League, the Youth Movement, and general sympathizers from cooperating with the Alien Registration Act, passed in June 1940. Under this sweeping law, designed to remove potential foreign enemies within the United States' borders, alien residents had to fill out extensive forms to prove they were not beholden to the potential overthrow of the American government. Membership in any groups such as the German-American Bund had to be declared in the paperwork. By Kunze's decree, all Bundists should deny their affiliation on these forms.[1]

On the July 4, Denton Quick, Andover's sheriff, raided Camp Nordland. Kunze, Klapprott, and several others were arrested and charged with violating New Jersey laws against racial hatred. They were released pending trial for later in the year.[2]

In September President Roosevelt signed the Selective Service Act, a military draft bill in preparation for what increasingly seemed like the inevitable entry of the United States onto the battlefields of Europe. Kunze told Bundists to register but refuse service if called up for conscription, claiming the act violated the American Constitution. What's worse, it diluted every Bundist's sense of what it meant to be loyal to the Fatherland. The order was largely ignored. The foolhardy few who obeyed Kunze were jailed for evading the draft or subversive action against the government.[3]

Things turned darker for Kunze when on September 12, the Hercules Powder Plant, a New Jersey Factory which manufactured gunpowder and other explosives, was ripped apart by an enormous blast. Sabotage was suspected, though most likely the explosion was the result of a terrible accident. Regardless, Bundist involvement was suspected and a second raid was staged at Camp Nordland the next day. One local politician supported the raid, claiming if legal authorities had not gone in, outraged citizens wielding clubs would have taken the matter into their own hands. Various anti-Semitic propaganda was seized, as well as a rifle outfitted with a telescopic sight.[4]

In January 1941, Kunze, Klapprott, and their codefendants were found guilty at their race hatred trial. In his decision, Judge John Lose declared that the guilty men were in violation of the Constitution on the principle that all people in the United States are equal. There was enough Bund money left to scrape together bail for Kunze, Klapprott, and a third man while the verdict was appealed.

In the wake of the Hercules disaster, Camp Nordland was under intense scrutiny. On May 30, Sheriff Quick led a team of his deputies, several FBI agents, and a contingent of politicians into the camp and announced it was being shut down as a "public nuisance." More literature was seized, as well as a few rounds of ammunition. A notebook bearing the names of top Nazi officials and Bund sympathizers was discovered. One page contained a curious notation: "Lindbergh will take command of the United States when Hitler wins."[5]

By now Kunze was desperate. In August he presided over a Bund convention in Chicago, an anemic affair, where he announced his resignation. All bank accounts had been frozen by the Federal Government and the Bund could not pay any of its bills. Kunze wanted out. His membership refused this request.

In response Kunze went on the lam.

With their leader now AWOL George Froboese, the Midwestern gau leader, took charge of the withering Bund. On November 13, in what was a superfluous move at best, he announced that Kunze was no longer *Bund Führer*. He instructed Willy Leudtke, a secretary of limited power, to find the missing Kunze and deliver the news. It was an unenviable mission that was about to be rendered pointless.

On December 2, 1941, Froboese sent a letter to the few steadfast loyalists remaining within the sputtering group. "We all wanted the fight," he wrote, "we have therefore the obligation to persevere.... We must carry on, comrades!" It was less a call to arms than it was a desperate final gasp of a dying creature.[6]

And then, the inevitable.

On the morning of December 7, 1941, the American Naval base at Pearl Harbor, Hawaii, was hit and hit hard by a surprise Japanese air attack. The next day Congress declared war on Japan.

Hitler seized the opportunity. His Reich, the *Führer* declared four days later, was now at war with the United States. Roosevelt and the United States Congress responded in kind. America joined the Allied Forces of Great Britain, France, the Netherlands, the USSR, and others in the battle against the European Axis Powers of Germany and Italy. For the second time in a little over twenty years those of German heritage living in the United States were hyper conscious how they might be perceived by their fellow citizens. Those who had openly called for an America akin to Nazi Germany's principles and philosophies were under particular scrutiny.

Fritz Kuhn's dream of a Swastika Nation ended not with the German-American Bund flag flapping proudly in the breeze over the White House, but in a dank little room in an anonymous Manhattan location. On Tuesday, December 16, the top Bundists gathered together in one last secret meeting. Unbeknownst to anyone present, an FBI informant was in their midst. He did not provide any names to his handlers as to who was present, though they likely included Froboese, Klapprott, and Leudtke. The once-proud uniformed leaders of a national movement were now just faceless and beaten bureaucrats. Everything was gone. Offices shuttered. Businesses shut down. Membership, its numbers never fully established, was reduced to a handful of battered partisans.

A vote was taken. The forgone results were unanimous. The German-American Bund and all affiliates were officially dissolved. Perhaps they could continue in some form, but there would be no national headquarters. In defeat, there would be no cooperation with the government. The men agreed not to provide government investigators with any keys to their desks or file cabinets.

And that was that. Fritz Kuhn's vision of a Swastika Nation was over.[7]

34

Arrests

GERHARD KUNZE WAS ON the run. During the Chicago convention he had connected with Count Vonsiatsky, who was sympathetic to the fallen *Bund Führer*'s plight. Vonsiatsky dipped into his personal fortune, providing Kunze with $2,800. The $2,000 was to help with the legal troubles in New Jersey. The remaining $800 was to skip out to Mexico.[1]

Despite Kuhn's strong edicts that the Bund was not an espionage wing for Nazi Germany, Kunze did some freelance work in the western United States, looking for potential flaws in the American home defense plans.[2] On November 9, just days before he was officially kicked out of the Bund, Kunze crossed into Mexico at the El Paso border. He connected with Dr. Wolfgang Bell, a Bundist living in El Paso who ferried Kunze down to Chihuahua. From there Kunze went to Mexico City and the German Embassy. Not wishing to incur the wrath of their host country, embassy officials told Kunze they could not help him. All was not lost. Kunze found an appropriately corrupt Mexican politician.[3] A few pesos later, Kunze had a brand-new name and a brand-new birth certificate. He was now Alfonso Graf Carbides, the proud son of a Mexican mother and German father. Kunze holed up in the small coastal town of Boca del Rio, along the Gulf of Mexico. With his remaining Vonsiatsky funds, he planned to purchase a boat, somehow make his way across the Atlantic Ocean to the Azores islands off the coast of Portugal, and from there on to Germany to deliver his goods. Instead, Kunze was found and arrested, and on the direct order of Manuel Avila Camacho, Mexico's president, delivered to the waiting hands of FBI agents in Brownsville, Texas.[4] Kunze was found guilty of espionage and given a fifteen-year sentence.[5]

Fritz Kuhn was paroled on June 18, 1943, having served three and a half years of a potential five-year sentence. He was released from Clinton Correctional Facility, in Dannemora, New York, where he'd been transferred from Sing Sing. He would not step out as a free man.[6]

In January, Kuhn had been indicted under the Nationality Act of 1940, charged with remaining loyal to Nazi Germany even though he was a naturalized American citizen. In his defense, Kuhn said that he officially became an American citizen on December 3, 1934, six years before the new law went into place. He also claimed that his work as *Bundesführer* was to foster "understanding between the two nations."

Nobody was buying it. Kuhn's citizenship was revoked on June 1, about two weeks before he was paroled. Kuhn was released from state custody into the federal internment camp system for wartime enemy aliens.[7]

He was sent to Texas, first to a facility in Crystal City and then Camp Kennedy. For a time Kuhn taught mathematics to other prisoners, but these classes quickly turned into diatribes of Nazi ideology. Elsa and Walter Kuhn left the United States in 1944 on a boat bound for Lisbon, and presumably back to Germany from there.

Kuhn maintained his arrogance inside internment camp walls. Texas officials finally had enough and in August 1944 sent Kuhn to Fort Stanton in New Mexico. Nine months later Hitler committed suicide and the Third Reich lay in ruins. With the Japanese surrender in August 1945, World War II was over. In September Kuhn was kicked out of the United States, and sent back to Germany.[8]

"Kuhn was denaturalized and deported—but there is no invention to delouse him," wrote the gleeful Winchell. "He sailed on the S. S. *Winchester Victory*—the only boat with a name close enough to that of the columnist who first exposed his activities here in 1933 . . . he was arrested for practically spitting on the sidewalk when he should have been shot for treason . . . The lucky rat! He is *ON* the *Winchester*—instead of having one *AIMED* at him."[9] The two American military policemen who accompanied Kuhn back to Germany paid a visit to Winchell after fulfilling their duties. Kuhn had asked them to deliver a message to the columnist, a threat Winchell enjoyed passing along to his readers.

"Fritz said, 'Tell Herr Vinchell, I vill liff to piss on his grafe.'"[10]

Upon his arrival in Germany Kuhn was taken into U.S. military custody and sent to Hohenasperg, an ancient fortress near Stuttgart now being used as a prison for war criminals. He was assigned menial tasks, working at times in the prison baggage room, dyeing plant, and—reminiscent of his days at Ford—in an X-ray laboratory. Kuhn's health was bad; he suffered two heart attacks while imprisoned.

United States authorities declared Kuhn was of no diplomatic concern in postwar Germany, posed no danger to occupying American troops, and therefore could be released from prison. Nearly a year to the day after Hitler's suicide, Kuhn returned to his hometown of Munich, where Elsa, Waltraut, and Walter—now twenty-two and nineteen respectively—lived in a three-room apartment. "I want to live a private life," Kuhn told reporters. "Since 1939 I've been locked up and have not opened my mouth. I should have been forgotten, but I am not. Now I want to be left alone to make a new start.

"I'll never go back to politics again," he assured anyone who might have thought this was even a remote possibility.[11]

The postwar legal system continued to dog Kuhn. In early 1947, he was taken into custody by German officials on a denazification indictment, held for three days and released after the charge was dropped. Kuhn was again arrested for denazification in July and sent to Dachau, the former Nazi concentration camp, now fittingly turned into a prison for German war criminals.[12] Though a broken man, Kuhn still had some friends left; other inmates were jealous that he had better meals thanks to gifts of food sent by his smattering of supporters remaining in the United States. Perhaps the nutrition helped Kuhn maintain a cagey mind. In January he somehow finagled his way past prison guards and into elusive flight.[13]

A fresh version of an old story emerged in the wake of Kuhn's escape. Though disgraced in both his adopted and home countries, Kuhn's enigmatic appeal to women was as strong as ever. Hedwig Munz, a thirty-two-year-old divorced waitress with two children, came forward with a public statement. The blond-haired, blue-eyed woman told reporters that she had met Kuhn at a restaurant. Their chance encounter blossomed into an instantaneous romance. "We became engaged almost at once," Munz said. "He calls me Hedi. He is a very affectionate man." Now living in a small apartment with her sister, brother-in-law, children, and ex-husband, Munz had no clue where Kuhn was. "I will hear from him very soon," she said. "He won't let me wait long in uncertainty."

After revealing her romance with Fritz Kuhn, Munz was fired from the American Army snack bar where she waited tables.[14]

For her part, Elsa Kuhn once again stood by her husband, questioning the veracity of Munz's story. "How can she expect to marry my husband when he is still married to me?" Mrs. Kuhn told the press. "That's silly."[15]

Kuhn was tried in absentia in a trial that lasted all of five hours. Otto Gritschneider, Kuhn's attorney, didn't bother showing up to the proceeding. With his client remaining at large, the counselor saw no point in wasting time providing a futile defense at a trial where the outcome was an almost certainty. Evidence presented before the court consisted of documents showing Kuhn's connections to Adolf Hitler, and the *Bundesführer*'s own attempts to create a Swastika Nation in America. The verdict: ten years of hard labor should Kuhn ever be found, plus a fine of twelve thousand marks (a value at the time of about twelve hundred American dollars). Kuhn's entire financial worth was seized, save for three thousand marks.[16]

That June, in Bernkastel—a German town in the postwar French military zone about 250 miles northwest of Munich—a fleshy man aged fifty-two applied for a chemist's license. When asked for his name, the man replied "G. Kuhn."

The surname clicked with authorities. "G. Kuhn's" fingerprints were compared to those of the fugitive ex-*Bundesführer*. They were a perfect match.

He put up no fight during his arrest. Had he not been captured, Kuhn told a reporter, he planned to make a new life for himself in the region. Conceivably this would have been with his "Hedi" or perhaps a new paramour. Instead, Kuhn claimed that at last, after his many years as an unrepentant lothario, he was a domestically reformed husband to his long-suffering Elsa. "I am staying with my wife, from now on." He also said he would appeal his ten-year sentence.

Munich Police President Franz Pitzer, who took Kuhn into custody, sneered at his prisoner. "If you hadn't worked for a guy like Hitler, you wouldn't be here today."

Replied Kuhn, "Who would have known that it would end like this?"[17]

35

Aftermath

As he promised "Hedi," Kuhn appealed his verdict. He did not expect much. "You don't get justice in a German court," he claimed, adding that he would prefer to face the American judicial system "anytime."[1] Kuhn must have been surprised then when the German Appellate Court reduced his sentence to time served. Having served two years of his ten-year sentence, in July 1949 Fritz Kuhn emerged from a prison cell for the last time.[2] It was at best a hollow victory. In March he appealed to the United States government to reinstate his American citizenship and allow him to return. He was categorically turned down. However, the feds made a provision that should Kuhn return to the United States, he would promptly be arrested and stand trial for "traitorous activities while being protected by the Constitutional Rights as a citizen of the United States." The memo denying Kuhn's request was forwarded to President Truman, Watson Miller, Attorney General Tom Clark, J. Edgar Hoover, head of the Immigration and Naturalization department, and a few senators, including future president Lyndon Baines Johnson.

A copy was also provided to Walter Winchell.[3]

He was freed from prison, but not bad health. For two years Kuhn lived in poverty and anonymity. December 14, 1951, almost ten years to the day that the German-American Bund was officially dissolved, the disgraced *Bundesführer*, Fritz Julius Kuhn died of unknown causes.

The news did not reach the United States for another two years, where it filled little space on obituary pages in February 1953. *The New York Times* piece described Fritz Kuhn as "a poor and obscure chemist, unheralded and unsung."[4]

Winchell told his readers of Kuhn's ignominious end through a small, almost negligible item in his February 6 column. *"Headline,"* he wrote. "'Hitler's U.S. Bund Chief Fritz Kuhn Died Friendless in Germany.' (Oh, the poor, poor feller). We own recordings of his voice telling his bed-mate (a planted agent): 'Undt ven I am in powah in de United Schnates Vincell will hang from hish favorett lamp-post in frunt of his Shtork Cloob. Ha, Ha!.'"

The item ended with Winchell's final thought on Kuhn and the *Bundesführer's* dream of a Swastika Nation.

"(End of shrug)." (parenthesis in original)[5]

In some form or other, Fritz Kuhn and the German-American Bund united a disparate cast of characters. A few, like Florence Camp and Virginia Cogswell, faded into obscurity, which probably was merciful given their unhappy connections to the *Bundesführer*. Others played out their lives in forums both private and public (and sometimes a mix of the two), all leaving their distinctive legacies to the world.

The Bundists

Life after the Bund's dissolution became difficult for its leaders and loyalists. The organization, ended by its top officials in the wake of Pearl Harbor, was officially outlawed by the United States shortly thereafter.[6] Throughout the war years rank-and-file members were brought to trial by federal authorities. Some were charged with violating the draft laws, as per Fritz Kunze's orders. Many were denaturalized for taking American citizenship through fraud, remaining loyal to the Nazi government back in Germany because of their membership in the Bund. Like Kuhn, they were held at internment camps after being denaturalized.

On March 18, 1943, Judge John Bright, in the case of *United States vs. Fritz Kuhn and Nineteen Others*, ruled that a majority of the defendants—including top Bundist leaders—maintained complete loyalty to their Fatherland, never intending to honor their oath of American citizenship. "No alien can take this oath with any mental reservation [and he cannot] retain allegiances or fidelity to his homeland," Bright wrote in his decision. The guilty parties were summarily denaturalized, though some successfully later had their verdicts overturned.[7]

Many Bundists, including Kunze, Schwinn, and Klapprott faced charges in what became known as "The Great Sedition Trial." Defendants were accused of various conspiracies to overthrow the United States government. The trial dragged on for months, becoming a nightmare of legal paperwork, courtroom outbursts, charges and countercharges. Convictions were few. "What was once the best show in the town outside the monkey house of the National [Z]oo has been deserted by the public," wrote Chicago *Tribune* reporter Walter Trohan. ". . . [T]he accepted view of the public is that no one connected with the case knows what it's all about."[8]

The Kuhn Family

After Fritz Kuhn's death, his wife and children had nothing left for them in a denazified, politically split East and West Germany. Walter moved to Mexico where he enlisted in the military; Elsa and Waltrut joined him shortly thereafter.[9]

Walter Kappe

After returning to Germany in 1937 Walter Kappe, the former editor of *Der Amerikadeutscher Volksbund* joined *Abwehr*, the Nazi wartime intelligence unit dedicated to espionage. Given his background, Kappe was chosen to lead a unique military operation: train a group of soldiers to slip into the United States via a German U-boat submarine, then have the men spread across the country and wreak havoc at selected manufacturing and business targets vital to the American war effort. Though the sixteen volunteers made it into the United States, the operation was a complete failure. All of the men were captured before they could carry out assignments, and put on trial. Some were sent to American prisons, while others went to the electric chair.

After the war Kappe floated from job to job in an alcoholic haze, spending his final days in the unlikely position as souvenir salesman near an American military base in Frankfurt. Kappe died in 1958.[10]

George Froboese

On June 17, 1942, a train en route to New York City made a stop in Water-loo, Indiana. One passenger got off, apparently to stretch his legs. He walked unseen down the tracks, lay down, put his head on the rail as though it were a pillow, and waited for the train to leave the station.

Police investigating the gruesome sight looked through papers found on the body. They identified the headless corpse as George Froboese, the final leader of the now defunct German-American Bund. He was on his way to New York to testify before a grand jury, face possible criminal charges, and ultimately be stripped of his United States citizenship. It seemed Froboese decided that a macabre public suicide was a better option than facing the American legal system.[11]

August Klapprott

Klapprott was stripped of his citizenship and sentenced to five years in prison for violating the Selective Service Act. He appealed the decision, fighting his way through the legal system well after the end of the war. Though he eventually was found not guilty of violating draft laws, his status as an American citizen was thrust into statutory limbo with no resolution.[12]

Walter Winchell

As his first marriage was falling apart, Winchell met June Magee, a vaudeville showgirl. He claimed they were wed on May 11, 1923, but like so many of the self-perpetuated legends surrounding Winchell, this wasn't true. His divorce from Rita Greene would not be finalized for another five years.[13] Winchell and June were never legally married during their nearly fifty years together. June had a two-year-old daughter, Gloria, whom Winchell formally adopted; rumor had it that the child was his though this was unlikely. A daughter, Walda, was born in 1927.[14] Gloria died of pneumonia on Christmas Eve, 1932; she was just nine years old.[15] They had one more child, Walter Junior, born in 1935.[16]

In the postwar era, Winchell took a hard ideological swing from Roosevelt lefty to hard-core McCarthyite. He was abandoned by old friends when he used his column as a nonstop platform to attack singer Josephine Baker as a Communist when she complained about racial discrimination at the Stork Club. His radio show was cancelled in 1957, but the worst was when his life's blood column came to an ignominious end after the *Daily Mirror* folded in on October 16, 1963. Parent company Hearst gave him some work for a few more years in a few of their lesser holdings, a charity position that ended in 1967.[17]

One of the happier jobs in Winchell's twilight days was as narrator of the ABC television series *The Untouchables*. The show, which ran from 1959 to 1963, portrayed the fictionalized adventures of 1930s lawman Elliott Ness, played with square-jawed temperance by Robert Stack. During the second season, the show broadcast an episode titled "The Otto Frick Story." The improbable plot had Ness breaking up an international Nazi narcotics operation run by a ringleader clearly modeled after Fritz Kuhn. Newsreel footage of the Bund's 1939 Madison Square Garden rally was incorporated into the story. Although the story held no bearing to the truth, Winchell's voice seemed to cackle with glee throughout this over-the-top fictional vilification of his old nemesis.

Dorothy Parker once quipped, "Poor Walter. He's afraid he'll wake up one day and discover he's not Walter Winchell."[18] Her witticism proved all too prophetic.

Desperate to regain footing in the business he loved, Winchell took out a full-page advertisement in *Variety*, under the dark heading "WW BACK IN SHOW BIZ." The ad included a list of recent credits, including a role in the drug-fueled 1968 exploitation film *Wild in the Streets*, some small television appearances, and work as radio voice for an automobile leasing company. He closed the ad with a cynical offer to *The Wall Street Journal*, *Women's Wear Daily*, or *The New York Morning Telegraph*, suggesting they hire him as a janitor. Winchell was briefly picked up by *The Morning Telegraph*, as well as by *Variety*, both papers offering him pitiful space buried in the back of their pages.[19] By and large, Winchell was a sad and ossified wreck of a man.

He grew estranged from his children. Walda moved to Scottsdale, Arizona to be with her mother who was now living there. Walter Junior fell into deeper personal depths. He dropped out of high school, served in the Marines, drifted across jobs, and reveled in dangerous public pranks, like blowing off a smoke bomb in a New York cafeteria or whipping out a revolver at a children's pizza party.[20]

His downward spiral continued when Walter Junior married the daughter of a former Nazi general. He took to marching into Manhattan saloons garbed in a Nazi getup and shouting "*Heil* Hitler!" Fights were the natural consequence. One public scuffle turned brutal when Walter Junior jammed the business end of a broken bottle into another man's face, causing the victim to go blind in one eye. Winchell spent considerable money to cover for his son and make the ugly story disappear.

Walter Junior, with his wife Eva and two children, moved to California. Depression and mental illness, fueled by copious use of prescription drugs and narcotics took the inevitable toll. On Christmas Day, 1968, he shot himself with a thirty-eight caliber pistol. Walter Winchell Jr. was thirty-three years old. His sister Gloria had died on Christmas Eve thirty-six years earlier.

June Winchell became a recluse after her son's suicide. She died of heart disease on February 5, 1970.[21] Winchell succumbed to cancer two years later, on February 20, 1972. Though estranged from her father, Walda took command of his remains. He was buried at Greenwood Memory Lawn Cemetery in Phoenix. A pair of funeral home employees served as pallbearers, and a rabbi officiated at the ten-minute service. As per Walda's demand, no one else was in attendance.[22]

Winchell's final resting place lays end to end above the graves of June, Walter Junior, and Walda, who died in 1987. His burial plot is marked by a simple memorial stone bearing a replica of Winchell's famous signature, the years of his birth and death of 1897–1972, and centered with a traditional *Magen David*, the Jewish Star of David. It bakes in the hot Arizona sun in a nondescript industrial neighborhood about eight miles from the Phoenix Sky Harbor Airport.

If there is any solace to be found here, it is that Fritz Kuhn was a wretched failure in his bitter vow: "Tell Herr Vinchell, I vill liff to piss on his grafe."

Meyer Lansky

Shortly before the outbreak of World War II Meyer Lansky, just shy of forty years, registered at his local draft board.[23] Though he'd pulled back from Bund bashing, ". . . I was still ready to do all I could to help America because it had adopted me." He was turned down for military service, but in

April 1942 government officials approached Little Man with a possible way he could help with the war effort. Sabotage was suspected along New York's corruption-filled waterfronts. Italians sympathetic to Mussolini were considered prime suspects. Perhaps they were feeding information to German spies. Nothing could be proven. The Navy needed someone who knew the score, and that man was Lansky's old colleague "Lucky" Luciano. At the time Luciano was ensconced in New York's Clinton Correctional Facility, a hard-core prison commonly referred to as "Siberia" among its residents.[24] "From the moment when I went to see Lucky and got his cooperation, nothing went wrong in the Port of New York," Lansky recalled. "No enemy agents as far as I know ever got any important information from the men who worked there, and no suspicious characters were allowed anywhere near the loading docks."[25]

In 1948, when Israel was in bloody, hard-fought infancy, Lansky pulled strings and arranged for guns to be shipped to the Jewish state's fledgling army. At his suggestion, fellow mobsters helped out and bought Israel Bonds.[26]

His loyalty to Israel became a hoped-for refuge twenty-two years later when Lansky faced jail time for tax evasion charges. In 1970 he fled to Israel, where Little Man hoped to spend the rest of his days. Under the country's Law of Return, established by the Israeli government in 1950, any Jew could immigrate there and attain citizenship. Lansky proved to be a major exception. The Israeli Supreme Court ruled in 1972 that due to a criminal past, Lansky should be expelled from the country.[27] Little Man went back to Miami, and was convicted of contempt of court for his would-be escape to Israel. Though sentenced to a year and a day for his actions, the verdict was overturned when Lansky was acquitted as a criminal tax cheat. The main witness against Lansky in his tax evasion trial, Vincent "Fat Vinnie" Teresa proved to be a man of limited veracity, turning the government's case into a complete washout.[28]

Lansky spent his final years in ill health, succumbing to cancer on January 15, 1983.[29] He was rumored to be worth some $300 million at the time of his death, but his last will and testament revealed him to be a man of modest means.[30] If Little Man had any money squirreled away, it was never found.

In the end, perhaps Lansky's golem life was summed up by his angry testimony to Senator Estes Kefauver during the 1950 senate investigation into organized crime. "I'm not a kneeling Jew who comes to sing songs in your ears," Lansky snarled. "I will not allow you to persecute me because I am a Jew."[31]

Abner "Longy" Zwillman

Zwillman maintained his empire, investing in legitimate businesses, criminal enterprises, and that shadowy area where the two worlds mingled. His fingers touched hotels and casinos both high class and seedy, auto parts manufacturing, post-Prohibition liquor distribution, cigarette machines, and the unlikely world of canned office music with investments in the Muzak corporation. Labor unions and politicians were in his pockets. Smitten by Hollywood, he dated now-forgotten starlets and bankrolled B-movies. He stored money in safes, shoeboxes, and sometimes banks, where tellers understood where the cash came from and how to handle it.[32]

Often that money was funneled into Jewish charities. Zwillman's long list of benefactors included United Jewish Appeal, the National Conference of Christians and Jews, and several area synagogues. He gave food to those in need during the Jewish holidays. Zwillman's generosity also extended to Catholic institutions and charities.

One year during the Days of Awe—the ten-day period between the Jewish New Year Rosh Hashanah and Yom Kippur, the Day of Atonement— Zwillman summoned a local rabbi to his Newark headquarters. "Rabbi," the gangster said, "I understand you're the only honest man in the Jewish community." Longie handed the rabbi fifty grand in cash with the instructions, "give it to any charity you want."[33]

Zwillman's easy monetary flow caught up to him; like Capone before him, Longy was charged with tax evasion. The 1956 trial resulted in a hung jury. The FBI suspected jury tampering and secreted microphones in Zwillman's office. A loose-lipped associate gave exactly what the government wanted when the unwitting thug revealed that two of the jurors deciding Zwillman's fate had been bribed.[34]

Agents swooped in and made arrests in February 1959. Zwillman was a nervous wreck. It seemed like there was no way out and jail was the last place he wanted to spend the rest of his days. On the morning of February 26, 1959, Mary Zwillman found her husband hanging from a noose in their basement. By all appearances it was a suicide.

Or maybe it wasn't. Rumors persisted that Longy was considering singing to the feds about mob activity to avoid a lengthy prison sentence. Speculation ran wild that underworld colleagues, worried he might turn on them whacked Zwillman and made it look like a self-induced death.[35]

Zwillman's former enforcer Max "Puddy" Hinkes, the ex-prizefighter who declared smashing Bundist bones with iron bars and baseball bats to be "one of the most happy moments of my life," remained a lifelong member in Longy's organization. His ties to the Jewish community also ran deep. In 1992, old and retired from mobster life, a dinner was held in Hinkes's honor at the Synagogue of the Suburban Torah Center in Livingston, New Jersey. He was praised throughout the evening for "wreak[ing] havoc and destruction" on Bundists "that would wish to do harm to Jewish lives."[36]

Mickey Cohen

Like Meyer Lansky, Mickey Cohen tried to serve his country during World War II by joining the army. He was declared 4-F thanks to an old psychological exam taken after the heat of a courtroom outburst.[37] In the late 1940s, he fought a wild touch-and-go battle for control of the Los Angeles underworld with rival Jack Dragna. Twice Cohen's house was bombed: once by dynamite and once by a heavy-duty torpedo.[38] The attempted killings were business, but what Cohen took personally was Dragna's anti-Semitism. "He would get in a little zing all the time . . . to [Bugsy Siegel] and Jews, and I kind of woke up to it," Cohen said.[39]

David Ben-Gurion, Israel's first prime minister and a man filled with *chutzpah*, impressed Cohen. Upon learning the country's army was short on guns and ammunition, Cohen offered his unique means of support to the fledgling Jewish state, enlisting fellow mobsters Albert Anastasia, Charlie "the Jew" Yanowsky, and an Irish mobster known as "Chopsie" in a operation to smuggle war surplus guns and dynamite into the right Israeli hands.[40]

When a story spread that Cohen converted to Christianity he squashed the rumor fast. Cohen felt genuinely hurt by this gossip. ". . . I had been strongly connected with the Israel cause," he wrote in his memoirs. "My name over there . . . added some strength to the youth of Israel. Now if anything like this would have been the truth, it would have been a terrible slap in the face to those Jewish youths."[41]

Journalist Herb Brin, a crime reporter who supported countless Jewish causes, was impressed by the gangster's commitment to Israel. "I knew who [Cohen] was and what he was," Brin recalled. "But when we talked about Israel he was a different person. He had tears in his eyes once when we talked about Israel."[42]

Cohen ended up in prison twice. Like his former boss Capone, he was locked up not for his mobster ways but tax evasion. In 1952, Cohen was sentenced to four years; a decade later he was given a fifteen-year sentence. During the second stint a cocky fellow prisoner wielding a lead pipe clubbed him in the head. Cohen was never the same after that, though he maintained his braggadocio personality to the very end, succumbing to stomach cancer in 1976.[43]

Jack Ruby

After moving to Dallas, Jack Ruby née Jacob Rubenstein wracked up a string of arrests for various infractions, ranging from assault to traffic violations to exhibiting "obscene" strip acts.[44] All the while he maintained a vestigial tie to his faith, attending synagogue for High Holiday services during Rosh Hashanah and Yom Kippur. After his father passed away in 1958, Ruby attended temple faithfully for the next year to recite traditional Jewish mourning prayers for the departed, even though his adult relationship with his father was held together by only the thinnest of blood ties.[45]

On Friday November 22, 1963, President John F. Kennedy was assassinated in Dallas. Police arrested a suspect named Lee Harvey Oswald and charged him with murder. Two days later, on Sunday, November 24, Ruby entered the Dallas Police Station and shot Oswald dead.

The Warren Commission investigating the assassination interviewed Ruby in his Dallas jail cell during June 1964, where he testified how devastated and distraught he felt after the president was gunned down. Fearing Mrs. Kennedy might face unbearable personal trauma if she faced her husband's assassin in court, Ruby decided there was only one course of action. He claimed to have taken Preludin, a prescription diet pill, the morning he shot Oswald. "I think [the drug] was a stimulus to give me an emotional feeling," Ruby explained. "I wanted to show my love for our faith, being of the Jewish faith . . . suddenly the feeling, the emotional feeling came within me that someone owed this debt to our beloved President to save [Mrs. Kennedy] the ordeal of coming back [for a trial]."[46]

As it was when he fought the Bundists in Chicago, Ruby saw himself as a protector, this time vanquishing a killer to defend the honor of the fallen president's widow and children.

In his final days before death from lung cancer on January 3, 1967, Ruby ranted and raved that Jews were being tortured as punishment for his killing of Lee Harvey Oswald. To the very end, Jacob Rubenstein of Chicago's West Side Jewish ghettos remained faithful to his people.[47]

Congressman Samuel Dickstein

Congressman Dickstein served in Congress through 1945, then served on the New York Supreme Court until his death in 1954. His Special Committee on Un-American Activities evolved into the House Committee on Un-American Activities, a public cauldron for exposing subversives in America from the late 1940s into the mid-1970s. At its highpoint in the 1950s, Senator Joe McCarthy served as the committee's unyielding overlord. Lives were destroyed by mere accusations without proof. Hollywood created an infamous "blacklist" of suspected communists. Spies were everywhere. Any and everyone—except perhaps United States congressmen and senators—were suspect.

After the fall of the Soviet Union, thousands of classified documents from the Cold War era were released for public scrutiny. Julius Rosenberg, long thought to be an innocent martyr after being executed with his wife Ethel for providing secrets of the atom bomb to the Soviet Union, turned out to be exactly what the government said he was: a Communist spy.

Another name turned up that surprised many. Samuel Dickstein, the self-aggrandizing force who exposed the Bund and fought communist

subversion through the power of his office, was a paid employee of the
NKDV, the Soviet spy agency that preceded the KGB, selling information
and visas to the Russians. He held this position from 1937 through 1940,
while at the same time leading the charge against Fritz Kuhn and the
German-American Bund.[48]

Thomas Dewey

Thomas Dewey vaulted from district attorney to a successful political career. He was elected governor of New York as a Republican, an office he had
run for the year before Kuhn's trial but lost to incumbent Democratic governor Herbert Lehman. In 1940, he enjoyed a brief moment as frontrunner
in the Republican race for president, a status that faded with the rising
popularity of the more liberal and eventual GOP candidate Wendell Willkie.
At age thirty-eight, many party heads felt Dewey was too young to run the
country; his anti-interventionist stance against American entry into the war
in Europe also worked against him.

In 1942, he again ran for governor and this time won the office. Dewey
leaped into the job with the same zeal he demonstrated as district attorney.
With his no-nonsense approach to government spending and strong advocate for education reform, Dewey grew into the role he coveted as a national
powerbroker in Republican politics. He was rewarded with the presidential
nomination in 1944, losing the election to Roosevelt but earning 46 percent
of the overall vote. He was reelected as New York Governor in 1946, and
repeated the pattern with his party's nomination for president in 1948. The
campaign against the incumbent Harry Truman was by all appearances a
path right into the White House. Polls and pundits assured Dewey would
have a stunning victory on November 2. Vote counting went well into the
night and Truman pulled out the unexpected upset but not before *The Chicago Daily Tribune* published the blunder of all blunder headlines, "Dewey
Defeats Truman."

Dewey once predicted "I will be President. It is written in the stars."[49]

Dewey was reelected governor one last time in 1950, and upon retirement in 1955 settled into a role as Republican Party powerbroker, king-
maker, and behind the scenes advisor to President Richard Nixon. Nixon

offered him a seat on the Supreme Court, a post Dewey turned down due to his age. He died of a massive heart attack on March 16, 1971.

Wrote his biographer Richard Norton Smith, "Neither a crusader nor a hero in the conventional sense, [Dewey] had instincts for thoroughness, order, and expertise . . ."[50]

Mayor Fiorello LaGuardia

In spring of 1941, Mayor LaGuardia was appointed by President Roosevelt to head up the Office of Civil Defense, a federal program designed to oversee coordination between state and national government for protection of American citizens in case of war emergency. He remained director of the OCD until Pearl Harbor and a permanent replacement was named.

His final years as mayor were plagued with increasing budget difficulties, putting the city on the brink of financial crises. LaGuardia's popularity plunged and he chose not to run for another term, rather than risk a humiliating defeat at the polls. In 1946, he was appointed to head the United Nations Relief and Rehabilitation Administration (UNRRA), a body that provided aid to victims of war throughout the world.

LaGuardia's passionate abhorrence for the Nazis was well known throughout Germany. He was vilified in the German press as a "dirty Talmud Jew." In a moment of sardonic humor he once was greeted by President Roosevelt with a stiff-armed Nazi salute and the words "*Heil* Fiorello!" LaGuardia responded in kind, "*Heil* Franklin!" Yet even though he was the son of a Jewish mother, LaGuardia believed he was not Jewish enough "to justify boasting about it."[51] Still, there was a deeper connection to his hatred of the Bund and Hitler than most people realized. LaGuardia's sister, Gemma LaGuardia Gluck, married to Jewish Hungarian Herman Gluck, was held in a concentration camp in the final year of WWII.

The Glucks lived in Budapest, where Herman worked as a bank administrator until the German invasion of Hungary in March 1944. On order from SS officers, Hungarian police raided the Glucks' home on May 12. The place was torn apart in search of a short-wave radio, which Nazi authorities believed Gemma was using to contact her brother back in New York. No radio transmitter was found.

A secret meeting was held on May 23 between Adolf Eichmann and Eberhardt von Thadden, a Nazi Foreign Office bureaucrat. It was von Thadden's idea that, because of her familial connection to New York's powerful mayor, Gluck be held captive as a possible bargaining chip rather than deport her to an extermination facility. The request was given serious attention from office through office in the Nazi chain of command. Gluck finally was arrested on June 7. On the orders of Heinrich Himmler she was sent to Ravensbrück, a women's concentration camp in northern Germany "as a political hostage." Her husband was also taken into custody.[52]

Gluck watched as her friends were taken away to the gas chambers. "Because I was the sister of LaGuardia, I was saved but the others of my poor comrades were killed," Gluck wrote. "The camp personnel director told me afterward that I was kept from the gas chamber because they were fearful that some harm would come to the Germans in New York in reprisal."[53]

On April 15, 1945, just days before Germany's fall to the Allies, Gluck, her daughter Yolanda, and fourteen-month-old grandson Richard were transferred outside the camp to other holding facilities. They ended up in a Berlin prison, in the Charlottenberg section of the city, then taken in by a local politician after the Russian invasion. In turn he tried to use Gluck's status as LaGuardia's sister for his own protection, to no avail. After the American forces entered Berlin, Gluck was able to send word to her brother in New York that she was alive. A radio broadcast was arranged, with Gluck and LaGuardia speaking live on the air.

Given his position as head of the UNRRA LaGuardia had to be careful to avoid accusations of special favors for his sister when so many people wanted to leave war ravaged Germany, but he pulled what strings he could. LaGuardia finally was able to arrange passage into Denmark for his sister, her daughter, and grandson, sending a letter to her via General Eisenhower. Shortly before the family left for Copenhagen, Gluck learned her husband was murdered at Mauthausen camp hospital.

LaGuardia reunited with Gemma in September, when he traveled to Denmark as part of a UNRRA tour. It took another year and a half before Gluck received authorization that she, Yolanda, and Richard could immigrate to the United States. They arrived in New York on May 19, 1947. LaGuardia had just months to live at this point, as the cancer burned through his body. He died on September 20, but not before making arrangements for his sister, niece, and grandnephew to have permanent residence in an apartment in a Queens municipal housing project.[54]

Judge James Garrett Wallace

Wallace remained on the bench until his retirement in 1953. The Fritz Kuhn trial was the most notable of his career; in another famous case the judge also presided the trial of Joseph "Socks" Lanza, a mob connected labor union racketeer who controlled New York's Fulton Fish Market.

Wallace's sideline as "the Singing Judge" thrived through the years. He served in the New York City Bar Association as both vice president and star in their amateur theatrical productions.[55] His talents were enough for the Bar Association to custom press a record album for him, *Judge James Garrett Wallace Sings of the Law and Lawyers*.[56] Judge Wallace died on November 29, 1956 after suffering a stroke.[57]

Peter Sabbatino

Peter Sabbatino continued his career as a criminal lawyer well into his seventies. He defended more than three hundred accused murderers, and earned a good reputation for earning them not guilty verdicts. In the years following his defense of Fritz Kuhn, Sabbatino became something of a go-to attorney for high profile and often despised clients. He was counsel for Army Sergeant John David Provoo, an American accused of collaborating with the Japanese while held as a POW during WWII. His client was found guilty, but Sabbatino fought back and Provoo's verdict was overturned on appeal. In 1966, when Sabbatino was seventy-five, he represented another unpopular defendant, Talmadge Hayer, one of the three gunman who shot down Malcolm X at the Audubon Ballroom on February 21, 1965.

At a dinner honoring Sabbatino on his seventy-fifth birthday Judge Hyman Barshay, a New York Supreme Court Justice, paid tribute to the man who devoted his life and work to see that justice would remain just. Barshay described Sabbatino as one of the great legendary criminal lawyers, "a learned, resourceful, fair and hard-hitting attorney." Sabbatino died in 1973 at age eighty-two.[58]

Henry Ford

Throughout the 1930s Ford scribbled into private notebooks, noting various trivia, miscellanea, and his strong dislike of the New Deal, labor unions, competitors, and—despite his public statements to the contrary—unrepentant anti-Semitism. After the American entry into World War II against Nazi Germany, Henry Ford neither renounced nor returned the Grand Service Cross of the Supreme Order of the German Eagle presented to him in 1938 by the Nazi government. (Neither did Charles Lindbergh.)[59]

Ford-Werke, a German subsidiary of Ford's empire, manufactured machines and parts that proved invaluable to the Nazi military throughout WWII—even after the United States declared war on Germany. A postwar inquiry conducted by civilian investigators concluded that support provided to *Ford-Werke* from its Michigan parent company was vital to the Nazi government and their war efforts.[60]

After Germany's defeat, when America at last could return to business as usual, Ford was asked if he would ever offer public shares of his eponymous empire. "I'll take down my factory brick by brick before I'll let any of the Jew speculators take stock in my company," was his blunt answer.

In May 1946, the United States government created the documentary *Death Stations*, an aptly titled movie, using footage shot at Nazi concentration camps. A private screening was arranged for Ford and his top executives. Unflinching images of Hitler's Final Solution bombarded the audience for one solid hour. The film ended. Auditorium lights were turned on for an audience drained by the depravity. And then more trauma.

Henry Ford was collapsed in his seat. Sometime during the screening, he had a massive stroke. Having at last borne witness to the end result of Hitler's dream and a world that he perhaps helped to forge, his brain was set ablaze. Eleven months later Henry Ford was dead.[61]

EPILOGUE

In the Rubble of the Swastika Nation

ON OCTOBER 9, 1987, a group of like-minded individuals congregated at the Holiday Inn in Irvine, California for something billed as "The Eighth Annual International Revisionist Conference." The meeting was organized by the Institute for Historical Review, a group of pseudo-historians who for reasons of their own fanaticism, fervently denied that the Holocaust could have or ever did happen.

Today was a unique day for the group, a chance to hear from an honored guest, eighty-one-year-old August Klapprott, the close associate of Fritz Kuhn, former *Bundesleiter* of the New Jersey branch of the German-American Bund.[1] In this group's world of historical illusions, Klapprott was a wizened elder. His speech unfolded like a modern-day version of old Bund talking points. Bruno Hauptmann was innocent of kidnapping and murdering Charles Lindbergh's infant son; the crime was a set-up by anti-German factions. The Bund was hounded and destroyed by the FBI. Klapprott spoke of his post-Bund years in prison where he was forced to fix broken beds for "jungle-dancing" African-Americans. In a wry moment, he bragged about killing six million cockroaches during his incarceration. That number, of course, was well known by the group, and the image that Klapprott linked it to raised hearty laughter throughout the room. Finally, in an affirmation of the "Institute's" irrational beliefs, Klapprott claimed to have met former Jewish concentration camp inmates who told him that none of their fellow Jews were turned to ashes in Nazi ovens.

Almost five decades had passed since the fall of the German-American Bund. August Klapprott remained unrepentant—an old man still proud and deluded, and an inspirational figure to like-minded acolytes boiling in fanatical ideologies.[2]

Others too, dreamed of a Swastika Nation. In the 1960s, George Lincoln Rockwell, a Korean War veteran, formed what he called the American Nazi Party and led counter marches to Dr. Martin Luther King Jr.'s civil rights demonstrations. Rockwell was murdered by one of his followers in August 1967.

Frank Collin, a Rockwell acolyte, created his own Nazi group, the National Socialist White People's Party of America in Chicago's southside Marquette Park neighborhood. In the summer of 1977, he became an notorious cause célèbre for the First Amendment after announcing his group would march through north suburban Skokie, a village now home to many Holocaust survivors. A deal was struck with the courts and the march did not take place; instead Colin and his men held a rally in downtown Chicago, hiding behind large shields while angry protestors shouted them down. It was subsequently revealed Colin's father was a man named Max Collin née Cohen, a Jewish survivor of Dachau. Collin was later jailed on child molestation charges. Upon being paroled Colin reinvented himself as "Frank Joseph," a New Age writer and pagan worshiper.

David Duke, a former Grand Wizard of the Ku Klux Klan and head of the fringe group he dubbed the National Association for the Advancement of White People, served briefly in the Louisiana House of Representatives. William Pierce founded the National Alliance, an anti-Semitic and racist organization extolling the philosophies and ideas found throughout *Mein Kampf*. Under the pseudonym "Andrew MacDonald," Pierce published a cult novel: *The Turner Diaries*, the story of a victorious underground race war fought by white Gentile Americans against Jews and blacks. This fiction inspired the real-life group The Order, a bloodthirsty bunch who robbed banks to help fund other white nationalists, and murdered Jewish radio talk show host Alan Berg in his driveway. *The Turner Diaries*, which included a pivotal scene of the FBI building leveled by a crude car bomb in Washington, D.C., was a muse for Timothy McVeigh in his 1995 bombing of the Murrah Federal Building in Oklahoma City.

Violent Aryan groups slithered in various forms into the twenty-first century, connecting from the rural hills of Arkansas to the thick woods of Oregon via the Internet. They posted copies of *Mein Kampf* and *The International Jew* on Web sites. Throughout the United States armed white supremacists steeled themselves in bunkers and hideaways, constantly preparing themselves for what they believed would be a modern version of what the Bund called *Der Tag*—"The Day"—a time when marauding Jews and African Americans would try to wrest loose what these frightened survivalists believed to the core was an Aryan birthright.

The Nazi dream, driven by arrogance, ignorance, and fear, seethes in all corners of the United States. But no one has ever come so close or fallen so far as Fritz Kuhn in the inglorious pursuit of an American Swastika Nation.

NOTES

Part I: The *Bundesführer*

1. FBI Report, Newark, New Jersey, April 27, 1942, 4.

1. Fritz Julius Kuhn

1. Toland, John. *Adolf Hitler* (Hertfordshire, UK: Wordsworth Editions Limited, 1997), 155.
2. Ibid, 98.
3. Ibid, 153.
4. Gordon, Harold J. Jr., *Hitler and the Beer Hall Putsch* (Princeton, NJ: Princeton University Press, 1972), 284–285.
5. Toland, 156.
6. Herzstein, Robert E., *Roosevelt & Hitler: Prelude to War* (New York: John Wiley & Sons, 1994), 146.
7. FBI Report, September 13, 1939, page 3.
8. Kuhn, Mary. Author interview, November 10, 2012.
9. Hitler, Adolf. *Mein Kampf*, trans. Ralph Manheim (Boston: Houghton Mifflin Company Sentry Edition, 1943), 126.
10. Dawidowicz, Lucy S. *The War Against the Jews 1933–1945* (New York: Bantam, 1981), 16.
11. Toland, 55.
12. Watt, Richard M., *The Kings Depart: The Tragedy of Germany: Versailles and the German Revolution* (NY: Simon and Schuster), 293.
13. Meyer, G. J., *A World Undone: The Story of the Great War, 1914 to 1918* (NY: Delacorte Press, 2006), 5–7.
14. Dawidowicz, 17.
15. Diamond, 226.

16. Whelan, Frank. "The American Fuehrer Fritz Kuhn's Neo-nazi Rally in Sellersville Was His Last Hurrah," *The Morning Call*, May 12, 1985. Accessed June 10, 2011, http://articles.mcall.com/1985-05-12/news/2472315_1_nazi-berlin -nazi-masters-myths
17. Dawidowicz, 17.
18. Passant, E. J., *A Short History of Germany: 1815–1945* (London: Cambridge University Press, 1966), 158–159.
19. Toland, 75.
20. Michael Burleigh, foreword to *A Brief History of the Birth of the Nazis: How the Freikorps Blazed a Trail for Hitler,* by Nigel Jones (London: Constable & Robinson Ltd., 2004).
21. Toland, 75.
22. Jones, Nigel. *A Brief History of the Birth of the Nazis: How the Freikorps Blazed a Trail for Hitler* (London: Constable & Robinson Ltd., 2004), 61–74.
23. Larson, Erik. *In the Garden of the Beasts: Love, Terror, and an American Family in Hitler's Berlin* (New York: Crown, 2011), 49.
24. Jones, 75–76.
25. Winter, Jay and Blaine Baggett, *The Great War and the Shaping of the 20th Century* (NY: Penguin Studio, 1996), 336.
26. Ibid, 376.
27. Jones, 76.
28. Diamond, 227.
29. Jones, 151–152.
30. Ibid, 199.
31. FBI memo. May 29, 1939, 1.
32. Rollins, Richard. *I Find Treason: The Story of an American Anti-Nazi Agent* (New York: William Morrow and Company, 1941), 122.
33. Toland, 75.
34. Rollins. *I Find Treason*, 122.
35. FBI memo. June 9, 1939.
36. FBI memo. Undated.
37. FBI memo. May 29, 1939, 1.
38. Diamond, 227.
39. *Investigation of Un-American Propaganda Activities in the United States: Hearings Before a Special Committee on Un-American Activities*, 76th Cong. 3726 (1939) (testimony of Fritz Kuhn), 3786–87.
40. Gangi, Robert J. "The German American Bund as a Unique *American* Phenomenon: The Amalgam of *Deutschtum*, Americanism and National Socialism" (master's thesis, William Paterson University of New Jersey, 2008), Part II, Section I, http://germanamericanbund.synthasite.com/part -two.php
41. Diamond, 227.
42. Tamm, E.A. Memorandum for the Director Re: Fritz Julius Kuhn, May 13, 1939.

43. Tolzmann, Don Heinrich. *The German-American Experience* (Amherst, New York: Humanity Books, 2000), 268.

44. Canedy, Susan. *America's Nazis: A Democratic Dilemma* (Menlo Park, CA: Markgraf Publications Group, 1990), 10

45. Tolzmann, 291.

46. Canedy, 9.

47. Tolzmann, 291.

48. Pietrusza, David. *1920: The Year of Six Presidents* (New York: Basic Books, 2008), 45.

49. Tolzmann, 271.

50. Ibid, 298–305.

51. FBI memo. October 8, 1943.

52. Watts, Steven, *The People's Tycoon: Henry Ford and the American Century* (New York: Alfred A. Knopf, 2005), 134.

53. Lee, Albert. *Henry Ford and the Jews* (New York: Stein and Day, 1980), 78–79.

54. Baldwin, Neil, *Henry Ford and the Jews: The Mass Production of Hate* (New York: Public Affairs, 2003), 145.

55. Hitler, 639.

56. FBI Memo. June 14, 1939.

57. FBI Memo. May 13, 1939.

2. Friends

1. Diamond, 102–106

2. Grover, Warren, *Nazis in Newark* (New Brunswick, NJ: Transaction Publishers, 2003), 74.

3. Diamond, 121–122.

4. Miller, Julie, rev. Mary Bowling, "Introduction: Emerson Family Papers, ca. 1840s–1976." The New York Public Library Humanities and Social Sciences Library Manuscripts and Archives Division." May 1989, rev. 1991.

5. House Committee on Un-American Activities, *Report on the Axis Front Movement in the United States, Appendix VII, First Section Nazi Activities*, 78th Cong., 1st sess., (1943), 56–57.

6. Diamond, 123–126.

7. Ibid, 128.

8. Ibid, 129–130.

9. Ibid, 130–133.

10. Ibid, 143–148.

11. Canedy, 55.

12. "Berlin Hears Ford is Backing Hitler," *New York Times*, December 20, 1922.

13. Raymond Fendrick, "'Heinrich' Ford Idol of Bavaria Fascisti Chief," *Chicago Tribune*, March 8, 1923.

3. The Rise of Fritz Kuhn

1. FBI report, June 22, 1943.
2. Diamond, 164.
3. Ibid, 172.
4. FBI memorandum, May 14, 1939.
5. FBI memorandum, January 7, 1943.
6. Diamond, 175–180.
7. Ibid, 185–186.
8. FBI memorandum, July 31, 1939.
9. *Investigation of Un-American Propaganda Activities in the United States: Hearings Before a Special Committee on Un-American Activities*, 76th Cong. 3726 (1939) (testimony of Fritz Kuhn), 3728–29.
10. Wolter, Erik V. with Robert J. Masters, *Loyalty on Trial: One American's Battle with the FBI* (Lincoln, NE: iUniverse, Inc., 2004), 67.
11. Diamond, 124.
12. Wolter, 66.
13. Diamond, 154.
14. Ibid, 103–105.
15. Ibid, 155–156.
16. *Charleston, West Virginia Gazette*, August 13, 1934
17. Bayor, Ronald H., *Neighbors in Conflict: The Irish, Germans, Jews, and Italians of New York City, 1929–1941*, 2nd Edition (Urbana and Chicago: University of Illinois Press, 1988), 68–70.
18. *Freunde Des Neun Deutschland, Ortsgruppe* yearbook, June 3, 1934.
19. *Miami News-Record*, August 28, 1934.
20. Smith, Geoffrey S., *To Save A Nation: American "Extremism," the New Deal, and the Coming of World War II* (Chicago: Ivan R. Dee, 1992), 92.
21. Diamond, 173–174.
22. "U.S. Nazi Witness," *Chicago Daily Tribune*, November 4, 1933.
23. Grover, 82.
24. Canedy, 63.
25. Grover, 83.
26. Diamond, 177.
27. Grover, 83.
28. "Hitler Cheers and Fists Fly at Inquiry on Nazis; Police Break Up Fight at Hearing," *Chicago Daily Tribune*, October 18, 1934.
29. Grover, 83.
30. Wolter, 65.
31. Canedy, 64.
32. Diamond, 184.
33. *Investigation of Un-American Propaganda Activities in the United States: Hearings Before a Special Committee on Un-American Activities*, 76th Cong. 3726 (1939) (testimony of Fritz Kuhn).

34. FBI memorandum, January 7, 1943.
35. "Nazi Activity Here Limited By Hitler," *New York Times*, December 25, 1935.
36. Smith, Geoffrey S., 93.
37. *New York Times*, December 25, 1935.

Part II: The Rise of the German-American Bund

1. Brantley, Dwight. Letter to FBI Director, June 9, 1939.

4. Bundesführer

1. Diamond, 222.
2. "German Group Hits Communism." *Buffalo Evening News*, March 30, 1936.
3. *Syracuse Herald*, March 29, 1936.
4. *Buffalo Evening News*, March 30, 1936.
5. *Ontario Daily Messenger*, March 30, 1936.
6. Shirer, William L., *The Rise and Fall of the Third Reich: A History of Nazi Germany* (New York: Fawcett Crest, 1983), 406fn.
7. *Sheboygan Press*, March 30, 1936.
8. Diamond, 231.
9. From *Awake and Act! Aims and Purposes of The German American Bund. An Appeal to all Americans of German Stock* by Fritz Kuhn, President of the German American Bund, New York April 17, 1936. Excerpted in undated FBI Memo.
10. Canedy, 73.

5. Order

1. Canedy, 73.
2. Ibid, 81
3. FBI Report, November 17, 1941, 90–91.
4. FBI report, November 1942
5. Diamond, 230.
6. Canedy, 84–86.
7. Bell, Leland V., *In Hitler's Shadow: The Anatomy of American Nazism* (Port Washington, New York, London: Kennikat Press, 1973), 30–31.
8. Diamond, 245–246.
9. Bell, 32.
10. FBI memo, May 14, 1939, 32.
11. FBI memo, May 13, 1939, 30.
12. Bell, 32.
13. FBI memo, May 14, 1939, 29.
14. Canedy, 124.

Part III: Swastika Nation

1. Undated FBI File.

6. Olympia

1. Shirer, *The Rise and Fall of the Third Reich: A History of Nazi Germany*, 322
2. Infield, Glenn B., *Leni Riefenstahl: The Fallen Film Goddess* (New York: Thomas Y. Crowell Company, 1976), 115.
3. Large, David Clay, *Nazi Games: The Olympics of 1936* (New York: W. W. Norton & Company, 2007), 70–71.
4. Ibid, 78–79.
5. Shirer, *The Rise and Fall of the Third Reich: A History of Nazi Germany*, 322.
6. Shirer, William L., *Berlin Diary: The Journal of a Foreign Correspondent, 1934–1941* (New York: Popular Library, 1961), 53.
7. Canedy, 143.
8. Diamond, 273.
9. Burleigh, Michael, *The Third Reich: A New History* (New York: Hill and Wang, 2000), 223–228.
10. Shirer, *The Rise and Fall of the Third Reich: A History of Nazi Germany*, 365.
11. Burleigh, 223.
12. Bell, 40.
13. FBI memo, May 14, 1939, 59.
14. Ibid.
15. Diamond, 274.
16. Shirer, *The Rise and Fall of the Third Reich: A History of Nazi Germany*, 363–365.
17. FBI memo, May 14, 1939, 60–61.
18. Miller, Marvin D. *Wunderlich's Salute: The Interrelationship of the German-American Bund, Camp Siegfried, Yaphank, Long Island, and the Young Siegfrieds and their relationship with American and Nazi institutions.* (Smithtown, NY: Malamud-Rose, 1983), 23.
19. FBI memo, May 14, 1939, 60–61.
20. Diamond, 275.
21. Ibid, 276.
22. FBI memo, May 14, 1939, 61.
23. Reuth, Ralf Georg, *Goebbels*, translated from the German by Krishna Winston (New York: Harcourt Brace & Company, 1993), 110–13
24. FBI memo, May 14, 1939, 61.
25. Diamond, 278–279.
26. Dodd, William E. and Martha Dodd, editors with an Introduction by Charles A. Beard, *Ambassador Dodd's Diary, 1933–1938* (New York: Harcourt, Brace and Company, 1941), 340.
27. FBI memo, May 14, 1939, 50.
28. FBI Report, April 27, 1942, 3.

29. Ibid, 5.
30. Herzstein, 283.
31. FBI Report, April 27, 1942, 6.
32. Ibid.
33. Medoff, Rafael, "Alf Landon, Unlikely Friend of the Jews," *Jewish Ledger: Serving Connecticut's Jewish Community*, jewishledger.com, December 2012, accessed March 31, 2012.
34. FBI Report, April 27, 1942, 6.
35. *New York Times*, October 16, 1936
36. "Says Kuhn's Bund had 6,617 in 1937." *The New York Times*, April 4, 1939.
37. Bayor, Ronald H. *Neighbors in Conflict: The Irish, Germans, Jews, and Italians of New York City, 1929–1941* (Urbana and Chicago: University of Illinois Press, 1988. Second Edition), 61.

7. Nazi Fighter with a Typewriter

1. Gabler, Neil. *Winchell: Gossip, Power and the Culture of Celebrity* (New York: Vintage Books, 1994), 5–9.
2. Winchell, Walter, introduction by Ernest Cuneo. *Winchell Exclusive: "Things That Happened to Me—and Me to Them"* (Englewood Cliffs, New Jersey: Prentice-Hall, Inc., 1975), 10–11.
3. Gabler. *Winchell*, 28–31.
4. Ibid, 35.
5. Winchell, 15
6. Winchell, 25–26.
7. Stuart, Lyle. *The Secret Life of Walter Winchell* (New York: Boar's Head Books, 1953), 43–44.
8. Gabler. *Winchell*, 63.
9. Ibid, 71.
10. Thomas, Bob. *Walter Winchell: The Man and the Myth* (New York: Berkley Medallion Books, 1972), 48–49.
11. Ibid, 35.
12. Ibid, 51.
13. Ibid, 59–60.
14. Blumenthal, Ralph, postscript by Shermane Billingsley. *Stork Club: America's Most Famous Nightspot and the Lost World of Café Society* (Boston, New York, London: Back Bay Books, 2001), 9.
15. Weiner, Ed. *Let's Go to Press: A Biography of Walter Winchell* (New York: G. P. Putnam's Sons, 1955), 66–67.
16. Ibid, 69–70.
17. Klurfeld, Herman. *Winchell: His Life and Times* (New York: Praeger Publishers, 1976), 66.
18. Gabler. *Winchell*, 195.
19. Forster, Arnold, foreword by Elie Wiesel. *Square One: The Memoirs of a True*

Freedom Fighter's Life-long Struggle Against Anti-Semitism, Domestic and Foreign (New York: Primus, Donald I. Fine, Inc., 1989), 57–58.

20. Larson, 4–5.
21. Klurfeld, 65.
22. Gabler. *Winchell*, 195.
23. Klurfeld, 65.
24. Gabler. *Winchell*, 195–196.
25. Klurfeld, 66.
26. Weiner, 85.
27. Ibid, 86.
28. Klurfeld, 67.
29. Winchell, 127.
30. Weiner, 90.
31. Thomas, 99.
32. Klurfeld, 67.

8. Family and Youth

1. "Talk of the Town." *The New Yorker*, July 13, 1940.
2. Carlson, John Roy. *Under Cover: My Four Years in the Nazi Underworld of American—The Amazing Revelation of How Axis Agents and Our Enemies Within Are Now Plotting to Destroy the United States* (New York: E. P. Dutton & Company, Inc., 1943).
3. "Nazi Names Mark A Realty Project In Yaphank Tract." *The Mid-Island Mail*, January 20, 1937.
4. "Talk of the Town." *The New Yorker*, July 13, 1940.
5. Carlson. *I Find Treason*, 109.
6. "5,000 Members of German American Club at Yaphank Festival." *The Mid-Island Mail*, July 22, 1936.
7. Ewing, Helen W. "The 'Friends of New' Germany Establish Nazi Camp in Yaphank." *The Mid-Island Mail*, July 31, 1935.
8. Miller, 1–2.
9. Monahan, Roy P. testimony. *Committee of Un-American Activities, House of Representatives, Res. 282, Volume 2*, 1938, 1086.
10. Carlson. *Under Cover*, 108–109.
11. "Large Nazi Outing All But Peaceful." *The Mid-Island Mail*, July 7, 1937.
12. "Judge Neuss Registers Complaint Against Nazi Crowds at Yaphank." *The Mid-Island Mail*, June 23, 1937.
13. "Town Board Says Ask U.S. Attorney About Nazi Camp." *The Mid-Island Mail*, June 30, 1937
14. *The Mid-Island Mail*, June 23, 1937.
15. "Town Board Says Ask U.S. Attorney About Nazi Camp." *The Mid-Island Mail*, June 30, 1937.
16. "Swastika-marked Knife is seized." *The Mid-Island Mail*, August 4, 1937.

17. *The Mid-Island Mail*, June 23, 1937.
18. "Camp Head Says This Is Plan If Brookhaven Town Board Does Not Stop 'Picking on Us.'" *The Mid-Island Mail*, July 28, 1937.
19. Miller, 54.
20. Monahan testimony, 1083.
21. Diamond, 267n.
22. "Nazis Teach Children Here to Hate Jews." *The Brooklyn Eagle*, March 27, 1938.
23. Carlson. *Under Cover,* 109.
24. *The Brooklyn Eagle*, March 27, 1938.
25. Bell, 24–26.
26. Monahan testimony, 1085–87.
27. *Committee of Un-American Activities, House of Representatives, Res. 282, Volume 6,* 1939, Testimony of Helen Vooros, 3900–01.
28. Ibid, 3893.
29. Ibid, 3902.
30. Monahan testimony, 1086.
31. Miller, 179.
32. Vooros testimony, 2928.
33. *The Brooklyn Eagle*, March 27, 1938.
34. Vooros testimony, 3920–35.

9. It Can't Happen Here

1. Grover, 194–198.
2. Benter, Steven. "The Hidden Past," *The Cedarburg Graphic Pilot*, May 2, 1988.
3. Lewis, Sinclair, introduction by Michael Lewis. *It Can't Happen Here* (New York: The New American Library, 1970), 24–25.
4. Jung, Wolfgang T. Letter to Town Clerk, October 25, 1937.
5. Southbury Historical Society Bund Timeline, 1.
6. Manley Reverend Felix A. Letter to Roscoe Nelson, December 13, 1937.
7. "Two Southbury Pastors Attack Pro-Nazi Camp." *The Waterbury Republican*, November 22, 1937.
8. Letter by The Kettletowners, undated.
9. "Southbury Folk on Record As Opposed To Bund Camp; Demand Government Action." *The Waterbury Republican*, November 24, 1937.
10. "Two Southbury Pastors Attack Pro-Nazi Camp." *The Waterbury Republican*, November 22, 1937.
11. "Southbury Pastor Denounces Nazi Camp in Stirring Sermon." *The Waterbury Republican*, November 22, 1937.
12. "VFW to Act Monday at Southbury Community Hall to Form Resolution Condemning Nazi Camp." *The Waterbury Republican*, November 22, 1937.
13. "Southbury Folk on Record As Opposed To Bund Camp; Demand Government Action." *The Waterbury Republican*, November 24, 1937.

14. "Nazi Camps Scored by Farmer Session." *The New York Times*, November, 24 1937.
15. Chase, Geo. C. Letter to Reverend M. Edgar N. Lindsay, December 10, 1937.
16. Anonymous. Letter to Reverend M. Edgar N. Lindsay, November 24, 1937.
17. Brown, Lois Lindsay. Interview by author. Chicago, IL. 22 July 2012.
18. "Southbury Halts Bund Activities By Two Arrests." *The Waterbury Republican*, December 6, 1937.
19. Anonymous. Letter to Harold Hicock, undated.
20. Southbury Historical Society Bund Timeline, 1.
21. "Southbury's Zoning Code Bars Use Of Bund Camp For Recreation Or Drills." *The Waterbury Republican*, December 8, 1937.
22. "Zoning Draft in Southbury Wins Approval." *The Waterbury Republican*, December 14, 1937.
23. "Bund Charges Are Dismissed By Southbury." *The Waterbury Republican*, December 27, 1937.
24. "Bund Activity Is Investigated By Federal Men." *The Waterbury Republican*, December 16, 1937.
25. "Deed for Southbury Bund Campsite Transfer." *The Waterbury American*, October 11, 1940.
26. Mindell, Cindy. "On the Right Side of History." Jewish Ledger: Connecticut Edition. Accessed December 1, 2012. http://www.jewishledger.com/2012/11/on-the-right-side-of-history
27. Hubbell, Bernice. Letter to G. Kenyon Moore, April 7, 1938.
28. Bell, 56–58.
29. FBI Report. April 27, 1942, 20–21
30. Miller, 38.
31. Bell, 60.
32. FBI Report. April 27, 1942, 30.

10. New Moon and Red Cloud

1. Townsend, Kenneth William. *World War II and the American Indian* (Albuquerque: University of New Mexico Press, 2002), 33–35.
2. "American Indian Federation." Oklahoma Historical Society's Encyclopedia of Oklahoma History & Culture. http://digital.library.okstate.edu/encyclopedia/entries/A/AM006.html, accessed November 12, 2012.
3. Townsend, 47–48.
4. Sonneborn, Liz. "Jemison, Alice Mae." *A to Z of American Indian Women*, Revised Edition, A to Z of Women. New York: Facts On File, Inc., 2007. *American Women's History Online*. Facts On File, Inc. http://www.fofweb.com/activelink2.asp? ItemID=WE42&iPin=AIW064&SingleRecord=True (accessed November 12, 2012).
5. Townsend, 50–56.

6. Carlson. *Under Cover*, 46.
7. Carlson, John Roy. *The Plotters* (New York: E. P. Dutton & Company, Inc., 1946), 26.
8. Townsend, 55–56.
9. Carlson. *The Plotters*, 26–28.
10. Townsend, 42–45.

11. Disturbances

1. Dobbs, Michael. *Saboteurs: The Nazi Raid on America* (New York: Vintage Books, 2005), 56.
2. Miller, 26.
3. Dobbs, 56–57.
4. Monahan testimony, 1085–86.
5. Wolter, Erik V. with Robert J. Masters. *Loyalty on Trial: One American's Battle With the FBI* (Lincoln, NE: iUniverse, 2004), 81.
6. Carlson, *Under Cover*, 30–31.
7. Monahan testimony, 1085–86.
8. Baylor, 135–137.
9. "Nazis Send 10 to Hospitals in N.Y. Bund Riot." *Chicago Daily Tribune*, April 21, 1938.
10. "U.S. Veterans Loose Battle With Germans in Manhattan." *Life Magazine*, May 2, 1938, 19.
11. Newark, Tim. *Mafia Allies: The True Story of America's Secret Alliance with the Mob in World War II* (St. Paul, MN: Zenith Press, 2007), 74.
12. "U.S. Veterans Loose Battle With Germans in Manhattan." *Life Magazine*, May 2, 1938, 19.
13. "Nazis Send 10 to Hospitals in N.Y. Bund Riot." *Chicago Daily Tribune*, April 21, 1938.
14. Newark, 74.
15. "Nazis Send 10 to Hospitals in N.Y. Bund Riot." *Chicago Daily Tribune*, April 21, 1938.
16. Newark, 74.
17. U.S. Veterans Loose Battle With Germans in Manhattan." *Life Magazine*, May 2, 1938, 19.
18. Newark, Tim. *Mafia Allies: The True Story of America's Secret Alliance With the Mob in World War II* (St. Paul, MN: Zenith Press, 2007), 74.
19. "Nazis Send 10 to Hospitals in N.Y. Bund Riot." *Chicago Daily Tribune*, April 21, 1938.
20. "Jew Defends Nazi." *Chicago Daily Tribune*, April 22, 1938.
21. Bell, 69.
22. Spivak, John L. *Secret Armies: The New Technique of Naz Warfare* (New York: Modern Age Books, Inc., 1939), 93.

23. Bell, 69.
24. Joint Fact-Finding Committee on Un-American Activities in California, *Report to California Legislature*, California Senate, 54th sess., 1943.
25. "Photostat Copy of Official Publication List—German Bund." Aryan Bookstore, undated.
26. Sounes, Howard. *Charles Bukowski: Locked in the Arms of a Crazy Life* (New York: Grove Press, 1998), 8–9.
27. Ibid, 18–19.
28. Bukowski, Charles. *Ham on Rye* (New York: Ecco, 2002), 236.
29. Pleasants, Ben. "When Bukowski was a Nazi, Part 1." Hollywood Investigator, April 8, 2003. Accessed July 7, 2010. http://www.hollywoodinvestigator.com /2003/bukowski1.htm.
30. Bell, 21.
31. Gabler, Neal. *An Empire of Their Own: How the Jews Invented Hollywood* (New York: Anchor Books, 1989), 295–296.
32. "San Francisco Landmarks." NoeHill in San Francisco. Accessed July 10, 2012. http://www.noehill.com/sf/landmarks/sf174.asp
33. Bell, 69.
34. "Protests of Nazi Bund Meetings." The Virtual Museum of the City of San Francisco. Accessed July 10, 2010. http://www.sfmuseum.org/hist1/bund.html
35. Bell, 69.

12. Hollywood

1. Gabler. *An Empire of Their Own*, 5.
2. Ibid, 272–273.
3. Marx, Groucho. *The Groucho Letters: Letters From and To Groucho Marx* (New York: Simon and Schuster), 21.
4. "Suicide of the Hollywood Motion Picture Industry." October 20, 1936.
5. Ceplair, Larry and Steven Englund. *The Inquisition in Hollywood: Politics in the Film Community, 1930–1950* (Berkeley: University of California Press, 1983), 104–112.
6. Hollywood Anti-Nazi League for the Defense of American Democracy. "The Menace of 'Hitlerism in America.'" Undated.
7. Hollywood Anti-Nazi League for the Defense of American Democracy. "Three Major Events in the Anti-Nazi World." Undated.
8. Riefenstahl, Leni. *Leni Riefenstahl: A Memoir* (New York: St. Martin's Press, 1993), 237–238.
9. Bach, Steven. *Leni: The Life and Work of Leni Riefenstahl* (New York: Vintage, 2008), 333n.
10. Riefenstahl, 238.
11. Baldwin, 284.
12. Bach, 170.
13. Riefenstahl, 238–239.

14. Gabler, Neal. *Walt Disney: The Triumph of the American Imagination* (New York: Vintage Books, 2007), 363.
15. Eliot, Marc. *Walt Disney: Hollywood's Dark Prince* (New York: Birch Lane Press, 1993).

Part IV: Golems

1. Cohen, Mickey as told to John Peer Nugent. *In My Own Words: The Underworld Autobiography of Michael Mickey Cohen* (Englewood Cliffs, NJ: Prentice-Hall, Inc., 1975), 2.

14. Little Man

1. Renck, Ellen Sadove. "History of Grodno." JewishGen, 2009. Accessed June 19, 2012. http://www.jewishgen.org/belarus/info_history_of_grodno.htm.
2. Eisenberg, Dennis, Uri Dan, and Eli Landau. *Meyer Lansky: Mogul of the Mob* (New York & London: Paddington Press, Ltd., 1972), 26.
3. Lacey, Robert. *Little Man: Meyer Lansky and the Gangster Life* (Boston: Little, Brown and Company, 1991), 17.
4. Eisenberg et al, 26–29.
5. Lacey, 19–21.
6. Eisenberg et al, 41.
7. Lacey, 24.
8. Eisenberg et al, 33–39.
9. Ibid, 46–48.
10. Ibid, 54–57.
11. Ibid, 52–53.
12. Lacey, 284.
13. Telushkin, Rabbi Joseph. *Jewish Literacy: The Most Important Things to Know About the Jewish Religion, Its People, and Its History* (New York: William Morrow & Company, Inc., 2001), 49.
14. Dimont, Max I. *Jews, God and History (50th Anniversary Edition)* (New York: Signet Classics, 2004), 374.
15. "Stephen Samuel Wise." Jewish Virtual Library. Accessed June 22, 2012. http://www.jewishvirtuallibrary.org/jsource/biography/wise.html.
16. Eisenberg et al, 184.
17. "Nathan David Perlman." Jewish Virtual Library. Accessed June 22, 2012. http://www.jewishvirtuallibrary.org/jsource/biography/nperlman.html.
18. Lacey, 113.
19. Wise, Rabbi Stephen S. "What is an American?" *Free Synagogue Pulpit: Sermons and Addresses, Volume V, 1918–1919* (New York: Bloch Publishing Company. 1920), 2.
20. Eisenberg et al, 184–185.
21. Ibid, 48.
22. Rockaway, Robert A. *But He Was Good to His Mother: The Lives and Crimes of*

Jewish Gangsters (New York & Jerusalem: Gefen Publishing House, 2000), 228–229.

23. Eisenberg et al, 185–186.
24. Lacey, 113.
25. Eisenberg et al, 185.
26. Lacey, 113.
27. Eisenberg et al, 185–186.

15. King of Newark

1. Stuart, Mark A. *Gangster: The True Story of the Man Who Invented Organized Crime* (London, England: A Star Book published by the Paperback Division of W. H. Allen & Co., 1986), 15–20.
2. FBI memo, June 7, 1950, 1–5.
3. Rockaway, Robert A. *But He Was Good To His Mother: The Lives and Crimes of Jewish Gangsters* (New York & Jerusalem: Gefen Publishing House, 2000), 32.
4. Stuart, 18–24.
5. Grover, Warren. *Nazis in Newark* (New Brunswick, NJ: Transaction Publishers), 42–43.
6. FBI Memo, June 7, 1950, 1–5.
7. Ibid, 74.
8. FBI Memo, June 7, 1950, 3.
9. Stuart, 80–97.
10. FBI Memo, January 15, 1958, 37.
11. Higham, Charles. *Howard Hughes: The Secret Life* (New York: St. Martin's Griffin, 2004), 58–59.
12. Grover, 4.
13. Ibid, 23–25.
14. Ibid, 47–49.
15. New Jersey Boxing Hall of Fame Web Site. Accessed June 29, 2012. http://www.njboxinghof.org/cgi-bin/henryseehof.pl?493
16. Grover, 50–51.
17. Rockaway, 231.
18. Grover, 52–53.
19. Ibid, 27–31.
20. Rockaway, 224–225.
21. Ibid, 231–232.
22. Grover, 27–31.
23. Ibid, 53–56.
24. Rockaway, 231–232.
25. Grover, 214–215.
26. Konigsberg, Eric. *Blood Relation* (New York: Harper Perennial, 2006), 53.
27. Rockaway, 229–230.

16. The West Coast Racketeer

1. Rockaway, 175.
2. Buntin, John. *L.A. Noir: The Struggle for the Soul of America's Most Seductive City* (New York: Harmony Books, 2009), 20–24.
3. Cohen, 7.
4. Ibid, 6–8.
5. Ibid, 9.
6. BoxRec Web Site. Accessed June 29, 2012. http://boxrec.com/list_bouts.php ?human_id=166332&cat=boxer
7. Buntin, 44.
8. Cohen, photo insert.
9. Rockaway, 44–46.
10. Cohen, 21.
11. Ibid, 29–30.
12. Buntin, 63.
13. Newark, Tim. *Mafia Allies: The True Story of America's Secret Alliance With the Mob in World War II* (St. Paul, MN: Zenith Press, 2007), 113.
14. Buntin, 85.
15. Newark, 113–114.
16. Cohen, 35.
17. California Legislature, Fifty-Fifth Session "Report Joint Fact-Finding Committee on Un-American Activities in California," 1943, 260–261.
18. Cohen, 67–68.
19. Lewis, Brad. *Hollywood's Celebrity Gangster: The Incredible Life and Times of Mickey Cohen* (New York: Enigma Books, 2007), 26.
20. Cohen, 68.

17. The Chicago Avenger

1. Cutler, Irving. *The Jews of Chicago: From Shtetl to Suburb* (Urbana and Chicago: University of Illinois Press, 1996), 153.
2. Wills, Gary and Ovid Demaris. *Jack Ruby* (New York: Da Capo Press, Inc. 1994), 96–98.
3. Cutler, 153.
4. Wills and Demaris, 98.
5. *Report of the Warren Commission on the Assassination of President Kennedy* (New York: Bantam Books, 1964), 694–695.
6. Wills and Demaris, 99.
7. *Warren Report*, 697.
8. "Illinois Nazis' Membership Put at 4,000 to 6,000." *Chicago Tribune*, January 6, 1938, 3.
9. "Germania Club Bans Meetings of Nazi Groups." *Chicago Tribune*, March 9, 1938, 4.

10. "Stench Bombs Halt Dance Attended by Bund Leader." *Chicago Tribune*, March 8, 1939, 9.
11. "Protest Plans to Hold German Folk Festival." *Chicago Tribune*, July 10, 1938, 13.
12. "Bund Speakers Assail Jews and Press at Picnic." *Chicago Tribune*, July 25, 1938, 5.
13. *Warren Report*, 696.
14. Century, Douglas. *Barney Ross* (New York: Nextbook Schocken, 2006), 151.
15. Wills and Demaris, 99.

Part V: Girlfriends

1. Monahan testimony, 1086.

18. On the Town

1. Rollins, 108.
2. "Talk of the Town: Chez Bundesführer." *The New Yorker*, March 18, 1939, 14.
3. Plummer, Elizabeth. "Glamour Girls and Boys of Gotham Have Busy Nights." *Prescott Evening Courier*, Prescott, Arizona, December 13, 1939 (AP Story)
4. Rollins, 108.
5. Sharkey, Joe. "Weekend Excursion: Traces of the Place at High Tide." *New York Times*, November 30, 2001.
6. Diamond, 253.
7. Klurfeld, Herman. *Winchell: His Life and Times* (New York: Praeger Publishers, 1976), 67–68.
8. Winchell, Walter. "On Broadway." New York *Daily Mirror*, May 12, 1939.
9. Mefford, Arthur. "Wife's Letter Tells Romances of Kuhn." New York *Daily Mirror*, May 31, 1939.

19. The Edict

1. Larson, 344–345.
2. Canedy, 159–163.
3. FBI Report, April 27, 1942, 30.
4. Canedy, 164.
5. Diamond, 311–312
6. FBI Report, April 27, 1942. 30–33.
7. "Foreign News: Land of Justice." *Time* magazine, May 9, 1938.
8. Baylor, 63.
9. "Kuhn Admits Lies About His Romance." *The New York Times*, November 23, 1939.

20. The Golden Angel and Miss America

1. "Kuhn Is Cleared On 5 Of 10 Counts." *The New York Times*, November 25, 1939.
2. "Cogswell, Virginia. "How to Hold a Husband." *San Antonio Light*, San Antonio, Texas April 10, 1938.
3. Sasser, Tate, Business Manger, Miss Georgia Pageant, Columbus, GA. Author interview, June 7, 2011.
4. Puro, June, Liz Puro, Office Administrator, Miss America Organization, Linwood, NJ, email to author, June 7, 2011
5. Cogswell.
6. Ibid.
7. Rollins, photo insert 116.
8. Cogswell.
9. Rollins, 110–113.
10. Brantley, Dwight. Letter to Director of FBI, June 9, 1939.
11. Rollins, 114–118.

Part VI: George Washington's Birthday

1. "Free America! The German American Bund at Madison Square Garden, February 20, 1939. Speeches by J. Wheeler-Hill, Rudolf Markman, George Froboese, Hermann Schwinn, G. William Kunze and The Bund Fuehrer: Fritz Kuhn," February 1939, 2.

21. Madison Square Garden

1. Winchell, Walter. "On Broadway" New York *Daily Mirror*, February 10, 1939.
2. "Nazis Hail George Washington as First Fascist." *Life*, March 7, 1938, 17.
3. Peters, C. Brooks. "Reich Denies Link to American Bund." *New York Times*, February 26, 1939.
4. "22,000 Nazis Hold Rally in Garden; Police Check Foes." *New York Times*, February 21, 1939.
5. Maloney, Russell. "Heil Washington!" *The New Yorker*, April 4, 1939.
6. New York *Times*, February 21, 1939.
7. "Bund Rally Bomb Rumor Fails to Worry Mayor," *New York Times*, February 21, 1939.
8. "22,000 Nazis Hold Rally in Garden; Police Check Foes." *New York Times*, February 21, 1939.
9. Maloney.
10. "22,000 Nazis Hold Rally in Garden; Police Check Foes." *New York Times*, February 21, 1939.
11. Maloney.
12. "22,000 Nazis Hold Rally in Garden; Police Check Foes." *New York Times*, February 21, 1939.
13. Maloney.

14. "22,000 Nazis Hold Rally in Garden; Police Check Foes." *New York Times*, February 21, 1939.
15. Maloney.
16. "22,000 Nazis Hold Rally in Garden; Police Check Foes." *New York Times*, February 21, 1939.

22. The Rally

1. Jenkins, Philip. *Hoods and Shirts: The Extreme Right in Pennsylvania, 1925–1950* (Chapel Hill, NC: The University of North Carolina Press, 1997), 139.
2. Ibid, 150.
3. "Free America," 1–2.
4. "22,000 Nazis Hold Rally in Garden; Police Check Foes." *New York Times*, February 21, 1939.
5. "Free America," 3.
6. "Free America," 4–7.
7. Thompson, Dorothy. "Goodbye to Germany." *Harper's Magazine*, December 1934, 12–14.
8. Kurth, Peter. *American Cassandra: The Life of Dorothy Thompson* (New York: Little Brown & Company, 1990), 287–288.
9. Maloney.
10. Kurth, 288.
11. Maloney.
12. "Bund Foes Protest Policing of Rally," *New York Times*, February 22, 1939.
13. Winchell, Walter. "On Broadway" New York *Daily Mirror*, February 26, 1939.
14. Ibid, February 23, 1939.
15. "Free America," 10.
16. "22,000 Nazis Hold Rally in Garden; Police Check Foes." *New York Times*, February 21, 1939.
17. "Free America," 9–14.
18. Ibid, 15.
19. Jeffers, H. Paul. *The Napoleon of New York: Mayor Fiorello LaGuardia* (New York: John Wiley & Sons, Inc., 2002), 278.
20. "Free America," 15–20.
21. Lasky, A. Victor. "One Punch Izzy Still in There Punching," *Stars and Stripes*, December 8, 1944.
22. "Bund Foes Protest Policing of Rally," *New York Times*, February 22, 1939.
23. Maloney.
24. "Bund Foes Protest Policing of Rally," *New York Times*, February 22, 1939.
25. "Free America," 20.
26. Maloney.
27. "22,000 Nazis Hold Rally in Garden; Police Check Foes." *New York Times*, February 21, 1939.
28. Maloney.

29. "22,000 Nazis Hold Rally in Garden; Police Check Foes." *New York Times*, February 21, 1939.
30. "Bund Foes Protest Policing of Rally," *New York Times*, February 22, 1939.
31. Lasky.

23. Reactions

1. Peters, C. Brooks. "Reich Denies Link to American Bund," *New York Times*, February 26, 1939.
2. "See A Challenge to Bund," *New York Times*, February 22, 1939.
3. Winchell, Walter. "On Broadway" New York *Daily Mirror*, March 15, 1939.
4. "Anti-Nazis in Los Angeles Toss Eggs at Bund Chiefs." *Chicago Daily Tribune*, February 23, 1939.
5. "LaGuardia Order Bans Bund Guards; Hall Owners Must Hire Their Own Ushers," *New York Times*, February 28, 1939.
6. "Public Officials and Clergy Rally to Denounce Bund," *New York Times*, March 4, 1939.

Part VII: Cracks in the Madhouse

24. Legalities

1. *The New York Times*, March 3, 1939.
2. Canedy, 198–199.
3. Diamond, 346.
4. Richards, Guy. "Photo of Kuhn With a Blonde Rips His Alibi," New York *Daily News*, May 11, 1939.
5. "Kuhn Is Arrested in Theft of $14,548 Of Bund's Funds." *The New York Times*, May 26, 1939.
6. Richards. New York *Daily News*, May 11, 1939.
7. FBI Report, June 6, 1939.
8. "Complaint Is Filed On Kuhn As Citizen." *The New York Times*, May 9, 1939.
9. "Mayor Halts Issuance of Passports to Kuhn And Two Bund Aides After One Slips Away." *The New York Times*, May 13, 1939.
10. "Mayor Blocks Kuhn Move to Leave U.S." New York *Daily Mirror*, May 13, 1939.
11. "Mayor Halts Issuance of Passports to Kuhn And Two Bund Aides After One Slips Away." *The New York Times*, May 13, 1939.
12. "Bund Tax Evasion Charged; Mayor Asks Dewey to Act." *The New York Times*, May 18, 1939.
13. "Dewey Gets Criminal Charges Against Kuhn." New York *Daily Mirror*, May 18, 1939.
14. "Bund Tax Evasion Charged; Mayor Asks Dewey to Act." *The New York Times*, May 18, 1939.
15. Rice, William and Gerald Duncan. "Mayor and Dewey Vie for Kuhn Scalp." New York *Daily News*, May 19, 1939.

16. "Dewey Calls Kuhn in Inquiry on Bund." *The New York Times*, May 19, 1939.
17. Rice, William and Gerald Duncan.
18. "Nation 'Waking Up,' Bund Leader Asserts." *The New York Herald-Tribune*, May 22, 1939.
19. "Bund Leaders Visit Dewey." *The New York Sun*, May 22, 1939.
20. "Kuhn Stalks Out On Failure to Get Immunity." *The New York Herald-Tribune*, May 25, 1939.
21. "Bund Leaders Visit Dewey." *The New York Sun*, May 22, 1939.
22. "Grand Jury Hears Kuhn's Lieutenant." *The New York Times*, May 23, 1939.

25. Arrest

1. "Dewey's Men Seize Kuhn in Pennsylvania." *The New York Herald-Tribune*, May 26, 1939.
2. "Kuhn Is Arrested In Theft of $14,548 Of Bund's Funds." *The New York Times*, May 26, 1939.
3. "Kuhn Out On Bail On Theft Charge." *The New York Times*, May 27, 1939.
4. "Kuhn Is Arrested In Theft of $14,548 Of Bund's Funds." *The New York Times*, May 26, 1939.
5. "Kuhn Out On Bail On Theft Charge." *The New York Times*, May 27, 1939.
6. "Dewey's Men Seize Kuhn in Pennsylvania." *The New York Herald-Tribune*, May 26, 1939.
7. "Kuhn Is Arrested In Theft of $14,548 Of Bund's Funds." *The New York Times*, May 26, 1939.
8. "Kuhn Freed on Bail After Woman's Visit." *The Washington Post*, May 27, 1939.
9. "Fritz Kuhn Freed on $5,000 in Theft Case." *The Washington Herald-Times*, May 27, 1939.
10. "Kuhn Freed on Bail After Woman's Visit." *The Washington Post*, May 27, 1939.
11. "Kuhn in Seclusion, Prepares Defense." *The New York Evening Journal-American*, May 27, 1939.
12. "Fritz Kuhn Freed on $5,000 in Theft Case." *The Washington Herald-Times*, May 27, 1939.
13. "Kuhn in Seclusion, Prepares Defense." *The New York Evening Journal-American*, May 27, 1939.
14. FBI Report, April 27, 1942.
15. "Kuhn, Out on Bail, Speaks Before Milwaukee Bund." *New York Herald-Tribune*, May 28, 1939.
16. Benter.
17. "Using The American Flag As A Carpet At A Nazi Camp!" *Click: The National Picture Monthly*, June 1939, page unknown.
18. "The Latest Crop of Lies." *Deutscher Weckruf und Beobachter*, May 18, 1939.
19. Carlson. *Under Cover*, 45–47.
20. Diamond, p. 347.

26. Confessions of a Nazi Spy

1. Gabler. *Empire of Their Own*, 342.
2. Doherty, Thomas. "The Saga of the Warner Brothers, Hollywood's Studio Family." History News Network, George Mason University. Accessed October 19, 2010. http://www.hnn.us/articles/124269.html
3. Robinson, Edward G., with Leonard Spigelgass. *All My Yesterdays: An Autobiography* (New York, Hawthorn Books, Inc., 1973), 2.
4. MacDonnell, Francis. *Insidious Foes: The Axis Fifth Column and the American Home Front* (Guilford, Connecticut: The Lyons Press, 2004), 64.
5. Doherty.
6. Ross, Steven J. "*Confessions of a Nazi Spy:* Warner Bros., Anti-Fascism and the Politicization of Hollywood," in *Warners' War: Politics, Pop Culture & Propaganda in Wartime Hollywood*, ed. Martin Kaplan and Johanna Blakley (Los Angeles: The Norman Lear Center Press, 2004), 54.
7. Robinson, 206.
8. *Confessions of a Nazi Spy*. Internet Movie Data Base. Accessed July 12, 2010. http://www.imdb.com/title/tt0031173/trivia?ref_=tt_ql_6
9. Ross, 54.
10. MacDonnell, 67–70.
11. Schallert, Edwin. "'Confessions of a Nazi Spy' Vigorous, Documentary Film," *Los Angeles Times*, May 5, 1939.
12. "National Board of Review Exceptional Films 1939." National Board of Review. Accessed July 12, 2010. http://www.nbrmp.org/features/nbrmagazine_review.cfm?id=16
13. Sandeen, Eric J. "*Confessions of a Nazi Spy* and the German-American Bund," in *American Studies*, Vol. 20, No. 2: Fall 1979 (University of Kansas), 74.
14. Wolter, 28.
15. Sandeen, 74.
16. Fernett, Gene. *Hollywood's Poverty Row, 1930–1950* (Satellite Beach, Florida: Coral Reef Publications, Inc., 1973), 6–7.
17. *Hitler—Beast of Berlin*. Internet Movie Data Base. Accessed July 12, 2010. http://www.imdb.com/title/tt0031427/?ref_=fn_al_tt_2
18. "Movie 'Beast of Berlin' Will Stay Banned in City." *Chicago Daily Tribune*, November 17, 1939.

27. Hindenburg Park

1. Rasmussen, Cecilia. "Nothing Sleepy About This Past," *Los Angeles Times*, May 14, 2006.
2. "La Crescenta Picnic Grounds: Your ideal picnic grounds." Brochure, undated.
3. "Giant Pro-American Rally." Flyer, April 30, 1939.
4. "Bund Chieftain Fritz Kuhn Arrives to Address Meeting." *Los Angeles Times*, April 29, 1939.

5. "Bund's Chief Tells Program." *Los Angeles Times*, May 1, 1939.
6. "Housewife Breaks Up German Bund Meeting." *Sarasota Herald-Tribune*, April 30, 1939.
7. "Bund's Chief Tells Program." *Los Angeles Times*, May 1, 1939.
8. "Housewife Breaks Up German Bund Meeting." *Sarasota Herald-Tribune*, April 30, 1939.
9. "Bund's Chief Tells Program." *Los Angeles Times*, May 1, 1939.
10. "Wanted For Kidnapping: Adolf Hitler." Undated handbill.
11. "Bund's Chief Tells Program." *Los Angeles Times*, May 1, 1939.
12. "Dies Warns Against Foes Boring Within." *Los Angeles Times*, May 2, 1939.
13. Patenaude, Edward. "Kuhn's Comeuppance Fondly Remembered," *Telegram & Gazette*, Worcester, MA., July 27, 1995.
14. Patenaude, E. "Display Holds War Memories," *Telegram & Gazette*, Worcester, MA., July 20, 1995.
15. "People," *Time* magazine, July 24, 1939.
16. Patenaude, Edward. "Kuhn's Comeuppance Fondly Remembered," *Telegram & Gazette*, Worcester, MA., July 27, 1995.
17. "Kuhn Pays $5 Fine On Plea Of Guilty." *The New York Times*, July 21, 1939.
18. Patenaude, E. "Display Holds War Memories."
19. Kuhn Pays $5 Fine On Plea Of Guilty." *The New York Times*, July 21, 1939.

Part VIII: Trials

1. "Kuhn Says Press Persecutes Him, Sees Plot Behind Larceny Charge." *The New York Herald-Tribune*, June 2, 1939.

28. Un-American Activities

1. Kuhn testimony, 3712.
2. Ibid, 3756.
3. Ibid, 3735.
4. Ibid, 3764.
5. Ibid, 3774–76.
6. Ibid, 3831–33.
7. Ibid, 3777–78.
8. Ibid, 3827.
9. Ibid, 3861–62.
10. Ibid, 3889.
11. "Acts to Hold Kuhn If He Tries Flight." *The New York Times*, August 30, 1939.
12. *Investigation of Un-American Propaganda Activities in the United States: Hearings Before a Special Committee on Un-American Activities*, 76th Cong. 3726 (1939) (testimony of Helen Vooros), 3903–07.
13. Pope, Ernest R. "Hitler's Baby Boomerang." *Coronet Magazine*, May 1942.
14. Vooros testimony, 3921–22.

29. *The People v. Fritz Kuhn*

1. Winchell, Walter. "Walter Winchell On Broadway" September 7, 1939.
2. "Bail of Fritz Kuhn Boosted to $50,000 and He Goes to Jail." *The Chicago Daily Tribune*, September 30, 1939.
3. "Nazi Bund Chief Loses in Effort to Reduce Bond." *The Chicago Daily Tribune*, October 5, 1939.
4. "Kuhn Stays in Tombs; Lawyer Maps Appeal" *The New York Times*, December 1, 1939.
5. Fletcher, H. B. Letter to J. Edgar Hoover, October 16, 1939.
6. "Dewey is Upheld on Kuhn Records." *The New York Times*, November 2, 1939.
7. "Talk of the Town." *The New Yorker*, June 11, 1949.
8. "Jury Completed in Theft Trial of Bund Chief Kuhn." *The Chicago Daily Tribune*, November 10, 1939.
9. "Kuhn Again Loses Plea to Stay Trial." *The New York Times*, November 9, 1939.
10. "12 Business Men Put on Kuhn Jury." *The New York Times*, November 10, 1939.
11. "Jury Completed in Theft Trial of Bund Chief Kuhn." *The Chicago Daily Tribune*, November 10, 1939.
12. "People." Time Magazine, November 20, 1939.
13. "Kuhn Spent Bund Cast on Woman, Declares State." *The Chicago Daily Tribune*, November 11, 1939.
14. FBI Memo, April 14, 1942.
15. "Aides Depict Kuhn as Czar of Bund" November, 11, 1939.
16. Considine, Bob. New York *Daily Mirror*, November 11, 1939.
17. Winchell, Walter. "Winchell in Blunderland: Reviews Kuhn vs. People," New York *Daily Mirror*, November 11, 1939.
18. Winchell, Walter. Da Ist Wieder Der Vincell! New York *Daily Mirror*, November 14, 1939.
19. Winchell, Walter. "Unser Volter's Veenchill-View," New York *Daily Mirror*, November 15, 1939.
20. Winchell, November 14, 1939.
21. Winchell, November 17, 1939.
22. Winchell, November 15, 1939.
23. FBI report, November 1942.
24. "Kuhn Acts to Call Dewey as Witness." *The New York Times*, November 17, 1939.
25. Considine, Bob. "Kuhn Lovegrams Kept Wires Hot." New York *Daily Mirror*, November 14, 1939.
26. "Physician Links Fuehrer Kuhn to Georgia Peach." *The Chicago Daily Tribune*, November 15, 1939.
27. "Kuhn Acts to Call Dewey as Witness." *The New York Times*, November 17, 1939.
28. Canedy, 180–181.
29. Miller, 69–75.
30. "Kuhn Paid Bills of Woman Friend From Bund Fund, Sent Her 'Kisses.'" *The New York Times*, November 14, 1939.
31. Miller, 82.

32. "Kuhn Story False, Lawyer Declares." *The New York Times*, November 15, 1939.

33. "Kuhn Paid Bills of Woman Friend From Bund Fund, Sent Her 'Kisses.'" *The New York Times*, November 14, 1939.

34. "Kuhn Story False, Lawyer Declares." *The New York Times*, November 15, 1939.

35. "Kuhn Accountant Inspects Bund Books." *The New York Times*, November 16, 1939.

36. "Testimony At Odds On Kuhn Payment." *The New York Times*, November 21, 1939.

37. "Mayor and Dewey Placed on Stand by Kuhn Defense." *The New York Times*, November 18, 1939.

38. Ibid.

39. "Kuhn Takes Stand, Denies The Theft Of A 'Single Cent.'" *The New York Times*, November 22, 1939.

40. Rollins , 117–118.

41. "Kuhn Admits Lies About His Romance." *The New York Times*, November 23, 1939.

42. "Kuhn Is Cleared On 5 Of 10 Counts." *The New York Times*, November 25, 1939.

43. "Plea To Kuhn Jury Charges Politics." *The New York Times*, November 28, 1939.

44. "Kuhn Jury To Get Theft Case Today." *The New York Times*, November 28, 1939.

45. "Kuhn Found Guilty On All Five Counts; He Faces 30 Years." *The New York Times*, November 30, 1939.

46. Ibid.

47. "Yorkville is Apathetic." *The New York Times*, November 30, 1939.

48. "Kuhn Is Sentenced to 21/2 To 5 Years As A Common Thief." *The New York Times*, December 6, 1939.

30. The Encounter

1. "Kuhn in Sing Sing; Is A 'Little Upset.'" *The New York Times*, December 7, 1939.

2. "The Talk of the Town." *The New Yorker*, December 16, 1939.

3. Lee, 97.

4. Wallace, 139.

5. Wallace, 137.

6. Tamm, E. A., FBI memorandum, May 14, 1939.

7. Lee, 97.

31. Prison

1. "Kuhn in Sing Sing; Is A 'Little Upset.'" *The New York Times*, December 7, 1939

2. "Lawyer for Kuhn Censured by Court," *The New York Times*, December 14, 1939.

3. Donegan, T. J. Letter to J. Edgar Hoover, April 25, 1940.

4. Diamond, 362.

5. Diamond, 362–363.

Part IX: The Fall of the German-American Bund

1. Diamond, 366.

32. Honored Guests

1. Grover, 259.
2. Carlson. *Under Cover,* 152.
3. Grover, 288.
4. Miller, 122–123.
5. Grover, 288.
6. Miller, 123.
7. Miller, 123. Grover, 288–289.
8. Miller, 122–123.
9. Grover, 288.
10. Carlson. *I Find Treason,* 152–153.
11. Miller, 123.
12. Carlson, 153.
13. Grover 288.
14. Miller, 123.
15. Testimony of Gerhard Kunze. *Committee of Un-American Activities, House of Representatives, Res. 282, Volume 2,* 1938, 8358.
16. Testimony of August Klapprott. *Committee of Un-American Activities, House of Representatives, Res. 282, Volume 2,* 1938, 8292.
17. Ibid, 8299.
18. Testimony of Richard W. Werner, *Committee of Un-American Activities, House of Representatives, Res. 282, Volume 2,* 1938, 8338–49.
19. Ibid, 8382–88.

33. Dissolution

1. Miller, 128.
2. Glaser, Martha. "The German-American Bund in New Jersey." *New Jersey History 92* (Newark: New Jersey Historical Society), 43–44.
3. Diamond, 365.
4. Glaser, 44.
5. Grover, 308–309.
6. Diamond, 365–366.
7. Ladd, D. M. FBI Memo, December 17, 1941.

34. Arrests

1. "Vonsiatsky Espionage." Federal Bureau of Investigation: Famous Cases & Criminals. Accessed December 28, 2012. http://www.fbi.gov/about-us/history/famous-cases/vonsiatsky-espionage

2. Abella, Alex and Scott Gordon. *Shadow Enemies: Hitler's Secret Terrorist Plot Against the United States* (Guilford, CT: Lyons Press, 2003), 67.
3. "Vonsiatsky Espionage."
4. Abella and Gordon, 67.
5. "Vonsiatsky Espionage."
6. "Kuhn, ex bund-chief paroled for Internment." *The Chicago Daily Tribune*, June 19, 1943.
7. Diamond, 367–369.
8. Canedy, 226.
9. Winchell, Walter. "Walter Winchell in New York" New York *Daily Mirror*, September 18, 1945.
10. Winchell. *Walter Winchell Exclusive*, 128.
11. "Fritz Kuhn Set Free; He'd Like to Return to U.S." *The Chicago Daily Tribune*, April 26, 1946.
12. Canedy, 226.
13. "Foreign News: Old Refrain." *Time* magazine, February 16, 1948.
14. "Divorced Waitress Said Girl Friend Of Fritz Kuhn." *North Tonawanda Evening News*, February 7, 1948.
15. "Foreign News: Old Refrain." Time Magazine, February 16, 1948.
16. "Kuhn Convicted in Germany as Nazi Offender." *The Chicago Daily Tribune*, April 21, 1948.
17. "Nab Fritz Kuhn, Ex-Bund Chief in French Zone." *The Chicago Daily Tribune*, June 18, 1948.

35. Aftermath

1. "People: Just Deserts," *Time* magazine, February 28, 1949.
2. *The New York Times*, July 17, 1949.
3. Miller, Watson, undated letter. FBI file, April 12, 1949.
4. "Fritz Kuhn Death in 1951 Revealed." *The New York Times*, February 2, 1953.
5. Winchell, Walter. "Walter Winchell of New York." *The Daily Mirror*, February 6, 1953.
6. Smith, Geoffrey S., 181.
7. Diamond, 368–369.
8. Trohan, Walter. "Sedition Trial, Once a Bedlam, Now Dull Show." *The Chicago Daily Tribune*, August 8, 1944.
9. "Fritz Kuhn Death in 1951 Revealed." *The New York Times*, February 2, 1953.
10. Dobbs, 278.
11. "Bund Leader's Suicide Linked To Jury Probe," *The Chicago Daily Tribune*, June 18, 1942.
12. Warden, Philip. "Freed Bundist Fights To Regain His Citizenship." *The Chicago Daily Tribune*, October 17, 1947.
13. Gabler. *Winchell*, 58.

14. Ibid, 95–99.
15. Ibid, 163–165.
16. Ibid, 218.
17. Weinraub, Bernard. "He Turned Gossip into Tawdry Power; Walter Winchell, Who Climbed High and Fell Far Still Scintillates." *The New York Times*, November 18, 1998.
18. Gabler. *Winchell*, xv.
19. Thomas, 10–11.
20. Gabler. *Winchell*, 482–486.
21. Ibid, 541–544.
22. Gabler. *Winchell*, 549.
23. Lacey, 116–117.
24. Dan, 186–187.
25. Ibid, 203.
26. Lacey, 163–164.
27. Ibid, 348.
28. Ibid, 378.
29. Ibid, 421.
30. Ibid, 426.
31. English, T. J. *Havana Nocturne: How the Mob Owned Cuba and Then Lost It to the Revolution* (New York: William Morrow, 2008), 85–86.
32. Stuart, 127–149.
33. Rockaway, 242.
34. Rosen, A. FBI memo to J. Edgar Hoover. January 22, 1959.
35. Stuart, 236–237.
36. Rockaway, 232.
37. Cohen, 65.
38. Rockaway, 176–177.
39. Cohen, 63.
40. Ibid, 92.
41. Ibid, 108.
42. Rockaway, 252.
43. Ibid, 177–178.
44. Warren Report, 706.
45. Ibid, 710.
46. AARC The Assassination Archives and Research Center, Warren Commission Hearings Volume V. Accessed July 12, 2012. http://www.aarclibrary.org/publib/jfk/wc/wcvols/wh5/html/WC_Vol5_0105a.htm
47. Wills and Demaris, 99
48. Stone, Kurt. F. *The Jews of Capitol Hill: A Compendium of Jewish Congressional Members* (Landham, MD: Scarecrow Press, Inc., 2010), 123.
49. Smith, Richard Norton. *Thomas E. Dewey and His Times* (New York: Simon and Schuster, 1983), 17.

50. Ibid, 643.
51. Jeffers, H. Paul. *The Napoleon of New York: Mayor Fiorello LaGuardia* (New York: John Wiley and Sons: 2002), 233.
52. Saidel, Rochelle G. *The Jewish Women of Ravensbrück Concentration Camp* (Madison, WI: The University of Wisconsin Press, 2004), 111–113.
53. Gluck, Gemma LaGuardia. S. L. Shneiderman, ed. *My Story* (New York: David McKay Company, Inc.), 74.
54. Saidel, 114–120.
55. "James G. Wallace, Ex-Jurist, is Dead," *The New York Times*, November 30, 1956.
56. *Judge James Garrett Wallace Sings of the Law and Lawyers*, http://www.Amazon .com/James-Garrett-Wallace-Lp-Lawyers/dp/B007VRWRSS. Accessed September 15, 2012.
57. "James G. Wallace, Ex-Jurist, is Dead," *The New York Times*, November 30, 1956.
58. "Peter Sabbatino, Lawyer, 82, Dead." *The New York Times*, December 8, 1983.
59. Baldwin, 268–269.
60. Wallace, 332.
61. Ibid, 358–359.

Epilogue: In the Rubble of the Swastika Nation

1. Lee, Martin A. *The Beast Reawakens: Fascism's Resurgences from Hitler's Spymasters to Today* (New York: Routledge, 2000), 228.
2. Miller, insert.

SELECT BIBLIOGRAPHY

Newspapers

The Chicago Daily Tribune
The New York *Daily Mirror*
The New York Times

Government Documents

Federal Bureau of Investigation files on Fritz Kuhn, German-American Bund
*Investigation of Un-American Propaganda Activities in the United States, Hearings Before
a Special Committee of Un-American Activities House of Representatives, Seventy-Sixth
Congress, First Session, Vol. 6, August 1939*

Books

Baldwin, Neil, *Henry Ford and the Jews: The Mass Production of Hate* (New York: Public
Affairs, 2003).
Bell, Leland V. *In Hitler's Shadow: The Anatomy of American Nazism* (Port Washing-
ton, New York, London: Kennikat Press, 1973).
Buntin, John. *L.A. Noir: The Struggle for the Soul of America's Most Seductive City* (New
York: Harmony Books, 2009).
Canedy, Susan. *America's Nazis: A Democratic Dilemma* (Menlo Park, CA: Markgraf
Publications Group, 1990).
Carlson, John Roy. *Under Cover: My Four Years in the Nazi Underworld of American—
The Amazing Revelation of How Axis Agents and Our Enemies Within Are Now Plot-
ting to Destroy the United States* (New York: E. P. Dutton & Company, Inc., 1943).
Cohen, Mickey as told to John Peer Nugent. *In My Own Words: The Underworld
Autobiography of Michael Mickey Cohen* (Englewood Cliffs, NJ: Prentice-Hall,
Inc., 1975).

Diamond, Sander A. *The Nazi Movement in the United States 1924–1941* (United States: Disc-Us Books, Inc., 2001).

Eisenberg, Dennis, Uri Dan, and Eli Landau. *Meyer Lansky: Mogul of the Mob* (New York & London: Paddington Press, Ltd., 1972).

Gabler, Neil. *Winchell: Gossip, Power and the Culture of Celebrity* (New York: Vintage Books, 1994).

Grover, Warren, *Nazis in Newark* (New Brunswick, NJ: Transaction Publishers, 2003).

Herzstein, Robert E. *Roosevelt & Hitler: Prelude to War* (New York: John Wiley & Sons, 1994).

Hitler, Adolf. *Mein Kampf*, trans. Ralph Manheim (Boston: Houghton Mifflin Company Sentry Edition, 1943).

Jeffers, H. Paul. *The Napoleon of New York: Mayor Fiorello LaGuardia* (New York: John Wiley & Sons, Inc., 2002).

Jones, Nigel. *A Brief History of the Birth of the Nazis: How the Freikorps Blazed a Trail for Hitler*, (London: Constable & Robinson Ltd., 2004).

Klurfeld, Herman. *Winchell: His Life and Times* (New York: Praeger Publishers, 1976).

Lacey, Robert. *Little Man: Meyer Lansky and the Gangster Life* (Boston: Little, Brown and Company, 1991).

Larson, Erik. *In the Garden of the Beasts: Love, Terror, and an American Family in Hitler's Berlin* (New York: Crown, 2011).

Lee, Albert. *Henry Ford and the Jews* (New York: Stein and Day, 1980).

Lewis, Brad. *Hollywood's Celebrity Gangster: The Incredible Life and Times of Mickey Cohen* (New York: Enigma Books, 2007).

MacDonnell, Francis. *Insidious Foes: The Axis Fifth Column and the American Home Front* (Guilford, Connecticut: The Lyons Press, 2004).

Miller, Marvin D. *Wunderlich's Salute: The interrelationship of the German-American Bund, Camp Siegfried, Yaphank, Long Island, and the Young Siegfrieds and their relationship with American and Nazi institutions.* (Smithtown, NY: Malamud-Rose, 1983).

Rockaway, Robert A. *But He Was Good to His Mother: The Lives and Crimes of Jewish Gangsters* (New York & Jerusalem: Gefen Publishing House, 2000).

Rollins, Richard. *I Find Treason: The Story of an American Anti-Nazi Agent* (New York: William Morrow and Company, 1941).

Shirer, William L., *The Rise and Fall of the Third Reich: A History of Nazi Germany* (New York: Fawcett Crest, 1983).

Stuart, Mark A. *Gangster: The True Story of the Man Who Invented Organized Crime* (London, England: A Star Book published by the Paperback Division of W. H. Allen & Co., 1986).

Thomas, Bob. *Walter Winchell: The Man and the Myth* (New York: Berkley Medallion Books, 1972).

Winchell, Walter, introduction by Ernest Cuneo. *Winchell Exclusive: "Things That Happened to Me—and Me to Them"* (Englewood Cliffs, New Jersey: Prentice-Hall, Inc., 1975).

ACKNOWLEDGMENTS

In August 2009 I went to see Quentin Tarantino's film *Inglourious Basterds*, blithely unaware this simple action would forever change my life. After hooting and hollering at the happiest climax to a movie ever, I left the theater wondering about real stories of Jews battling back Nazis during the Hitler era. After much digging, I discovered the forgotten story of Fritz Kuhn, the German-American Bund, and their many disparate foes. What started as an entertaining afternoon at the movies turned into a three-year journey researching and writing about an improbable cast of characters that proved to be an author's dream. So thanks, Quentin, for lighting the spark. Give me a call. Drinks on me.

Sources were many. The FBI graciously answered my numerous requests for decades-old files, which proved a treasure trove of information. I also relied on newspaper accounts of the day, endless pages of congressional hearing transcripts, and numerous books. Through these many documents I fit together voluminous pieces of a widely scattered historical puzzle.

This epic undertaking, sometimes exhilarating, sometimes grueling, yet always fascinating was made all that much easier by the good graces, charming wit, and deft skills of my editor at St. Martin's, Daniela Rapp. Not only is she a wonderful editor, Daniela knows how to nurture an often overwrought author (specifically me) through thick and thin. Daniela, thanks. And then some.

Michele Rubin took on the story with zeal. From the nascent start to full-blown completion, her belief in this book made things happen. Your impact on my life has been profound, Michele, and I cannot praise you enough for this. Thanks to my agent Leigh Feldman for seeing me through to the finish. And of course Jean Garnett, Brianne Johnson, and everyone at Writers House.

The many other thank-yous: Leigh Harken for reading and ripping apart my proposal, two days of microfilm tedium, and bringing this into the final drafts. A writer and friend of unparalleled caliber (p.s., a tip of the hat to Andy for his support). Thanks beyond thanks to my mom and dad Sheila and Gene Bernstein and in-laws Nancy and Chuck Diddia, for your infinite patience, infinite wisdom, infinite love; Michelle Allen and my Bath friends who helped open a door I've been banging on for years; Phil Koek for his considerable help with the Los Angeles sections (Jives says thanks as well); my legal troika of Barbara Jacobson Dutton, Matthew J. Frawley, and Bran Harvey for answering many questions on points of law and the courts; the patient staff of the New York Public Library, for the Performing Arts; the many people and resources of the Chicago Public Library system (especially Rosa Petrizzi and my cheerleaders at the Mt. Greenwood branch); Allison Platt and her crew at The Bookies Paperbacks & More in Chicago, and Augie Aleksy at Centuries & Sleuths Bookstore in Forest Park, IL. Support your local independent bookstores! Randy Albers and everyone at the Columbia College–Chicago Fiction Writing Department, with notable kudos to my thesis advisor Andrew Allegretti; Lee Jacobson, for bailing me out with book hunting at the last minute possible; Richard H. Levey, the consummate New Yorker Groucho Marxist and impeccable host; the great people of Southbury, Connecticut for their many insights into Bund fighting: Reverend Shannon Rye Wall of South Britain Congregational Church UCC, Lois Lindsay Brown, and everyone at the Southbury Historical Society; Amelia Cotter of the German National Congress in Chicago; staff of New York's Stephen Wise Free Synagogue, Mary Kuhn, and Meyer Lansky II, for their insights on major players of this story; Sharon Woodhouse and Lake Claremont Press, for taking a chance on me when no one else would; Rabbi Ellen Dreyfus, for suggestions and help early on; Meghan Leigh Diddia, the greatest file sorter on the planet; assorted stuff from Bethany Duvall, Rebecca Fournier, Rick Kogan, Maureen Moynihan, Lisa Pevtzow, June Skinner Sawyers; and the many family, friends, and writing *consiglieres* who provided help, support, advice, assistance, and so on ad infinitum.

A large shout out to my hundreds of composition students over the years, for teaching me how to be a better writer.

And last but really foremost, Cheryl Diddia-Bernstein, the real brains behind the outfit, the strongest person I know, and without whom this book (and so much more) would be impossible.

INDEX